[digital] LIGHTING & RENDERING

Second Edition

New Riders

JEREMY BIRN

Digital Lighting and Rendering, Second Edition
Jeremy Birn

New Riders
1249 Eighth Street
Berkeley, CA 94710
510/524-2178
800/283-9444
510/524-2221 (fax)

Find us on the Web at: www.newriders.com
To report errors, please send a note to errata@peachpit.com

New Riders is an imprint of Peachpit, a division of Pearson Education

Project Editors: Davina Baum, Kristin Kalning
Development Editor: Davina Baum
Production Editor: Andrei Pasternak
Copyeditor: Emily Wolman
Tech Editor: Jesse Brophy
Compositor: Maureen Forys, Happenstance Type-O-Rama
Proofreader: Corbin Collins
Indexer: Joy Dean Lee
Cover design: Aren Howell
Interior design: Maureen Forys, Happenstance Type-O-Rama

ISBN 0-321-31631-2

9 8 7 6 5

Printed and bound in the United States of America

Table of Contents

Foreword

To help you make better 3D renderings, this book fuses information from several fields. In these pages you will find concepts and techniques from professional cinematography, design principles from traditional visual arts, practical advice based on professional film production experience, and plain-English explanations of the latest science behind the scenes.

Who Should Read This Book?

You should read this book when you have at least a working knowledge of how to use a 3D package, and are interested in taking your 3D rendering further.

- For professional users of 3D rendering software, this book is designed to help with real-world production challenges and contribute to the ongoing growth of your work.
- For students of computer graphics, this book will help you develop more professional rendering skills.
- For dedicated 3D hobbyists, this book can help you improve the artistic quality of your 3D renderings and learn more about professional approaches to graphics production.

This book is written to be clear, but not condescending. Every effort has been made to define terms the first time they are used, and to illustrate every concept and technique with figures and sample renderings. This book is designed to complement, rather than to replace, your software's manuals and help files. Most of the information you find here is not in your software's manual, even if some of it should be.

Software Requirements

This book covers techniques and concepts that are applicable to work in almost any 3D rendering software. 2D Paint and compositing software is also recommended.

3D Software

No single program is going to support every feature, function, and rendering algorithm described in this book. Hopefully you won't mind learning about a few functions that aren't in your particular software yet. However, most sections show several alternate approaches or work-arounds so that you can achieve any effect that is described, no matter which program you use.

Being non-software-specific doesn't mean that this book doesn't discuss particular software, though. If there's a noteworthy feature in Renderman, Mental Ray, 3D Studio Max, Maya, Softimage, Lightwave, or any other program, it will be mentioned when it comes up.

This book is dedicated to the idea that, with an awareness of the art and computer graphics principles that go into a rendering, and a little bit of creative problem solving, you can accomplish great work in almost any rendering package.

2D Software

Any good 3D system should be complemented with 2D software to create and manipulate texture maps, and to composite together layers and render passes. Ideally you should have a paint program such as Adobe Photoshop (used in many texture-creation examples in this book), Paint Shop Pro, or Fractal Painter. Free alternatives such as The Gimp or Paint.NET will also work just fine. A dedicated compositing program, such as Shake, Digital Fusion, or After Effects, is useful when compositing together render passes, although you could also do basic compositing of still images in your paint program.

About This Edition

This is the second edition of the popular book *[Digital] Lighting & Rendering*. The first edition became the standard text on the art of 3D lighting and rendering, and introduced many artists to the field. Since it was published in 2000, it has met with great critical and commercial success. I am sincerely grateful to each teacher who has chosen to assign my book to students, everyone on the Internet who has posted a recommendation, and every artist who has shown my book to a friend or colleague.

This new edition has advanced along with changes in technology, in software, and in the industry. To keep up with an evolving field, every chapter has grown with new techniques and concepts. Issues such as occlusion and global illumination, which had been relegated to single sections in the first edition, are now woven throughout the book, in discussions of different issues from architectural rendering to render passes. A new chapter has also been added on understanding studio production pipelines—how professionals work together in different positions to create feature-film visual effects and computer animated features.

In computer graphics, we say our work is never really completed, only abandoned. Shots always could be better, always could be tweaked and revised a little more by perfectionist artists. Crashing into a deadline is what finally forces us to let go of the projects we love. The same is true in releasing a book. I'm glad that what I abandoned in 2000 has made so many people happy. The first edition represented the best of what I had to say that year. Since then I have continued to work in the industry, gaining experience in visual effects and animated feature production, working with different applications and renderers, teaching courses on lighting and rendering, and I have had ample time to regret every word that I wrote. Being able to revisit and revise all of this material has been a great pleasure, and it is with great pride that I abandon this new edition to you.

[CHAPTER ONE]

Fruit Bowl images by Donal Khosrowi (top) and Andrzej Sykut (lower).

Fundamentals of Lighting Design

The craft of lighting design was practiced for centuries prior to the advent of computer graphics, in fields such as theater, painting, photography, and cinematography. 3D artists have a great deal to learn from the traditions of earlier lighters. This chapter provides an introduction to some of the key terms and concepts in the field of lighting design, and looks ahead to some of the important issues and challenges that will be raised in this book.

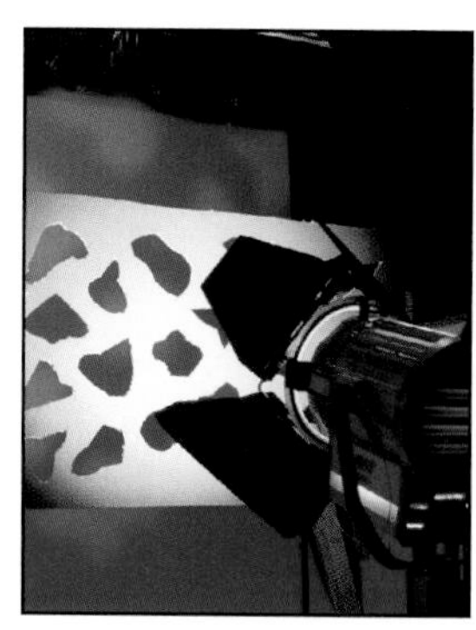

Motivation

Before you add a light to your scene, you should know its *motivation*. Motivation is the cause or original source for each light in your scene.

You probably wouldn't begin to animate a character without knowing what the character was doing or trying to do, or paint a texture map without knowing what material you were trying to create—and yet many people add lights to their scenes in just this sort of random manner, without thinking about what kind of light they are trying to depict.

Motivation should inform every decision you make in adjusting your lights. Once you know a light's motivation, you know what qualities of real light you are trying to depict, and what kind of light sources you should study or think about when creating an appearance in 3D.

Off-Screen Space

Off-screen space is the area that isn't visible in your shot, such as the space above the camera. The illumination, shadows, and reflections you see in a photograph are often motivated by off-screen sources, rather than by light sources that are visible within the frame. An important part of your job in designing lighting for any scene is to imagine what exists in off-screen space, so that you can light your scene with lights that appear to be motivated by real light sources.

To see how lighting can be shaped by off-screen space, take a look at the four photographs in Figure 1.1. The objects in the frame don't change, and yet based on the light coming from off-screen, you can tell a great deal about where each picture was taken.

If the light coming from off-screen space in a photograph can provide this much information, how do we make the lighting in our 3D scenes appear just as distinctive to communicate the same things? The answer starts with studying the visible qualities of light from each kind of light source.

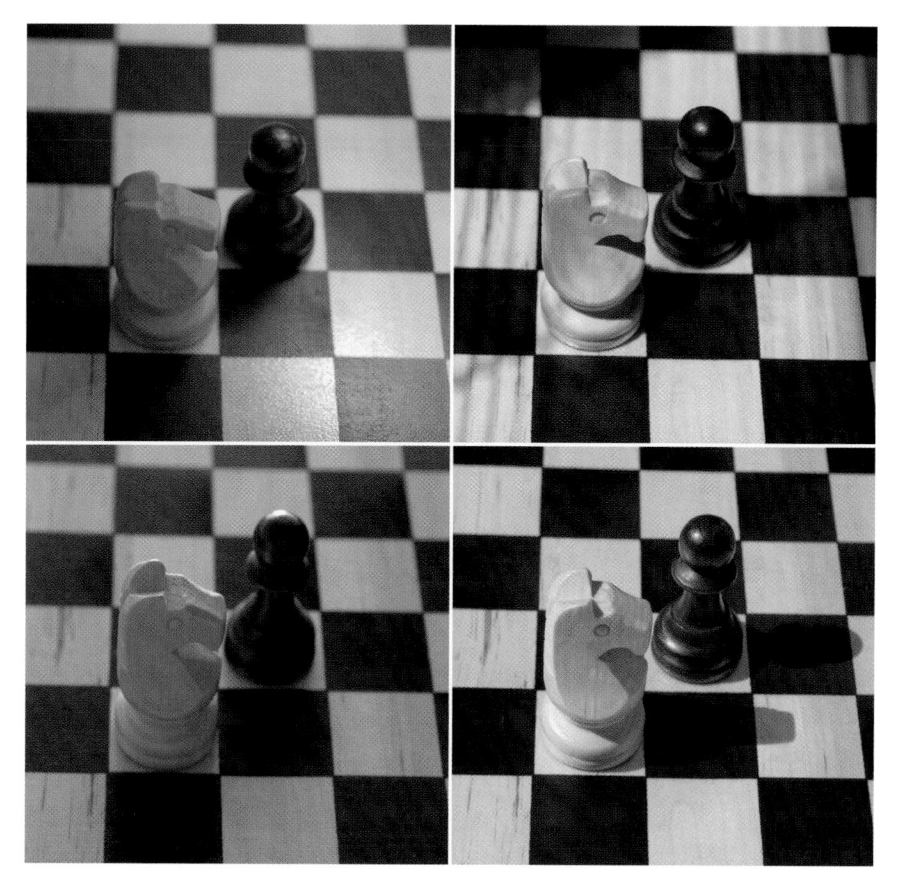

[Figure 1.1]
You can recognize a scene lit by a lamp (upper left), by light through a window (upper right), under a cloudy sky (lower left), and in direct sun (lower right).

Qualities of Light

We recognize different sources of illumination by the different *qualities of light* they add to the scene. The main qualities of light that we notice in a picture are color, brightness, softness, throw pattern, and angle.

- Every type of light source has a distinctive *color temperature*, which, when combined with the white balance of the camera, determines the color of the light. Chapter 8, "The Art and Science of Color," has charts of real light sources' color temperatures.

- *Brightness*, like color, is all relative to how the camera is adjusted—this time based on the exposure settings of the camera. Chapter 6, "Cameras and Exposure," describes a real camera's exposure process, and how to make sure your own renderings are exposed properly.
- *Softness* is a function of several settings on a light. The penumbra of a spotlight sets the softness of the edge of its cone. The decay or drop-off of a light sets how it fades away with distance. Most importantly, soft shadows create the impression of soft, diffused light while crisply defined shadows indicate hard light. Figure 1.1 showed the hard-edged shadows of the chess pieces lit by direct sun, and the much softer shadows cast by the cloudy sky. Chapter 3, "Shadows and Occlusion," discusses several approaches to rendering hard and soft shadows.
- *Throw pattern*, or the shape of a light, is another noticeable quality of light. Figure 1.1 showed the pattern of the light filtered through Venetian blinds as the throw pattern of sunlight that has passed through a window. Chapter 2, "Lighting Basics and Good Practices," discusses projecting cookies from your lights to simulate different throw patterns.
- A light's *angle* tells you where it is coming from. For example, a late afternoon sun will come from a lower angle than light in the middle of the day. To a lighting designer, angle also helps determine the visual function of a light, such as whether it functions as a key light, a kicker, or a rim. Aiming lights at the correct angle to achieve different visual functions is described in Chapter 5, "Lighting Creatures, Characters, and Animation."

Almost any adjective you use to describe light could be considered a quality of light. I sometimes consider animation, such as whether a light is flickering or consistent, to be a quality of light. I have heard other people describe the level of contrast as a quality of light, although I consider the amount of contrast in an image to be a function of the brightness and softness of the lights in the scene.

The one thing that ties all of these qualities of light together is that you can study them in real life, and work to imitate them with the lights in your 3D scene. Knowing which kinds of light you want to study in real life starts with imagining what kinds of light sources are motivating your scene's illumination.

Direct and Indirect Light

Direct light shines directly from an original source, such as a lightbulb or the sun, to an object that it illuminates. *Indirect light* is light that has reflected or bounced off one surface already, before it indirectly illuminates other objects. For example, if a floor lamp aims light at the ceiling, then the circle of light on the ceiling is direct light. The light that has reflected off the ceiling to softly illuminate the rest of the room is indirect light.

Direct light sources are usually the motivation for most of the brighter lights in your scene, but indirect light, such as light that has bounced off the ground or a wall, is also a motivation for light that can fill in or illuminate parts of your scene. Chapter 4, "Lighting Environments and Architecture," explains how to set up extra lights to simulate indirect light bounces in an environment, as well as global illumination functions that automate the simulation of indirect light.

Cheating

Cheating is an intentional departure from what's motivated, done in a way designed not to appear noticeably wrong to the audience.

As a simple example of cheating, Figure 1.2 shows the environment that I built to represent the off-screen space surrounding the fruit bowl on the cover of this book. It contains the window that will be reflected on the surface of the fruits. That window in the reflection is also the motivation for the key light (the main, brightest illumination) illuminating the left side of the fruits in the scene.

[Figure 1.2] A textured environment surrounds the fruit bowl in the lower right.

If we weren't doing any cheating and stuck with what was motivated, then the key light would be positioned exactly where the window is, so that the illumination on the fruit came from the same angle as the reflection of the window. However, doing this would light the fruit too frontally, which would appear to flatten out the round forms. The shape of the fruit will be better defined by light that comes more from the side instead of the front. To accomplish this, the position of the light is cheated away from the window that motivates it, as shown in Figure 1.3.

[Figure 1.3]
The motivated position for the key light (orange) would match the reflection, but the new key light position is cheated away from the window (green).

Figure 1.4 compares the fruit lit from the actual window position to the fruit lit from the cheated angle.

Cheating is performed, to some extent, on almost every project done in 3D. Shadows cast from one character to another are moved or removed if they are distracting. Light on a character that appears to come from a lamp may actually come from a position far away from the lamp if it lights a character better. Rims of light perfectly outline forms, even if there was no light in exactly the right place to motivate the rim.

[Figure 1.4] Illumination from the original angle (left) doesn't shape all of the fruit as well as light from the cheated position (right).

Cheating in Live Action

Knowing how to cheat and fake things is a crucial part of creating 3D graphics, but it is also an established part of the art of live-action cinematography.

A pool of light on the floor that appears to have come from a window may actually come from a light above the set. An actor running into a dark forest may have his face fully lit when in reality he would have been in darkness. Even the walls of the set are sometimes mounted on wheels (this is called a *wild wall*) so that they can be moved out of the way, or rotated independently from other walls.

So why do lighting designers cheat? Why not just make the lighting be as accurate and true-to-life as possible? The short answer to these questions is that lighting and cinematography are arts, not just sciences. A more in-depth answer starts with understanding the *visual goals* that a lighting designer is trying to achieve in lighting a scene.

Visual Goals of Lighting Design

There is more to lighting a scene than simply running a simulation of real-world parameters. Lighting is also designed to achieve certain visual goals that help a viewer better appreciate a scene. How well a lighting artist accomplishes these goals determines how the lighting will enhance or detract from a shot.

Making Things Read

Much like photography, cinematography, and painting, 3D rendering is a process of producing two-dimensional images that depict three-dimensional scenes. To give your renderings solidity and presence, and to fully communicate the three-dimensional form of an object or character to an audience, you need to define your models with careful lighting. Some people call this process *modeling with light*, because it is your lighting that lets the viewer perceive an object's 3D form. Defining a character with light is one of the main focuses of Chapter 5.

Making Things Believable

Computer graphics can be rendered in many different visual styles. Some projects require *photorealism* (images that can be mistaken for a photograph), while other projects are stylized in different ways or designed to create more illustrated or cartoon-like looks. However, whether or not the visual style you adopt is photorealistic, your lighting still needs to be *believable* to the audience.

A believable image is at least internally consistent, with lights balanced in a way that would be motivated in real life. For example, if there is a beam of direct sunlight entering a room, the viewer expects the sunlight to be brighter than the light of a table lamp. Even in a cartoon, basic expectations of weight and balance still exist, and sometimes getting small details right in your lighting can even help "sell" a scene that otherwise would be impossible to believe.

Often the key to creating believable lighting is studying real life. Before beginning a project, try to study how light behaves in situations similar to what you will be rendering. In visual effects work, studying the *live-action footage* (the images filmed with a real camera) can show you a great deal about how a subject should appear in an environment. For projects created entirely in 3D graphics, collect *reference images* that you can study to see how color and light would appear in a real scene. Whether you photograph the reference images yourself, find them on a photography website, or grab still frames from rented DVDs, your collection of reference images can be useful throughout your project to compare with your renderings as you design and adjust your lighting.

It is a poor artist who blames his tools for his work. Part of making a scene believable is compensating for the failures, flaws, and limitations inherent in your rendering software. Almost every physical effect discussed in this book, from indirect light bouncing off walls to the translucency in human skin, can be simulated through careful texturing, lighting, and compositing, even when your software doesn't fully or automatically simulate everything for you. When someone sees the picture or animation that you have lit, they want to see a complete, believable picture, not to hear excuses about which program you used.

Enhancing Shaders and Effects

Frequently in 3D graphics you will find it necessary to add lights to a scene to help communicate the identity of different surfaces and materials. For example, you might create a light that adds highlights to a character's eyes to make them look wetter, or puts a glint of light onto an aluminum can to make it look more metallic. Many effects that, in theory, could be created exclusively though developing and adjusting surfaces and textures on 3D objects are often helped along during production by careful lighting designed to bring out the surface's best attributes. No matter how carefully developed and tested the shaders on a surface were before you started to light, it's ultimately the lighting artist's responsibility to make sure all that is supposed to be gold actually glitters.

Visual effects such as explosions, fire, water, smoke, and clouds also need a good deal of attention from lighting, usually including special dedicated lights. For example, if a fire is supposed to appear to be glowing and illuminating objects around it, or if raindrops are supposed to have highlights making them visible against a dark sky, then lights must be added in close coordination with these effects elements.

Maintaining Continuity

Working on longer projects in which many people are involved in lighting different shots, maintaining continuity is a key concern. All the shots must come together to maintain a seamless experience for the audience. Many tactics are employed to maintain continuity, from comparing images of different shots to your own while you light, to different lighting artists sharing lighting rigs for sets and characters, to screenings of sequences focused on continuity where any errors or discrepancies might be found.

In visual effects, continuity becomes a more complex problem, because you will be matching and integrating your 3D graphics with live-action plates. During a day of shooting, the sun may move behind a cloud while filming one shot, and be brighter or have moved in the sky when another shot is filmed. While integrating a creature or spaceship with the lighting from the background plate may be the key to making your shot believable, the continuity of the sequence as a whole is just as high a priority, and sometimes you need to adjust your shot's lighting to match the lighting in adjacent shots as well.

Directing the Viewer's Eye

In a well-lit scene, your lighting should draw the viewer's eye to areas that are important to the story, animation, or key parts of the shot. Chapter 7, "Composition and Staging," will cover more about what makes a part of the frame attract the viewer's eye or command attention.

Besides making the intended center of interest visible, good lighting avoids distracting the audience with anything else. In viewing an animated film, the moment something unintended catches your eye—whether it's a strange flicker or artifact, a highlight where it doesn't belong, or a shadow that pops or changes suddenly—your eye has been pulled away from the action and, worse than that, your attention has been pulled away from following the story. Good lighting can add a lot to a film, but first and foremost you must do no harm to the experience of watching the animation.

Emotional Impact

When they are absorbed in the story and watching what happens to the characters, most of your audience will never consciously *see* your lighting as they watch a movie, but instead will *feel* it. Helping create a mood or tone that enhances the emotional experience of watching a film is the most important visual goal of cinematic lighting design.

One of the main focuses of Chapter 8 is the different moods and associations created by simple things such as the color scheme chosen for a shot. While staying within what is motivated and believable, you can think about what kind of look or mood you are trying to achieve in lighting a scene. Is it very starkly lit, with high contrast and harsh shadows? Is it softly lit, with subtle lighting and soft shadows? Is the scene very colorful with lots of saturated tones, or gloomy and desaturated? Is there a point in the scene when there should be a shift in tone, something changing? Knowing the story and, of course, discussing the main points of the scene with the film's director are the keys to planning the type of mood you will try to achieve.

Achieving the visual goals of good lighting design is an artistic process, grounded in the tradition of cinematography, which in turn borrows a great deal from painting. Technology may change some aspects of the process of 3D lighting. This book covers a number of the key technologies that are speeding up or changing the process of lighting, from hardware acceleration to image-based lighting and global illumination. However, mastering the craft of lighting a 3D scene is, at its heart, a timeless skill whose value will not go away with any new button or switch added to future graphics software.

Lighting Challenges

Most of the time spent on lighting is not spent setting up lights in your scene. More time is actually spent on adjusting your lighting, getting feedback on your work, and revising things, than on the initial set-up. Re-rendering scenes with better and better lighting, while getting feedback on your versions, is essential to perfecting your lighting skills.

To help you get more practice with lighting, and to get feedback on your scenes as you light them, you can browse through an ever-expanding set of "Lighting Challenge" scenes, which are available to download from this book's companion website, www.3dRender.com, in a variety of file formats. On the Lighting Challenges discussion forum, you can see how other artists have lit each scene; see breakdowns of the lights, the render passes, and other elements of people's work; and, most important, post versions of your own work to get feedback. I'll be there too, to give you feedback on your work and post suggestions.

There's no resource more valuable than the Internet in learning about 3D rendering, from researching the latest and most esoteric of plug-in shaders for your renderer, to getting critiques and feedback on your work. I'm on the Web almost every day, often while waiting for frames to render. In fact, an ideal time for you to read this book is while waiting for frames to render, running your own tests and trying the Lighting Challenge scenes as you read these chapters.

The plan is that Lighting Challenge scenes will be added about once a month, including indoor and outdoor environments, characters, products, and scenes that present specific challenges such as lighting hair or lighting underwater. The scenes and the discussion forum are free to join, and are a wonderful complement to this book. In fact, even the cover image was rendered from one of the challenge scenes. Figure 1.5 shows several of the other entries by different artists in the fruit bowl Lighting Challenge scene. Feel free to download the scene and take a stab at lighting it yourself.

[Figure 1.5]
The Fruit Bowl Lighting Challenge, as lit by Angel Camacho (upper left), Lazhar Rekik (upper right), Florian Wild (middle left), Yohann da Geb (middle right), Holger Schömann (lower left), and Ctrlstudio (lower right).

Your Workspace

Before you start work on lighting your 3D scene, pay some attention to the lighting in your own office or the area around your computer.

Working in a room with sunlight coming in through a window, or too bright a light from the ceiling lights or lamps, can limit your perception of the scene you are trying to light. Before you begin lighting a scene, turn your office lights down or off, and make sure there is no screen glare or reflections visible on your monitor.

As a general rule, conventional CRT monitors are capable of a greater range of contrast and more accurate colors than a flat LCD monitor. However, monitors do not last forever; if you have a monitor that is more than five years old and has had daily use, it is not likely to be as bright as it once was, and it will not perform as well as a new monitor. A new flat-panel monitor can easily outperform an old, worn-out CRT.

In terms of proceeding with this book, you shouldn't need new hardware, but take a moment to check that your current monitor is adjusted well. As a simple approach to calibrating your monitor, visit www.3dRender.com and view the image shown in Figure 1.6 on your screen. Make sure you can read all of the gray numbers at the top and bottom of the image; if any are unreadable, you are missing a part of the dynamic range of your images. Check both the controls on your monitor as well as the software control panel to make sure you don't have the brightness or contrast adjusted to a level that hides bright or dark tones from you.

[Figure 1.6] Viewing this image on your monitor, make sure that you can read all of the numbers along the top and bottom.

If you are ever creating printed output, then the most accurate way to calibrate your monitor is to print a test image first, and then adjust your monitor to match the printer's output. The calibration will never be completely perfect for every color, but you should be able to get a reasonably good preview of what you will get if you adjust the monitor side by side with printed output.

Even a well-calibrated monitor may shift its appearance during the first hour or two after being turned on. At many studios, monitors are left on continuously instead of being turned off over night, so that the calibration will not be lost in the morning.

Creative Control

You probably learned this lesson in dining at seafood restaurants: *If it smells like fish, it is not good fish.*

A similar principle applies in computer graphics: *If it looks like computer graphics, it is not good computer graphics.* When an image is well lit and well rendered, the technology behind the image does not call attention to itself. Viewers will notice only a compelling image, a realistic scene, or an innovative new visual style. When viewing a great rendering, the fact that a computer was used in creating the image will not be the first thing that strikes a viewer's mind.

When you, the artist, are truly in control of your 3D rendering, then it is your hand that the viewer will see in your work, rather than the impression that a computer has made the picture.

The goal of this book is to help you take control over the lighting and rendering process, so that every aspect of your rendering is the result of your own deliberate and well informed decisions. Every chapter deals with an issue or aspect of lighting and rendering a 3D scene, and discusses how it works and how you can make it work better.

[CHAPTER TWO]

Lighting Basics and Good Practices

There aren't many "happy accidents" in 3D graphics. To achieve professional results, you need to be in control of every step of the lighting process, from choosing the appropriate type of light for each purpose, to test-rendering each light and adjusting its controls and options, to lighting in production and managing multiple versions of your scene until you can please your client or director.

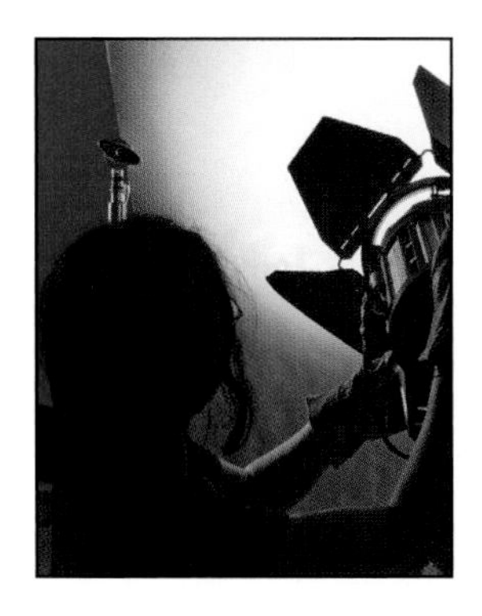

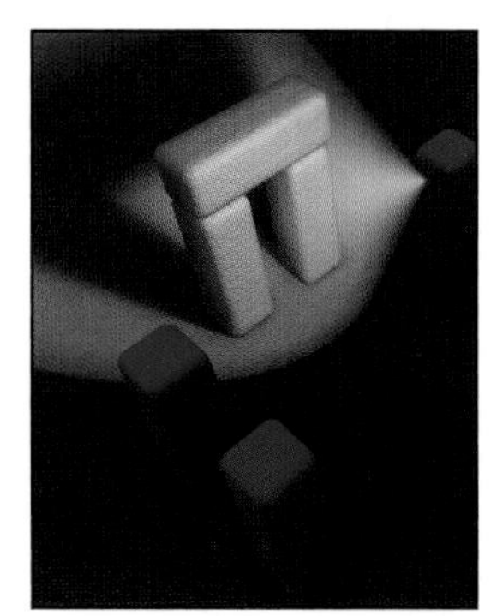

Starting Points

Where does the lighting process start? The answer varies widely between companies and projects. Sometimes, especially at smaller companies or on smaller projects, it is as simple as having a conversation with the client or director. He may tell you that the scene is set at night outside the theater at a movie premiere, and he wants a blue or purple gradient for the sky, camera flashes illuminating the characters from all directions, and spotlights sweeping through the sky in the background. From that verbal description, you can sit down and develop some test images to show the director the next day.

If your lighting begins with a conversation, you should start adding, collecting, and discussing reference images as soon as possible. Gather images from the Internet, frames from rented movies that contain similar scenes, and books, magazines, and stock photography catalogs. The sooner you can put some images in front of the director and agree on what your project is supposed to look like, the sooner you can be sure that your work is headed in the right direction.

If you are working on visual effects shots, lighting creatures or vehicles that will be composited into a live-action movie, then you will be given the *background plates* (the digitized frames that were filmed as a part of the movie.) Usually you will also get some reference images of a sphere or other simple objects held in front of the camera from which you can attempt to match the lighting of the shooting location. Your background plate will be your bible in lighting your visual effects shots, and you'll observe every detail you can in it, such as the angle and sharpness of the shadows, and the colors, tones, and level of contrast in the scene, then incorporate your observations into your lighting. Matching the lighting from real locations is discussed in detail in Chapter 11, "Rendering Passes and Compositing."

If you are working on an animated production, the art department will have started working on the look of the scenes long before you begin to light them. There are likely to be paintings or illustrations of what each scene should look like. The lighting artist will use the art from the art department to draw inspiration, and to suggest the colors and tones that should appear in the image. However, she will make her own decisions about exactly how to implement the lighting design using the many types of lights and options available in 3D graphics.

Types of Lights

You begin setting up lighting in a 3D scene by choosing which types of lights to add. The actual lights that you can use in a 3D program are roughly based on real-world types of light sources. Each has its own uses and advantages, so it pays to know your tools and choose them carefully for each project.

Point Lights

Point lights, also known as *omni* or *omnidirectional lights*, are the simplest light sources to use in 3D. As shown in Figure 2.1, a point light emits light uniformly in all directions.

[Figure 2.1]
A point light emits light uniformly in all directions, casting shadows that radiate out from the light's position.

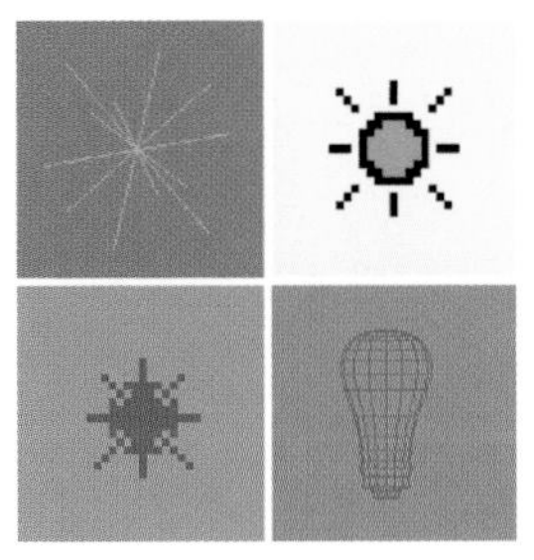

[Figure 2.2]
Icons for a point light in Lightwave 3d, a Radial light in Electric Image, a point light in Maya, and a point light in Softimage. All perform similar functions.

A point light in 3D graphics is best compared to a lightbulb hanging in the middle of a room—as shown in Figure 2.2, some programs even represent point lights with a lightbulb icon. Yet unlike a real light bulb, a point light is infinitely small, so all of the light emitted from it comes from exactly the same point in space.

When point lights are set to cast shadows and you model a light fixture around them, the shadow of the light fixture will limit and shape where the light can shine, as shown in Figure 2.3. However, most lighting artists prefer to use spotlights for this kind of effect, because spotlights provide more control over exactly where the light is aiming.

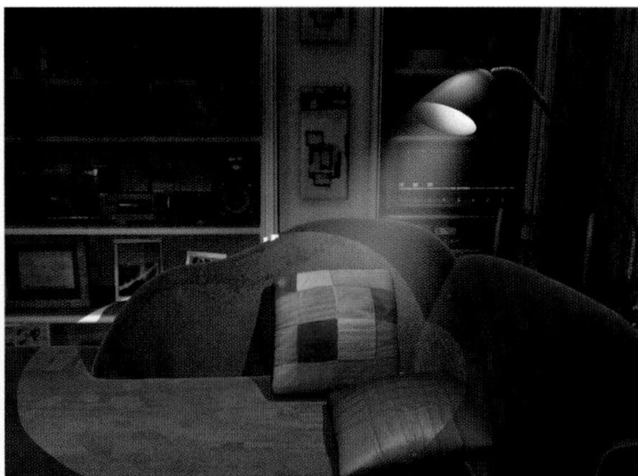

[Figure 2.3]
When positioned within a light fixture and set to cast shadows, a point light can appear similar to a spotlight.

Spotlights

Spotlights (also called *spots*) are the most popular type of light in lighting design for computer graphics, because they can be controlled and adjusted so completely. Just like a point light, a spotlight simulates light radiating from an infinitely small point. However, instead of aiming in all directions, it is limited to a specified cone or beam of light in a certain direction, as shown in Figure 2.4. The spotlight's rotation can determine where the beam is aimed, or a *target* or *interest* may be linked to the light so that the light is always aimed toward the target.

You could do almost all of your lighting with spotlights; even when light needs to be aimed in different directions, you can use several spotlights together, as shown in Figure 2.5.

[Figure 2.4]
A spotlight's illumination is limited to a cone aimed in a specific direction.

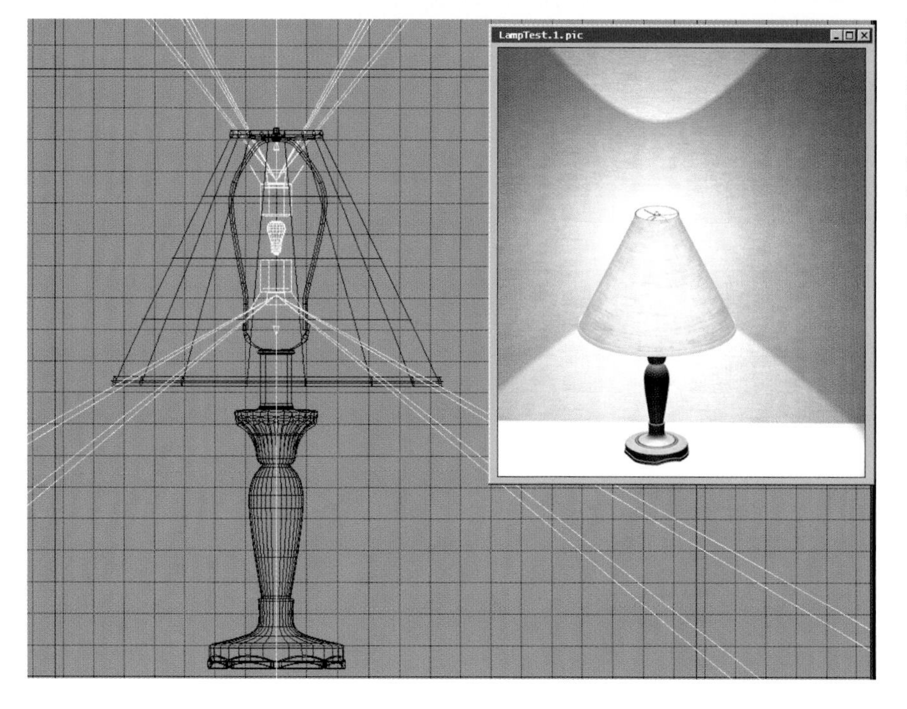

[Figure 2.5]
Multiple spotlights can be aimed in different directions, giving the appearance of an omnidirectional light while allowing more control over where the lights are aimed.

Spotlights have handy controls that you can adjust to shape exactly where light will fall. The *cone angle* determines the width of the spotlight's beam, while the *penumbra angle* (also called *falloff* or *spread angle*) determines the softness of the edge around the spotlight's beam. At a penumbra of 0, the beam will have a perfectly sharp edge, as shown on the left side of Figure 2.6. As you increase the penumbra, the spotlight beams will gain a soft edge, as shown in the center of the figure. With a very soft beam, you no longer notice the shape of the spotlight at all. As shown on the right side of Figure 2.6, spotlights can add subtle illumination to a scene, with each light gently brightening the area where it is aimed, but all of the spotlights blending together seamlessly. Chapter 4, "Lighting Environments and Architecture," describes how to place lights as shown in this figure.

[Figure 2.6] With hard-edged lights (left), you can see every spotlight cone distinctly. As the penumbra angle is increased (center), the lights begin to merge; when the lights are soft enough (right), they merge together so that you cannot distinguish between the individual sources.

Spotlights also have an option called *barn doors*. In real life, barn doors are metal flaps mounted in front of a spotlight, as shown in Figure 2.7, which can be folded in front of the light to crop it horizontally or vertically. Barn doors in 3D graphics give you the same kind of creative control, enabling you to crop out a square or rectangle of light.

Spotlights are also popular in computer graphics because they work efficiently with some kinds of shadows. In Chapter 3, "Shadows and Occlusion," I will discuss why spotlights are usually the most efficient kind of light when rendering depth map or shadow map shadows.

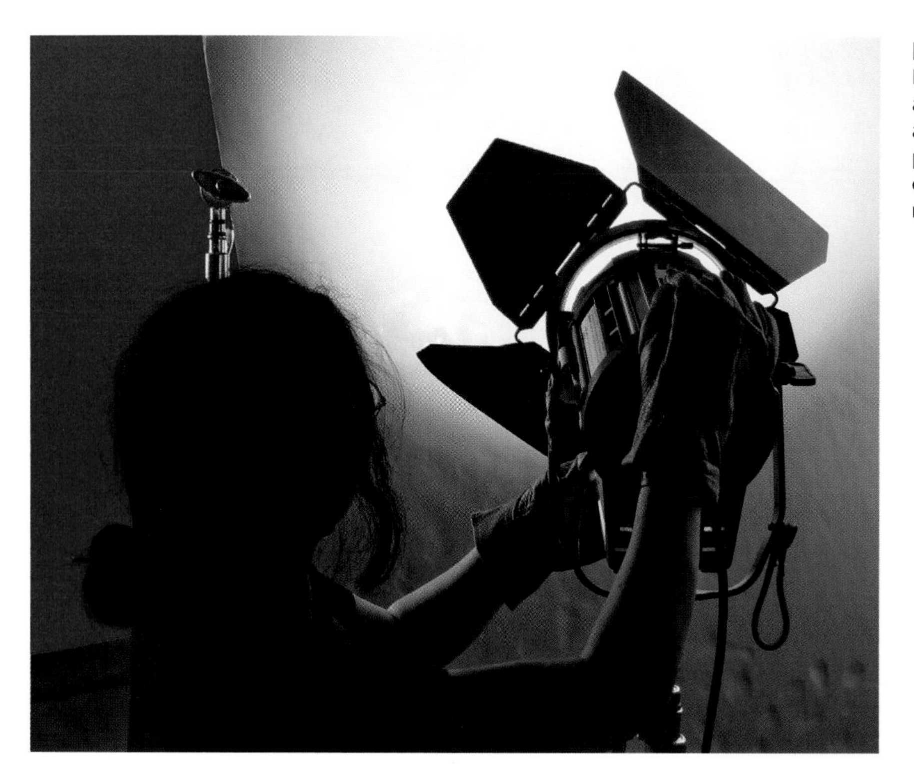

[Figure 2.7]
Besides having control over aiming a light, barn doors also allow a cinematographer to limit the coverage of a spotlight to less than its natural cone angle.

Directional Lights

A *directional light*, which is particularly useful for simulating direct sunlight, is also known as a *distant*, *direct*, *infinite*, or *sun light* in different programs; the different icons are indicated in Figure 2.8.

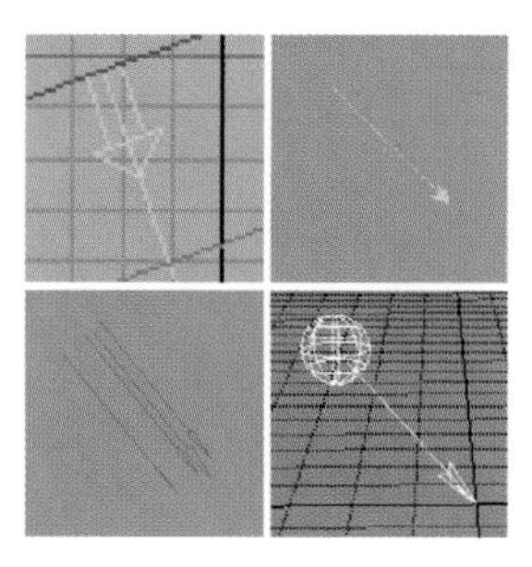

[Figure 2.8]
A 3D Studio Max target direct light, directional lights in Alias Power Animator and Maya, and an Infinite light in Softimage, all serve the same purpose

A directional light illuminates every object from the same angle, no matter where the object is located relative to the light. In Figure 2.9, the directional light aims down and to the left, causing every object to be illuminated as if it were being lit from the upper left.

[Figure 2.9]
A directional light creates parallel shadows and illumination that strikes each object from the same angle.

Although the directional light in Figure 2.9 is right in the middle of the scene, it simulates light as if it came from very far away. All of the shadows cast from a directional light are parallel, which is something you normally would only see in shadows from a very distant light source such as the sun. Contrast these shadows with the shadows cast by point lights and spotlights, where the shadows diverge away from the light at different angles.

Area Lights

An *area light* is a type of light that simulates the size of a physical light source in real life. With point, spot, and directional lights, scaling up the light in your scene only scales up the icon, and doesn't change the illumination. As you scale up an area light, however, it will accurately simulate illumination from a larger panel of light. If an area light is scaled very small, its illumination will appear similar to a point light. As shown on the right in Figure 2.10, illumination from a larger area light will appear softer, creating softer shadows and emitting illumination that can wrap around nearby subjects.

[Figure 2.10] An area light creates softer illumination and shadows as it is scaled larger.

Area lights are often available in a variety of shapes, including spherical area lights, rectangles, discs, and linear lights. If you have a choice, use the shape that best fits the type of light source you are trying to simulate. For example, a linear light can be perfect for simulating a fluorescent tube.

The quality of light and shadows achievable with area lights can make them an excellent choice for some realistic renderings. However, soft shadows from an area light are slower and more complex to render than shadows from a point light or spotlight. This is because the renderer needs to scatter multiple rays to sample whether different parts of the area are causing a partial shadow, versus tracing rays to just one point. Many artists avoid using area lights for larger animated projects simply because they can take so long to render. See Chapter 3 for more information about soft-shadow rendering options.

Models Serving as Lights

In some programs, any 3D model in your scene can be designated to function as a light source. With this feature, even nontraditional shapes of light, such as a neon sign, can be used as a true light source, as shown in Figure 2.11.

[Figure 2.11]
Using an object as a light allows for odd shapes such as fluorescent rings or neon tubes.

Any renderer that supports *global illumination* (the simulation of indirect light bouncing from one object to another, discussed in Chapters 3 and 4) will allow objects to illuminate other objects. When rendering with global illumination, applying a high incandescence or a bright ambient color to an object will allow it to work as a light source.

While using arbitrarily shaped models as light sources is becoming possible in many programs, it is not a common or efficient solution for most professional lighting work. In most cases, professionals avoid it because it makes rendering too slow. You can usually fake something similar by putting some point lights inside your model and assigning a bright or glowing shader to the surface.

Environment Spheres

An *environment sphere* (also called a *sky dome*) is a special light source that surrounds and provides illumination from all around your scene. Environment spheres are perfect for simulating light from the sky. They also make great *fill lights*, the secondary lighting that you need to fill in areas unlit by your main light source. Figure 2.12 is lit entirely by an environment sphere, with no other light sources added.

[Figure 2.12] An environment sphere surrounds the scene and lights objects based on the colors mapped to the sphere.

When you map environment spheres with an image, the colors from that image are used to determine the brightness and color of the illumination from each angle. This technique, called *image based lighting* (IBL), is covered in Chapter 4.

Ambient Light

In real life, *ambient light* means the light that is all around you. It includes light from the sky, light that has reflected back up at you from the ground or floor, and light from any other light source. If you hold your fist out in front of you, you can see that there is light illuminating every side of it, but notice that the light contributes different colors and intensities at different angles. Real-life ambient light is different in every environment, but it rarely is very flat or uniform.

In computer graphics, many programs have an ambient light (sometimes called *global ambience*) that uniformly brightens your objects in an unrealistic way. It makes every side of every surface the same color, robbing your scene of shading and diversity. The general rule with this kind of ambient light is this: Don't use it. Figure 2.13 shows the flat, unrealistic shading that comes from using ambient light as a fill light.

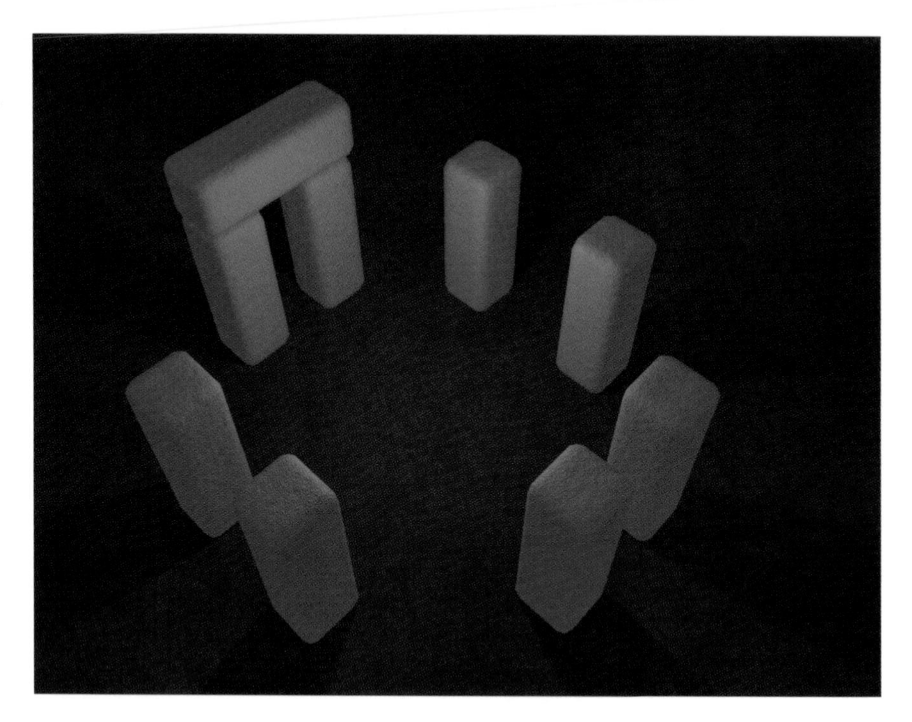

[Figure 2.13]
Ambient light flattens the scene and robs it of richness and shading.

If your scene needs to be brighter, you can add any kind of light discussed above to fill in the illumination where it is getting too dark. Any other type of light will make better fill lights than a flat, uniform ambience.

A variation on ambient light that makes it less uniform is an *ambient shade* parameter. When used, it makes an ambient light function more like a point light, only with light that wraps farther around each object as the ambient shade parameter is lowered.

You should always start lighting in complete darkness, so that when you add your first spotlight and test-render your scene, you see no illumination except that light. Getting rid of any extra light, including default lights or global ambience, is critical to accurately adjusting and controlling your lighting.

Controls and Options

After you've added a light to your scene, the next step is to *solo* the light so that you can adjust it more precisely. To solo a light means to hide all the other lights in the scene, and render the scene illuminated by just one light. By isolating each light, you know exactly how it contributes to the lighting and shadows in the scene, and you can accurately adjust the controls and options on the light.

Decay

Decay (also called *attenuation* or *distance falloff*) controls how the intensity of a light decreases with distance. The image on the left side of Figure 2.14 is an example of a light with no decay: It lights the farthest rock as brightly as the near ones. The right side of Figure 2.14 shows a light with an *inverse square* (also called *quadratic*) decay—it lights the rocks near it much more brightly than the distant rocks.

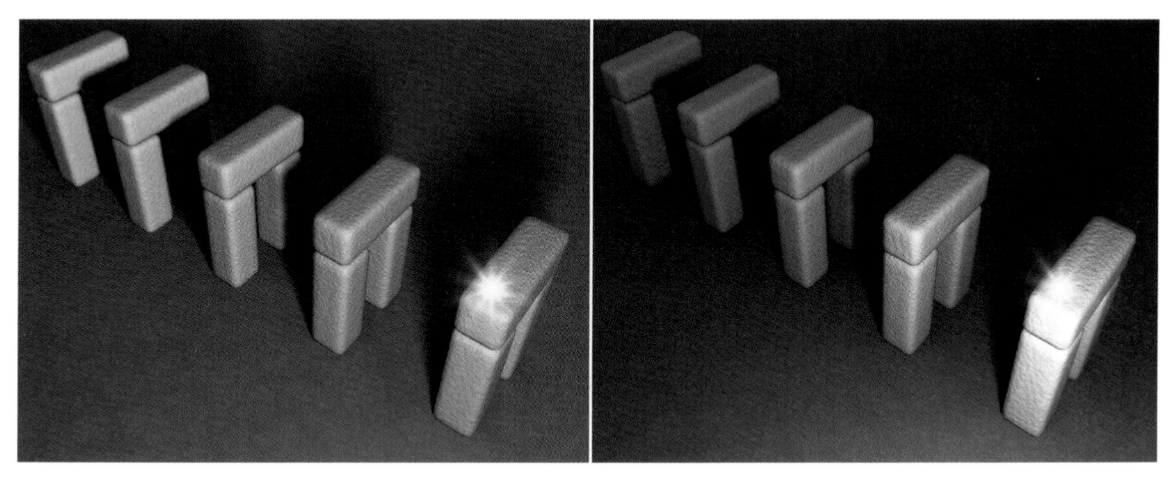

[Figure 2.14] Without decay (left), objects far from the light are illuminated as brightly as nearby objects, while inverse square decay (right) makes objects near the light source much brighter than objects farther away.

Some software offers a multiple-choice setting between three or four specific types of decay. Another way to adjust decay is by using a numeric value, usually labeled *decay* or *exponent*. The numeric approach is more flexible, because you are not limited to whole numbers. For example, if you wanted less than a decay of 2 (inverse square), but more than 1 (linear), you could type a number such as 1.8. Your main choices are shown in Table 2.1.

[Table 2.1] Decay Rates

NUMERIC VALUE	TYPE OF DECAY
0	None
1	Linear (inverse)
2	Quadratic (inverse square)
3	Cubic

Inverse Square Decay

An inverse square decay (also called *quadratic* or a decay rate of 2) is the most physically correct setting; this is the type of decay seen in real light sources. In real life, decay is a function of light rays geometrically spreading out over space, not of the rays decreasing in energy. Real rays of light can travel huge distances—they can keep traveling for light years—without wearing out or growing dimmer. However, as they travel farther away from their source, rays spread out geometrically so that they are more and more scarce.

Figure 2.15 shows how a plane moving twice as far from a source gets half as many rays of light over its height. This also happens across the width of a surface, so that it will become one-quarter as bright every time you double the distance between the surface and the light. The geometric spreading-out of photons is simulated by using an inverse square decay on your lights.

If a light source is visible in your shot, as in Figure 2.16 where a character has just lit a match, or you have modeled a lamp on a table and it is turned on, then it is a good idea to use an inverse square decay. Also, when working with global illumination, inverse square decay is a geometric property of how indirect light is bounced between surfaces, so using it on your primary lights can add to the consistency and realism of the rendering.

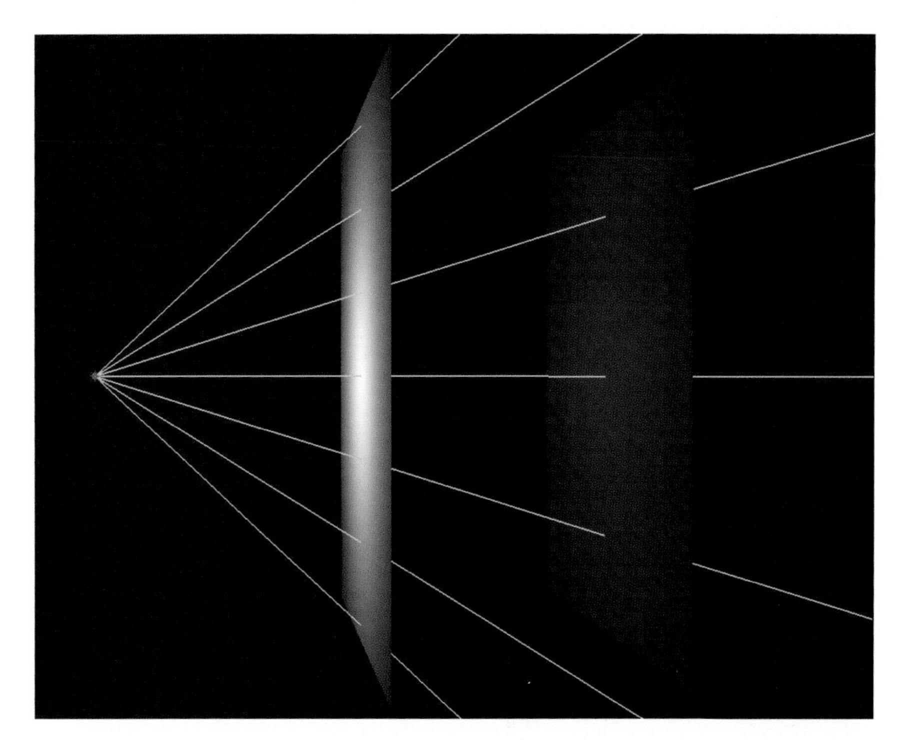

[Figure 2.15]
Six rays of light hit a nearby surface, while half as many hit a surface at twice the distance. This difference over the height and width of a surface makes an object twice as far away receive one-quarter as much light.

[Figure 2.16]
An inverse square decay is useful when a light source (such as this match) is visible within a scene. Character by Rini Sugianto.

Using No Decay

There will be situations when you will not want to use inverse square, and you may prefer to use no decay at all. Lights with inverse square often need a very high intensity in order to light distant objects. As a result, the lights end up overexposing nearby surfaces. A light with no decay, however, can be easily adjusted to light a large space consistently.

If you are simulating a very distant light source, like the sun, then using no decay can sometimes look the most realistic. For example, the sunbeam entering the room in Figure 2.17 would not get dimmer between the table and the floor. Real sunlight, which had just traveled millions of miles to reach the earth, would not suddenly decay during the last few feet of its journey.

[Figure 2.17]
A sunbeam entering a room is an example of light that does not need any decay.

Other Decay Settings

Using a decay of 3 (cubic) makes a light decay more rapidly than a real light would in the vacuum of space, but you could use it to simulate a light in a thick fog or under murky water. Very high decays can also be useful if you are adding a light that needs only to influence a surface right next to it, such as positioning an extra highlight in a particular place on a car's bumper.

A decay of 1 (linear) can be a useful compromise between full inverse square and no decay at all. If you have simulated light bouncing up from the ground, you'll want some decay. However, since inverse square might be too much, using a linear decay may work well.

In addition to different decay settings, many programs also let you set specific distances at which your light will decay or attenuate. For example, you could set a light to begin growing dimmer at 50 units, and disappear completely at 100 units from the light. This might not be physically correct, but it is certainly convenient. If you know that a light should not reach a certain object, setting it to cut off by a specific distance is a more reliable way to limit it than just using inverse square by itself.

Diffuse and Specular

In real life, diffuse and specular are two ways that light can be reflected off a surface. In *diffuse reflection,* light rays are scattered in all directions. Think of light hitting a plaster wall or a piece of fabric, or anything that is not glossy or shiny—that is diffuse light reflectance. *Specular reflection* occurs when rays of light are not scattered at all, but instead are reflected in parallel, creating a perfectly focused image. A mirror, or anything with a mirror-like reflection, shows you specular light reflectance.

When 3D surfaces are rendered, they can reflect the illumination from your light source in both diffuse and specular ways, as shown in Figure 2.18. The diffuse illumination is the primary shading, covering the side of the surface that faces the light, while the specular highlight simulates a reflection of the light source itself. In the case of point lights or spotlights, which are infinitely small points in space, an accurate specular reflection would be less than a pixel in size. To correct for this, a cheat is programmed into the renderer that adds an adjustable highlight size to each surface, simulating a reflection of an area bigger than the tiny point.

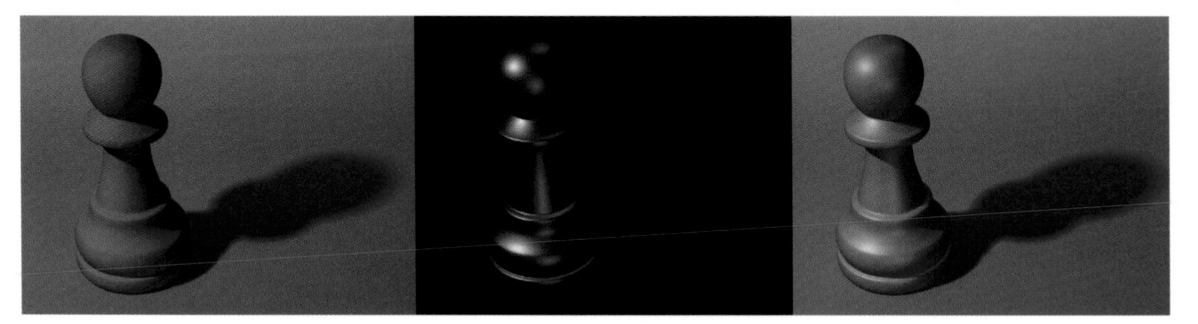

[Figure 2.18] A light can emit diffuse illumination (left), specular illumination (center), or both (right).

You can control whether each light emits diffuse or specular illumination, and often you will want a light that emits one or the other, but not both. If you wanted to add highlights to your character's eyes, but didn't want to over-light the whole eyeball, then you could set a light to emit specular only. If you added lights to simulate illumination bouncing up from the ground (which would be a very soft source of illumination without a concentrated source), then you could set those lights to emit diffuse only, so that there wouldn't be unmotivated highlights on the bottom of a shiny surface.

Some renderers, like Pixar's RenderMan, allow you to set different levels for a light's diffuse and specular light emission. In such programs, you might give the sun a specular level of 1.0 to 1.2, fill lights representing the sky specular levels between 0.3 and 0.5, and lights representing illumination reflected back from the ground levels between 0 and 0.25. These numbers are just starting points; as you test-render, you will usually want to tweak the diffuse and specular levels from each light. If your renderer only lets you turn specular emission on or off, but you really want a level in between, try making two lights—one for diffuse and one for specular—and adjust their colors and intensities separately.

Light Linking

If you have a light that you only want for a specific purpose, such as adding highlights to a character's eyes, then you can use *light linking* (also called *selective lighting*), which allows you to associate specific lights with specific objects. You could create a point light, set it to emit only specular illumination, and then link the light to the character's eyeballs. If this light is kept reasonably close to the camera position, you're guaranteed that the character's eyes will always have highlights when it looks toward the camera. And because of light linking, you'd know those highlights won't affect anything else in the scene.

You can also use light linking to gain more precise control over how different objects are lit. If you have a light illuminating many objects in your scene, you might find that it looks good on most of the objects, but somehow appears to light other objects with the wrong intensity, color, or angle. Instead of settling for a compromise, you can make a second copy of your light, and link it to the objects that weren't well lit. Once you unlink the old light from those objects, you can adjust the second light in however you want.

In Softimage | XSI, there are two selective lighting modes, *inclusive* and *exclusive*. In inclusive mode, once the light is associated with some objects, it will only illuminate those objects. In exclusive mode, the light will illuminate all objects except for the ones with which it is associated.

Figure 2.19 shows an example of how you can use light linking to gain more precise control over how different objects are lit. There are two different lights used to represent the illumination from the match. One is linked to the character's hand and clothing, but not to his head. This one is positioned exactly at the match flame, so that the hand and arm will be lit from a realistic angle. The other light is linked only to the character's head, and it is cheated forward, so that the match light will better define his face.

Light linking is a marvelously powerful cheat, but can make an unrealistic image if you aren't careful. Whenever you set up a scene with light linking, you need to test-render it and make sure that what you've done makes sense and doesn't depart too obviously from what's plausible.

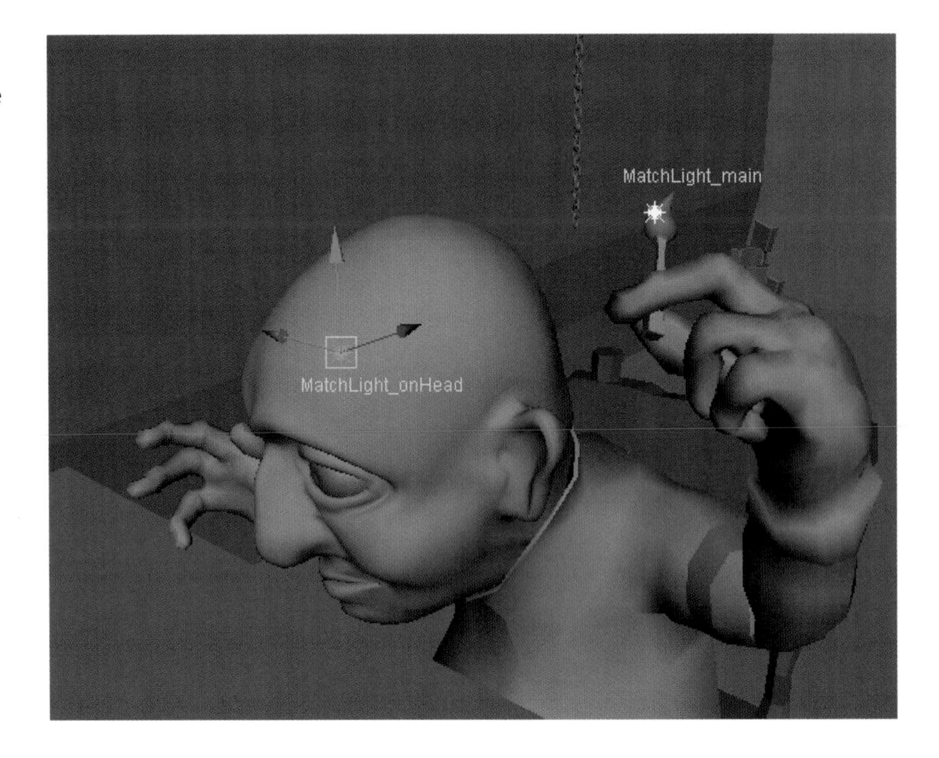

[Figure 2.19] Light linking allows you to cheat, and illuminate some objects using a light with a different angle, color, or intensity than what illuminates other objects.

Cookies

In lighting for movies, television, and theater, a *cookie* (also called a *cucoloris* or *gobo*) is a piece of metal, wood, or cardboard with holes or shapes cut out of it. Cookies are designed to break up a light or project a pattern into the scene. The exact origin of all these terms is not clear, but in the early days of movies, when lights were very hot, metal cookie sheets were used to make a cookie. Cucoloris could be a contraction of *cookie* and *iris*, and *gobo* could be short for *go-between*. Figure 2.20 shows a real cookie in action.

It is possible to model a cookie as a 3D object and put it in front a light that casts shadows. However, a more direct way to create a similar effect in computer graphics is to map an image onto a light. In most 3D programs, the color of a light is mappable with any image you choose. You could use an image as shown on the left side of Figure 2.21 as a cookie, mapping it to the color of a spotlight. On the right side of the figure, you can see the pattern projected into a scene.

[Figure 2.20] A real-life cookie has holes cut out to shape or dapple a spotlight's illumination.

[Figure 2.21] A texture map used as a cookie (left) breaks up your lighting as if the sun had filtered through the trees (right).

Lighting in Production

Now that you've added lights to your scene, and adjusted their options and controls, you press Render. Your first render is, at best, a rough draft of what you want to develop into a professional final product. Most of your time in lighting is spent revising and improving the setup—this is where the real work gets done. The art of lighting is essentially the art of *revising* lighting, to get it to look as good as possible by your deadline.

When to Light

When you are working in the early stages of a project, like modeling, rigging, or layout, you probably don't want to spend too much time on lighting. At most, you could use a simple lighting rig that allows you to see the models.

By the time animation is being test-rendered, it is a good idea to have at least one light casting a shadow. If you render animation without any shadows, it is easy to overlook physical contact mistakes, like a foot not making contact with the ground. These kinds of mistakes will become apparent in a fully lit scene, so it is best if you can see them when testing animation.

The real lighting process begins when your layout is done: You know where your camera will be positioned and how the shot is composed, your animation is complete, and you can see where the characters will appear throughout the shot. Also, your shaders and textures are finished, so you can see how objects will respond to light.

Sometimes production schedules will force you to do lighting work while revisions are being made to the animation or even to the camera. This is an unfortunate necessity. Lighting a scene that is still changing will waste a lot of your time, because you will need to go back and change your lighting (sometimes multiple times) in reaction to changes made to the animation, shaders, or textures.

The Feedback Loop

An essential part of refining your scene is the feedback loop: making changes, waiting to see the results of each change, evaluating those results, and then making more changes. The key here is a tight feedback loop, which means seeing results as soon as possible after making changes. This leads to a quicker work pace and allows more refined results on a tight schedule.

How can you get feedback faster? For some types of changes, such as changing the position of a light or adjusting the size of a spotlight's cone, most modern 3D software supports real-time feedback, which shows you the basic illumination, highlights, and shadows as you drag the light. What's visible in real-time is limited, however, and usually doesn't show you how everything will appear in a final render.

When you are doing software test-renders, you should always think of ways to save rendering time.

- Leave visible in your scene only those objects that you really need to see in each render; hide everything else. If there are any particularly complex models in your scene, sometimes a simpler object can be used as a stand-in while you adjust lights around it.
- If you are adjusting one specific light or shadow, hide all the other lights in your scene, so you are rendering only with that light. As mentioned above, soloing a light gives you a clearer view of exactly what the light is contributing to the scene, but it also saves valuable rendering time by skipping the calculation of the other lights and shadows in your scene.
- Most changes can be made while looking at only part of your image—crop a region that only shows you what you need to see, rather than rerendering the entire frame.
- Even when lighting film resolution shots, render your earlier tests at a video resolution, and render only a few frames from the shot at full resolution until you have the lighting approved.
- Turn off any functions or effects that aren't a part of what you are currently adjusting. You can light a character without her hair visible in the shot for most of your test renders, and then do only a few tests with hair visible when you are working on the hair lighting. You do not need time-consuming functions such as raytracing, global illumination, or high-quality anti-aliasing turned on during all of your test renders.

Since computers are getting faster, you may wonder why you even need to learn all of these optimization and test-render tricks. Even though computers get faster every year, computer graphics productions also continue to get more complex and push the limits of even the newest hardware. Learning to work smart and think strategically before each render is a skill you'll need later in your career.

Chapter 11 discusses another key factor in your feedback loop. If you render elements in separate passes and layers, you can make many changes to your scene in a compositing program, which allows some kinds of changes to be made interactively without rerendering.

Naming Lights

Naming becomes especially important when you are installing lights that more than one person will use or edit. If you expect other people to be able to make sense of your lighting design, or if you want to avoid mistakes that arise from confusing one light and another, take care to label every light clearly.

The most informative names refer to the type of light, its motivation, and what it is illuminating. For example, "Spec_fromMatch_onEyes" will tell you that a light is designed to create specular highlights, motivated by a match, illuminating the character's eyes. "Bounce_fromRedCarpet_onSet" describes light bouncing off the red carpet onto the rest of the set. Most studios have much more exacting naming conventions. Exactly which conventions you follow doesn't matter as much as making sure that everyone follows the same set of rules, consistently trying to create helpful names for each light.

Organizing your lights into clearly named groups is also important. If you have some lights used for similar purposes—such as exterior lights coming in through windows of a set, interior lights on the set, lights added around a particular character, or lights associated with a particular effect, then grouping the lights and giving the groups intuitive names makes them easy to find and adjust, and easier to save as separate files and reuse in another shot.

Managing Versions

You will go through many versions of a scene before you achieve a final, approved lighting setup. When you save your versions, be sure to save the rendered images, and also save the lights in the scene used to render it. If you have just shown a version of a scene to the client, you might make a folder with a backup of the 3D files and the rendered images from that version, so that you can go back and retrieve that version if needed. Often you will go backward—clients do request changes one day and then ask you to revert to a previous iteration. Often when you make two versions of something, you will be asked to "split the difference" between a previous version and the current one, making it vital to maintain an association between the 3D scenes used and the images that you show to the client.

When you compare two versions of an image, it's best to compare them in the same window, flipping back and forth between the old and new images. Viewing images side by side, it would be difficult to detect every change, but when viewing both versions in the same window, you can see even the most subtle changes, because they appear as motion on the screen when you flip between them. Comparing a pair of frames before and after a change is great for testing your own work, and is also useful in showing requested changes to a client or director.

Exercises

A review of lighting basics may have been old news for some readers, but new to those just getting started. Here are some ideas for readers who want to go further with the material covered in this chapter:

1. The essential process of soloing a light—hiding all other lights and rendering your scene with just one light visible—is the best way to explore what each light is doing in your scene. If you have any older scenes that you have lit before reading this book, load them up and try soloing some of the lights. See if you discover any surprises, such as lights in your scene that don't actually do anything, or lights that aren't illuminating the intended subject.

2. Run some tests in your software to explore each type of light available. While most scenes can be lit entirely with spotlights, be sure you go through and test each of the other lighting tools available to you.

3. Try using the different decay options available in your software. In some cases, you may need to use very high light intensities to compensate for higher decay rates, but it is worthwhile to experiment with decay and all of the other options available to you on each light.

[CHAPTER THREE]

Shadows and Occlusion

Setting up shadows takes just as much time and attention as setting up lights. You can think of all of your illumination as one half of your lighting design, and shadows as the other, equally important half. Shadows can add richness to the tones and shading of your image, tie elements together, and improve your composition. Besides their artistic importance, rendering shadows is a key technical area to master. Making the best choices of shadow-casting algorithms, building up a bag of tricks to cheat and manipulate your shadows, and knowing how to optimize your shadows for the best possible rendering speeds are essential skills for any 3D artist. This chapter will explore both the visual and the technical sides of shadows and occlusion in 3D graphics.

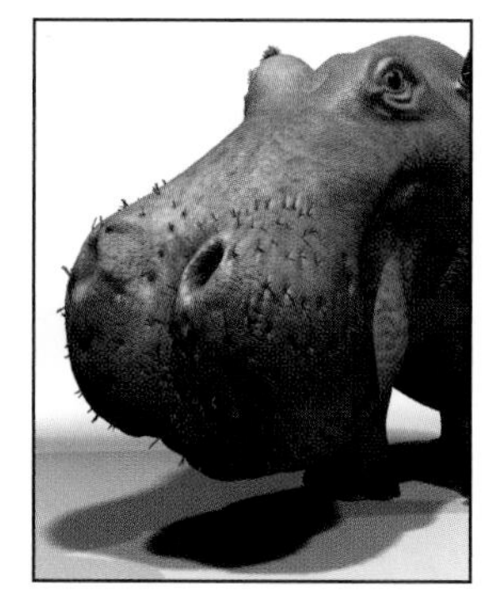

The Visual Functions of Shadows

People commonly think of shadows as obscuring and limiting vision. But shadows can often reveal things that otherwise would not have been seen. Here are some of the visual functions that shadows serve in cinematic images and computer graphics.

Defining Spatial Relationships

When objects cast shadows onto each other, the spatial relationships between the objects are revealed. For example, compare the scene in Figure 3.1 before and after shadows are added. Without shadows, you can't tell exactly where each ball is located. On the right side of the figure, the added shadows reveal how close some of the balls are to the back wall, when a ball is on the ground, and when two balls are near each other.

[Figure 3.1]
On the left side, you cannot tell how close the large upper ball is to the back wall. The most basic use of shadows is to show spatial relationships between objects, as in the right side of this figure.

The way shadows visually indicate spatial relationships is both a blessing and a curse. When a scene is rendered with shadows, the shadows can reveal mistakes and inaccuracies in your animation, such as if a character's feet are floating above the ground instead of planted firmly on it. Animation that was created and approved without shadows may need to be fixed once it has been test-rendered with shadows and any flaws are made visible.

If you are reading this book indoors, look around the room at all the places where furniture meets the floor. At a glance, you can probably tell whether each piece is directly touching the floor or is held above the floor by wheels or casters, just by looking at the shadows each piece of furniture is casting. As you look around the room, your eye interprets small differences in the shadows almost instantly, determining the spatial relationship between the furniture and the floor.

Revealing Alternate Angles

In addition to spatial relationships, a well-placed shadow can also disclose new angles on a subject that otherwise might not be visible. In Figure 3.2, the woman's profile is brought out by a shadow, without which we would see only the front of her face.

[Figure 3.2]
The shadow reveals a character's profile, which otherwise would not be seen in the rendering.

You can think of the light casting shadows as something like a second camera, with its own angle of view and perspective on the character. Most 3D programs enable you to view the scene from a light's point-of-view, as an aid to positioning and aiming the light. The outline of what you see—the profile of the subject from the light's point-of-view—shows you the shape that will be rendered as the shadow.

Be careful that no part of the character is much closer to the point-source or spotlight, lest it become disproportionately enlarged in the shadow. Also, be sure that any cheats that the animator has created don't look strange from the shadow's perspective. For example, if the animator has stretched a character's arm to an extra long length in order to bring the hand into the foreground, that cheated pose might look believable from the point of view of the camera, but look strange where the character's shadow is visible on the side wall. To fix this, you may need to change the angle of your shadows, or might even have to use a second version of the character without the cheat as a shadow object (shadow objects are discussed below).

Enhancing Composition

Shadows can play an important role in the composition of your image. A shadow can lead the viewer's eye to a desired part of the rendering, or create a new design element to balance your composition. Figure 3.3 shows how a well-placed slash or other shadow can "break up" a space, adding variety to what otherwise would be a monotonous rear wall.

Adding Contrast

Figure 3.3 also shows how a shadow can add contrast between two elements that might otherwise appear similar in tone. In the right frame, the shadow behind the vase adds depth and definition to the rendering by increasing the contrast between the vase and the similarly colored wall behind it. The vase now pops out much more clearly from the frame, so that people will clearly notice its shape, even in a briefer shot.

[Figure 3.3]
A slash breaks up the space and adds to the composition, making the image on the right a more attractive rendering.

Indicating Off-Screen Space

A shadow can also indicate the presence of off-screen objects. The sense of "off-screen space" is especially important when you are telling a story or trying to set a mood for a small scene. A shadow that appears to have been cast by objects not visible on the screen indicates that there is more to the world you are representing beyond what's directly visible in the shot. The shadows in Figure 3.4 suggest a great deal about the other elements that might be in the off-screen environment. Sometimes you can just project an image, mapped to the color or intensity of the light, to simulate shadows from off-screen objects.

[Figure 3.4] The shadow indicates what might exist in off-screen space.

Integrating Elements

By cementing the relationship between objects, shadows can also create a kind of integration between the elements in a scene. In the fanciful or implausible scenes often created in computer graphics, realistic shadows may be the only threads of reality available to tie together and sell the whole image. Even the commuting hippo in the subway car in Figure 3.5 looks more natural and present in the scene with shadows underneath him. Building a solid sense of contact between 3D sets and characters, between human actors and digital creatures, or even between 3D characters and real environments, is perhaps the most essential function of shadows. Without this contact, many scenes would fall apart into an apparent collage of disjointed images.

[Figure 3.5] Shadows help integrate otherwise incongruous elements.

Which Lights Need Shadows?

In real life, all lights cast shadows; there is no equivalent in real life to having a light with shadows turned off. In computer graphics, you could imitate this rule by turning on shadows from all of your lights. More often, however, 3D artists are highly selective about which lights need to cast shadows and which don't.

Shadow Clutter

Next time you watch a television comedy that was filmed in front of a studio audience, take a look at the floor. Around the actor's feet, you often see a pattern of overlapping shadows, each aiming a slightly different direction. The overlapping shadows are caused by the grid of spotlights overhead, which light the actors and the set. These shadows would not be motivated by the light in most real rooms.

You may even notice that the set itself was designed and built to hide many of the extra shadows. For example, the living room sofa in a situation comedy would be out in the middle of the stage, with a lot of space behind it. Often there will even be a staircase filling the rear wall of the set, so that the actors would never be sitting or standing right in front of a wall that would accumulate too many of those unmotivated overlapping shadows.

When you see how far designers go to hide unwanted shadows, you can appreciate how lucky we are in 3D to be able to turn off any shadow we don't like. In animation, living room sofas can be pushed right against a wall, with no unwanted shadows behind the characters.

When used judiciously, the power to leave shadows turned off for selected lights is a wonderful option. Figure 3.6 shows how much cleaner and simpler a scene can look with one unified shadow compared to a clutter of several overlapping shadows.

[Figure 3.6]
Which do you like better? In most cases, simpler, unified shadows are better than many overlapping shadows.

Secondary Shadows

In complex scenes, you usually need more than one light casting shadows. Trying to get away with only one shadow-casting light will especially hurt you in areas that are already in a shadow. For example, the ball in the left frame of Figure 3.7 does not look fully "attached" to the ground because it does not cast a shadow. Since the ball is in an area where one shadow is already being cast, it is being lit only by a secondary light, which does not cast shadows. In the right frame of Figure 3.7, turning on shadows from the other light better attaches the ball to the ground, even though it is in a shadow area.

[Figure 3.7]
Without secondary shadowing (left), the ball casts no shadow. Scenes without secondary shadowing can look very flat in shadow areas. With shadows (right), the ball appears better attached to the ground.

Any light that *doesn't* cast shadows creates risks: It could shine straight through walls, illuminating the inside of a room as brightly as the outside. A light from behind a character, meant to illuminate a character's hair and shoulders, could end up brightening the inside of the character's mouth. It could also make parts of your scene look very flat in places where you would expect smaller objects to shadow each other.

Shadow Color

In real life, shadows often appear to be a different color than the area around them. For example, outdoors on a sunny day, shadows can appear to be tinted blue. The shadows appear blue because the bright yellow light from the sun is blocked from the shadow area, leaving only indirect light and blue light from other parts of the sky.

There is a parameter on most lights called *shadow color*, which adds color to the shadows cast by that light. Pure black is the default shadow color, which means that no extra color or brightness is added to a shadow. When shadow color is set to any value above pure black, it brightens the shadow by letting some of the original light leak into the area where it should be blocked. A shadow color of pure white would look the same as turning off shadows completely.

If you have a scene where the shadows are too dark or need color added, as on the left frame of Figure 3.8, one option would be to adjust the shadow color of your light. The middle frame of Figure 3.8 shows the results with the shadow color set to a deep blue. That was quick and easy, and didn't require any new lights to be added to the scene, but it's not very realistic. Notice how the blue in the middle frame fills in only the shadow itself; it does not extend naturally into the unlit side of the object.

[Figure 3.8]
A black shadow looks unnatural (left), but the shadow color parameter lightens only the cast shadow, not the unlit side (middle). Colored fill lights added to tint shadows achieve more believable results (right).

The best way to re-create blue outdoor shadows is not to use the shadow color parameter at all. Adding blue fill lights to the scene, which will naturally become more visible where the sunlight is blocked, is a better option. The right frame of Figure 3.8 shows a more natural result; the shadow color parameter is turned back down to pure black, and blue fill lights are added around the scene. The fill light can come from multiple spotlights or sky-dome–type lighting, but any source of light that comes from different angles will add color more naturally than the shadow color parameter. You may need to tint the key light color to compensate for the fill light, removing blue from the key so that the color balance of the scene does not shift.

In realistic lighting, adjusting your shadow tones by adding colored fill lights should always be your first choice, and the shadow color parameter should be used sparingly, if at all. The only physically correct setting for your shadow color parameter is pure black, because that means that an opaque object would block all of the light from the light source. Using the shadow color parameter at all is a cheat. If it is adjusted cautiously, with very dark color values, the shadow color parameter can make a shadow a little lighter or add a subtle tint to a shadow. If used too visibly, shadow color creates a mismatch between the cast shadow that it lightens and the unlit side of your subject that it does not lighten. Setting the shadow color parameter too high also creates the unrealistic situation of having a light that partially leaks through opaque objects.

Some artists generalize that shadows should always be of complementary colors to the objects casting them or to the key light. As a creative decision, you may use shadows with complementary colors to make colored objects pop out more visibly, but this is an artistic stylization, not something that always happens as a rule in real life. For example, the combination of yellow light with blue shadows that you often see outdoors would be unrealistic if recreated in an indoor scene that lacked a motivation for the blue fill light.

Testing Shadows

Even if you avoid using the shadow color parameter as a part of your general lighting, it is a handy tool for highlighting a shadow during test renders.

Cranking the shadow color up to a bright red, as shown in Figure 3.9, is a great way to isolate exactly where a particular light's shadow is going. Use this whenever there is room for confusion between several overlapping shadows, or if you are not sure which shadow comes from which light. If you make adjustments while the shadow color is bright red, you can see what you're doing even when adjusting shadows that will be subtle in the final render. When you're done with your adjustments, just set the shadow color parameter back to pure black.

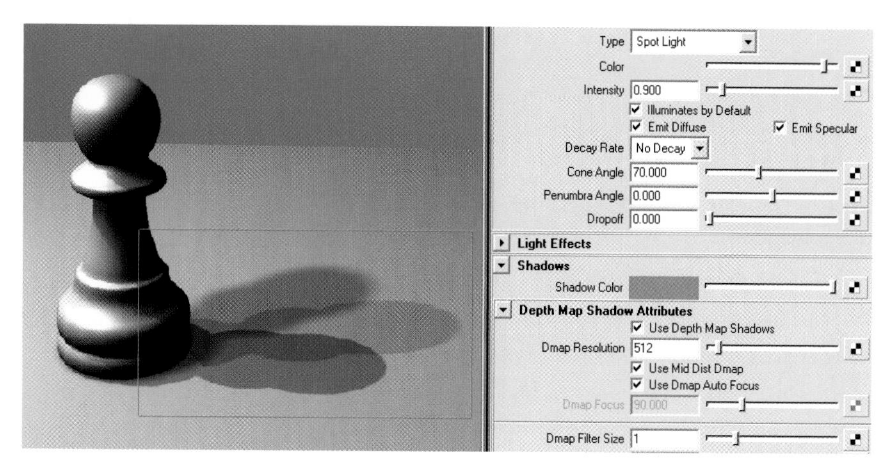

[Figure 3.9] Temporarily assigning a bold shadow color makes it easier to see and adjust an individual shadow within your scene.

Shadow Size and Perspective

The location of a light source relative to the object casting shadows determines the size of the shadows. For example, a light that is far away from your subject will cast a shadow similar in size to your subject, as shown on the left in Figure 3.10. Alternatively, moving the light closer to the subject will enlarge the shadow, making the shadow much bigger than the subject itself, as shown on the right side of the figure.

Adjustable shadow size works only with shadows coming from a point source, such as a spotlight. If you were using directional or infinite lights, they would always make shadows the same size as the object casting them, regardless of position.

[Figure 3.10] What size do you want your shadow to be? Move the light farther away for a smaller shadow (left) or up close for a larger shadow (right.)

Shadows look different, and even take on different shapes, when cast from different perspectives. For example, there is something visibly wrong with the sunbeams on the left side of Figure 3.11. They were produced by putting one spotlight directly outside of each window in the room. You can see how they splay outward, aiming away from the nearby lights. Moving the lights much farther back, as shown on the right side of the figure, makes the shadows appear parallel. On the right side of the figure, the left and right sides of the sunbeams appear parallel, as they would in real life. Using an infinite or directional light instead of a spotlight could also create parallel sunbeams.

[Figure 3.11] Sunbeams that spread out from an unnaturally close perspective (left) give away that sun lights were placed too close to the windows. Moving lights farther away (right) creates parallel sunbeams.

Shadow Algorithms

Many rendering programs let you choose between two popular techniques to calculate shadows:

- *Depth map* (also called *shadow map*) *shadows* are typically the quickest and most efficient to render, but have a finite resolution and sometimes need to be adjusted (as described below) to avoid artifacts.
- *Raytraced shadows* are easy to use and accurate at any resolution, but usually take more rendering time to compute.

The following sections discuss how to use depth map shadows and raytraced shadows, along with their advantages, disadvantages, and options for adjusting their appearance.

Depth Map Shadows

Depth map shadows are currently the most popular kind of shadows used in professional lighting work for film. This kind of shadow works by precomputing a depth map to determine where shadows will be rendered.

A *depth map* (sometimes abbreviated *dmap;* also called a *shadow map*) is an array of numbers representing distances. Before the renderer even begins rendering the scene viewed by the camera, it computes a depth map from the point of view of each light that will cast depth mapped shadows. For each direction that the light shines, the depth map stores the distance from the light to the nearest shadow-casting object found in that direction, as shown in Figure 3.12.

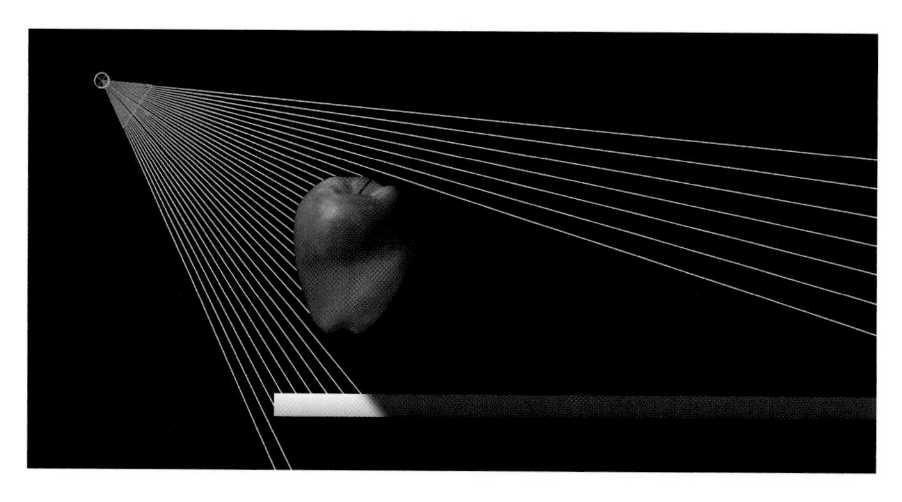

[Figure 3.12]
A depth map shadow is based on an array of distance measurements from the light to the nearest visible geometry, shown here as white lines.

During the rendering, the light will be cut off at the distances specified by the depth map, so that it does not shine farther than the distance stored for each angle. When rendering a surface under the apple, for example, the renderer needs to check only the depth map to see which parts of the ground are shadowed and which aren't. This saves a tremendous amount of rendering time, because the renderer doesn't need to repeatedly check through the scene to verify where objects come between the ground and the light.

Figure 3.12 shows only one row of depth measurements, as would exist in one "slice" of a depth map. A depth map would actually run both horizontally and vertically over the area illuminated by the light. For example, a depth map with a resolution of 512 would actually be 512 distance measurements wide by 512 distance measurements high.

Resolution and Memory Use

A single distance measurement within a depth map is stored as a *floating point value*. Floating point values can store just about any number, from tiny fractions to huge distances, but use 4 bytes to store each value. The resolution of a shadow map is used for both the horizontal and vertical dimensions of the map, meaning the number of bytes used is actually 4*(resolution^2). Table 3.1 shows the memory used by common shadow map resolutions, in megabytes.

[Table 3.1]

Shadow Map Memory Use

DEPTH MAP RESOLUTION	MEMORY USED
128	0.06 MB
256	0.25 MB
512	1 MB
1024	4 MB
2048	16 MB
4096	64 MB

As Table 3.1 shows, increasing your shadow map resolution will rapidly deplete your system's memory. As general defaults to start with, on a well-framed spotlight, a shadow map resolution of 512 will usually be adequate for television, and a resolution for 1024 will usually be good for final shots in a feature film.

Depth Map Framing

To make shadow maps work efficiently, you need to frame your shadow map so that it covers the geometry in the shadow and not too much extra empty space around it.

Spotlights are the lighting tools of choice for most projects that use depth map shadows. You can aim and control a spotlight to put your shadow exactly where it's needed. If you used an omnidirectional (point) light, then the software would need to calculate multiple depth maps in order to calculate the shadows cast in each direction. If you used a directional (infinite) light, then the depth map shadow might be stretched over too broad an area to optimize its resolution.

If you are lighting with a spotlight, make sure that the cone angle is focused as tightly as possible around your subject, so that you don't waste samples in your depth map shooting off into empty space. Figure 3.13 shows how a shadow map works efficiently for a narrow cone angle, but becomes lower resolution at a wider cone angle, as its samples are wasted over a wider area. If the light is very far away from your subject, you may be able to use a very narrow cone angle. You can check your framing by viewing the subject from the light's point of view, to make sure there isn't too much empty space around the subject within your shadow map.

[Figure 3.13] A spotlight that is poorly aimed, with its cone angle covering too wide an area, will waste most of the samples within a shadow map and produce inaccurate results (left), while a spotlight with a cone tightly focused around the subject uses the shadow map efficiently for an accurate shadow (right).

There may be situations when it seems impossible to properly frame a depth map for everything that needs to be shadowed. For example, if the sun were lighting a very large scene including a tree, a house, and an animated character, you'd really want a depth map framed neatly around each of these things. In programmable renderers such as Mental Ray and Renderman, studios can implement solutions providing control over which objects are in each shadow map, and which shadow maps a given light uses. In most off-the-shelf 3D software, however, there is no option to specify an arbitrary list of shadow maps that will be used by a light, nor is there an option that allows you to frame each of those shadow maps differently. When you are stuck with a shadow map covering too wide an area, and can't frame it any tighter because of the number of objects it needs to light, you have several choices:

- Replace your light with several spotlights, each covering a smaller area. This will add a little bit of natural variation to the lighting, which is often a good thing.
- Turn off shadows in the main light, and instead use shadows-only lights (described later in this chapter) to create shadows beneath each object.
- Use different well-focused spotlights for each shadow in a separate shadow pass, then use the shadow pass to darken the scene in compositing software. (Chapter 11, "Rendering Passes and Compositing," goes into detail about this.)
- Raise the resolution of the shadow map as high as necessary. Be mindful of the memory and performance hit that this solution will take, though. If test renders show that you need to go above 2048 or 4096, you may even find that a raytraced shadow (discussed below) could be more efficient in some cases.

Depth Map Bias and Self-Shadowing Artifacts

Artifacts like bands or grid patterns (as shown in Figure 3.14), are often caused by having a parameter called depth map bias set too low. For scenes built on a very large scale, you may need to raise the bias of some shadows to eliminate such artifacts.

[Figure 3.14] A depth map bias that's too low causes artifacts that appear to be stripes, grids, or moiré patterns, shown at a bias of 0.005 (left), 0.02 (middle), and 0.25 (right).

Bias is a number that gets added to each distance measurement in the shadow map, pushing the shadow-start-distance further out from the light. Increasing the bias slides the shadowing effect out a little further away from the surface casting the shadow, so that it doesn't accidentally start too soon and cause artifacts. Artifacts such as banding or grid patterns appear because points on the surface essentially begin shadowing themselves, in areas where the limited number of depth samples have under-estimated the actual distance from the light to the surface.

The bias is set in the distance units of your software, so a scene built on a larger scale might need a higher bias, or a scene built on a very small scale might need a lower bias.

Fixing Light Leaks

Too high a bias can cause visible gaps between the object casting a shadow and the point where the shadow itself starts. A high bias can even let light "leak" through walls and corners that should be blocking the light, as shown in Figure 3.15.

If you have light leaking through corners, there are some things you should do to isolate and fix the problem:

- Hide all the other lights in your scene, so that you are test-rendering only one light.
- If you are using a spotlight, make sure the cone is as narrow as possible to aim it just where it needs to shine.

- Reduce the depth map bias.
- Reduce the filtering or softness applied to the shadow, which extends light into shadow areas in much the same way as an increased bias.

A light leak is not always the fault of the lighting; often, it is a problem with your modeling. Here are some tips to fix your models to avoid light leaks:

- Build thicker geometry in your architecture, instead of using infinitely thin surfaces. Walls of real houses have a thickness, and yours should too.
- Add a polygon outside a building to block light where it is not needed.
- Make sure that all corners are properly beveled, not perfect 90-degree angles.
- If a part of your geometry isn't casting shadows, try adding another surface, such as a primitive shape, inside the part.

For some beginners, raising the shadow map resolution seems to be their first response to any shadow problem, even though this takes more memory and rendering time. If a problem with your shadows can be fixed by adjusting the bias, which does not add to your rendering time, then get the bias right first. If your shadows are not working well with a particular model, sometimes you need to fix the model.

[Figure 3.15] A depth map bias that's too high, combined with thinly built geometry, can cause light leaks (left). Lowering the bias (right) is one way to fix this problem.

Transparency Support

You expect a transparent object to cast a lighter shadow, and an opaque object to cast a darker shadow. However, conventional depth map shadows do not respond correctly to transparency, and are not any lighter when blocked by a transparent object For example, in Figure 3.16, the shadow becomes as dark under a transparent material as it is under an opaque material. Remember that each point in the depth map stores only one distance at which the light will be cut off, so it either stops at the glass or it doesn't, with no shades possible in between.

[note]

The conventional depth map shadows described here are what you get in most programs, but alternatives do exist. Most notably, deep shadow maps provide different levels of transparency in renderers that support them.

[Figure 3.16] A limitation of conventional depth map shadows is that different levels of transparency in objects do not cause lighter shadows.

You may be able to work around the lack of transparency support in scenes that have a small amount of glass by setting glass objects not to cast shadows, or by using light-linking to remove them from some of the shadow-casting lights. However, in scenes with a large amount of glass (in which you will probably be raytracing already to achieve refraction), you may want to bite the bullet and switch to raytraced shadows.

Raytraced Shadows

Raytraced shadows are shadows computed by tracing rays of light between light sources and illuminated objects. Raytraced shadows are computed one pixel at a time as you render rather than being pre-computed and stored in shadow maps. Raytraced shadows have a number of advantages over shadow maps:

- Raytraced shadows become lighter when shining through transparent surfaces, and they can even pick up color from colored transparent surfaces, as shown in Figure 3.17.
- With raytraced shadows, you don't run into many of the problems associated with shadow maps, such as needing to adjust bias to prevent artifacts or fix light leaks.
- Raytraced shadows do not use a fixed-resolution map, so they can always be crisp and accurate in any resolution rendering.
- Raytraced shadows support higher quality, more realistic soft shadows, when used with area lights as described below.
- Raytraced shadows work equally well from most types of lights, with no efficiency advantage pushing you toward spotlights.

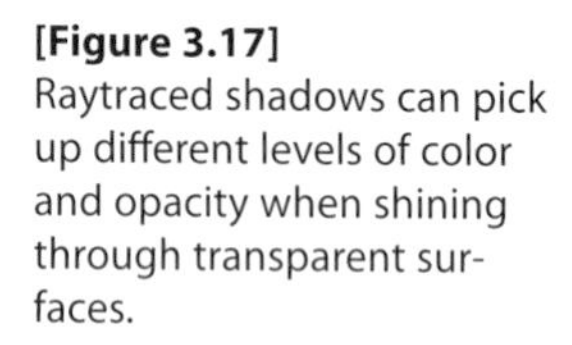

[Figure 3.17]
Raytraced shadows can pick up different levels of color and opacity when shining through transparent surfaces.

So, if raytraced shadows are so wonderful and easy to use, why didn't I write about them first? And why do most feature films still rely primarily on shadow maps? There are two simple answers:

- Raytraced shadows generally take longer to render than shadow maps. For complex scenes, the difference can be huge.
- Employing raytracing in your scene increases memory use, and effectively limits the complexity of the scenes you can render on your computer.

Thus, raytraced shadows may be the first choice of a beginner or someone working on simpler scenes, but currently they're less desirable for professionals working on larger, film-resolution projects or doing animation work on tight deadlines.

How Raytraced Shadows Work

Conventional raytracing works backwards in the sense that each ray is computed starting at the camera, instead of starting at the light source as in real life. For each pixel in your image, a ray is traced out from the camera at the appropriate angle until it hits part of a surface that needs to be rendered, as shown by the white lines in Figure 3.18.

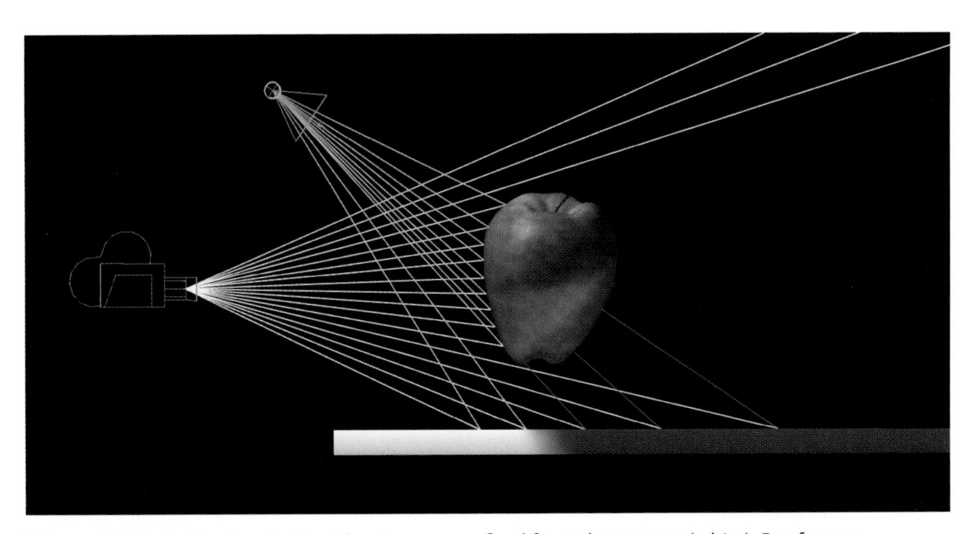

[Figure 3.18] Raytracing starts with primary rays fired from the camera (white). But for raytraced shadows, rays need to be fired from each rendered point towards the light, to see if the path is clear (yellow) or blocked and requiring a shadow (red).

For each point on a surface, the renderer needs to determine which lights will be illuminating that point. If a light uses raytraced shadows, then the renderer needs to trace a path from the surface point to the light. If any polygons are found to be blocking that path, then the light will be blocked from the points on the surface. The area where the light is blocked from points on the surface forms the raytraced shadow. The yellow rays in Figure 3.18 show rays followed to the light; red rays show rays that were blocked by geometry, indicating that the point being rendered is in shadow.

If there is more than one light casting raytraced shadows, then the process of checking through space to see whether there are any polygons blocking a ray needs to be repeated for each light with raytraced shadows. All of this needs to be repeated at least once for each pixel, and usually more than once per pixel when rendering with anti-aliasing (anti-aliasing techniques will be discussed in Chapter 9 , "Shaders and Rendering Algorithms.")

The result is that raytraced shadows slow down even the fastest computers. Furthermore, the time required to raytrace the shadow is only a part of the performance hit taken by raytracing. All of the polygons in your scene that might be casting a shadow need to be stored in memory in a way that can be searched through. Instead of allowing the rendering software to focus on a small part of your scene at one time, the raytracing process requires continual access to large amounts of data, usually stored in memory in many sorted lists of polygons. The result is that raytracing a large, complex scene uses up far more memory than rendering without raytracing.

Trace Depth

One concern of using raytraced shadows is *trace depth*, the idea that raytracing is always limited to a finite number of steps. Raytracing without limits could potentially get caught in an infinite loop—leaving your computer rendering a reflection of a reflection of a reflection—if it were not limited to a finite number of calculations. These limits can cause problems with missing raytraced shadows. If your raytraced shadows don't appear within a reflection, or don't appear when seen through layers of refractive glass, chances are you've run into a limited trace depth. The image on the right-hand side of Figure 3.19 shows the consequences of a shadow not appearing in a reflection.

[Figure 3.19]
With a ray depth limit (trace depth) of 1, the raytraced shadow appears in the rendering but is not reflected in the bottom of the ball (left). With a depth of 2, you can see a reflection of the raytraced shadow (right).

Besides having a trace depth or ray depth limit setting on your light, trace depth may also be limited globally to your scene's render settings. Trace depth being set too low in either place can prevent your raytraced shadows from appearing in reflections or through refractive transparent surfaces.

Depth map shadows don't have a trace depth setting. A depth map shadow on a surface will tend to appear in any raytraced reflection of the surface, without regard for trace depth.

Hard and Soft Shadows

By default, most shadows are *hard* (having crisply defined, sharp edges, as shown in Figure 3.20). Some people dislike hard shadows, especially the very crisp ones achieved through raytracing, because traditionally they've been an overused staple of most 3D renderings.

In many cases, using *soft shadows* (which are less distinct and fade off toward the edges, as in Figure 3.21) for some of your lights tends to look more realistic than using only hard shadows.

[Figure 3.20] Hard-edged shadows indicate light from a small point source.

[Figure 3.21] Soft shadows come from larger light sources.

Hard and Soft Light

For realistic results, soft shadows should be used in conjunction with other signs of softer or less direct light in a scene. For example, if you compare Figures 3.20 and 3.21, notice that a penumbra has been added, giving the spotlight's cone a soft edge, to roughly match the softness of the shadows.

If you are lighting shiny or reflective subjects, take a careful look at the specular highlights and reflections, and make sure they look like reflections of a large enough light source to motivate your soft shadows. In some cases, you may need to replace specular highlights with a reflection of a larger light source to be believable with very soft shadows.

Before getting into soft shadow options, here are some scenarios in which you would want to use hard light as a creative choice:

- To simulate illumination that comes directly from a small, concentrated light source, such as a bare light bulb.
- To present direct sun on a clear day, which produces hard light.
- In space scenes, where light reaches objects without being diffused through an atmosphere.
- To call attention to an artificial light source, such as when a spotlight is focused on a circus performer.
- To project shadows with clearly defined shapes, such as when you want your audience to recognize a villain by watching his shadow on a wall.
- To create a harsh or inhospitable environment.

On the other hand, you would use soft lighting in these situations:

- To produce natural light on cloudy days, when you would not get very bold shadows.
- To create indirect light, such as light that has reflected off walls or ceilings, or light from the sky, which is generally very soft.

- To simulate light that has been transmitted through translucent materials, such as curtains or lampshades.
- To make many environments look more comfortable or relaxing, and make most subjects look more natural or organic. Most interior lighting fixtures in a home are designed to either diffuse or bounce light to soften the light from a lightbulb.
- To portray characters favorably or make them look beautiful. Close-up shots of many movie stars, especially female lead actresses in Hollywood movies, are frequently soft-lit.

If you look around and pay attention, you'll find a combination of soft and hard shadows in many situations where a quick glance might have made you think that only a hard shadow existed. For example, on a sunny day, you quickly notice the hard shadows from the sun, but if you look closely, you'll also see the soft shadows of light from the sky darkening areas underneath large objects.

Soft shadows work differently depending on whether you have chosen depth map shadows or raytraced shadows (both discussed earlier in this chapter) for your lights, so the next two sections discuss the specific options separately.

Soft Shadows with Depth Maps

You can soften a depth map shadow by increasing a *filter* (also called *dmap filter* or *shadow softness)* setting. Shadows softened through basic depth map filtering will produce a uniform softness, as shown on the left side of Figure 3.22, instead of getting softer farther from the object, as shown with the raytraced soft shadows on the right of the figure. If you are using a small amount of depth map filtering, this usually isn't a problem. If the object casting the shadows doesn't touch the ground, such as the shadow of a fish onto the ocean floor, then this kind of softening isn't a problem even with larger amounts of filtering. However, especially when physical contact needs to be shown, using too high a filter value can be unconvincing.

[Figure 3.22]
A depth map shadow is softened uniformly from beginning to end (left), whereas a soft raytraced shadow grows softer with distance (right).

Figure 3.23 shows a solution to making shadows that become softer with distance, using only basic depth map shadows: using several lights, each with their own depth map shadows, in a row or an array.

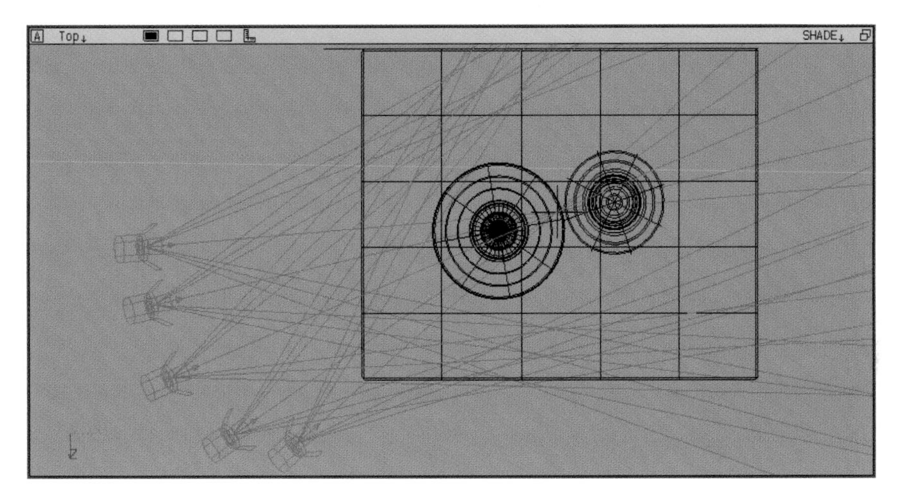

[Figure 3.23]
Viewed from the top, an array of multiple lights create overlapping soft shadows.

This forms the overall impression of one shadow getting softer, as shown in Figure 3.24. In this figure, you can still see the edges of the overlapping lights on the right side, because there are only five lights in the row. More lights would make these bands more subtle so that they could blend together better, but in a production with more complex surfaces and texture maps, these bands would not be as noticeable as they are in the figure.

[Figure 3.24] Several shadows blend together to form the impression of one larger source.

The filter is proportionate to the resolution of your shadow map. In other words, if you double the resolution of your shadow map, you might need to double the amount of filtering in order to get an equally soft shadow.

High filter values can be slow to compute, especially on higher-resolution shadow maps. Often you can get similar results if you lower the shadow resolution, instead of just raising the filter value. For example, if your shadow resolution is 1024, and a filter value of 16 isn't soft enough for you, try lowering the shadow resolution to 512 instead of doubling the filter size. The result will be similar, but much faster to render.

Soft Raytraced Shadows

Soft raytraced shadows can be particularly slow to render, but they are very pretty if you can afford the extra rendering time. By default, raytraced shadows from a point-source light are very sharp. In fact, they can often appear *too* sharp—more perfectly crisp than shadows cast by any light in real life.

Luckily, there are several options for getting soft, natural-looking raytraced shadows, with most programs supporting several types of area lights, or a light radius parameter to soften shadows from a point light.

Area Lights

An area light is the most conceptually elegant source for soft shadows, because it is designed to closely resemble the effects of a larger light source in real life. As in real life, a larger light source, such as a fluorescent ceiling panel, casts softer shadows than a smaller light source, such as a bare light-bulb. With area lights, you can simply scale the light larger to make a softer shadow, as shown in Figure 3.25.

[Figure 3.25]
A small light source (left) makes harder shadows, while larger light sources (right) create softer shadows.

Areas lights in some programs are available in a variety of shapes. Common shapes include a line, cylinder, rectangle, disc, and sphere. Each simulates a different shape light source; for example, a line or cylinder could be a good simulation of light from a fluorescent tube. If fewer shapes are available, often other shapes can be scaled to resemble them, such as scaling a rectangular area light down in one dimension to match a line.

In some programs, specular highlights will even take on the shape and size of your area lights. If they don't, then in some cases it will look better to turn off specularity from the light, and either do without highlights completely or add a raytraced reflection of a similarly shaped object.

Light Radius

Another option for creating soft raytraced shadows in some programs is a *light radius* parameter on the light. As a raytraced shadow option, light radius creates the impression of a larger light source, like a spherical area light, when calculating raytraced shadows. Increasing the light radius to 3, for example, is the same as having used an area light with a 3-unit radius.

Using a light radius parameter does not create any visible change to your rendering compared to using a round area light. It only changes how you control the softness (by adjusting this parameter instead of scaling the light), and gives you the flexibility to use different kinds of lights, such as a spotlight, to create soft raytraced shadows.

Sampling

Soft raytraced shadows tend to scatter rays and produce a noisy, dithered pattern, as shown on the left side of Figure 3.26. Turning up the number of Shadow Samples or Shadow Rays will smooth out the shadow, although increasing the sampling will slow down your rendering, making the raytracer do many times more work in computing the shadow. Increasing your scene's anti-aliasing quality will also help smooth out grainy shadows (and will also help slow down your rendering.)

[Figure 3.26] Raytraced soft shadows can appear grainy (left), so increased sampling is needed to smooth them out (right.)

Occlusion

Occlusion, in brief, is blocking, as in when an object blocks light. Technically, you could say that all regular shadows are kinds of occlusion, but most people reserve the term occlusion for a reference to other kinds of light-blocking that aren't regular shadows from a light. The few examples that follow should shed some light on different kinds of occlusion.

Ambient Occlusion

Ambient occlusion is a function designed to darken parts of your scene that are blocked by other geometry or less likely to have a full view of the sky. You can use ambient occlusion as a replacement or supplement to the shadows in your fill lights.

The main idea behind ambient occlusion is *hemispheric sampling* or looking around the scene from the point of view of each point on a surface. Figure 3.27 shows how rays are sampled in all directions from a point being rendered. The more of these rays hit an object (instead of shooting off into empty space), the darker the ambient occlusion. Ambient occlusion can usually have a maximum distance set for the rays, so that only nearby objects will cause the surface to darken.

[Figure 3.27]
This diagram illustrates the rays that would be sampled in rendering just one pixel with ambient occlusion. Ambient occlusion looks around the whole scene from the point being rendered, and darkens the point based on how many nearby objects are encountered which might be blocking light.

Ambient occlusion can be a terrific substitute for soft shadows from your fill light. You might still want your main light source, such as the sun, to cast a shadow, but your could turn off shadows from the surrounding fill lights, such as lights simulating illumination from the sky. In Figure 3.28, the brightest light source casts a raytraced shadow. The fill lights do not cast shadows, but ambient occlusion softly darkens the areas underneath and between objects, even in areas that are entirely within the raytraced shadow.

[Figure 3.28] A scene with no shadowing on its fill light can look very flat (left), but adding ambient occlusion (right) provides extra shading that darkens areas that would not be exposed to the sky.

It would be possible to use ambient occlusion by itself, with no shadows at all in a scene, but this might produce too uniform a darkening effect in each area where two surfaces came together, and the audience might notice the lack of distinct shadows cast in a specific direction.

Compared to raytraced soft shadows from an area light, ambient occlusion can provide similar looking shading in your scene, but usually takes less time to render.

Occlusion in Global Illumination

Global illumination (abbreviated GI) is an approach to rendering in which indirect light is calculated as it interreflects between surfaces in your scene.

GI is different from ambient occlusion, which functions solely to darken parts of the scene. GI adds light to the scene, to simulate bounced or indirect light, essentially replacing both fill lights and their shadows.

With GI, objects block light by reflecting it away, just as real objects would. In Figure 3.29, occlusion is seen where the ground is darkened underneath the sphere. It looks very similar to a soft shadow from a light, but it is actually a natural part of global illumination, which grows darker in areas from which light has been reflected away.

[Figure 3.29]
Occlusion is an intrinsic part of global illumination, darkening the area under the sphere where light is reflected away.

It is possible to illuminate a GI scene with absolutely no lights. To prevent the scene from being pure black, you would need to provide something brightly shaded to start it off, such as the white cube in Figure 3.30, which has a high incandescence level on its shader. With global illumination, the bright white cube illuminates the whole scene, as if it were an area light. Where light bounces off the sphere, it does not reach the floor, so parts of the floor are occluded as a natural part of the GI process.

[Figure 3.30]
With global illumination, any bright object can be a light source and cast its own shadows, even in a scene with no lights.

In theory, productions could be lit entirely with incandescent objects. This would provide interesting options, such as the ability to model any shape you want and use it as a light source. However, this would also make the lighting and rendering process inordinately slow. In productions that use global illumination at all, it is most often used to supplement the direct illumination from conventional lights.

Other Types of Occlusion

Final gathering and image-based lighting are two more algorithms that are related in that they provide extra illumination, usually with built-in occlusion.

Final gathering (sometimes abbreviated FG) serves as a simplified form of global illumination. By itself, it can provide a relatively quick, single-bounce solution to adding both indirect light and soft occlusion to a scene, and it is becoming increasingly popular for this purpose. FG can also be used in conjunction with a full GI solution where it serves to smooth out and improve the quality of the global illumination.

Image-based lighting (abbreviated IBL) is an approach to rendering in which a sky dome surrounding the scene is mapped with an image of an environment, and the colors and tones from that image are used to illuminate the scene. The process of rendering with IBL often uses a similar rendering technique to those used in rendering GI, and it will often include similar built-in occlusion. In renderers that do not provide built-in occlusion in IBL renders, IBL can be combined with ambient occlusion.

Chapter 4, "Lighting Environments and Architecture," will talk more about GI, FG, and IBL.

Faking Shadows

Sometimes you want more creative control over your lighting than regular shadows and occlusion can provide. This section discusses some handy cheats and tricks to help you create "fake shadows"—things that look like regular shadows or occlusion, but really aren't. These techniques will give you more ways to control the shape and location of your shadow and will even save rendering time.

Negative Lights

Negative lights, which are simply lights with their intensity (also called brightness or multiplier) set to a negative number, can be useful tools for darkening parts of your scene. For example, if you wanted to softly darken a corner of a room or the area underneath a table without using any soft shadow or occlusion techniques, you could just put a negative light in the area you wanted to darken. As shown in Figure 3.31, the negative light will suck the light out of that area.

[Figure 3.31] A light with a negative intensity (left) under the table makes a difference between the area looking too bright (middle) and extra darkness (right).

Generally, a negative light should not be set to cast shadows, nor should it emit any specular light; negative specular highlights would be unnatural black dots. If you want to add a colored tint to the area, remember that the light color specifies the color that will be subtracted, not added, so you may need to set the light to a complementary color of the tint you'll see in the scene. For example, to darken an area and give it a blue cast, you'd set the negative light's color to yellow.

You can use almost any type of light as a negative light; a simple point or omnidirectional light can work well. Remember that these lights are still emitting their negative light from a specific point, however, so just like a positive light, they will affect the surfaces facing them, not surfaces facing away from them. For example, a negative point light might not work well to darken the interior of a character's mouth, because from the center of the mouth it would hit the insides of the teeth, not the outsides of the teeth.

Negative spotlights can be handy for aiming at a specific area of the ground you want to darken with something that looks like a soft shadow. They can even be constrained or grouped to move with vehicles and characters for this purpose. For this kind of use, you'll typically want to use light-linking to light the ground with the negative light exclusively, not light the objects above the ground that motivate the fake shadow.

In Maya, there is a kind of light called a *volume light*, which seems ideal for negative lighting. A volume light influences only the area within its own radius, or within a selected shape such as a cube or cylinder, so you can scale the light to surround the exact region you want to darken. With a volume light, you can turn off the Emit Diffuse and Emit Specular options, and use only Emit Ambient. This means it will softly darken every surface in the region, without any regard to whether a surface is facing towards the light or away from it.

Shadows-Only Lights

Sometimes you want to add a shadow to your scene, but you don't want to add any light along with it. Most 3D packages enable you to create a *shadows-only light*, a light that doesn't brighten anything, but adds only an extra shadow. Yet this functionality exists as a hack or cheat you can set up, not a clearly labeled option.

In many programs, you can create a shadows-only light by sliding the light color down to pure black and setting the shadow color to a negative value, as shown in Figure 3.32.

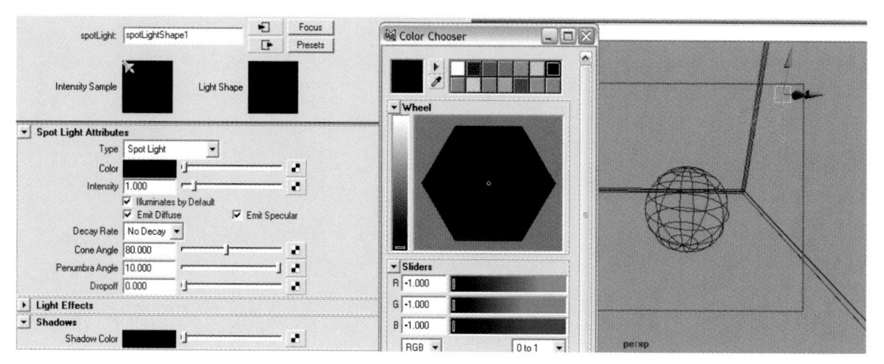

[Figure 3.32] In Maya, you can create a shadows-only light by giving a light a black color and a negative shadow color.

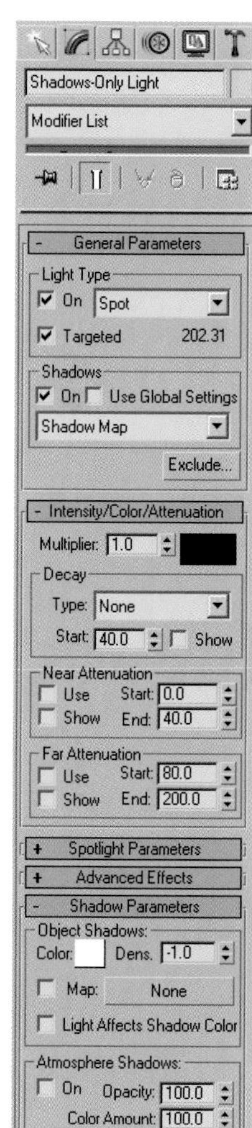

[Figure 3.33] A shadows-only light in 3D Studio Max uses a black light color, white shadow color, and a shadow density of –1.

In 3D Studio Max, you aren't allowed to set a color to a negative value, but an alternate technique for making a shadows-only light is to set the light's color to black, the shadow color to white, and the shadow density to –1, as shown in Figure 3.33.

If your software does not support either of the techniques above, there's an alternate way to create an identical effect. This works in any program that supports negative lights: Start with two copies of a spotlight in the same place. Give the first light a positive intensity of 1 and set it to cast shadows. Give the second light a –1 intensity but do not set it to cast shadows. As a pair, the first light will add illumination (except where it is shadowed); the negative light will subtract all of the illumination added by the first light, effectively canceling it out, but will also take light away from the area where the first light was shadowed.

Shadows-only lights can be tremendously useful if you want to control the exact size, angle, and perspective of your shadow without changing the lighting of the scene. You can even light the scene with several lights that don't cast shadows—such as the red, green, and blue lights in Figure 3.34—and then use a shadows-only light to add a single, consolidated shadow to an object, thus avoiding shadow clutter.

[Figure 3.34] Multiple shadows (left) can be replaced by a single shadows-only light (right).

Shadow Objects

Objects in most programs can be adjusted to cast shadows or not, whether or not they are directly visible in the render. This means that you can always add extra objects to your scene that cast shadows but are otherwise invisible. These are called *shadow objects*.

If you want to make an extra shadow, fill in gaps in an existing shadow, or plug any kind of light leak, adding a shadow object (which could be a primitive cube) can be a simple approach. Shadow objects are also handy if you plan to do any compositing. For example, if a real car were going to be composited into a 3D environment, you might add a shadow object the shape and size of the car to create proper shadows in the scene.

Shadow objects provide a marvelous degree of creative freedom that goes beyond the control a photographer or cinematographer would have when shooting in real life. Cinematographers use all sorts of blockers, flags, and other objects to cast shadows and control where a light can shine, but they have to put them in places that will not also be visible in the scene or block the camera. With shadow objects, you can shadow or block any light from any angle or position you want, and the surfaces you add to block the light will never appear in your rendering by accident.

You can also make a pair of two objects in the same place, with one being a shadow object (casting shadows but not directly visible) and the other being the regular object that will appear in the rendering but not set to cast shadows. Figure 3.35 shows an example of this: Because the regular object is a flat card textured to look like a tree, the shadows it would cast from the side would be very thin and un-tree-like. By turning off the tree card's shadow casting and adding a shadow object that is rotated toward the light, acceptable shadows can be cast.

[Figure 3.35]
A shadow object (green) helps cast a shadow from the side of the flat card textured as a tree.

Baking Lighting

Baking lighting is a process of computing all of the light and shadows that hit a surface and storing it as a texture map. Programs have different names for the functions that bake lighting, sometimes calling it "render to texture" or "convert to file texture." Once illumination has been baked into texture maps, the surface can be rendered very quickly, because lighting and shadows do not need to be calculated.

As an example of baking, suppose that you wanted a soft shadow of a shelf to appear a wall, as shown in Figure 3.36. Rendering a good-quality soft shadow from an area light takes a significant amount of rendering time, so you might not want to do that at every frame of an animation. Instead, the lighting and shadows can be baked into a texture map that gets applied to the wall.

Once converted into a texture map, as in Figure 3.37, the rendered lighting appears the same, even if the area light isn't present. The only downside is that the shadow would not change automatically if the lighting changed or something on the shelf moved.

Be careful about baking anything onto moving characters. The end result of a light-baking process is lighting that essentially seems "painted on" to surfaces. If the surface were on a moving character, the light would turn and move with the character instead of reacting to the lights in your scene. In fully rendered projects, baked-in occlusion should be limited to specific areas where you are sure you will want darkening throughout the whole production, such as the throat and nostrils.

[Figure 3.36] A soft shadow does not need to be recomputed for every frame if it can be baked into a texture map.

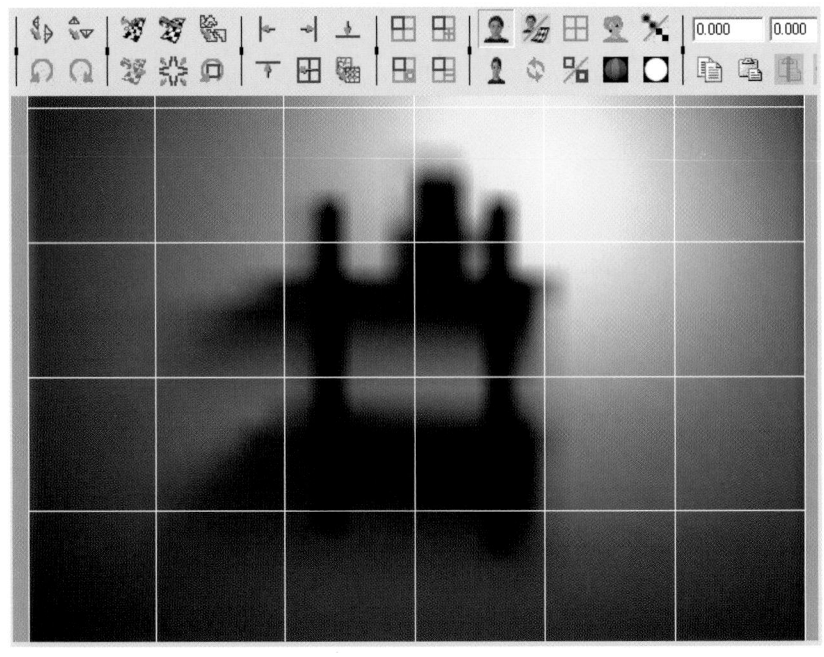

[Figure 3.37] A texture map on the wall stores a baked shadow.

For real-time games, a much greater amount of lighting, shadows, and occlusion is integrated into character textures, because it is often the only way possible to achieve certain looks. Even techniques such as global illumination can appear in an interactive game level if you bake your GI solution into textures on the walls and floor.

Conclusions

Use your own judgment regarding whether you need to apply any cheats or manipulations to your shadows. With computers getting faster and production schedules always placing demands on your own time, it might not always be worthwhile to spend extra time setting up a fake shadow just to speed up a rendering.

On the other hand, learning to think on your feet and cheat or manipulate any aspect of your rendering is a valuable skill. You are always better off knowing ten ways to achieve something rather than being boxed in to a single solution.

Some cheats and tricks are useful not just for saving rendering time, but for giving you more convenient and direct control over your output, which enables you to create the most appropriate shadow qualities for your scene.

Exercises

When you pay attention to shadows, the improvement to your renderings can be well worth the effort and experimentation you invest in them. Ask yourself some questions about the use of shadows that you see in movies and photographs that you admire, and in your own work.

1. Rent a movie, and pause it at some specific frames. Where do you see shadows? Are they all cast from the same light? Are the shadows hard or soft? Does the darkness of the shadows seem to match the level of contrast in the scene?

2. Examine a close-up picture of a person. Are there shadows on the person's face? Can you tell the angle of the lighting from the shadows?

3. Look at some of the renderings you have created previously. Do the shadows serve any of the visual functions that were mentioned in this chapter? Are the quantity, darkness, and softness of the shadows appropriate to the scene? Is there enough secondary shadowing in the shadow areas?

[CHAPTER FOUR]

Music Room rendered by Amilton Diesel.

Lighting Environments and Architecture

Lighting environments and architectural spaces with natural light requires an awareness of the world around you. Direct light from the sun, soft illumination from the sky, and indirect light blend their colors and tones in subtle ways. Naturally lit scenes will look different depending on the time of day or night, weather conditions, and angle of the sun. The shadows and contrasts of these variables set different moods. Artificial light—from desk lamps to street lights to the glow of a monitor—require an equal amount of care in simulating realistic throw patterns and illumination in your scene. Finally, global illumination simulates how all of these lights are transmitted from one surface to another. Global illumination is a key component to realistically rendering a space, so this chapter explores not just lighting with natural and artificial light sources, but also different types of global illumination, and how to simulate indirect lighting without it.

Daylight

You can create a simple outdoor lighting set-up by adding three elements to your scene: First, daytime scenes are often dominated by sunlight, illumination coming directly from the sun. Second, light from the sky needs to be added. In real life sky light might actually be light from the sun that has been transmitted through the atmosphere, but in 3D graphics we consider sky light as a separate source of illumination. Finally, indirect light must be added. This is light reflected off other surfaces in the scene; it doesn't come directly from the sun or sky. This section will look at these three steps, and some of the options and decisions you need to make along the way.

Sunlight

Think about your scene. What time of day is it? If it's outside, is there direct sunlight? You'll want to address the sun first, because the sun will be your *key light*—the most important, main light in defining your scene. The angle of the sun also comes from the time of day, but remember that your audience doesn't usually know whether the camera is facing east or west, so you have enormous creative latitude in picking the angle of the sun that lights your scene well.

Sunlight does not need any decay or attenuation based on distance. The light has already traveled billions of kilometers from the sun to reach your scene, so it is unlikely to wear out appreciably in the last few meters.

Make the sun a yellow color for most of the day, turning orange or red only during sunrise or sunset. Here are some sample colors, listed in both 0-255 and 0-1 format, depending on how you enter colors into your 3D software. There are more detailed color tables in Chapter 8, "The Art and Science of Color," but these should be good as a starting point.

[Table 4.1] Sample RGB Values for Sunlight

SOURCE	RGB (0–255)	RGB (0–1)
Sun at sunrise or sunset	182, 126, 91	.71, .49, .36
Direct sun at noon	192, 191, 173	.75, .75, .68
Sun through clouds/haze	189, 190, 192	.74, .75, .75

If you test-render your scene with just the sunlight and no other lights, it will appear very stark, as in Figure 4.1. Before you add any other lights, make sure that you are completely happy with which areas of the scene will be in sun, and which won't.

[Figure 4.1] Sunlight by itself looks contrasty.

Choosing an Infinite Light or a Spotlight

What kind of light source should you use for the sun? There are merits to using an infinite (or directional) light. You'll remember from Chapter 2 that an infinite light will cast all light and shadows in parallel. If you are rendering with raytraced shadows, and do not need to map the light with a cookie, then an infinite light is probably a good type of source to use for the sun.

If you use a spotlight instead of an infinite light, there is a risk that shadows could diverge unrealistically, instead of all appearing parallel. However, moving a spotlight far away from the scene and focusing it with a narrow cone angle can convey a similar appearance to an infinite light, while providing you with more control.

You can aim a spotlight precisely at the area of the scene that is visible in your shot. This means that depth map shadows will be more efficiently focused only where they are needed. Also, if you add a cookie to the sun—for example, if you want to simulate partial shade from overhanging leaves—the cookie can be more precisely aimed with a spotlight.

Adjusting Shadow Appearance

The shadows from the sun are the most important shadows in an outdoor scene. Be sure to adjust and test-render the sun shadows, and make sure you like their shape and direction, before you move on to adding any other lights.

Shadows from the sun are not completely sharp. The sun can be thought of as an area light, casting shadows that are slightly soft and that become softer with distance. The sun usually fills an area of about 1 percent of the sky around us, and the shadows from the sun can become considerably softer on a hazy day or around sunset.

It is best to leave the *shadow color* parameter of your sunlight set to pure black. The blue cast that appears in shadow areas will appear later, when we fill in the scene with sky light.

Choosing Raytraced or Depth Map Shadows

If you use a raytraced shadow, you may find that a single shadow is enough to cover your entire scene. If you are using depth map shadows, however, one light might not be enough to cover a large area. Stretching a depth map over too broad an area can cause it to lose accuracy. To work efficiently with depth maps, sometimes the sun must be represented with an array of lights, each providing light and shadows to one region of the scene. Using multiple depth maps, each with a reasonable resolution such as 512 or 1024, is usually more efficient than cranking up the depth map resolution above 2048 or 4096.

While a raytraced shadow is much easier to set up than a depth map, you may not always have a choice. Complex elements such as grass, fur, or vegetation could crash your computer if you try to render them in a raytraced shadow, so in some environments you have no choice but to use depth maps.

A paddock or field full of grass would be one example of an environment you'd want to light with depth map shadows. If your renderer supports *deep shadow maps* or *detailed shadow maps*, features designed to make shadow maps work better with transparency and fine details such as grass, then this is the best choice for fields of vegetation. Larger fields may require many depth maps coming from an array of lights.

Sky Light

Adding realistic sky light will lessen the contrast, fill in your shadow areas with a soft blue illumination, and bring the scene into a neutral color balance. Figure 4.2 shows a test-render of the scene with sky lights only (left) and the scene with both sky light and sunlight (right).

One way to add sky lights is to start with a copy of your sunlight, then swing the copy around about 90 degrees away from the sun position. Lower the intensity of the light to about 50 percent of the brightness of the sun, and then change the color from yellow to blue. To create softer shadows from your sky lights, either lower the shadow map resolution or increase the blurring or filtering.

[Figure 4.2] Test-render your sky lights by themselves (left) first, then render with the both the sunlight and sky lights visible (right) to see how they combine.

Test-render your sky light to make sure you like its dim blue illumination and soft shadows. If you like the test-render, make several more copies of your sky light, each coming from a different angle around your scene, as shown in Figure 4.3.

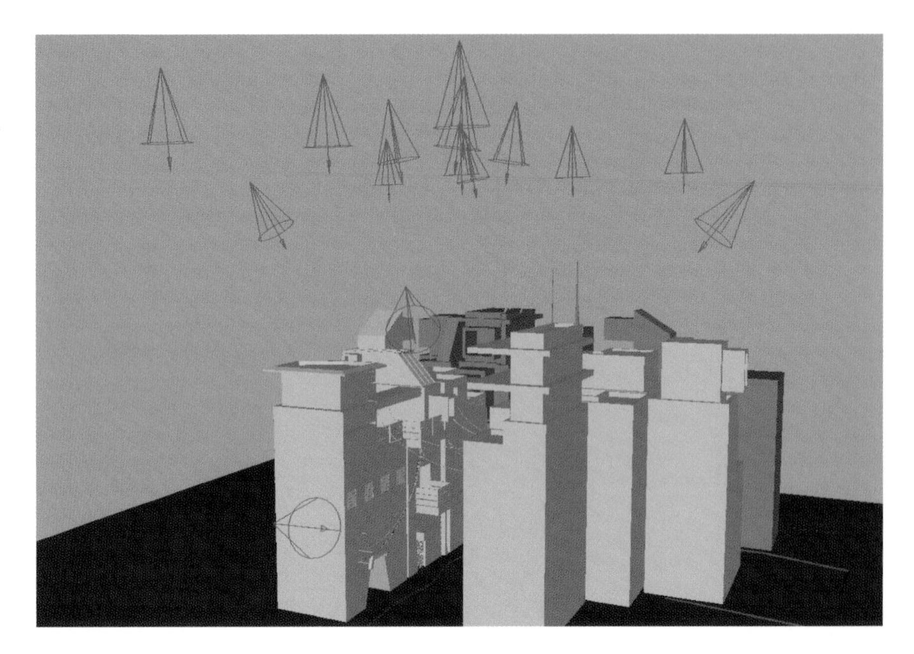

[Figure 4.3] Spotlights representing sky illumination (shown in orange) surround the scene, while a single directional light (in green) simulates the sun.

You may want to set your sky light to emit only diffuse illumination and little or no specular illumination. On a shiny surface, highlights in specific places on a model would give away that the sky was being simulated with only a few spotlights. Turning down the specular highlights from your sky lights and adding an environment map to create a more realistic, continuous reflection of the sky will help create realistic results without requiring an unreasonable number of lights.

Color Balance

In a sunlit scene, the warm color of the sun and the cool color of the sky should balance out so that they appear almost white where they overlap. Areas where the sun is blocked so that you see only sky light may look blue. If you render your scene with the sun and all of your sky lights visible, you can see the overall color balance of your scene.

A golden yellow overall tint for your scene might be desirable for a late afternoon or sunset, and a blue tint might be useful for dusk or a gloomy overcast day. For a normal daylight balance, however, you don't want your full scene to look blue tinted or yellow tinted overall. You may need to go back and adjust the sun's brightness or color to achieve a natural-looking balance and make it cancel out the blue of the sky.

We'll return to the issue of color balance in detail in Chapter 8, "The Art and Science of Color."

Image-Based Lighting

Image-based lighting (IBL) provides an alternative approach to simulating sky light. With IBL, instead of adding multiple lights, you map an image to a sky dome surrounding the scene, and the colors and tones from that image are used to illuminate the scene. Figure 4.4 is a test-render of the scene lit only by a texture map of a sky and clouds.

[Figure 4.4]
This test render shows a scene lit entirely by IBL instead of lights.

If your 3D software doesn't have a specific sky dome or image-based lighting feature, you can still use similar techniques with global illumination (discussed later in this chapter). With global illumination turned on, any sufficiently bright surface—including a giant sphere surrounding your whole scene—can be a source of indirect light.

IBL holds the promise of great convenience and realism, if you happen to have a texture map that perfectly matches the environment you are simulating. IBL also has the advantage that whatever map you make to represent the environment can also be used in reflections. However, IBL tends not to be as easy to adjust and control as having several lights in the scene working together to simulate light from the sky. If there's an area that is looking too dark and gloomy, for example, manually aiming extra light there is easier than creating a new version of the texture map and hoping that the right area will brighten.

Indirect Light

The sunlight and sky lights give you most of your illumination, but a realistic daylight scene also requires *indirect* or *bounce* light. Bounce lights simulate illumination from the sun and sky bouncing off the ground or other surfaces and indirectly illuminating other objects.

A bounce light is similar to a sky light in that it should not emit much specularity, because you don't want unmotivated highlights on the bottom of a reflective surface.

You should base the color of your bounce light on the color of the ground and the light hitting it. Sampling colors directly from a rendered image of the ground can be a good starting point for your bounce light colors.

Usually you will need several bounce lights—enough to cover a broad area of your scene. Position bounce lights beneath the ground, aiming up toward your buildings, characters, or other objects that require indirect light. Some attenuation is usually needed to make the lights decay with height.

If there are any walls that receive a great deal of direct light, then this can motivate some bounce light from walls as well. Place some bounce lights behind a wall, aiming through the wall at the ground and other nearby buildings, as shown in Figure 4.5.

[Figure 4.5] Bounce lights (shown in green) shine up through the ground and back through the sunlit wall to simulate indirect light.

Sometimes bounce lights need to cast soft shadows, especially if they are illuminating characters, so that they don't make the interior of a character's mouth appear too bright. If your lights are beneath the ground and need to shine through it, you should use light linking to unlink the lights from the ground, so that the ground will not cast a shadow blocking all of the bounce light.

Because bounce lights will be dim and subtle, it's usually a good idea to hide all of your other lights and test-render an image with only the bounce lights visible, so that you can see that they uniformly cover the surfaces of your scene. Figure 4.6 shows a test-render of bounce lights by themselves (left) and the complete scene, including sun, sky, and bounce (right).

We'll return to the important issue of indirect light in the "Simulating Indirect Light" and "Global Illumination" sections, later in this chapter.

[Figure 4.6] A test-render with only bounce lights visible (left) and a complete daylight look with all lights visible (right)

Night Scenes

You can create night scenes using the same basic principles as daylight, with a few modifications. Moonlight and night sky light can be created in much the same way you would create light from the sun and sky in daytime, while using a much dimmer light for the moon.

At night, light from the sky usually should be a very soft blue glow. Moonlight can be either blue or yellow. Most often, it appears yellow in scenes where light comes only from the moon and the night sky. If you see moonlight in addition to light from light bulbs, the moonlight will appear more blue.

The key to lighting night scenes is not to underexpose the entire scene, but to use a lot of contrast. The scene may be dominated by shadows, but the darkness should be broken up by bright highlights and selectively applied rims and glints of light.

You may have noticed that most night scenes in Hollywood movies feature wet pavement, which looks as if it had just rained. This will be true even in dry cities like Las Vegas. Cinematographers are always looking for ways to capture extra glints of light and reflections in their night scenes. Since they have discovered that spraying water on the streets is a great way to get the city lights to reflect off the street, and make prettier night scenes with more highlights in them, they do this even when it is obviously a cheat.

If you have any surface in your scene that could be reflective, feel free to use it wherever you need more contrast or visual interest. Reflections on the street were amplified in rendering Figure 4.7, using an extra light at the far rear porch set to emit specular only and exclusively light linked to the street. It was not set to decay rapidly like the other porch lights, so it brings out a texture in the entire street. Light linking was also used to add a light exclusively illuminating the hanging cables. These extra glints of light create interesting lines and contrast, even within a scene that was made up mostly of dark tones.

[Figure 4.7]
A night scene brings contrast that accentuates every glint and highlight.

Practical Lights

Practical lights are the light sources that are visible as models within your scene. Outdoors, practical lights include street lamps, vehicle headlights, illuminated signs, and lights on buildings. Indoor examples of practical lights include lamps, light fixtures, television sets, or any other model you've built that emits light.

There are two different aspects to simulating the illumination from a practical light. You need to light the source itself (such as the actual lamp or lightbulb), and then you need to light the surrounding set as if the lamp were casting illumination into the scene.

Lighting the Light

If you want to illuminate a bulb model using a light, you can position a point or omnidirectional light in the middle of it where a filament would be located, and give the outside of the bulb a translucent shader that will get brighter when backlit by the interior light source. To get realistic variation in brightness across the bulb's surface, give the light source inverse square attenuation.

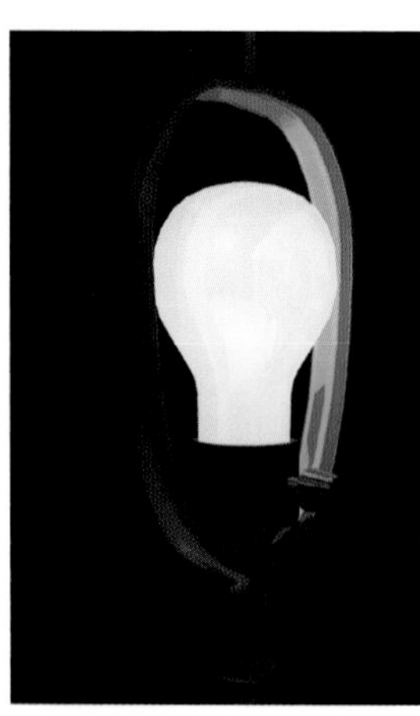

[Figure 4.8] Lightbulbs can be mapped with gradients brightening the center more than the top and bottom.

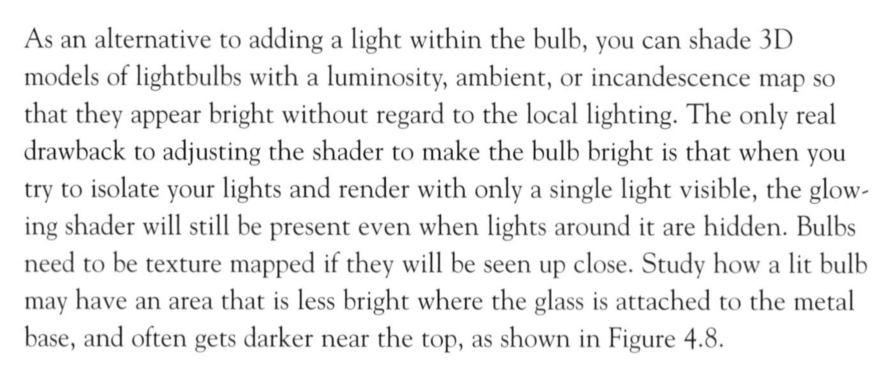

As an alternative to adding a light within the bulb, you can shade 3D models of lightbulbs with a luminosity, ambient, or incandescence map so that they appear bright without regard to the local lighting. The only real drawback to adjusting the shader to make the bulb bright is that when you try to isolate your lights and render with only a single light visible, the glowing shader will still be present even when lights around it are hidden. Bulbs need to be texture mapped if they will be seen up close. Study how a lit bulb may have an area that is less bright where the glass is attached to the metal base, and often gets darker near the top, as shown in Figure 4.8.

The immediate area around a light source often requires some dedicated lighting. For example, a lamp surrounded by a lampshade would receive a great deal of bounce light as light is reflected off the interior of the shade. You could add bounce lights to illuminate the lamp itself with its own indirect illumination.

If you are positioning any light inside of a 3D model of a lightbulb, and that light casts shadows, then you may want to unlink the light from the bulb model so that it can shine through the bulb and illuminate the surrounding area. Otherwise, the bulb model might cast a shadow that effectively blocked any of the light from reaching the rest of the scene.

Set Lighting from Practical Lights

Just because you are simulating a single practical light source doesn't mean that you need to light it with a single light in 3D. Often you will observe several different effects on the set from a single practical light, and use a light in 3D for each of these effects. For example, the lamp in Figure 4.9 emits a soft glow through the shade, as well as a cone of light aimed up through the top of the shade, and a cone of light aimed down from the bottom. This is simulated with a point light that shines out through the shade, plus spotlights aimed upward and downward to simulate the upward and downward cones.

[Figure 4.9]
A lampshade breaks illumination into upper and lower cones.

Outer Glow

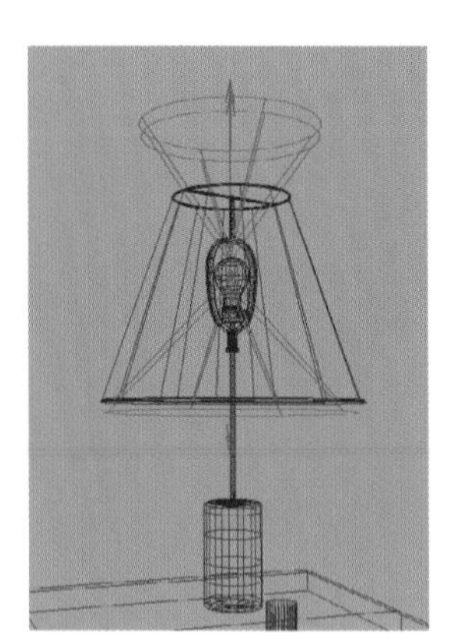

[Figure 4.10] With two spotlights aimed up and two aimed down, an outer glow is simulated along with the main illumination.

Often projecting one spotlight in a particular direction isn't enough. You sometimes see a broader, dimmer cone of light around the main light source. For example, if you used one spotlight for the illumination cast upward from a lamp, you might need another spotlight, with a slightly broader cone and a much dimmer intensity, to add a glow around the area. Figure 4.10 shows how the lighting in Figure 4.9 was created: two spotlights aiming upward and two aiming downward, including the main cones and the outer glows. The outer glows could simulate light that had bounced off the lampshade instead of being aimed directly from the bulb.

Throw Patterns

The *throw pattern* is the shape or texture of the light that is cast into the scene from a light source. We can recognize distinctive throw patterns from car headlights, flashlights, burning torches, and many other kinds of light sources. In real life, often a complex throw pattern is caused by reflection or blocking by structural elements within the light fixture. Figure 4.11 shows a throw pattern cast by a flashlight. When you study them, you see that no two models of flashlight cast exactly the same pattern into the scene.

[Figure 4.11] The throw pattern of a common household flashlight.

In 3D graphics, throw patterns can be created by modeling geometry around the light source, or by applying a cookie or map on the light source. If you used an image such as Figure 4.11 as a cookie on a light, it would help simulate a flashlight's beam as well as its outer glow, all in the same spotlight. A cookie can also be used to tint the edges of a spotlight's beam. In many real spotlights, there is a more saturated or reddish tint near the edge of the beam, just before it falls off to black. A cookie with a reddish edge can help simulate this and make softer, more naturalistic throw patterns for your spotlights. If all you wanted out of a cookie was to tint the outer edges of a spotlight, then a procedural ramp or gradient texture could also be used, and you wouldn't even need to paint a map.

Any time you are tempted to aim a spotlight into the your scene and have it add a plain circle of light, stop and think if a more complex throw pattern could be more natural looking.

Lighting Windows

The task of simulating light coming through windows presents a special challenge. If it is a sunny day, then you expect to see both sunlight and sky light entering a window. Sunlight would never enter by itself. If there is a sunbeam shining directly through a window, then you also expect to see light from the sky entering the window from a broader range of angles, as shown in Figure 4.12.

Direct sun is usually the brightest type of light in a room, and will cast the sharpest, most visible shadows. It should be test-rendered by itself before adding other lights. Usually an infinite or directional light is the best choice to simulate sunlight, in order to cast shadows that are parallel from each window.

[Figure 4.12] Sunlight and sky light enter a room through the windows.

After you position and test-render the direct sunlight, you need to add the sky light. The sky casts illumination through a window at a broad range of angles, reaching the floor below the window and sometimes all the way up to the ceiling above the window. Figure 4.13 shows spotlights aimed through each window to targets on the floor and walls inside the room. They do not cast shadows of the walls or window frames. Just as with daylight, you need to test-render your sunlight and sky lights to make sure they blend together naturally before you proceed to adding indirect light.

If you are lighting a scene that already has a background image, make sure that the angle of the sun coming into the room appears to match the angle of sunlight in the background plate. For example, if the background plate shows long shadows from late afternoon sun, then the sun should come in at a low angle. A cloudy day without much contrast would call for much softer shadows; a sharply defined sunbeam would look out of place.

If there is glass in a window, make sure in your test-renders that the glass doesn't cast too dark a shadow. If the window glass is blocking your light, the easiest changes are either to set the glass object not to cast shadows at all, or to use light linking to disassociate the glass from your outdoor lights.

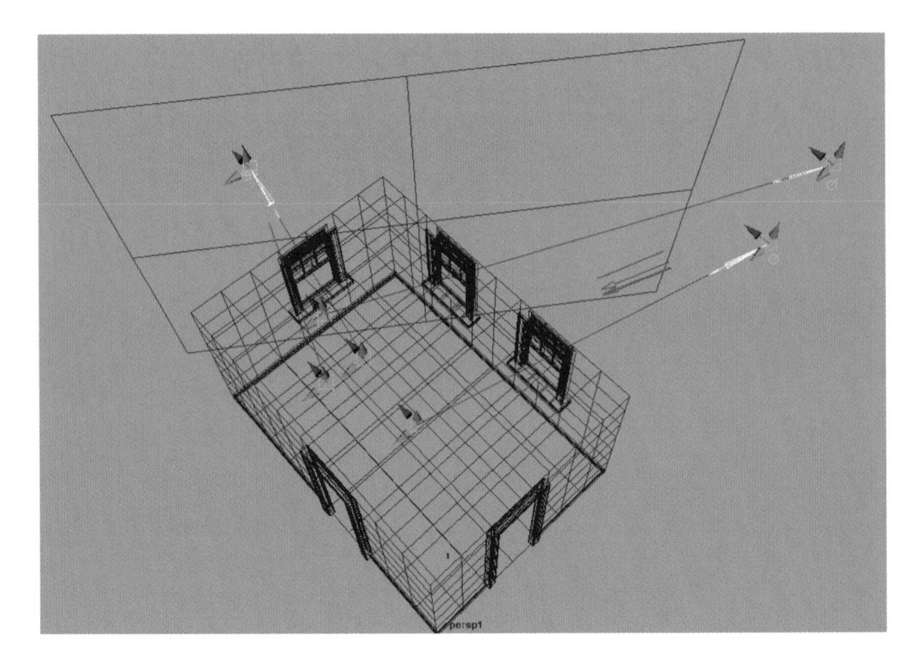

[Figure 4.13]
Sky lights (white) are aimed through windows to complement sunlight (orange) as it enters the room.

Simulating Indirect Light

Indoor scenes or enclosed spaces often have more complex indirect light or bounce light set-ups than outdoor environments. Scenes with many walls need bounce lights added to simulate light bouncing between each wall, the ceiling, and the floor. Some people call the process of lighting architectural spaces with many bounce lights *simulated radiosity,* although that term is falling out of favor.

Sunbeams tend to brighten everything around them. Figure 4.14 shows a photograph of a real sunbeam—notice the bounce light that appears on the nearby lampshade. For the sunbeams on the floor, add spotlights underneath the floor, aimed up at the ceiling. Test-render with the light bouncing on the ceiling to make sure the spotlights are nice and soft, and that they don't look like conspicuous circles.

[Figure 4.14] A real sunbeam casts indirect light onto nearby objects.

After hitting the obvious areas above the sunbeams, the next area that will need bounce light is the windows. There's no law of physics that says that light should bounce back directly toward a window, but real-life observation shows that the area around a window often tends to receive some illumination. Aim a spotlight through the floor or opposite wall if necessary, so that it brightens the area around a window. Figure 4.15 shows two bounce lights aiming up through the floor and one aiming at the center window.

Test-render the light aimed at the window to make sure that it is very soft, using a penumbra or drop-off to fade off softly toward its edges. These bounce lights should illuminate parts of the walls, ceiling, or floor without hitting much into the corners between them. The corners should remain darker. Figure 4.16 shows the room with bounced illumination added. Two bounce lights hit the ceiling above the sunbeams and one brightens the center window.

[Figure 4.15] Bounce lights are aimed up through the floor and in through the wall.

The light that was aimed at the center window can be duplicated and translated to aim at the window on the left, then the window on the right. For each bounce light, be careful that it is lighting the wall without making the corners get too bright.

Figure 4.17 shows the scene with bounce lights continuing along each of the walls. When you test-render the lights on the walls, they should look almost as if they blend into each other.

[Figure 4.16]
The scene with the first three bounce lights added.

[Figure 4.17]
Bounce lights added all the way around the set.

The ceiling and floor need the same treatment as the walls. Spotlights can be aimed down through the ceiling to light the floor and up through the floor to light the ceiling. They should brighten the ceiling and floor, as shown in Figure 4.18, without hitting the corners.

[Figure 4.18]
Bounce lights added on the floor and ceiling.

Finally, the room needs some dim, overall fill light to simulate the ambient light that has bounced more than one time. This will help the room better match the tone of the background image and will bring light all over the room, including the corners. Two fill lights are added in Figure 4.19—one aimed toward the floor and one toward the ceiling—but both are very broad, soft spotlights that illuminate the walls as well as the ceiling or floor.

[Figure 4.19]
Finally, fill light is added to brighten every surface.

Corners

Corners are the area where light most closely inter-reflects between walls. As a result, there should be continuity at the corners, a continuation of tones from one wall to another, rather than a sudden jump in brightness. If there were a huge difference between the amount of light on two walls in a corner, then it would look as if light were not reflecting between the walls.

Open spaces in the middle of walls tend to be exposed to the most ambient light bouncing around a room, so areas in the middle of a wall are often brighter than cracks or corners. Figure 4.20 is a photograph of a real corner, where you can see the soft progression from brighter walls into darker corners, and the continuity between the walls and ceiling where they meet.

An alternative approach to darkening your corners is to use *negative lighting*. Instead of carefully aiming bounce lights to avoid lighting the corners, you can use lights with a negative intensity to suck light out of the corners of a room. To use negative lighting in the corners, you just broadly illuminate the entire room with fill lights, then add lights focused in the corners with a negative intensity or brightness to darken those areas. The left side of Figure 4.21 shows how some negative lights are positioned along the corners of a room. In this case, they are volume lights in Maya, set to emit ambient but not diffuse or specular, with an intensity of -0.5. The rendered result is shown on the right, where you can see a soft darkening of the corners.

[Figure 4.20] A real corner shows darkening and the inter-reflection of light.

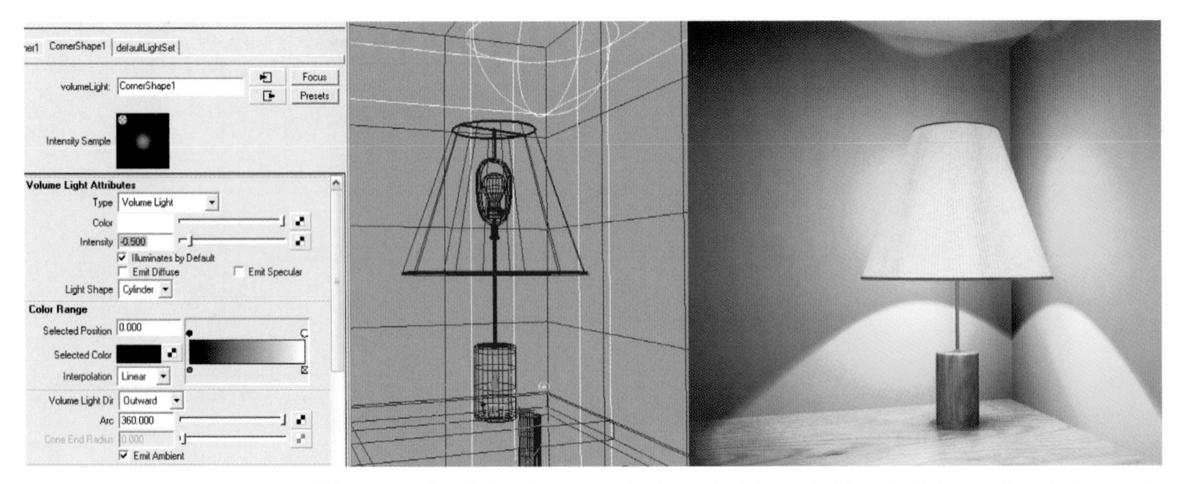

[Figure 4.21] A light with a negative intensity (shown in Maya, left), is positioned along each corner that needs to be darkened (center), producing a render with darkened corners (right).

A negative light is also used to darken the table underneath the lamp. Negative lights are handy for a quick fix where you need a crack or corner or an area underneath something to be made darker.

Sourcy Lighting

By the time you are done lighting a space, you should not be able to see the first bounce lights you added. In context, all of your illumination should blend seamlessly, and there should not be any pronounced circles of light. Individual bounce lights that are too visible or distinct are referred to as *sourcy lighting,* lighting that gives away the location of the individual light sources. Figure 4.22 shows an image with a sourcy light. You can distinctly see the circle of light cast by the spotlight on the center window on the left side of the figure. On the right side, the spotlight has been made less sourcy by making it softer.

As a final quality check to your scene, look around and make sure that none of your bounce lights stands out as too sourcy. To reduce sourciness, soften your spotlight cones, reduce the brightness of individual lights, and set bounce lights to emit only diffuse illumination without any specular.

[Figure 4.22] A sourcy light (left) calls attention to itself. When sourciness is reduced (right) you can't see the individual spotlights.

No matter how you look at it, simulating indirect light by carefully aiming many bounce lights at each surface in your scene can be a complex, time-consuming process. Fortunately, 3D artists have other choices for rendering with indirect light, through using *global illumination*, which is now available in most leading rendering software.

Global Illumination

Global illumination is any rendering algorithm that simulates the inter-reflection of light between surfaces. When rendering with global illumination, you don't need to add bounce lights to simulate indirect light, because the software calculates indirect light for you based on the direct illumination hitting surfaces in your scene.

Contrast the term global illumination with *local illumination*. Most rendering software uses local illumination as the default, unless you have activated a global illumination function. In local illumination, your rendering software considers only the surface currently being rendered and the lights directly illuminating it, without taking into account any other surfaces.

Using local illumination, if you add a single light to a scene, pointing down at the floor, then all of the light in the scene will be down where the light is aimed. This is illustrated on the left side of Figure 4.23. In real life, you'd expect a light like this to bounce off the floor and walls, and softly illuminate the whole room. However, with local illumination, the ceiling and shadow areas are pure black, because the directly lit surfaces are not reflecting light.

[Figure 4.23] A single light is rendered with local illumination (left) and global illumination (right).

Simply using raytracing, such as for raytraced shadows and reflections, is generally not considered global illumination. Even though a raytraced reflection could fit with the broad definition of having indirect light contribute to the rendering of a surface, only techniques in which indirect light can add to the diffuse illumination of objects are generally referred to as global illumination.

On the right side of Figure 4.23, you can see that light is bouncing off the walls and the green cube, adding indirect illumination to the scene. No bounce lights needed to be manually added; the simulation of indirect light was performed entirely by the software.

Global illumination makes lighting in 3D graphics much more similar to lighting for conventional cinematography. In filming live-action scenes, bounce light is always a factor. Light reflecting off of walls and floors is a natural source of fill light, softening the illumination of every scene. Filmmakers even use reflectors, as shown in Figure 4.24, to bounce sunlight back at actors, aiming reflected sunlight into a scene instead of needing to bring extra electric lights to a shooting location.

[Figure 4.24] Reflectors are used to bounce light onto actors or sets.

A phenomenon called *color bleeding* is visible in many renderings with global illumination. In real life, color bleeding is always happening around us, as light reflects off of differently colored surfaces. However, color bleeding is a subtle effect that is often unnoticeable. The situation in which you can most readily see color bleeding is when a brightly colored surface is much more brightly lit than a nearby white or gray surface. Figure 4.25 is a photograph in which natural color bleeding is visible. In the photograph, a sunbeam illuminates a red carpet brightly enough to cause red light to bounce up onto the white sofa.

Sometimes, in global illumination renderings, there is an unrealistic amount of color bleeding. For example, in Figure 4.26, the green cube almost appears to be glowing and illuminating the rest of the scene. The culprit is usually too much saturation in the shader, too much irradiance, or too high a photon intensity in your global illumination.

The basic workflow for lighting with global illumination starts out the same as for lighting without it. You add light from the sun, light from the sky, and any artificial light sources. But then, instead of adding bounce lights, you turn on and adjust your software's global illumination, and it essentially adds all of the bounce lighting for you. Figure 4.27 shows an example of this process. In this example, only three lights are added: a single area light for the sun, then two area lights representing sky illumination through the windows. After that, global illumination is responsible for all of the indirect light.

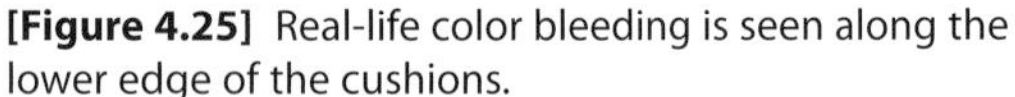

[Figure 4.25] Real-life color bleeding is seen along the lower edge of the cushions.

[Figure 4.26] Too much color bleeding can make global illumination renders unrealistic.

[Figure 4.27] Lighting for GI starts with direct light sources including the sun (left) and sky (middle). Global illumination completes the scene by adding indirect light (right). Images rendered in Lightwave by Jason Lee, otacon.kvaalen.com.

The difference between a test-render with only direct illumination, and your final render with global illumination, can be dramatic. If you plan to use global illumination, your direct light sources can leave much of the scene in shadow. Your initial test can look contrasty and bleak, with large black areas where sun, sky, and practical lights aren't directly aimed. As in Figure 4.28, the transition to using global illumination will fill in the black areas, making the whole scene brighter, and softening the illumination so that it wraps around more of the geometry in the scene.

[Figure 4.28] A test render showing only direct light (left) is darker and more contrasty than the scene rendered with global illumination (right). Images by Geoff Packer for Spiral Staircase Systems, spiralstairs.co.uk.

There are a number of different types of global illumination, including *radiosity*, *photon mapping*, *final gathering*, and *caustics*.

Conventional Radiosity

Radiosity is an approach to rendering global illumination in which indirect light is transmitted between surfaces by diffuse reflection of their surface color, and is stored in vertices of the surface meshes. Radiosity can be calculated progressively, so that light can bounce as many times as needed to create a refined, accurate simulation of real lighting. The number of bounces in a progressive radiosity solution is limited only by the amount of time available to compute the radiosity solution; it will keep running and calculating more light bounces forever, or until you interrupt it.

Radiosity was one of the first types of global illumination to become available in commercial rendering software. Some people incorrectly refer to all global illumination solutions as radiosity, just because they heard of radiosity first. The lighting style that actually simulates global illumination became known as *simulated radiosity* because of radiosity's early popularity.

Radiosity is usually calculated by storing shading information for each vertex of the polygonal objects in a scene. Figure 4.29 shows how the scene is subdivided during the radiosity calculation. More vertices are added where additional detail is needed in the shading, such as at the edges of shadows or highlight areas.

A disadvantage of this approach is that the resolution of your geometry is linked with the resolution of your global illumination solution. It is difficult to compute a quick approximation of the lighting for a scene with a high polygon count. The radiosity solution and subdivision of the geometry is also very difficult to recompute at each frame of an animated sequence, if major objects in a scene were moving.

Radiosity never became a very popular global illumination solution in the film industry, but it has become popular with architects. Architects often need to render fly-throughs, animations in which nothing moves except for the camera, and for that you can compute radiosity only once, and use the solution in every frame of the animation. In the film industry, in which animation usually involves moving geometry, other global illumination solutions such as photon mapping have become more popular.

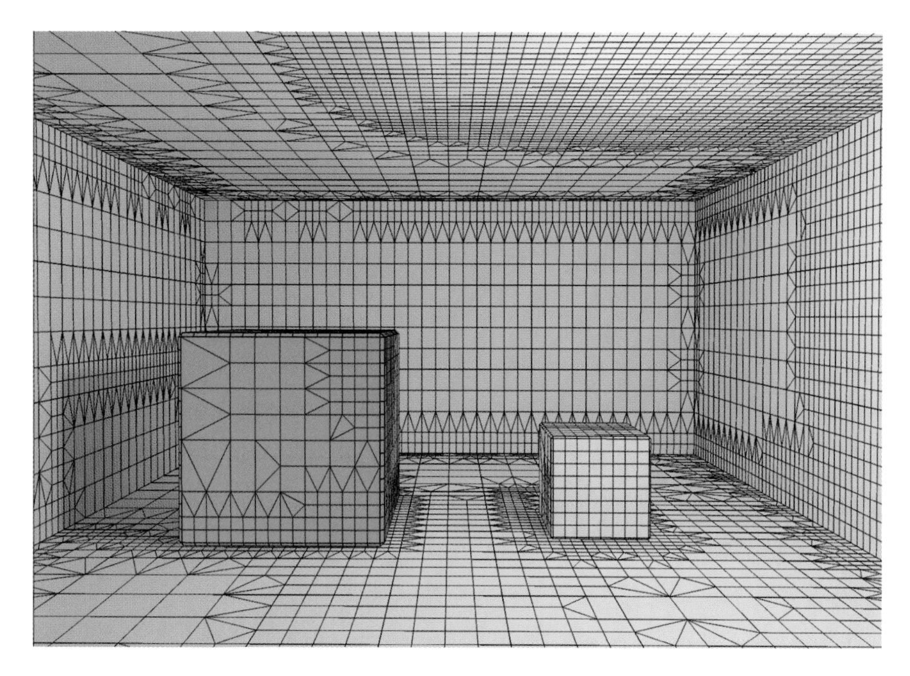

[Figure 4.29] Conventional radiosity stores irradiance information in polygon vertices.

Photon Mapping

The same kind of results that conventional radiosity calculates can also be rendered via *photon mapping*. With this approach to global illumination, a separate data type—the *photon map*—is created to store the global illumination solution. The resolution of a photon mapped solution is independent from the resolution of the geometry.

The speed and accuracy of photon mapped global illumination depends on the number of photons used. Extra photons take longer to compute, so for quick test-renders while setting up global illumination, you should start with a lower number of photons. When you render with fewer photons, the results will look blotchy, as shown on the left side of Figure 4.30, where the individual photons can be seen as paintball-like dots splattered onto every surface in the scene. As you turn up the number of photons, the results become smoother, more realistic, and less blotchy, as shown on the right side of the figure—although rendering with higher photon counts takes longer.

[Figure 4.30] Photon mapping with a low photon count (left) is very blotchy, but gets smoother with a high photon count (right).

You can think of photons in a photon map as very small particles of light. Photons can bounce around a scene in a global illumination solution, and are stored in a photon map where they bounce off a surface which should be brightened by indirect light. Photons don't necessarily duplicate all of the rules of real physics. For example, photons in CG can vary in size from pixel-sized dots up to the size of golf balls or sometimes basketballs. You can use a small number of photons set to a larger size for quick tests, and then use more photons for a more accurate final rendering. Most software has an adjustable photon size or radius, and also can choose a size automatically if the radius is left at 0, so that the size varies depending on the size of the surface to be covered and the number of photons.

You can set as many lights as you want to emit photons. The lights that are responsible for direct illumination should emit photons as well. It does not take any longer to render with two lights each emitting 50,000 photons than to render with one light emitting 100,000 photons, so don't worry about distributing your photon emission among the relevant lights. Your brightest lights should generally emit the most photons, while fewer photons should be needed for dimmer fill lights.

By itself, photon mapping can produce good results if enough photons are used. However, smooth renders can sometimes require a huge number of photons, which would be very slow to render. A solution to this problem is to use photon mapping in conjunction with final gathering.

Final Gathering

Final gathering is a rendering option that can be used in conjunction with photon mapped global illumination to smooth out your results, producing continuous illumination instead of the blotchy output you can get from photon mapping used alone. The left side of Figure 4.31 shows a scene with photon mapped global illumination; on the right, you can see the smoother results of turning on final gathering.

Basically final gathering does two things:

- If you're using photon mapped global illumination, it filters and smoothes out the result, to prevent blotchiness.
- It functions as a global illumination solution unto itself, adding an extra bounce of indirect light.

[Figure 4.31] Final gathering smoothes out photon mapped global illumination.

Final gathering performs both of these tasks by starting at each point on a surface being rendered, and looking around at all directions to see what is visible from that point. You can adjust how many rays or samples are taken by final gathering, to determine how many different directions it will look around into the scene. When final gathering is sampling rays in different directions, it looks at the color and illumination on nearby surfaces to add to the global illumination, and it also looks at nearby photons in a photon map, so that it can filter and smooth out photon mapped global illumination.

To use final gathering in conjunction with photon mapping, usually it's best to save the final gathering step for last. Adjust your photon mapped global illumination until the photon intensity (brightness) looks good to you, and you have a number of photons that accurately capture all of the indirect light bounces that you need in the scene. If the global illumination still looks a little blotchy, then as a finishing touch, turn on final gathering to smooth out the results.

You can also use final gathering by itself, without any photon mapped global illumination. When used by itself, final gathering provides a simple type of global illumination solution that usually works well for only a single bounce of light. Some renderers let you adjust the number of bounces that final gathering calculates, so that indirect light can bounce from one surface to another a number of times before providing illumination. However, this can be very slow. Most people use final gathering only for a single bounce, and use it in conjunction with photon mapping if they want a more complete multibounce global illumination solution.

Caustics

Caustics are the type of indirect light that remains focused instead of being diffusely scattered in all directions. While the previous sections have discussed approaches to rendering global illumination that could produce identical results, caustics are a visibly different type of indirect light. Caustics are distinctive in that they have a shape or pattern, instead of being scattered into soft, diffuse illumination. When you start looking for them, you will see that caustics are all around you in the real world:

- Light that refracts through a lens, magnifying glass, or prism is a caustic effect. You often see refracted caustics on top of a table next to glasses and bottles.

- Beams of light reflecting off a mirror are caustics, as are all the little glints of light reflected off a disco ball.
- Any shiny or highly specular surface creates caustic effects when hit by a bright light. On a sunny day, a car's chrome bumper or a building's window will create caustic patterns on the ground.
- The throw pattern of lights with built-in reflectors, including flash-lights and car headlights, are broken up with caustic patterns from the reflected light. (In 3D, this is usually more efficiently rendered by putting a map on the light.)
- Caustic patterns are perhaps best known for being the patterns reflected onto walls near water surfaces (as shown in Figure 4.32) or refracted into shimmering patterns on the bottom of swimming pools.

[Figure 4.32] Caustics are best known for shimmering water reflections.

Figure 4.33 shows two photographs of real-life caustics. On the left is an example of refracted caustics, caused by light traveling through a transparent bottle. On the right is an example of reflected caustics, caused by light bouncing off windows and metal panels on a building. You can see the most caustic patterns during hours when the sun is low in the sky, creating a lot of contrast between surfaces that receive sunlight and areas in shadow where caustics show up.

[Figure 4.33]
Caustic patterns can refract through a transparent object (left) or reflect off a shiny surface (right).

Caustics are often the brightest, most noticeable part of the indirect lighting in a scene. Caustics also tend to be a faster, simpler computation than rendering with full global illumination. Because caustics are very visible and relatively inexpensive to render, they are sometimes used by themselves, without activating a full global illumination solution for diffuse light. Figure 4.34 was rendered using caustics, without any other kind of global illumination. You can see caustics at work in both reflected and refracted light.

[Figure 4.34]
Caustics are used to create reflected and refracted light in this scene.

Figure 4.35 shows a comparison of the scene with and without caustics. The light bouncing off the mirror, refracting though the glass vase, and reflecting off the vase onto the top of the dresser are all added due to caustics.

One way to compute caustics is through photon mapping. If your renderer uses photon mapping to render caustics, then you will find that issues discussed above for photon mapped global illumination apply to caustics. Turning up the number of photons emitted from a light will make more accurate, less blotchy caustic patterns. Rendering caustic photons along with final gathering will provide smoother, more accurate results than photon mapped caustics by themselves.

[Figure 4.35] Compare the scene without caustics (left) and with caustics (right) to see the indirect light added from the mirror and vase.

Ambient Occlusion

Ambient occlusion is a type of shading that darkens areas enclosed in cracks and corners, or blocked underneath or between other surfaces. Places from which there would be a clear view of the sky or open spaces remain the brightest.

Ambient occlusion is not global illumination. It does not simulate indirect light bounces. It does not take into account the brightness, color, or lighting of nearby surfaces. It performs its shading based on the distance to other objects. Sometimes objects occlude themselves as well, such as when a character's nostrils or armpits become darker as they are surrounded by other parts of the character.

Figure 4.36 is rendered with ambient occlusion as a texture on all of the surfaces in the scene. Even though ambient occlusion bases its shading on the distance to other surfaces, not on lighting, the results resemble what would happen if a surface were surrounded by ambient light coming from every direction, brightening the surface where there was a clear view of the light, but darkening it where something got in the way.

[Figure 4.36]
A scene rendered with an ambient occlusion texture gets darker in cracks and corners.

Figure 4.37 shows what ambient occlusion is really adding to the scene. It has darkened every surface that was near to or facing a surface which might have shadowed it. Nothing you do with lights in the scene will change this output, so even though it may look similar to a soft shadow, you do not have the same degree of control over it. Rendering ambient occlusion shaders or textures by themselves can produce a useful render pass, which will be discussed in Chapter 11, "Rendering Passes and Compositing."

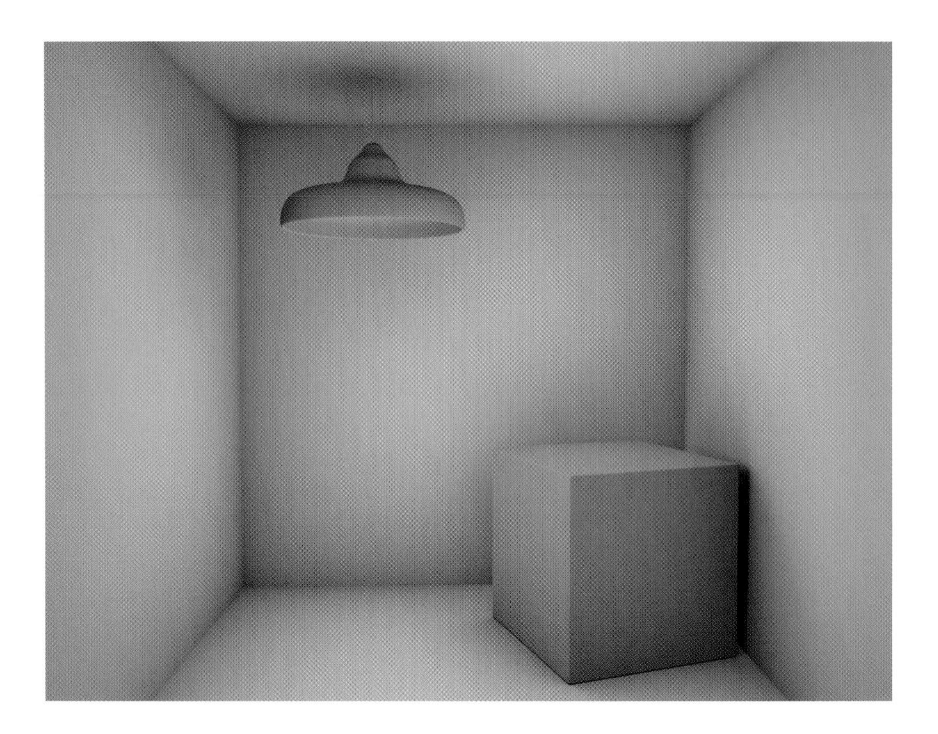

[Figure 4.37]
An ambient occlusion pass is shaded based on the proximity of surfaces.

Because ambient occlusion doesn't need to calculate the shaders or lighting on other surfaces, it is a faster, simpler process than full global illumination. Many productions use ambient occlusion in conjunction with manually adjusted bounce lights, as another way of darkening the corners in a scene rendered without full global illumination.

Exercises

Take a few moments to observe some of the phenomena described in this chapter as you go through your day. Keep your eyes open to observe real-world examples of lighting environments that you might use in your scenes.

1. In the room or environment you're in now, list what the sources of direct light are. Look around: are there any areas that are illuminated entirely by indirect light?

2. Go out with a camera late in the day, when the sun has a chance to glint off water, glass, or metal. Go on a "scavenger hunt" for real-world examples of caustics. Bonus points if you can also capture real-world examples where color bleeding is readily apparent.

[CHAPTER FIVE]

Scene by Kim Hyong Jun (www.kjun.com).

Lighting Creatures, Characters, and Animation

Good lighting can enhance animation in ways that are analogous to adding music and sound effects. When an animator keyframes a character, the initial animation tests are lacking in both lighting and sound. When the soundtrack is complete, sound effects will add definition and solidity to every motion, with every swish through the air, every footstep and thud created in sync with the animation. Likewise, good character lighting adds definition to the character, while shadows and occlusion create a sense of solid contact where feet meet the ground. Modeling with light defines the character's form, and makes the character appear to be present in the environment and actually moving through the space in which he appears. Like music, lighting helps set a mood and shape the emotional context of the scene, making a scene look foreboding, hostile, and scary, or bright, sunny, and cheerful. Whether you are adding a glint to a character's eye when she thinks of an idea, making sure the scales on a snake glisten as it slithers past the camera, or highlighting the profile of a character as he dances past a window, you are really completing the process of bringing a creature or character to life.

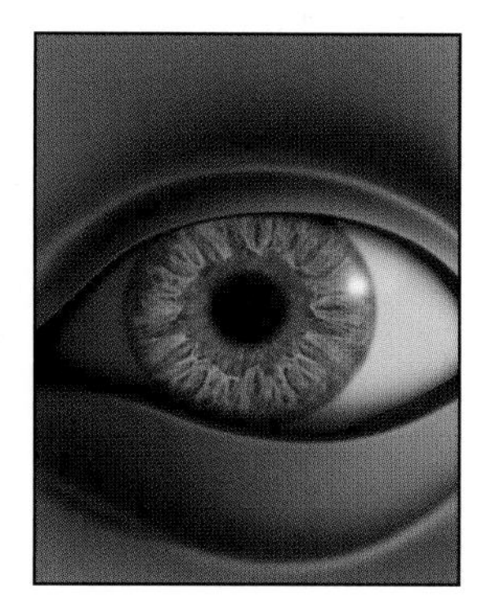
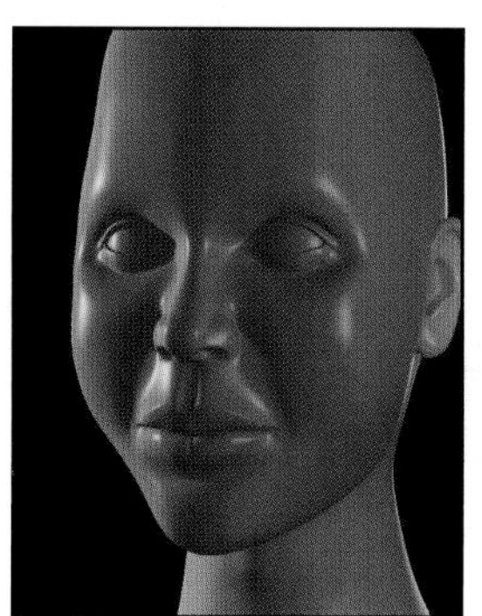

Modeling with Light

Modeling with light means lighting in a style designed to represent the full three-dimensional form of your models. Even though you are rendering a two-dimensional image, the shades and tones you add through lighting can help people perceive your models in three dimensions.

In real life, curved surfaces tend to get different amounts of illumination from different directions, creating a gradient running across the surface. If a part of your character is round in shape, it should not have flat shading. A key component to modeling with light is to try to create gradients that will indicate the curvature of each surface in a character.

In Figure 5.1, look in the yellow boxes to follow the gradients running across the animal's head, across its leg, and down its body. The head starts bright above the nose and shifts into a darker tone as it turns toward the jaw. The leg begins with its darkest tone facing the underside of the body, then transitions to a bright central core and back down again to a medium tone. Along the body, several features and wrinkles are each represented by shifts from bright to dark to bright again. The variety in these gradients conveys the curved shape of all of these forms.

[Figure 5.1]
Key gradients in shaping the form are enclosed in yellow boxes.

Directionality

One key aspect of how a form is lit is *directionality*, the cues that tell the audience where the light is coming from and where it is going. If the light on the character is centered and symmetrical, as on the left side of Figure 5.2, the result is visually monotonous. If the lighting is less symmetrical, coming more from one side, then the character appears more fully shaped by the light wrapping around each curved surface, as shown on the right in the figure.

[Figure 5.2]
Frontal light (left) flattens while asymmetrical light (right) defines the shape.

Nothing should split the character exactly in half. The left side of Figure 5.3 shows a situation where the terminator exactly bisects the form. The *terminator* is where the light turns into darkness, the edge of the visible illumination. When centered, it appears as a boring vertical line and doesn't bring out the roundness of the character. As demonstrated on the right side of the figure, sliding the terminator to one side turns it into a curve that better conveys the character's shape.

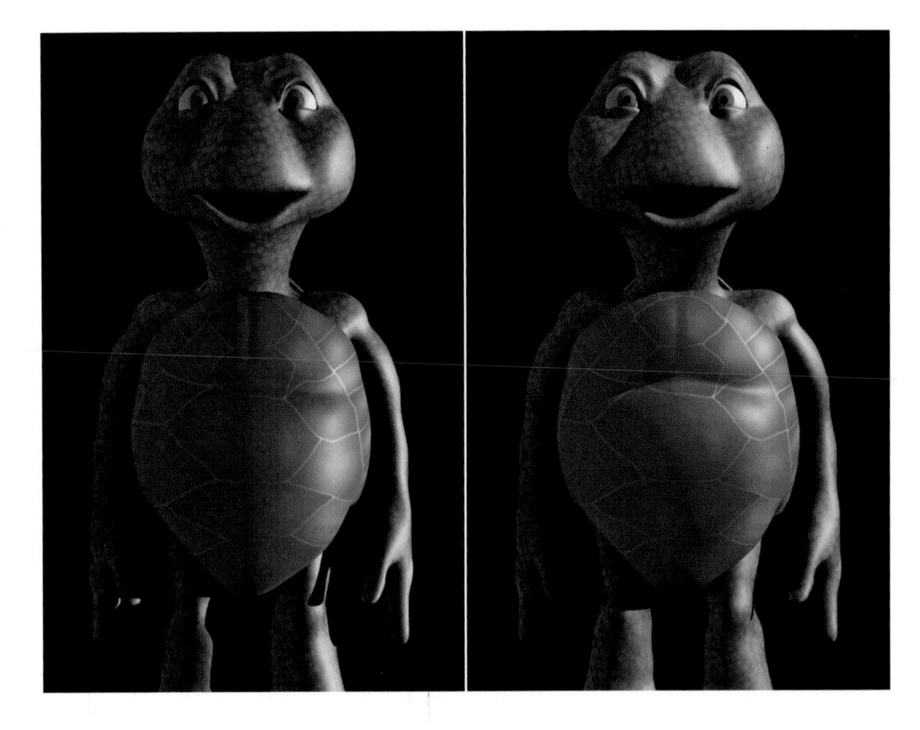

[Figure 5.3] Running vertically through the center of the shell, the terminator appears as a straight line (left), but it becomes a curve helping to define the shape when the light is moved to a new position (right).

The *core* of the character's lighting is the center of the gradient of shading running across a body. It tells you whether the light is coming from in front of or behind the character. The darker core, with brighter edges, as shown on the left side of Figure 5.4, makes a character look backlit. A brighter core, with some of the edges going darker, makes a character look more front-lit, as on the right side of the figure.

Definition

In any action or shot, you must decide which parts of your character most need definition. Based on what's going on or what's important to the story, some parts of a character will need to be clearly defined with lighting.

In defining a character's face, it is useful to think of the face as consisting of multiple planes. Imagine a head simplified into large, flat surfaces, as shown in Figure 5.5, representing the main angles of the head. To define the face well, each of the major planes of the face should receive a different shade or tone from your lighting, so that you see a shift in brightness or color wherever they intersect. For example, the front of the nose, the side of the nose, and the bottom of the nose should each have a different value. The right side of Figure 5.5 shows the face defined by the illumination hitting every plane.

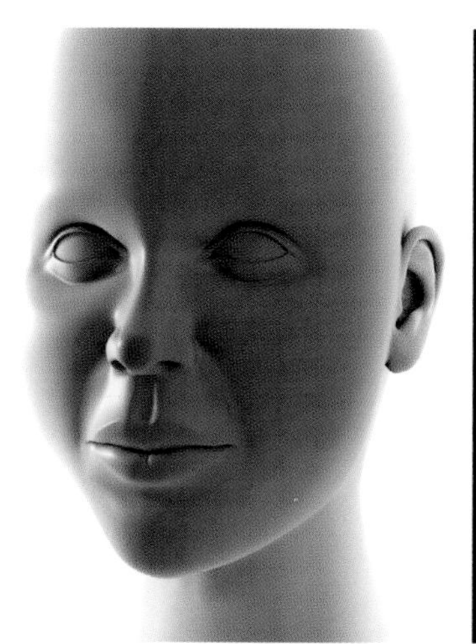

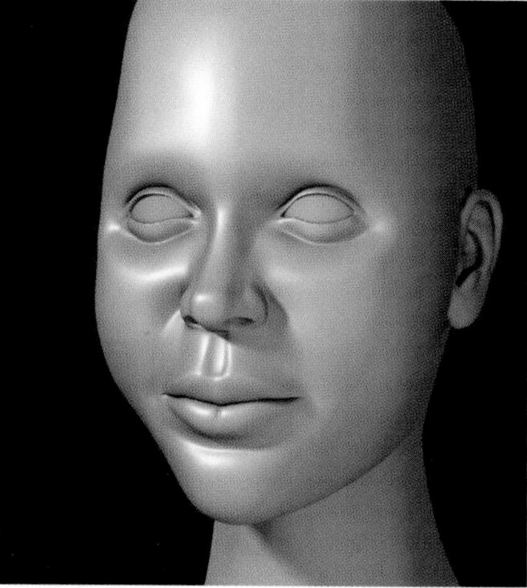

[Figure 5.4]
Shading with a darker core (left) and a bright core (right)

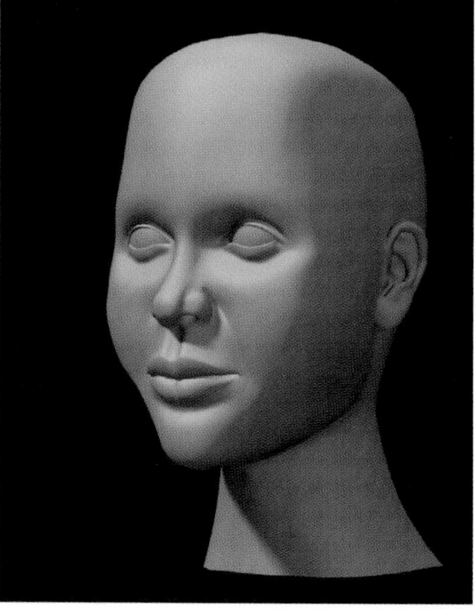

[Figure 5.5]
Selected planes of the face (left) show contrast that helps define the form of the head (right).

In cinematography, as in real life, a person's outline is not always fully defined. For example, when an actor wearing black pants stands in front of a dark piece of furniture, her legs won't be well defined. However, if her shirt and face are well defined, then she could be lit well enough for the audience to see her performance.

In lighting animated characters, on the other hand, the director of an animated film may consider the entire body important to a character's performance. Often the entire body is animated to anticipate or follow through with an action, and the director may want curves that flow through the entire body to be well defined in lighting. Even when you might think some scenes would look better if parts of a character fell into shadow, communicating the full animated performance to the audience is often more important to the director than simulating more subtle cinematography.

The brevity of a shot is another factor that forces you to add more definition. The shorter a shot, the less time the audience has to recognize what they are seeing and what's going on. If you are working on a sequence that will be rapidly edited, then you need to work much harder to make sure that everything the audience needs to see is clearly defined with light and contrast.

Even in a dark, shadowy scene, you must find ways to define a character against a background. If the character is half-lit, as shown on the left side of Figure 5.6, then sometimes you need to add some light to the background behind the darker side of the character, as shown in the center image.

Adding a rim of light around the character is another way to help define her silhouette, as shown on the right side of the figure.

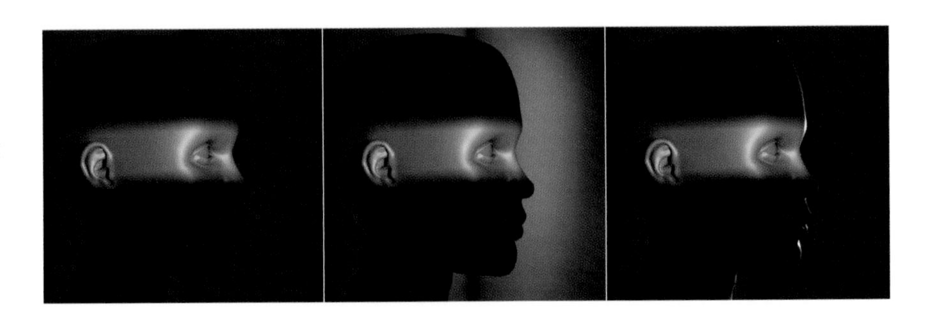

[Figure 5.6] When a character lacks contrast against the background (left), contrast can be boosted by adding light to the background (center) or adding a rim of light to the character (right).

Three-Point Lighting

One of the most basic and popular approaches to illuminating a subject is with a classic Hollywood lighting scheme called *three-point lighting*, a design that makes it easy to model your subject with light. Variations on three-point lighting can cast a favorable light on anything from a small prop to a movie star.

The three "points" in three-point lighting are actually three roles that light can play in a scene, each serving a specific purpose. The next section goes into more detail about how to create each of these in computer graphics, but it is useful to start with a background on how they are used in photography and cinematography:

- A *key light* creates the subject's main illumination and defines the dominant angle of the lighting. The key light is usually brighter than any other light illuminating the subject and is usually the light that casts the darkest, most visible shadows in your scene.
- A *fill light* softens and extends the illumination provided by the key light and makes more of the subject visible. The fill light can simulate the effect of reflected light or of secondary light sources in the scene.
- A *rim light* (sometimes called a *back light*) creates a "defining edge" to help visually separate the subject from the background. A rim light can glint off the subject's hair (and thus is sometimes called a "hair light") and add a defining edge to show where the subject ends and the background begins.

Figure 5.7 shows the three points being added one at a time to achieve portrait-style lighting.

At the left side of the figure, the subject is lit only by the key light. This main light illuminates most of her face, and the picture could look acceptably lit if we stopped here. However, part of her face remains black and unlit.

In the center, a fill light is added. Less than half as bright as the key light, and coming from the other side of her head, it fills in the area that the key light did not illuminate.

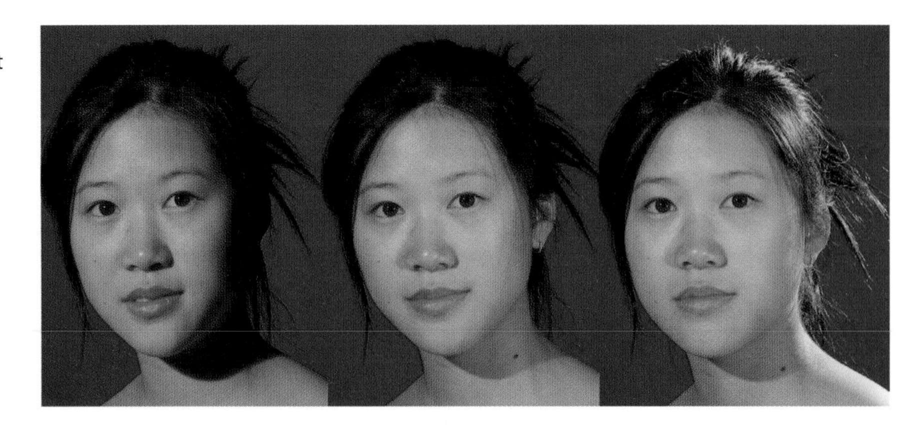

[Figure 5.7]
Photographs show key light only (left); key plus fill light (center); and key, fill, and rim light together (right).

On the right, a rim light is added. The rim light comes from behind the subject and creates a defining outline around her head and shoulders. The rim light adds definition to her silhouette, and helps separate her visually from the dark background. Even if her black hair was photographed against a black background, the rim light would bring out her hair's outline, texture, and detail.

Figure 5.8 shows the lighting placement used in this scene. A large 2000-watt light is used as the key and rim light, with a smaller 1000-watt light as the fill. The screens mounted in front of the key and fill soften the illumination and shadows.

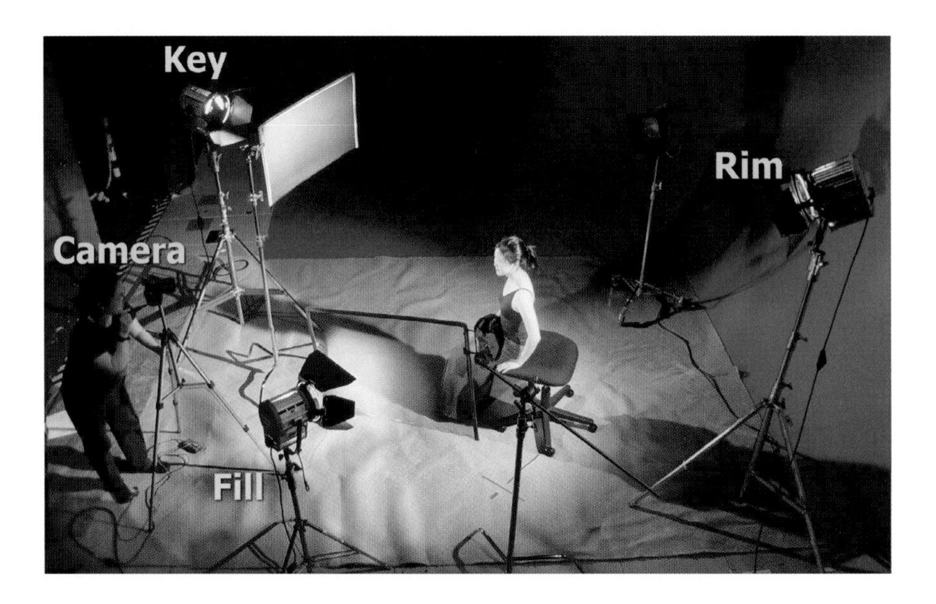

[Figure 5.8]
A three-point lighting set up is arranged around the subject.

Variations

You can make many tweaks and modifications to the basic three-point lighting set-up. Figure 5.9 shows the rim light added on the same side as the key, which adds contrast, reinforces the directionality of the lighting, and creates a more sunlit look.

The difference in brightness between the key and fill lights is called the *key-to-fill ratio*. For example, if the key were twice as bright as the fill, the key-to-fill ratio would be 2:1. A ratio of 2:1 would give you very bright, even lighting, without much contrast.

In a dramatic production, you don't want everyone lit with the same three-point lighting as if they were anchors on the TV news. A high key-to-fill ratio, such as 5:1 or 10:1, would give you a starker, higher contrast shot. Parts of the scene may become too dark to see clearly, but that may be acceptable to you. Figure 5.10 shows a scene with a 10:1 key-to-fill ratio,

[Figure 5.9] Rim and key can both come from the same direction.

[Figure 5.10] Upstage key and rim light leave a dark core.

with the key and rim lights behind the subject (moving the key behind the subject is sometimes called an *upstage key*). Only a small fill light was used, and some light has naturally bounced onto the subject's neck and chin. This is not conventional three-point lighting, but it is a use of a key light, fill light, and rim light.

Tools, Not Rules

It would be a mistake to adopt three-point lighting as a set of rules that you had to follow in every scene. Each scene is different. Simply saying that you are setting up three-point lighting is no excuse to add lights without thinking about a motivation for each light, and no excuse to position lights around a character that don't match the lighting used in the set.

Key lights, fill lights, and rim lights are tools you can use in creating your own lighting designs. Look around in the real world at how different people are lit. For example, you may find a time when a person's key light comes from a lamp on his desk, the fill light is reflected light bouncing off some papers, and he is rimmed by another lamp.

The main idea to take away from three-point lighting is that every light in your scene has a specific visual function. Functioning as a key, a fill, or a rim are three of the visual functions that a light could serve in your scene—and there are other functions covered below. As a lighting designer, you should be in control over exactly what each light adds to your image, and be able to name and describe each of your lights according to their function in the shot.

Functions of Lights

The previous section introduced three visual functions that lights can serve, but there are more than three common light functions. In this section, we will look at several functions of lights used on characters, and how to set them up in computer graphics:

- Key
- Fill
- Bounce
- Rim
- Kicker
- Specular

To serve these visual functions, lights must be positioned relative to the camera. They are generally set up after the camera has been positioned. If you later change your mind and decide to shoot your scene from a different angle, the lighting would also have to change.

Different studios have different standards for how lights are named. Most common naming schemes start with the function, or sometimes an abbreviation for the functions. If you name your lights something like Key_Sun_onDragon or Fill_Sky_onDragon, then anyone looking at your scene or copying your lighting rig will be able to understand the visual functions of each light.

Key Lights

As mentioned earlier, the key light is the main, brightest light in the scene, and establishes the scene's dominant angle for the illumination and shadows. Choosing an angle for your key light is one of the most important decisions in lighting your subject.

Putting the key light too close to the camera can flatten the form, as shown on the left side of Figure 5.11. Swinging the key light at least 30 degrees away from the camera will give some definition to the face you are lighting, as shown on the right side of the figure.

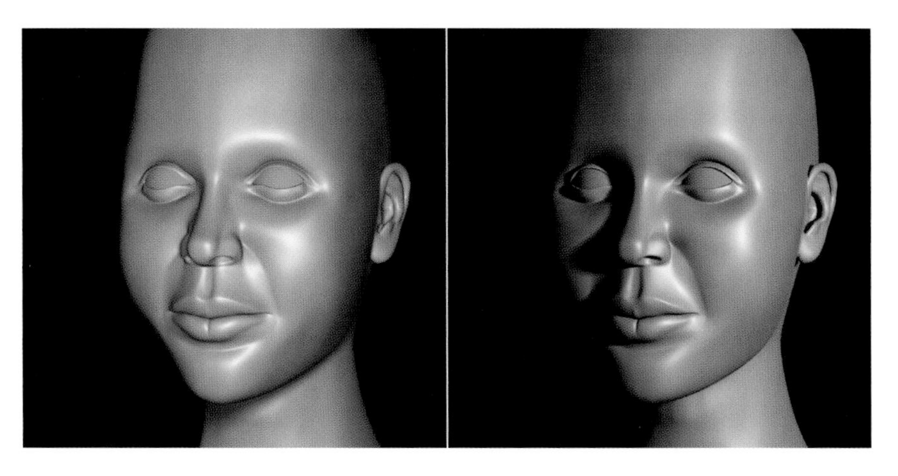

[Figure 5.11] A centered key light can flatten the subject (left); moving it to the side adds definition (right).

We are accustomed to seeing people lit from above, so it is most normal and natural to have light coming from overhead. Light from below your subject can look unnatural or spooky, as shown on the left side of Figure 5.12. Raising the key light above the eye level of your character, as shown on the right, looks more natural.

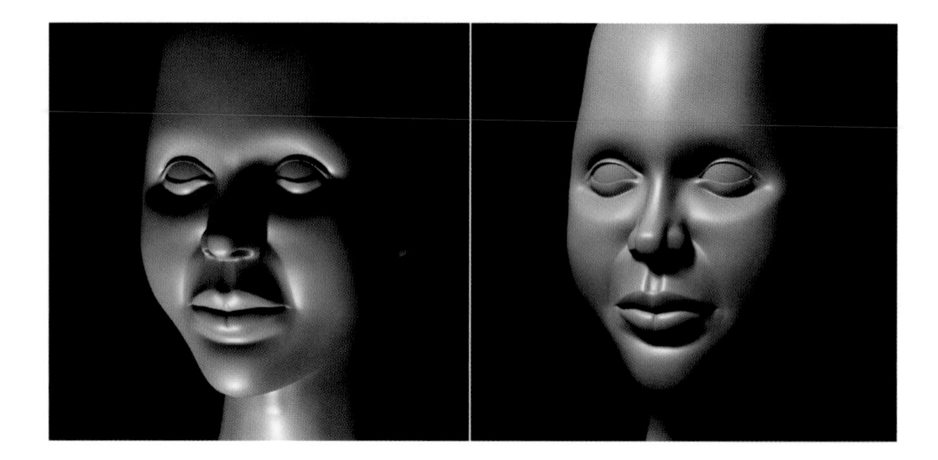

[Figure 5.12] Light from a low angle looks spooky (left), while an overhead key is more normal (right).

Your key might be positioned on the left or the right, depending on what is motivated in your scene, but keys will most often be positioned above your subject by 30 to 60 degrees, and to the side by 30 to 60 degrees, as shown in Figure 5.13.

Always test-render your key light in isolation, with no other lights visible in your scene. Make sure that you are happy with the illumination and shadows that your key light casts before you add any other lights.

Fill Lights

Fill lights extend the illumination beyond the key light, to make the rest of the character visible. While the key light might be motivated by the sun or a ceiling light fixture, fill light is often motivated by smaller lamps, indirect light, or the sky.

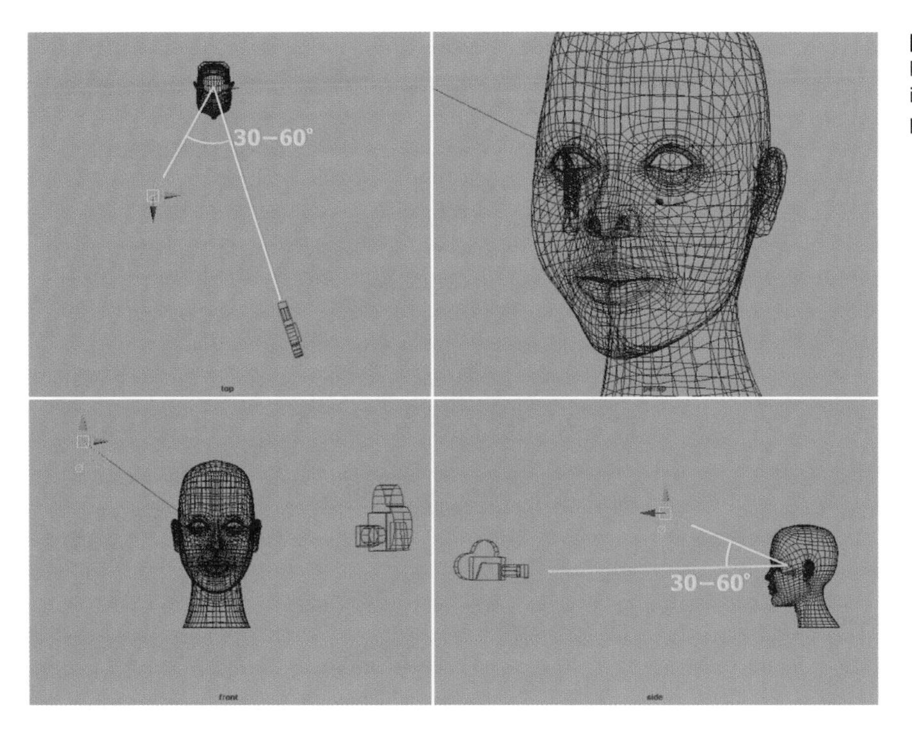

[Figure 5.13]
In wireframe, your key light is shown in a conventional position.

If you have already set up a key light aimed at your character and shadowing your character, then simply duplicating this light could be the quickest starting point to adding a fill. If you start with a copy of the key, be sure to rename the copy to make it clear that it is a fill light, and then swing it around to the position you want fill light to be in.

There are other things that you should adjust to make a fill light different from a key:

- Reduce the brightness of a fill light to less than half the brightness of the key.
- Give fill lights a different tint from the key. A complementary color (such as a blue fill with a yellow key) will do the most to help define the form of the character.
- The shadows cast by your fill lights should generally be softer than the shadows from the key.

Your first fill light will usually be aimed at the area in the key light's shadow. If you look at your test-render of the key by itself, as on the left side of Figure 5.14, it clearly has a black area in the areas where the key did not reach. On the right, fill light is added, continuing the illumination all the way around the character.

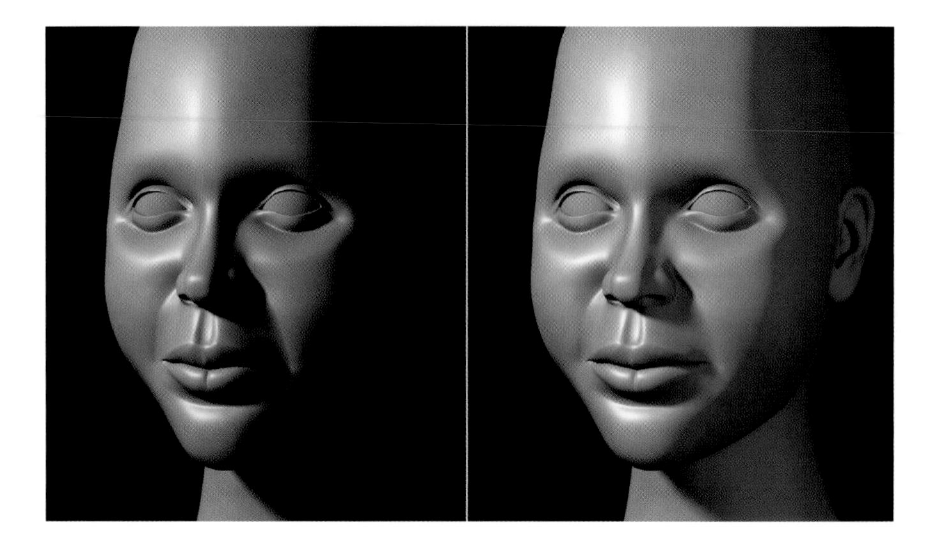

[Figure 5.14]
A model with the key light only (left) and with a fill light added (right).

To best fill in the area the key didn't hit, fill lights are generally positioned on the opposite side of the character from the key light. You can see the position of the fill in Figure 5.15, which shows the wireframe from Figure 5.14. Often fill light comes from a lower angle than the key. If the key light is coming from a high angle, then the fill might be at about eye level to your character, or lower.

You may need several fill lights to evenly light your character. Be careful that the fills don't add up to compete with the brightness of the key, which could reduce contrast and definition in the character. Very low key to fill ratios, such as 2:1 or lower, make it look like a cloudy day or a fluorescent-lit room.

In addition to the fills that light your whole character, you can also add fill lights that use light linking to selectively light certain body parts. For example, if your character's teeth were falling into shadow, and looking too dim and yellow in comparison to the white of his eyes, you might add a dim bluish fill light, linked exclusively to the teeth and gums.

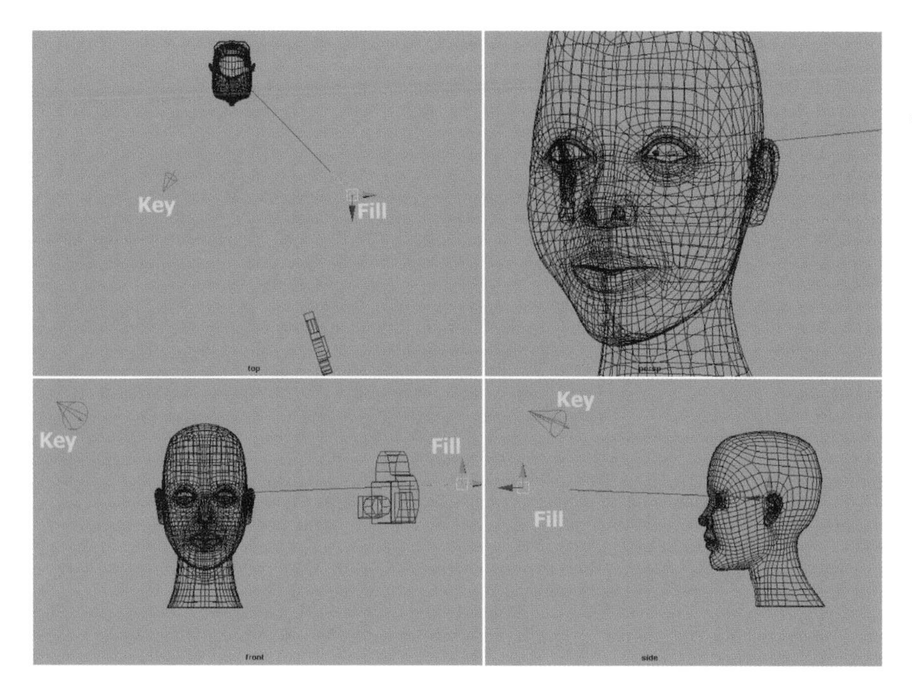

[Figure 5.15]
In wireframe, a fill light is added opposite from the key.

Bounce Lights

Bounce lights for characters are basically the same as bounce lights for sets, described in Chapter 4, "Lighting Environments and Architecture." Bounce lights can be considered a type of fill light; the only difference is that they simulate indirect light bounces instead of other sources of light.

To simulate light bouncing off the ground, you can aim bounce lights up through the ground. Bounce lights usually look best with a quadratic or inverse square decay, so the closer your character comes to the surface, the more the lights illuminate nearby parts of your character.

In lighting characters, you need to be especially careful that all of your bounce lights either cast shadows or are darkened by ambient occlusion, so that the inside of the mouth, nose, or other interior surfaces don't become too bright.

Also, bounce lights should not cast specular highlights. Nobody would believe that a highlight on the lower part of a character's eyeball was motivated by soft indirect light bounced off the floor.

The color of a bounce light is generally based on the color of the ground, or on whichever surface the light is supposed to have bounced off. Be careful to see how this color looks on your character, however. You may want to desaturate the bounce color if it is too striking a green, for example. To help breathe a little extra life into a character, sometimes it helps to tint bounce lights on characters a warmer color than you would use on a set, to simulate indirect light from the character's skin.

Light can sometimes bounce between characters, as well. Especially if your characters are out in the sun and brightly colored, there may be times when you should add a bounce light constrained to one character to add a small amount of illumination to another.

Rim Lights

As mentioned earlier in the chapter, rim lights are aimed to create a bright line defining the edge of the character. Rim lights have their origin in black and white photography and cinematography. Figure 5.16 shows how the foreground and background in a black and white picture can be similar shades of gray (left), but adding a rim light (right) can help separate the foreground from the background. As shown on the bottom, you can use rims to add punch to color images as well.

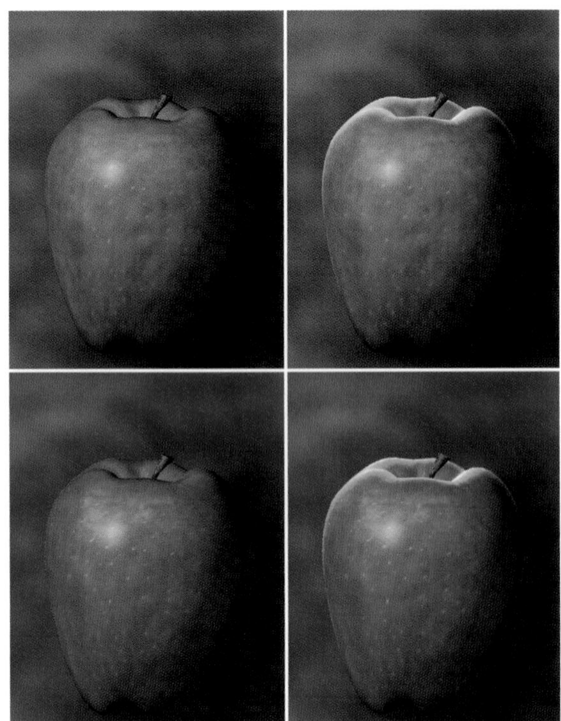

[Figure 5.16] Without rim light (left images), the apple has similar tones to the background; adding rim light (right images) makes it pop out.

There are many uses for rim lights in CG productions:

- Visually separating characters from backgrounds, especially in darker scenes.
- Adding a sense of directionality by brightening the key side of a character.
- Drawing the audience's eye to a particular character or action you want to highlight.
- Helping to match live-action background plates. (This is because many cinematographers like shooting when the sun is low in the sky or backlighting characters.)

Figure 5.17 shows a character without any rim light (left), and with rim light added on the left and right (right).

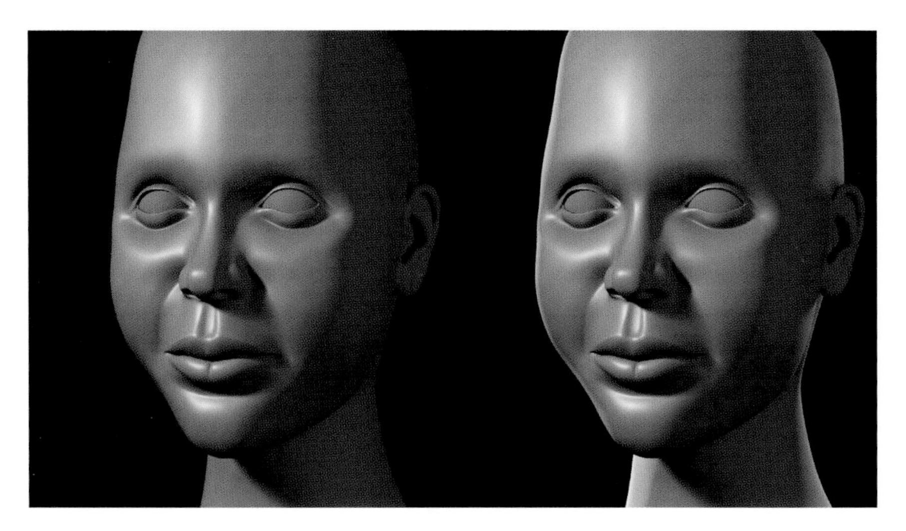

[Figure 5.17]
A figure without rim light (left) and with rims on both sides (right).

In live-action photography, a light directly behind a character will create a rim. In computer graphics, placing a light directly opposite an opaque object, as shown in Figure 5.18, will usually not produce any rim at all. Most often, the rim needs to be shifted above or to one side of the object, so that it is not directly behind it.

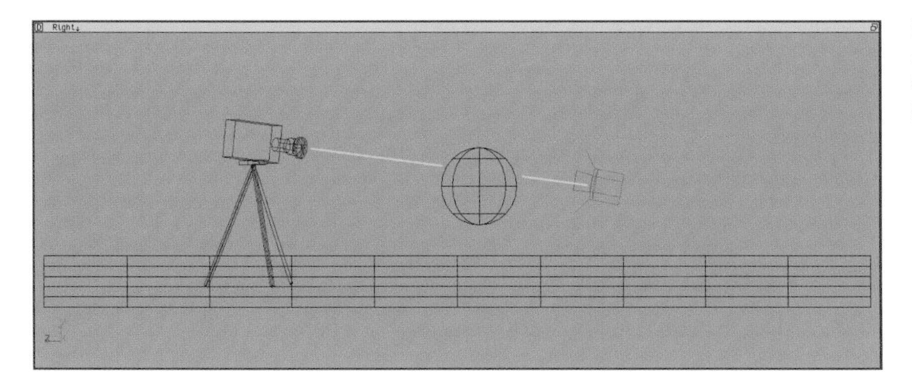

[Figure 5.18]
A rim light directly behind a 3D model is likely to completely disappear.

To aim a rim light, start with the light positioned behind the character, and move it so that you can see the light itself when you look through the camera or perspective view of your scene. You can control where the rim light appears on your character by where the light appears in your camera view. Figure 5.19 shows the two rim lights aimed at the head. If the rim is to the right of your character in the camera view, it will add a rim to the right side of the character. If the rim is above the character in the camera view, it will add a rim to the top of the character. Looking through your camera view, you can even line rim lights up beside specific limbs or parts of the head and shoulders, and get a rim on whichever parts of the body you want.

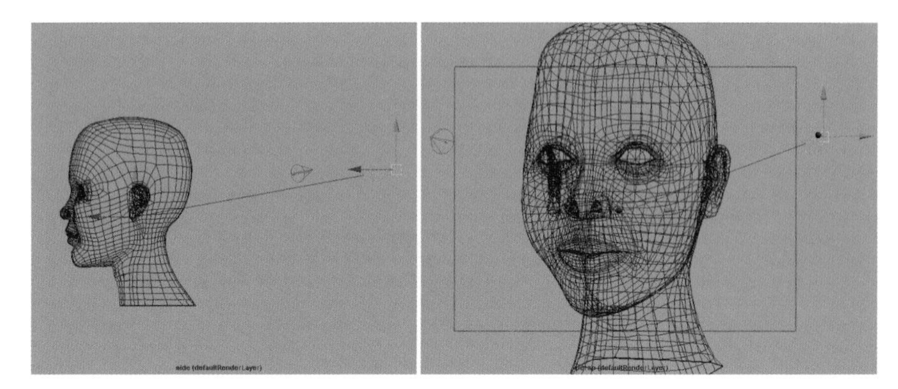

[Figure 5.19] The rim lights used in Figure 5.17 are positioned behind the subject (left) and aimed using the camera view (right).

You should usually link rim lights to your character, so that they illuminate only the character and not the set. To position a rim light correctly, sometimes it will need to shine through a wall behind the character. Rim lights need to cast shadows, otherwise the mouth interior or parts of the nose or ears could receive illumination leaking through your character.

When judged through your camera view, how far away from the character you position the rim light will control how wide and visible the rim will appear. To get a thinner or more subtle rim light, move it closer to the character in the camera's view until it is almost behind the character. To fatten up the rim and make it more visible, slide it farther away from the character, heading for the edge of the frame. To add a rim light on an especially smooth surface, sometimes you need to slide the rim slightly outside of frame.

Rim light is more apparent on real people than digital objects because in real life, people and clothing are usually covered with a translucent layer of hair, dust, stubble, or other fibers. This fine outer layer picks up and transmits rim light from directly behind a person.

If you add hair or fur to an object, then rim light suddenly becomes much more apparent, as shown in Figure 5.20. Because hair adds so many translucent strands that can each catch a rim light, sometimes there's a danger that rims can be too bright on hair—even if they've been properly adjusted for other parts of a character. If the hair is becoming pure white, you often need to use light linking to create a separate rim light for the character's hair, which might be dimmer or positioned more precisely behind the character.

[Figure 5.20]
Fur responds to rim light much more readily than smooth surfaces.

Special shaders or options on lights can also help a rim light wrap farther around an object. Figure 5.21 shows one way to achieve this—by connecting the facing ratio of a surface to a shader's highlight size, giving it much broader specular response near the rim.

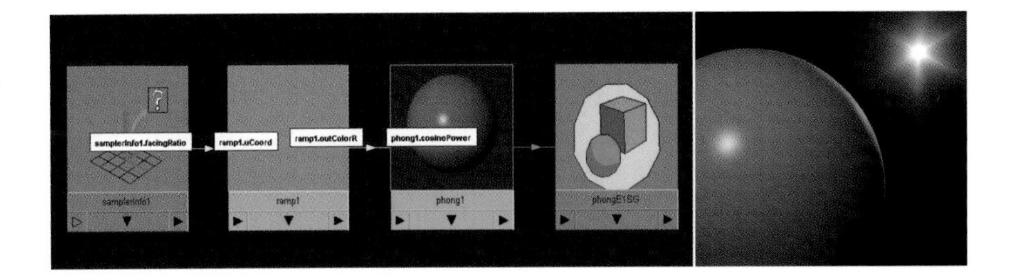

[Figure 5.21] In Maya's Hypershade window, facing ratio is used to boost highlight size at the rim of an object.

Kickers

A *kicker* is similar to a rim light, but wraps farther around the character, so that it lights one side or edge, as shown in Figure 5.22.

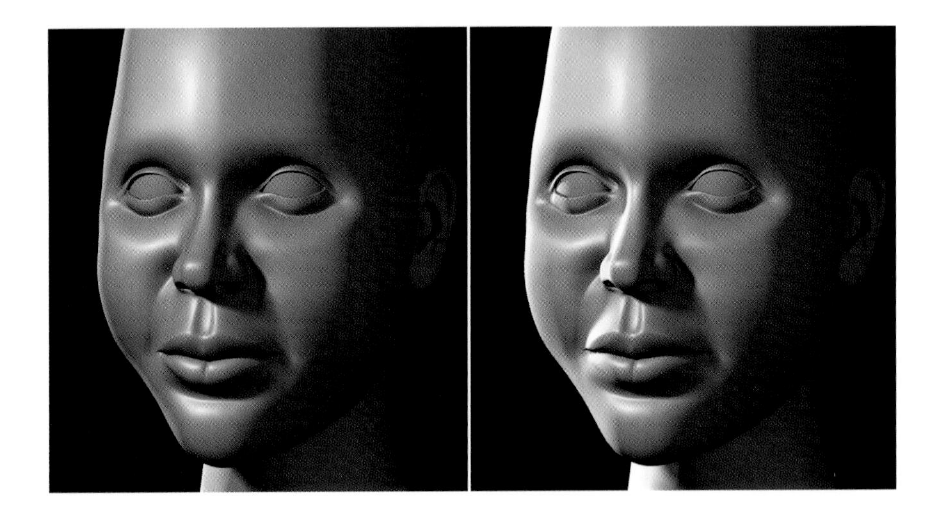

[Figure 5.22] A kicker (right) lights more of the character than a rim (left).

Visually kickers can perform many of the same functions as rim lights, but are much more apparent. Kickers also can add definition to an area on one side of a character, and can help add a lot of contrast in darker scenes.

Rim lights are often cheated into scenes in places where they are stylistically needed, but not exactly motivated by any light in the scene. Kickers are usually used more sparingly, only in cases where a bright light is clearly present to one side of the character. Figure 5.23 shows the position of a kicker, more to the side of a character, compared to a rim.

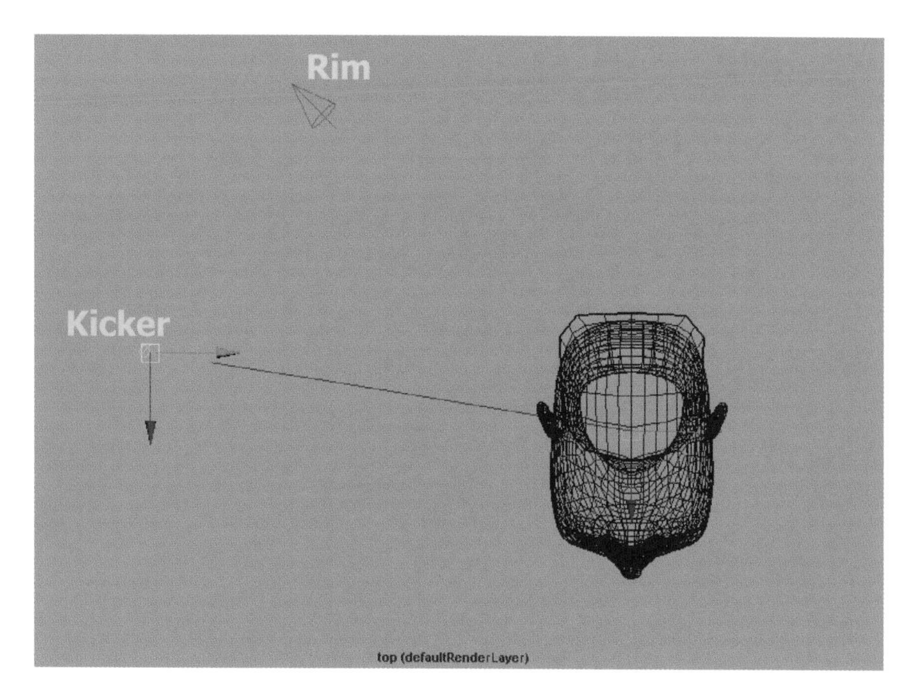

[Figure 5.23]
While a rim is behind a character, kickers are positioned more to the side.

Specular Lights

A *specular* or *spec light* is designed to add an extra specular highlight to a character. It can be any type of light source that is set not to emit diffuse illumination, but only specular.

If you are trying to make a character look wet, getting just the right highlights on his skin or hair is essential. As shown on the left side of Figure 5.24, reptile or lizard skin can look dry if it has no highlights or reflections, but adding some extra specular highlights (right) can fix that problem. To add highlights that will rake across a character's skin or hair, position the spec light roughly behind the character, much as you would a rim light.

As discussed below, spec lights are also ideal for adding highlights to eyes. If you want to make sure a highlight will appear in eyes, glasses, teeth, or other shiny parts of a character, position the spec light very close to the camera.

When a spec light is close enough to the camera position, you can get highlights that will remain visible no matter where a character moves during a shot.

[Figure 5.24] Lacking specularity, the snake looks dry (left); a specular light adds shine to the scales (right).

Issues in Lighting Character Animation

Lighting creatures and characters that change positions and poses is a far more complex task than lighting static geometry. A light that illuminated a character perfectly at one frame might not light her at all after she stepped into a shadow. A carefully aimed rim light that looked great at one frame might overexpose her hair after she turns a different direction.

It is technically possible to group or constrain lights to a character so that the lights move wherever she moves, and no matter where the character goes, all of the lights surround her from the same distance and angle. This would ensure that your lighting remains uniform, but it could also look fake if the lights appeared to follow the character around for no apparent reason.

Your character lighting will generally look more natural if the character is moving through the illumination of the scene and the light sources themselves remain static, as they would in real life. However, sometimes you can get away with cheating a little. Rim lights sometimes need to be animated in position just to maintain a nice consistent rim effect as a character moves. Sometimes a fill or bounce light can be constrained to a character, especially if it illuminates a specific area such as the mouth. Be careful about this; going too far with making lights move around that should really be static can make your lighting look fake, as if the character were in another world than the sets.

Test Frames

Because your character lighting is going to change over time, pick out a few representative frames from each shot where you want to develop and test the lighting. You might pick the first and last frame, or any frames that are extremes in terms of the character being as far forward or backward as he gets in the shot. Other good candidates worth testing are frames where a character's mouth is opened, so that you can see how the inside of the mouth looks, and any frames where two people or things come in contact.

Once you have a list of the frames that you want to test, you can move between them while lighting. If you work at one frame and aim a rim light or adjust your key, you will also want to switch to other frames and test-render the shot there, to see the results of what you have added or changed.

If you are working at film resolution, normally you won't be able to render all of your frames overnight. Instead, you should just render a new version of a few main frames at film resolution after you have changed the lighting. If you need to see your lighting in motion, you might also render the whole shot at a lower resolution, sometimes rendering every second or third frame for longer shots. Being very selective and careful about what you test-render is the key to getting your final rendering of all film-resolution frames done correctly the first time.

Linking Lights to Characters

Do characters even need their own lights? If you're lighting an animated film and there are already lights illuminating the set, couldn't you just let the set lights illuminate your characters? You can test-render your scene at a few different frames to see how your characters look when they are lit by the lights that are already there. Sometimes you may like the results. More often, however, you'll find that the lights illuminating the set aren't what you want to illuminate the character.

To gain more creative control over a character's lighting, you often need to create separate lights that are linked exclusively to your character. Then the lights illuminating the set will be linked only to the set, not to your character. The angle, brightness, and color of the lights on the characters should be similar to the set lighting. However, perfect technical continuity with your set should not outweigh concerns such as modeling with light or defining the character in a way that shows the animation and helps tell the story.

In many productions, each character has its own group of exclusively linked lights, or lighting rig. These lights can be adjusted in position and color to match different sets, wherever the character appears. In environments with many practical lights, however, such as in an office with many lamps, you should have the practical lights from the set illuminate the character, in addition to the key, fill, or other lights that are in the character's lighting rig.

Technology Changes

A lighting artist's toolkit keeps expanding, especially with more options for how to render fill and bounce light. Using spotlights with regular depth map shadows to create fill and bounce lights can work fine, but renderers today are loaded with alternatives including *ambient occlusion*, *image-based lighting* (*IBL*), and *global illumination* (*GI*). These were discussed in Chapter 4 for use on environments and sets. For use on characters, the animation industry has been adopting these techniques cautiously, and often in limited ways, simply because computing them for each frame of an animation can be such a slow process.

Ambient Occlusion on Characters

Ambient occlusion has changed over the past five years from something formerly considered too slow to use in most productions to being a staple of many high-quality productions. This change has come about from a combination of software improvements and faster computers.

If you are using ambient occlusion on your characters, you may not need fill lights to cast shadows. Ambient occlusion can darken the interior surfaces of a character, such as nostrils, armpits, behind the ears, and areas between any wrinkles in fabric, creating a look as if your fill lights were casting very soft shadows. Figure 5.25 shows ambient occlusion on a character, fill light without shadows, and then fill light multiplied by the occlusion.

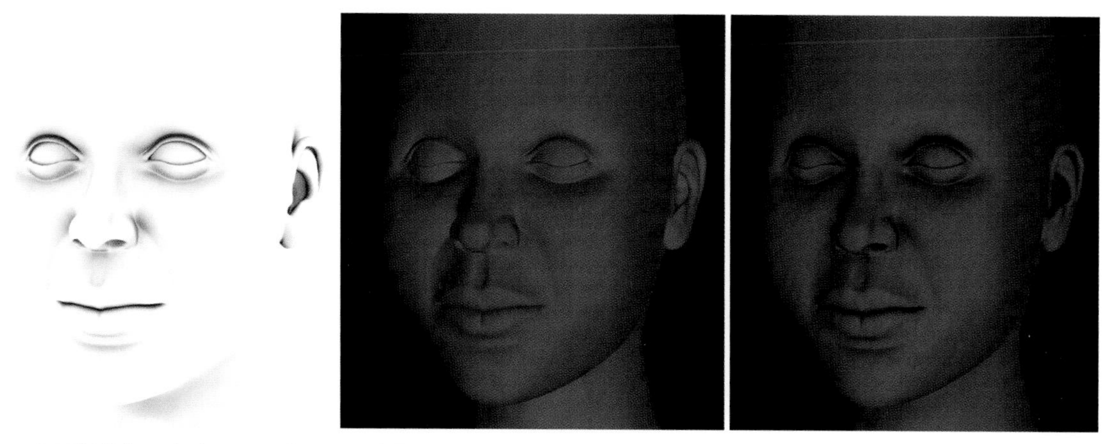

[Figure 5.25] With occlusion on a character (left), you can render fill lights that don't cast shadows (center), and when the occlusion is multiplied with the fill light the result will resemble fill shadows (right)

If your renderer allows you to connect ambient occlusion to specific light shaders, then for the most realistic results you should use ambient occlusion to darken the illumination from your fill lights and bounce lights, but not your key light. This way, your key light can be darkened by real shadows, cast in an appropriate direction, without being blocked by ambient occlusion; only your fill lights will be darkened by ambient occlusion. Especially if the key and fill lights are different colors, having them blend realistically in shadow areas can make your scenes more realistic. Selecting which lights will be darkened by ambient occlusion, and which lights won't, is not an option in every renderer; this is just a guideline to use if you have the option.

Sometimes people are tempted to overuse ambient occlusion until it becomes an unrealistically dominant part of a scene's shading. Making ambient occlusion appear as dark and prominent as your key light shadow is realistic only when you have a very low key-to-fill ratio, such as inside of room with soft lights, or outside on a cloudy day. While ambient occlusion is nice to look at, it's only one component of your lighting, and is sometimes very subtle.

If you need to render animation quickly and have decided that you can't use ambient occlusion at every frame, baking a more limited amount of ambient occlusion into a character is an option. You may want ambient occlusion baked into the character's texture maps for the interior of the nose, mouth, and in and around the ear. Be careful that your baked ambient occlusion doesn't visibly darken direct light from the key too much. It should mostly darken fill light.

IBL and GI on Characters

Image-based lighting is a terrific source of fill light and can be used on characters much as it is used on environments. You may find that you don't need to add many fill or bounce lights to a scene once you use IBL, especially if you are outdoors. IBL works best to simulate light coming from a great distance, so it could be a perfect source of fill from the sky, but not good for fill light from a nearby lamp.

Global illumination is usually deemed too slow to use on large character animation projects. When it is used, it is usually in a simplified form, providing only one bounce between surfaces, and computing indirect light based on simplified models instead of looking at the full set. Perhaps someday GI in animation will become as commonplace as ambient occlusion has become, but it will take faster computers to get to that point.

While a world of options exists for new ways to add fill and bounce light, other functions of lights are still best added as basic spotlights with depth map or raytraced shadows. Key lights, rim lights, kickers, and specular lights have not changed much in ten years, and don't seem likely to be replaced any time soon.

Subsurface Scattering

Many shaders in 3D software have a *translucency* parameter, which can make a thin surface such as a leaf, a lampshade, or a piece of paper appear translucent. However, for thicker objects such as characters, the translucency of skin is best simulated via shaders using *subsurface scattering*. Figure 5.26 shows a head with a regular, opaque shader (left). Rendered with subsurface scattering (right), the head shows a clear response to the bright rim light behind the left ear.

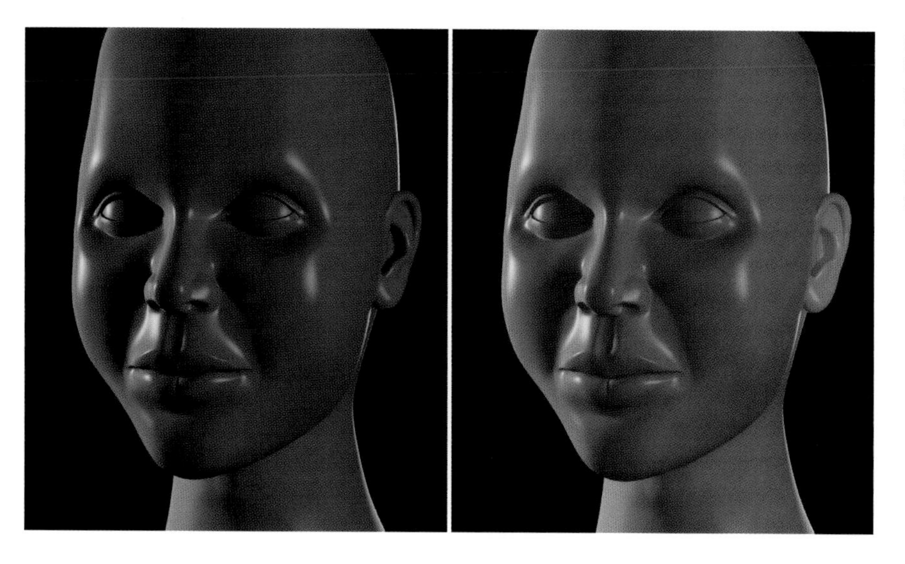

[Figure 5.26]
Without subsurface scattering (left) a character is opaque, with subsurface scattering (right) you can see where the light is positioned behind the ear.

Subsurface scattering simulates the way rays of light are dispersed within translucent materials. No matter how carefully you have texture mapped the surface of your skin, it can still look fake if it doesn't have realistic translucency. On skin, subsurface scattering is visible in three main areas:

- When bright light comes from behind thin parts of the body, such as the ears and nose, they can glow red. This is called *forward scattering* because the light enters on the far side of the surface and exits after scattering through to the front.
- The terminator where the light transitions into darkness takes on a reddish glow, also due to forward scattering.
- The edges of shadows on the skin can appear reddish. This is due to back scattering, or light entering the flesh, then coming out near the same point on the surface where it entered. This happens more on fleshy areas such as cheeks.

Figure 5.27 shows these effects in real photographs. Note that very bright light was used to make the effects very pronounced. In most cases, subsurface scattering is very subtle. However, human skin is a material with which we are all intimately familiar, and nailing subtle details of its shading is vital to making a lifelike, engaging character.

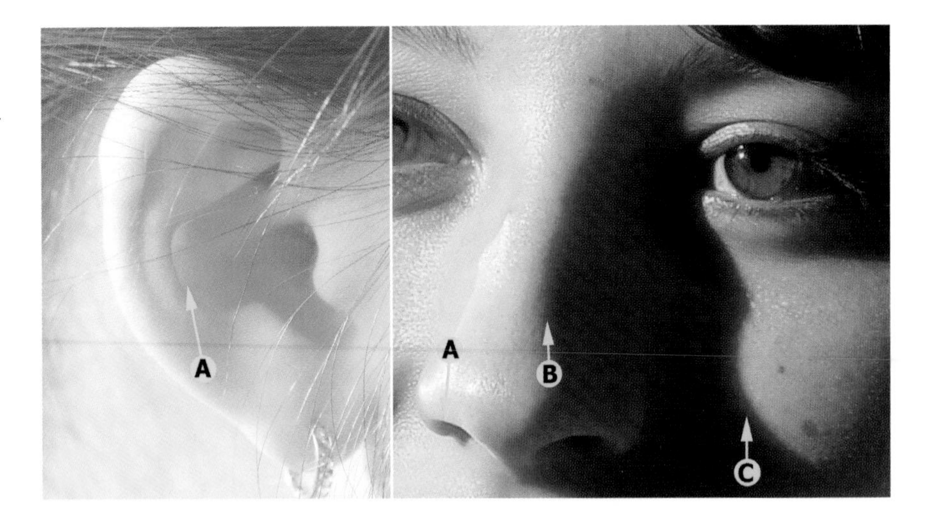

[Figure 5.27] Subsurface scattering photographs show forward scattering (A), a reddish terminator (B), and red edges of shadows (C).

Once subsurface scattering is used in a skin shader, it is usually a good idea to calculate scattering for all the other parts of the head, such as teeth and eyeballs, as well. Remember that subsurface scattering is a simulation of light passing through a model, so the interior parts of the head should be a part of the equation.

Mapping Variation

Images rendered with subsurface scattering can sometimes make a character's head look as if it were made of wax rather than of flesh and blood. The waxy look is actually a result of using subsurface scattering without painting maps to vary the scattering in different parts of the face. Completely uniform subsurface scattering looks waxy because wax is a very homogeneous material that scatters light uniformly.

Under your skin, you have a mixture of bone, muscle, cartilage, and fat—all of which scatter light differently and are distributed at different depths under your skin. To physically model all of this would be prohibitively complex for an animated production. However, the properties that you observe in real life can be reproduced by painting maps to control your subsurface scattering. For example, a back-scattering effect could be mapped to appear more pronounced in areas such as the cheeks, where there is more flesh beneath the skin, but painted darker in the forehead or chin, where there's bone immediately under the skin. You may need to paint one map to control the depth or scale of the subsurface scattering, to control how far it penetrates, and another map to control the colors of the indirect light, such as if it reveals veins or a tissue texture.

Faking Subsurface Scattering

An increasing number of shaders and solutions for soft, natural looking subsurface scattering are becoming available. However, they take time to set up properly and add to your rendering time. Some of the visual results of subsurface scattering can be faked through simpler adjustments to your shaders and lights:

- Tint the bounce lights on your character a warmer tone. Some pink or red will help create the feeling that the skin is tinting indirect light.
- Using a ramp shader or any shader with adjustable color gradients or remapping, adjust the shader so that its color appears red around the terminator instead of proceeding directly from white to black.
- Colorless wrinkles are a dead giveaway that you are using bump or displacement without subsurface scattering. When you texture map wrinkles onto a character's hands or face, also use your map to color the skin inside the wrinkle red or pink.

No matter what colors appear on the surface of a character's skin, it's what's underneath the skin, mostly red blood, that's most responsible for the tints added by subsurface scattering. Even green-skinned aliens have been rendered successfully with warm scattering tones added in the skin shaders.

Lighting Hair

Often a big concern in rendering hair and fur is how much they can slow down your rendering time. If you are rendering with depth of field (DOF) but a character is in perfect focus, it can save render time to render the character as a separate layer without calculating DOF for that layer. Hair and fur can greatly slow down raytracing, too. It is generally a good idea to exclude hair and fur from raytraced shadows or reflections altogether.

Hair is usually rendered with depth map shadows. Some renderers have special types of shadow maps designed to work well with hair, such as Deep

Shadow Maps in Renderman or Detail Shadow Maps in Mental Ray. Because hairs are so thin compared to individual samples in the shadow map, it is essential that shadow maps be tightly framed to focus on the hair itself. This is one reason to use separate lights to illuminate a character's hair.

Dedicating separate lights to hair also enables you to get more perfect rim lighting on hair. Hair tends to pick up rim light much more readily than most surfaces, so making a separately aimed, less intense rim light for the hair can provide a nice rim without making the hair go pure white.

Lighting Eyes

An eye has three main visible parts: the sclera (the white of the eye), the iris (the colored part), and the pupil (the black part in the middle). The sclera should be more gray than white; it certainly should not be as bright or white as a highlight in the eye. Often it is a pale gray or has shades of yellow, and when lit it grows darker near the edges.

The main shading of your sclera runs in an opposite direction from the shading on your iris. Figure 5.28 shows an eye lit from the upper left. The gradient running across the sclera is brightest on the upper left. The iris, on the other hand, is brightest on the lower right. Also notice that the iris is much flatter than the sclera, and doesn't vary as much in tone.

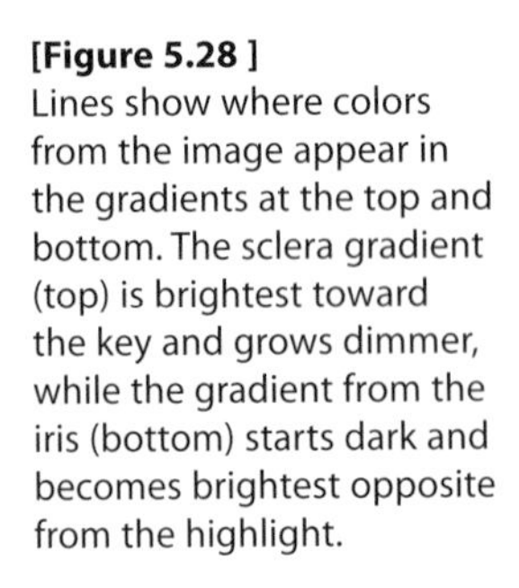

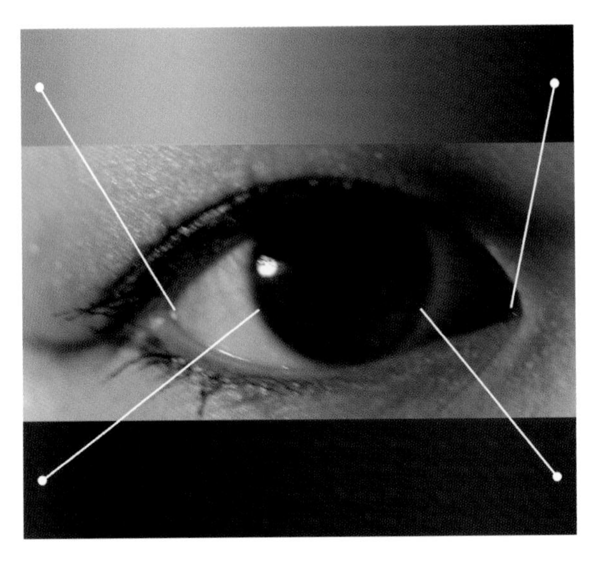

[Figure 5.28]
Lines show where colors from the image appear in the gradients at the top and bottom. The sclera gradient (top) is brightest toward the key and grows dimmer, while the gradient from the iris (bottom) starts dark and becomes brightest opposite from the highlight.

The shading you see in an eye is a result of the shape of the eye geometry. As shown in Figure 5.29, the iris is relatively flat, or angled inward into the eye, where it sits below the lens.

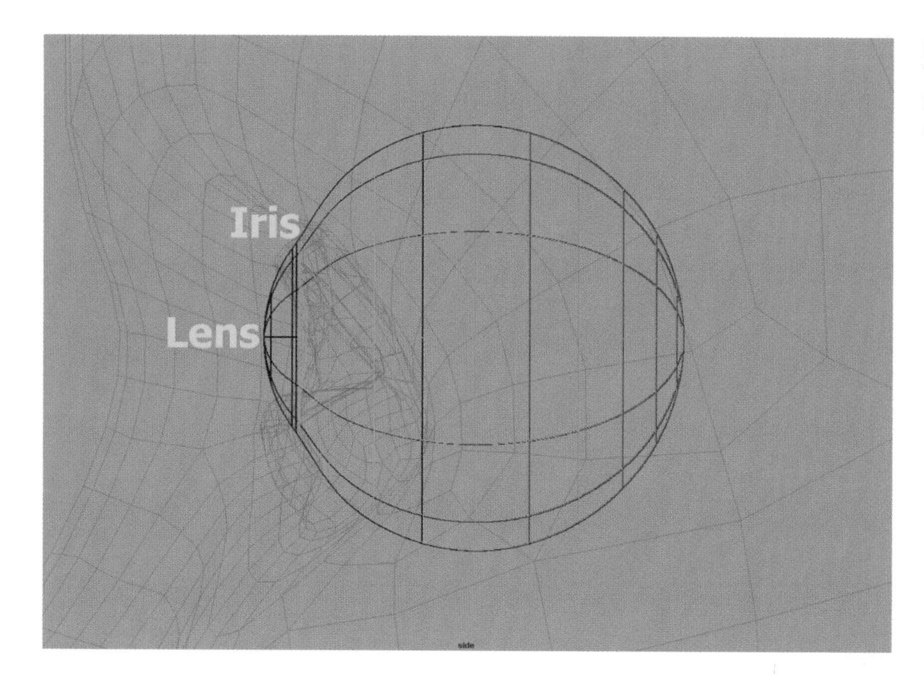

[Figure 5.29]
The geometry of an eye model built for realistic shading

You shouldn't necessarily build a character's eye model too similarly to a real human eye. A real eye depends on refraction to bring the color of the iris to the surface of the lens, even when the lens is seen from the side. If you don't want to raytrace all of your animation with refraction, simply putting the iris closer to the surface of the eye will probably give you better results.

Eye Occlusion

The edges of eyes are shadowed by eyelids and lashes. Even when lashes are too thin or small to see in a shot, they still contribute to the subtle shading that darkens the edges of the eyes. The extra shading can sometimes emphasize the roundness of eyes as well, bringing out their spherical shape.

Ambient occlusion can be used to darken the edges of eyes. Often you'll need a separately adjusted ambient occlusion shader for a character's eyeballs, so that they can respond to shading based on the very small distance from the eyeball to the lid. Occlusion on the eyes needs to be computed at every frame, not baked and held as a static texture map. Even if you use baked occlusion inside of the nose and ears, the eye occlusion needs to be recomputed for each eye pose, so that as the eyes close the eyelids will darken the appropriate parts of the eyeball.

Eye Highlights

Eye highlights help make a character look alive. Without highlights, a character's eyes look unnaturally dry. Even in wider shots, when highlights in a character's eyes might be only a few pixels in size, those will still be some of the most important pixels in the image.

You can start lighting eyes by giving them the same illumination as the rest of your character. Your key light or other lights on the character might contribute a specular highlight that works well enough to provide eye highlights in some shots.

If your key light is not enough to trigger nice eye highlight, create a new specular light. Use light linking to exclusively link it to your character's eyeballs, and of course set it to emit only specular light. You can start with the specular light positioned near your key light, but to make sure the highlights are visible in any animated shot, you can cheat the specular light very close to the camera. Once it is near the camera, moving the specular light a small amount to the side or upward can adjust the highlight position in the eye.

[Figure 5.30] An eye highlight near the key-side edge of the iris looks convincing.

Eye highlights should not appear immediately below the upper eyelid. Highlights should be shadowed or occluded by the upper lid so that they go away as the eye closes. Highlights along the bottom of the eye, against the lower eyelid, can make a character look as if he is crying or has a tear welling up in his eye.

Often the most convincing place for a highlight is right along one edge of the iris, as shown in Figure 5.30. This accentuates the convex shape of the lens of the eye, as though the edge of the lens had caught the highlight.

To keep pupils sharp and black, keep the highlights out of them. Putting the highlight too close to the center of the eye could gray out the pupil and make the character look dimwitted. If you want to achieve the look of a camera flash hitting the character in the center of the eye, then it is better to adjust your eye shader to make the pupil turn red than to leave a white or gray highlight in the middle of the eye.

Exercises

The illumination striking people and animals is something you can observe as you go through the day, and learn from every environment. Movies and photographs are another source of inspiration worthy of study. Most of all, keep practicing lighting your own characters in ways that best define them and fit with each scene.

1. A *one-light rendering* is an exercise in simplicity. Load up any 3D scene and try to light it with only one light. Allow blackness wherever the light is shadowed. With a good key light position, a one-light rendering can define the scene with its illumination, shadows, and terminator. If you are happy with your one-light rendering, then you have found a great starting point to either use global illumination, or to begin adding fill and bounce lights.

2. Grab a still from a DVD and study how the characters are lit. Try finding the gradients running across the characters as described in the "Modeling with Light" section. What does the gradient tell you about the subject and the source of the light? If you were lighting this scene in 3D, would the gradients running across the characters look the same?

3. If you aren't an animator yourself and you need experience lighting animated subjects, try to team up with a group project, either at a school or over the Internet. There's no experience except lighting a sequence of shots in an animated project that really gets you into character lighting.

[CHAPTER SIX]

Cameras and Exposure

Exposure is the all-important moment when the camera's shutter opens and allows light to reach the sensor or film. The adjustments that a photographer or cinematographer makes to control the exposure also influence the depth of field, motion blur, and other properties of the shot. 3D artists often need to match or simulate the effects of a real camera. Whether you are rendering visual effects elements that need to be integrated with live-action footage, or just trying to make a 3D scene look more believable or more cinematic, it helps to understand how real cameras work, and to be able to read the notations in a camera log regarding lenses, f-stops, and shutter angles.

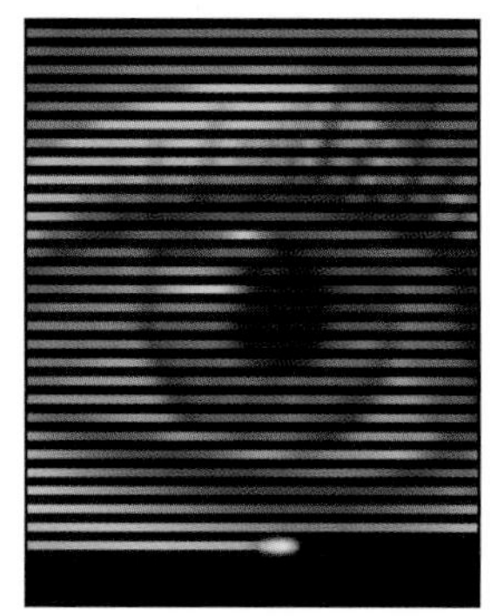

Understanding F-Stops and Depth of Field

[Figure 6.1] The camera's aperture dilates with a set of metal flaps. The hexagonal shape being formed here is sometimes seen as a feature of some lens flares.

Depth of field (DOF) determines how much of your scene will be in focus. With a narrow DOF, only a narrow slice of your scene will remain sharp near a specified focal distance; everything farther from or closer to the camera will be blurred. With a deep depth of field, more of the scene (sometimes all of your scene) will be in focus.

A photographer or cinematographer controls a camera's depth of field by adjusting the size of the *aperture*, the opening through which light travels in order to enter the camera. The aperture size varies via an arrangement of metal flaps, as shown in Figure 6.1.

The size of the aperture is measured in *f-stops*. The sequence of f-stops is shown on the lens of a camera in Figure 6.2. Each increase of one f-stop exactly cuts in half the amount of light hitting the film. Different lenses have different maximums and minimums, but often include the f-stops 1.4, 2, 2.8, 4, 5.6, 8, 11, 16, 22, and 32—if you are noticing a pattern here, the numbers are the square roots of all the powers of two.

A higher f-stop number, such as f64, indicates a narrow aperture, which allows in very little light, but creates a very large depth of field, which is sometimes called *deep focus*. Deep focus throws everything in focus at once, from objects very close to the camera to the distant background, as shown on the left side of Figure 6.3.

[Figure 6.2] The *aperture ring* on a camera lens is used to choose an f-stop. Some newer types of lenses lack an aperture ring because the f-stop is chosen electronically through the camera, but the f-stop numbers still work the same way.

A lower f-stop number, such as f1.4, specifies a wider aperture opening, which would let in more light. As light enters from a greater range of angles, this creates a shallow DOF, with fewer objects in focus, as shown on the right side of Figure 6.3. Any subject that stepped closer to the camera, or moved farther beyond the focal distance, would quickly fall out of focus.

DOF effects in 3D programs sometimes ask for an f-stop value to simulate depth of field. As shown in Figure 6.4, you can choose a low value such as f1.4 if you want a very limited depth of field, or a high number such as f64 if you prefer deep focus.

[Figure 6.3]
A small aperture creates a larger DOF (left), while a larger aperture produces a shallower DOF (right).

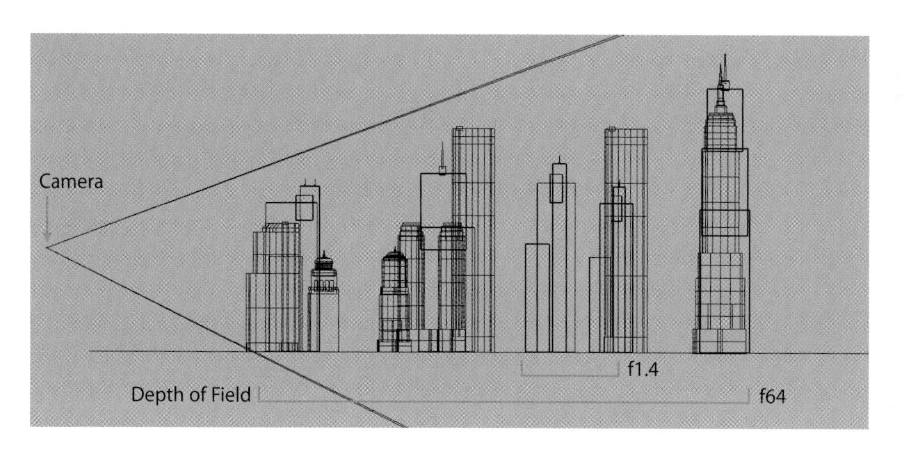

[Figure 6.4]
Adjusting your depth of field via simulated aperture controls gives a shallow DOF at lower f-stops.

Influencing depth of field is just a side effect of f-stop choice in a real camera; the primary function of the f-stop is to control how much light will reach the film or sensor. Each increase of one f-stop (such as from 1.4 to 2, or 2 to 2.8) exactly cuts in half the amount of light.

In 3D software, the f-stop you select to control depth of field will not affect the brightness of your scene, but you should remember the photographic relationship between brightness and aperture. A narrower DOF, with fewer things in focus, is expected in dark or dimly lit scenes, which would have been filmed with a lower f-stop number.

Matching Real Lenses

The *focal length* of a lens is the amount of magnification it provides. A greater focal length means that a lens is more zoomed-in or *telephoto*, providing more magnification to your image. A telephoto lens will tend to produce a more narrow depth of field, with a lot of blurring of the foreground and background. A wide-angle lens (low focal length) generally will have a deeper depth of field, with more things in focus. In many cases, this is a subtle distinction in comparison to the f-stop, but if you are simulating an extremely telephoto lens, such as the view through a telescope, bear in mind that the audience will expect a narrow depth of field.

A *macro* lens is a type of lens used for close-up photography and shooting very small things. A macro lens tends to have an extremely narrow depth of field. Because of this, people have come to associate a very narrow depth of field with miniature objects. If you want a part of your animation to look like macro photography of a tiny subject, a very narrow depth of field will help convey that effect, as in Figure 6.5.

Keep in mind that if you render a scene with too narrow a depth of field, it can make your characters look like miniatures in a dollhouse instead of life-sized people. Giving your scene a greater depth of field would make the scene's scale look more normal.

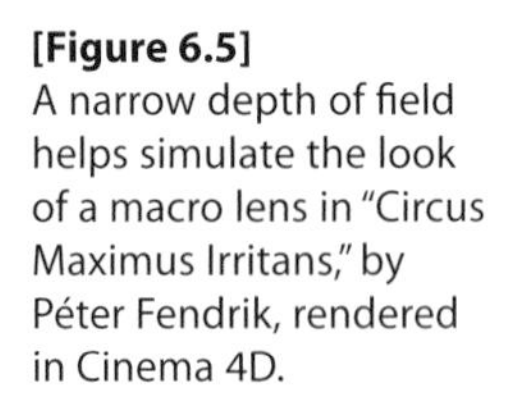

[Figure 6.5]
A narrow depth of field helps simulate the look of a macro lens in "Circus Maximus Irritans," by Péter Fendrik, rendered in Cinema 4D.

The Two-Thirds Rule

The *two-thirds rule* states that when a camera is focused to a specific focal distance, you can expect about one-third of the area in focus to be in the foreground, closer than the focal distance, and about two-thirds of the area in focus to be in the background, beyond the focal distance, as shown in Figure 6.6.

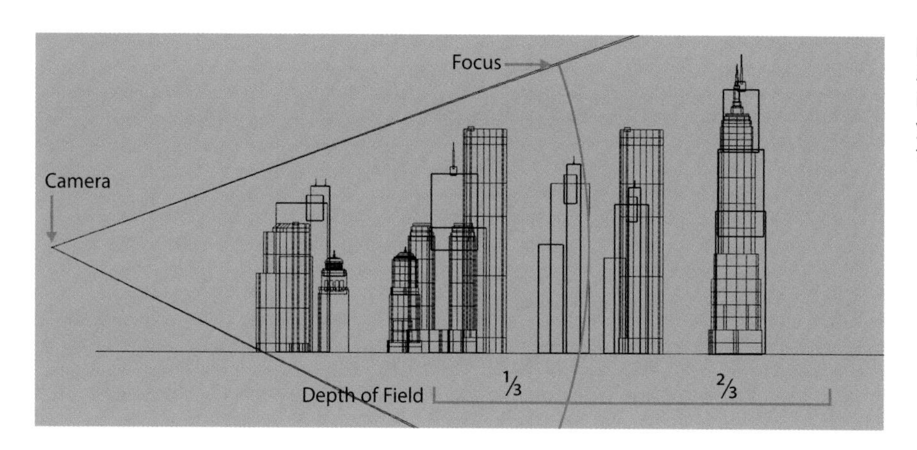

[Figure 6.6]
About one-third of the area in focus will be in front of your focal distance, and two-thirds will be beyond it.

If your software asks you to set an f-stop to control your depth of field, then the two-thirds rule is most likely already a part of the DOF calculation of your renderer. On the other hand, if your software allows you to set near and far focus distances manually, then paying attention to the two-thirds rule could lead to more realistic renderings.

Hyperfocal Distance

When a lens is focused at its *hyperfocal distance*, that means that everything in the background will be in focus, no matter how far away. In the foreground, focus begins at half the focal distance. For example, in Figure 6.7, if the camera is focused at 200 meters, everything from 100 meters to infinity will be in focus. Specifics depend on the lens, but the hyperfocal distance is usually reached when using a small aperture and when focused at least a few meters away. We often see outdoor scenes and landscape photography created with cameras focused at their hyperfocal distance.

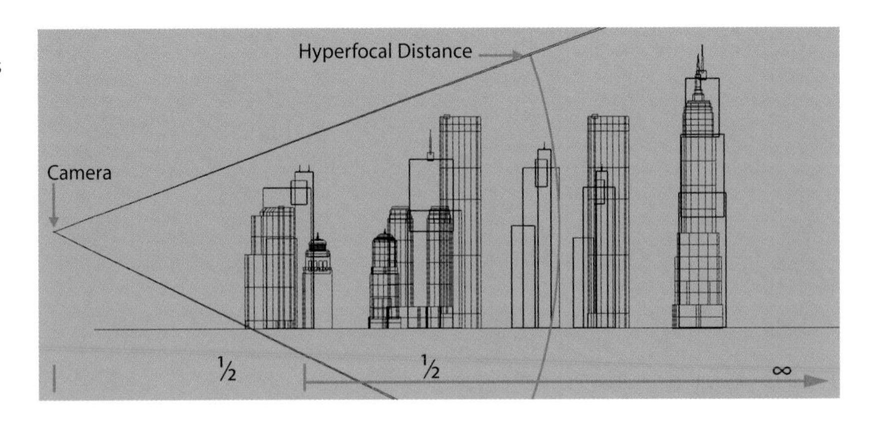

[Figure 6.7] When a lens is focused at its hyperfocal distance, everything in the background is in focus.

In bright daylight scenes, it can unrealistic to blur the background once the focal distance is more than a few meters from the camera. At night, or when indoors, backgrounds more often fall out of focus. If your background is an image mapped onto a sphere surrounding your scene, leave it fully in focus for most of your daylight shots. If you need to visually separate the foreground from the background, consider adding some mist or haze on your daytime backgrounds instead of blurring them.

[Figure 6.8] Highlights grow into beads of light as they fall out of focus. The bokeh (out-of-focus quality) of a lens gives each type of lens a unique signature.

Bokeh Effects

Bokeh (pronounced "bow-kay") is a word derived from Japanese that describes the "out of focus" quality of a lens.

With a real camera, when parts of a scene fall out of focus, they don't all get blurred as smoothly as a typical blur in computer graphics. Instead, things falling out of focus on a real camera tend to shimmer or glisten. Highlights or bright areas can bloom into little balls of light when they fall out of focus, as shown in Figure 6.8.

Lenses have different bokeh. Some lenses are described as very smooth and creamy; this means the lens blurs things in much the same way as a renderer's DOF, making areas look like they have been smoothly Gaussian blurred. Other lenses make very defined circles or seem to put rings around bright points of light when they fall out of focus.

At the time this book is being written, only a few renderers, such as SplutterFish's Brazil, support bokeh effects. If you lack this option in your rendering software, you could potentially simulate bokeh effects by applying treatments to highlights that get blurred during compositing.

Frame Rates

Video and motion picture cameras have a *frame rate*, which is usually measured in frames per second. The frame rate specifies how many individual frames or images are exposed per second of moving film or video.

Motion picture film is usually shot at 24 fps, which is called *sound speed*, because it is the standard speed for film with a synchronized soundtrack. Prior to the invention of sound, camera operators would crank movie cameras at slightly different rates for different shots, which they considered a part of their creative control over the flow of the film.

Different television standards around the world have different frame rates. The NTSC standard, common throughout North America and much of the Pacific Rim, uses a frame rate of just less than 30 fps. Two of the world's other major standards, PAL and SECAM, use 25 fps.

Realistic Motion Blur

The controls on a real camera that influence *motion blur*, the amount of movement or change captured during the exposure, are the shutter speed (in stills) or shutter angle (in motion pictures).

Shutter Speed and Shutter Angle

Shutter speed is a measurement of how long a camera's shutter opens to allow light to expose the film. Shutter speed is usually expressed as a fraction of a second, such as $^1/_{125}$. The longer the shutter is open, the more light reaches the film.

Doubling the amount of time the shutter stays open makes an image twice as bright. A shutter speed of one-quarter of a second would allow twice as much light to reach the film as a speed of one-eighth of a second. In the viewfinders and controls of many cameras, abbreviated labels show only the divisor (the second number in the fraction) to indicate a shutter speed. For example,

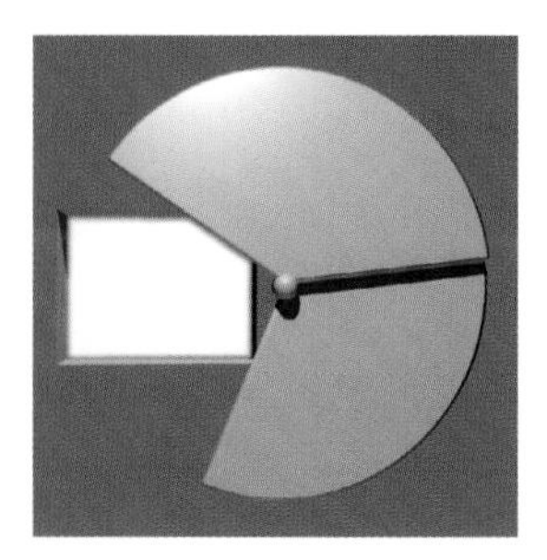

[Figure 6.9] An opening in a revolving shutter creates the shutter angle. The two halves of the shutter can rotate to make the opening wider or narrower.

$^1/_{250}$ of a second could be labeled 250, or $^1/_{2000}$ of a second could be 2000. In this case, what appear to be the highest numbers actually refer to the smallest fractions of a second.

In a motion picture camera, instead of shutter speed, you are more likely to see a control called the *shutter angle*. The shutter of most motion picture cameras is a revolving disc. The disc rotates 360 degrees for each frame that is exposed. A window behind the disc allows light through to the film when the shutter is open. The shutter angle controls the angle of the opening in the shutter, which can be made narrower by the position of a small metal flap, as represented in Figure 6.9.

A *shutter angle* control is also used to control motion blur in many 3D programs, including Renderman and Maya. In 3D software, you are allowed to type in numbers up to 360 degrees, or even higher. A 360-degree shutter angle would mean that the shutter never shut and no time was allowed to advance the film to the next frame. This is impossible with a real motion picture camera, but could be used in 3D rendering if you wanted longer streaks of motion blur.

The most common shutter angle of 180 degrees means that the shutter is open half of the time and closed half of the time. At a 180-degree shutter angle, the shutter speed would be equal to half of the frame rate. For example, at 24 fps, with a shutter angle of 180 degrees, the shutter speed would be $^1/_{48}$ of a second.

The shutter angle divided by 360 will tell you what portion of the frame rate is actually being used as the shutter speed for an exposure. For example, if the shutter angle was 90 degrees, then the shutter would be open one-quarter of the time. A 90-degree shutter at 24 fps would therefore be equivalent to a shutter speed of $^1/_{(4 * 24)}$, or $^1/_{96}$ of a second.

Different programs have slightly different ways to adjust motion blur. 3D Studio Max asks for a motion blur duration in frames, so that a value of one frame would equal a 360 degree shutter. If you have a logged shutter angle from live-action footage, divide the shutter angle by 360 to get the value in frames. For example, if a scene was shot with a 180-degree shutter, enter 0.5, which would produce results as seen in Figure 6.10.

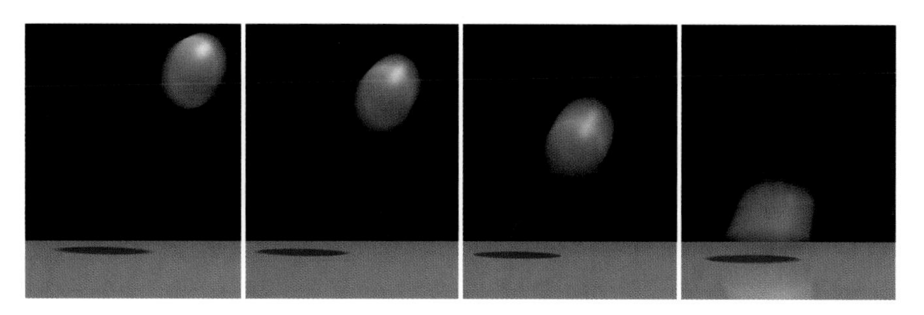

[Figure 6.10] A motion blur of 0.5 simulates a 180-degree shutter angle.

Motion blur is sampled over a fraction of the duration of a frame. For example, at 24 fps with a 180-degree shutter, the blur would show you the object's motion during the 1/48 of a second that the shutter was opened. To control this duration, Softimage XSI asks for a shutter open and shutter close time. For example, if you had shutter open at 0 and shutter close at 0.5, that would be a 180 degree shutter angle, sampling motion during the first half of the frame duration. If an animator wants to avoid having a particular pose motion-blurred at a particular frame, he can create a half-frame "hold." Making the character (or part of the character) hold still during the interval being sampled will produce a crisp image of the pose with no motion blur.

As a rule of thumb, keep your shutter angle between 90 degrees and 180 degrees for the most natural, realistic results. Too low a level of motion blur could make the action seem jerky or unnatural, while too high a number can create an after-image or trail behind objects as they move.

Always start your animation into motion prior to the first frame that will be rendered, and continue it through several frames beyond the end of the shot. This will ensure that you can have consistent motion blur at every frame. If the motion stopped at the first or last frame, you could be missing motion blur. If the character were in a different pose or position at frame zero, then jumped into position at frame one, the first frame could also have inconsistent motion blur. When animating a camera position, don't let the camera jump suddenly between frames, as if to simulate a cut; the motion blur would badly distort those frames.

To simulate the most photo-realistic motion blur possible, remember that slower shutter speeds are often necessary to let in enough light in darker environments, and very high shutter speeds are usually possible only in brightly lit environments.

The Comet Tail Myth

Some people imagine that motion blur lags behind a moving object, similar to how motion lines are drawn behind a running cartoon character, or a tail of flames appears behind a comet. In reality, motion blur is uniformly bidirectional, meaning that if something is filmed moving continuously left to right, it will have the same amount of blur on the left side as the right side.

When you look at a single frame from a movie, the motion blur does not indicate which direction something was traveling. If the subject moved at a constant speed throughout the exposure, then the motion blur will not be bright in front and fade out in the rear like the tail of a comet, instead will appear as streaks of a continuous brightness, as you can see in Figure 6.11. Even in a slow exposure capturing long streaks of motion blur, nothing about the motion blur would have looked different if the cars were driving in reverse.

[Figure 6.11] This shot would look just the same if all of the cars were driving in reverse. Motion blur does not fade off like a comet tail—it remains constant through the exposure if the brightness and speed of the subject remains constant.

Photographs can be created that appear to have trails fading off behind a moving object, but these are usually caused either by a camera flash triggered at the end of the exposure or by having the subject stop moving near the end of the exposure. If a subject was moving at a constant rate and illuminated evenly while the frame was exposed, the motion blur would be symmetrical and would not indicate whether the object was moving forward or backward.

Blurring Rotations

Rapidly rotating objects—such as the blades of a fan, spinning wheels, or a helicopter's propeller—are some of the hardest things to accurately motion blur. Rendering software must slow down and sample the motion several times per frame to render a fully round rotation, instead of a linear streak from one frame's position to the next. Further complicating things, rapid rotations don't always rotate in perfect synchronization with the frame rate, so sometimes a wheel can appear to be rotating backward.

Figure 6.12 illustrates the *wagon wheel effect*, the confusion sometimes caused by actions that repeat at a pace similar to the frame rate. The wagon wheel effect got its name from chase scenes in Western movies, which often featured speeding wagons. The rotating wheels often appeared to spin at the wrong speed, or even backward, when viewed on film. This was because similar-looking spokes changed places while the shutter was closed, making it difficult to follow their motion between frames.

[Figure 6.12]
The wheel turns counterclockwise between the first frame (left) and the second (right), but to the viewer it could look as if the wheel turned clockwise, if you mistake spoke **b** from the second frame for spoke **a** from the first.

Often, a cheated solution is the best solution to very rapid rotation. For example, you can replace a spinning fan blade with a flat disk, and transparency map it with a texture that is already blurred as if it were spinning. A simple textured surface can look like a rapidly spinning blade, without causing rendering headaches in every shot where it appears.

Video Fields

Most video cameras actually capture two separate exposures per frame, called *video fields*. A field is one half of a video frame, split by alternate *scanlines*—the horizontal lines of image information that make up a video frame, corresponding to one row of pixels running across your rendering—as shown in Figure 6.13.

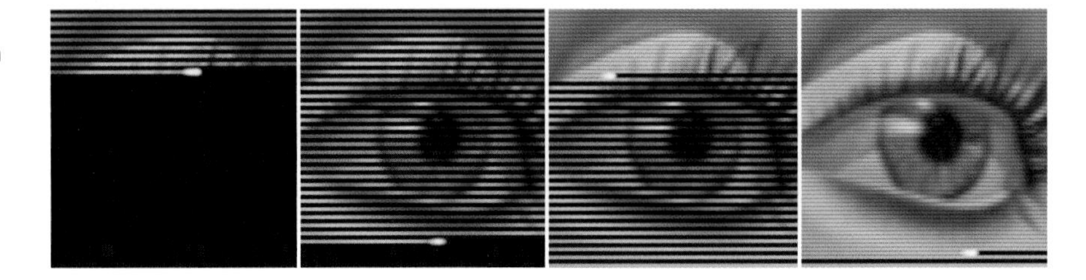

[Figure 6.13] Two fields are interlaced on a television screen to form a frame.

The field consisting of the odd-numbered scanlines is displayed first, then the other field is displayed, adding the even-numbered scanlines. When the two fields are interlaced to fit together, a full-resolution frame is created on the screen, taking advantage of all of the scanlines from both fields to reproduce the picture.

The advantage of splitting the frame into two fields is that moving subjects are effectively sampled at twice the frame rate, resulting in a smoother, more accurate reproduction of motion. Instead of having the shutter open only 25 or 30 times per second, it opens and captures a field 50 or 60 times per second. This means that moving subjects are scanned twice as frequently.

An alternative to interlaced fields is *progressive scan*, a type of display that does not split each frame into fields. Instead, it scans directly through all the scanlines of each frame in order. Progressive scan is used by computer monitors as well as some advanced television and high-definition television

(HDTV) systems. Some digital camcorders offer the option to record in progressive scan.

Rendering Fields

Most 3D rendering programs have an option to render motion in separate video fields. When activated, the renderer will output twice as many image files, rendered at each frame as well as at each half frame, so that the two field images show different points in time, but can be interlaced together to form a complete frame. This essentially simulates how an ordinary video camera would have recorded the motion.

By halving the shutter speed, the amount of motion blur is also cut in half by using field-rate video. Some 3D artists even turn off motion blur when rendering field-rate video output, although the complete lack of motion blur could look unrealistic. The renderings of an animated object in Figure 6.14 illustrate your different rendering choices for fields and motion blur; you can see that the motion blur matters less when rendering on fields.

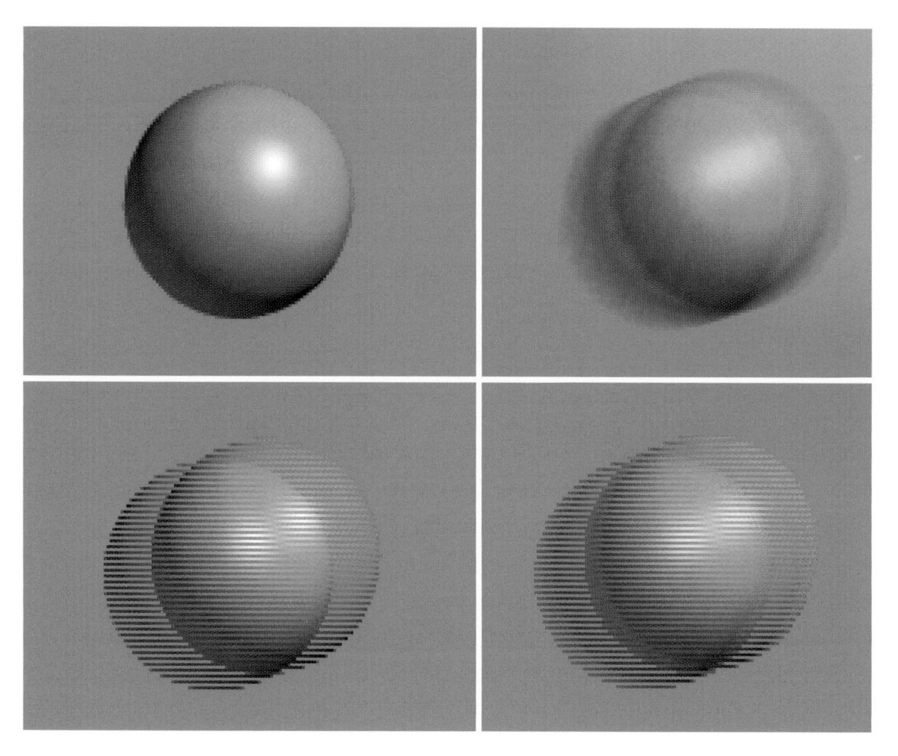

[Figure 6.14] An animated object with no motion blur or field-rate rendering (upper left) appears static. Motion blur is added to two renderings on the right, and field-rate motion is added to the lower two renderings.

Rendering 3D on fields is not recommended for most 3D animations. Field-rate computer graphics are a staple of corporate video production, "flying logo" style animated graphic design, and elements involving moving titles for television. Field-rate motion gives your output a "video" look (as opposed to a "film" look).

Generally, you shouldn't render character animation on fields. The half-frame interpolated poses created for field-rate rendering would hurt the quality of the animation.

3:2 Pulldown

When motion pictures, shot at 24 fps, are converted to NTSC (30 fps) video, they go through a process called *3:2 pulldown*. Every four frames of the original film are converted into five video frames by alternately recording two video fields from one film frame, then three video fields from the next film frame, as shown in Figure 6.15.

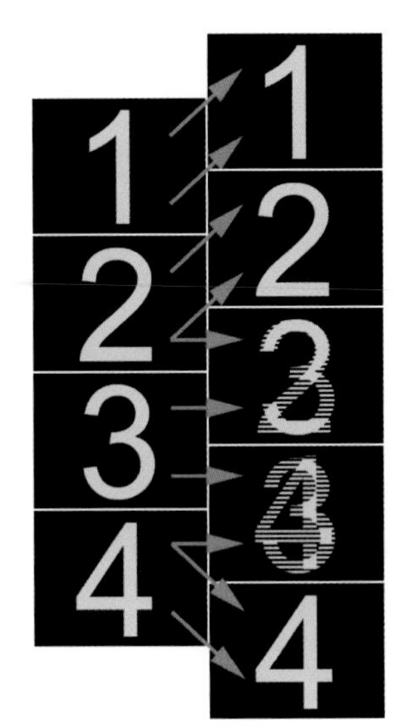

[Figure 6.15] In 3:2 Pulldown, film frames shot at 24 fps (left) alternately contribute two or three fields to produce 30 fps video frames (right).

3:2 pulldown produces some *jitter frames*, frames made of fields from two different film frames. Because jitter frames contain redundant information (fields also used in adjacent video frames), they are usually removed during visual effects work so that rendering and compositing can be done on a 24-fps basis. As a final stage, output will be expanded back to NTSC frame rate by simulating a 3:2 pulldown process in compositing software.

Film Speed

Besides aperture and shutter speed, the third main factor influencing a camera's exposure is the *film speed*. Some film stocks are more sensitive to light than others. A designated *film speed* measures how quickly a particular film stock responds to light.

Film speed is usually measured in ISO or ASA units. The International Organization for Standards (ISO) adopted the American Standards Association (ASA) standards for film speeds, so both refer to the same standard units. Low numbers such as 64 ISO or 100 ISO mean the film is less sensitive to light but is likely to be *fine-grain*, with sharp detail and not much visible grain. A high-speed film, such as 800 ISO or 1600 ISO, is more sensitive to light but usually has larger, more visible grain.

Just as you could choose a lower speed or higher speed film for a film camera, you can set a digital camera's ISO setting for similar results. At a lower ISO, the camera is less sensitive to light, but the image remains sharp, with very little noise (noise in a digital image means random variation in pixel colors, looking similar to grain in film). At a higher ISO, the signal from the imaging chip is amplified, but what amplifies the signal also amplifies the noise. A high-ISO image can lose quality and appear speckled with colored dots.

In visual effects work, compositors add simulated film grain when matching CGI to film stocks used in background plates. If you were simulating film or camcorder footage in an all-3D scene, consider adding more of a grain effect in low-light and indoor scenes than in sunny or outdoor scenes. Most importantly, pay attention to the issue of film speed as a part of understanding the trade-offs involved in controlling the camera's exposure process.

Photographic Exposure

So far in this chapter, we have discussed three main exposure controls on a real camera: aperture (f-stop), shutter speed, and film speed (ISO).

There is reciprocity between the three controls, so you can make tradeoffs between them. Photographers refer to each doubling of the amount of light captured as a *stop*. Opening to a wider aperture by one f-stop is a stop, but so is using twice as long a shutter speed, or using twice as fast a film speed. Because all of these controls have stops that exactly halve or double the amount of light, photographers can make trade-offs between them. For example, if a photographer were taking a portrait and wanted a soft-focused background behind her main subject, she would choose a wide aperture to achieve a shallow depth of field. To compensate for the extra light let in by the wide aperture, she could choose a faster shutter speed.

Apart from being manipulated to control side effects such as DOF and motion blur, the exposure controls have a primary purpose of controlling how much light gets captured in the shot. Learning how photographers make exposure decisions can help you in adjusting the intensity of the lights in a 3D scene.

The Zone System

When a casual photographer takes snapshots, the camera is usually left in an automatic mode. Automatic exposure adjusts exposure controls in the camera based on the average amount of light in the scene, essentially trying to bring the scene as close as possible to a medium gray. This provides an exposure that is "correct" in the sense that what is visible will be recorded on the film.

A professional photographer, on the other hand, starts designing a photograph based on his own impressions, to craft an image that uses the tones he chooses in each area of the frame. Instead of letting the camera bring a snow scene to an average gray level, he might prefer to make the snow white.

To achieve this level of control, photographers practice an approach called the *Zone System*, which describes tones that can be printed in 11 levels. Zone 0 is pure black with no detail, Zone 1 is the first perceptible value lighter than black, Zone 5 is medium gray, and so on up to Zone 10, which is pure white.

[Figure 6.16] An exposure meter tells photographers how to expose an area to produce a medium gray tone, or Zone 5, but adjusting the exposure to achieve other values is up to the creative control of the photographer.

A light meter, as shown in Figure 6.16, could be used to check the brightness of a particular area, such as a patch of snow. The meter displays a recommended exposure that would bring the snow to Zone 5. If the photographer wanted the snow to be printed in Zone 8, he could open the aperture by three stops compared to what his meter suggests.

To a practicing photographer, there's a lot more to the Zone System than this. Photographers can use special filters that darken the sky by a certain number of stops, develop and print the film in different ways to achieve different levels of contrast, and, as a last resort, adjust the brightness of different areas of the shot while printing in a darkroom. Throughout this process, every possible step is taken to adapt and control whatever light is available into the tones that the photographer wants to achieve in the final print.

How do we translate this into 3D graphics? How can we focus on controlling which tones will appear in our images as carefully as a professional photographer? A good place to start would be to look at a histogram.

Histograms

A *histogram* is a chart showing how frequently each possible tone appears in an image. Most paint and compositing software has a histogram function.

Figure 6.17 shows a typical histogram. For each of the 256 possible levels of brightness in the image, a vertical column is plotted. The height of each column is determined by the number of pixels in the image that use the tone. The columns on the left show the number of pixels using black and dark values, and the height of the columns on the right shows how many pixels use brighter tones, up to pure white on the extreme right.

You can view a histogram of one of your renderings, either for the entire image or for selected areas. A histogram is useful for spotting some common problems in renderings. For example, Figure 6.18 shows a histogram of an underexposed scene. Almost all of the columns are on the left side, showing that the whole image is lit using only the darkest 25 percent of the tones available.

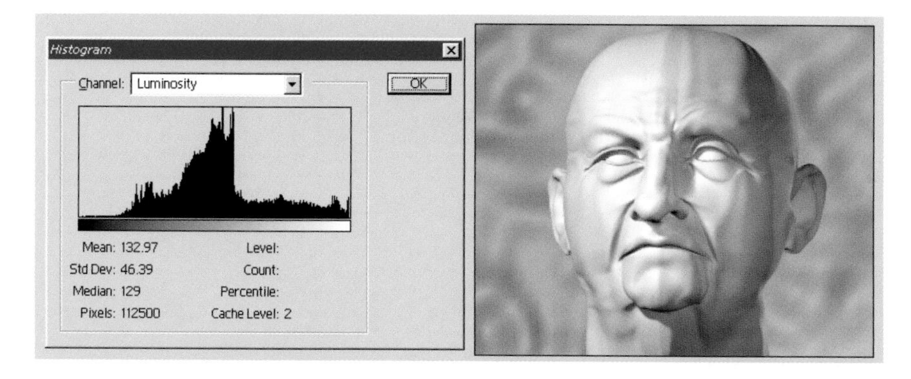

[Figure 6.17]
A histogram shows how you are using the tones available in each "Zone" of your rendered image.

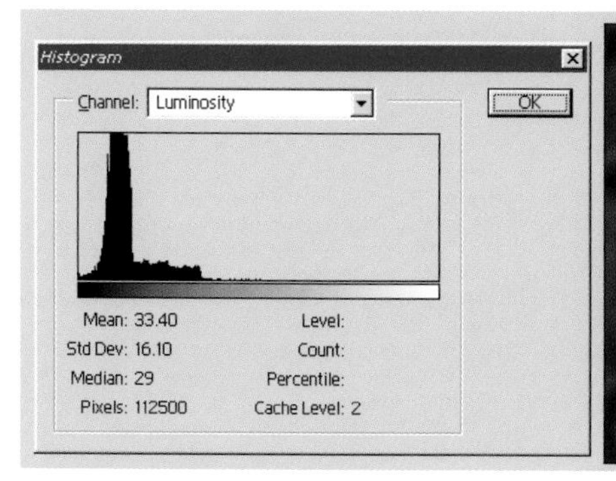

[Figure 6.18]
Underexposure appears as a concentration on the left side of the histogram.

Photoshop's Levels tool includes a histogram as a part of a powerful tool for changing the brightness and contrast of an image. As shown in Figure 6.19, immediately beneath the histogram are three triangles that you can slide into new positions along the histogram. The black triangle represents the level that will become black in the output image, and the white triangle represents the level that will become pure white in the output image. Between them, the gray triangle represents what will become medium gray. This triangle automatically stays at a midpoint between the black and white triangles as you drag them around; if you drag the gray triangle, then you will also be changing the gamma of your image.

[Figure 6.19] You can adjust Photoshop's Levels tool to isolate one Zone of brightness found in a 3D scene.

The cool thing about the Levels tool is that you can use it interactively to explore the different "zones" of your image. For example, Figure 6.19 shows the triangles framing the brightest tones in the scene. This causes every tone that was darker than where the black triangle points to disappear from your image, letting you see only where the brightest tones are used. You could also frame just the darkest part of the image by moving the white triangle to the left. If you are planning to composite 3D elements into a live-action plate, it is especially important to check that the black levels and white levels match the background plate.

In general, you should try to take advantage of the full range of tones available to you, so that a histogram from most of your renders shows columns in each zone. Students learning to light scenes often produce underexposed images in an effort to hide flaws in their scenes and make the lighting look more "subtle." Even if you are trying to depict a night scene or a dark closet, be selective with your lighting. To convey darkness, use high contrast and dark shadows rather than simply underexposing the whole scene.

Matching Lens Imperfections

In real life, lenses aren't perfect. Even the best lens can't reproduce the world around it as clearly as the virtual camera that renders our 3D scenes. Here's a look as some of the flaws of real lenses, and how to match or simulate them in 3D.

Lens Distortion

In most 3D rendered images, every line that was modeled as a straight line appears perfectly straight in the final rendering. This is not true in photography. In a real photograph, lens distortion often causes straight lines to appear bent.

The amount of curvature you get depends on what kind of lens is used. On many zoom lenses (lenses that have an adjustable field of view), zooming out to a wider angle causes moderate *barrel distortion*, in which the center of the image is bowed outward, and the edges and corners are compressed. More extreme curvature is seen in shots taken with a *fisheye lens*, which covers a very wide field of view, but often greatly curves and distorts the image, as shown in Figure 6.20.

On many zoom lenses, barrel distortion appears when the lens is zoomed out, but the opposite problem, *pincushion distortion*, appears when the lens is zoomed in. Pincushion distortion warps an image inward, making the center smaller, and is usually a result of an attempt to correct for barrel distortion in zoom lenses.

[Figure 6.20] A fisheye lens causes curvature in an image, as seen where the vertical tower appears bent.

Programmable renderers such as Mental Ray can have shaders written for them that mimic real lenses, including barrel distortion. However, even if you have such a shader, it would be difficult to frame shots in a wireframe or shaded viewport that didn't match the distortion of the final render. A more common approach to lens distortion is to render without distortion, and then warp the rendered image.

In visual effects, if you want to combine 3D renderings with a live-action plate, matching the lens distortion of the original shot becomes a pressing issue. Motion tracking software that matches real camera moves, such as 3D-Equalizer, often includes image-processing functions to correct for lens distortion. The workflow would be to undistort the background plate after it was digitized, composite in your 3D elements, then redistort the image if necessary.

Even for entirely 3D content, adding some barrel or fisheye distortion to shots that use a very wide field of view could add a touch of realism and make the shots more believable. Figure 6.21 shows the difference that a little distortion can make.

[Figure 6.21]
A 3D scene rendered with a wide field of view (left) can sometimes be made more natural by simulating barrel distortion (right).

Most compositing software includes warping functions that could simulate barrel distortion. If you wanted to distort images in a 3D program instead, you could texture map your rendered image onto a NURBS plane, scale up the center vertices of the plane to achieve your warping, and then render a view of the warped plane.

Adding barrel distortion has an added benefit in some shots: When the camera pans or tilts, the distortion almost resembles a perspective shift. If you are trying to "sell" a 2D matte painting as if it were more fully modeled 3D environment, then you don't want a pan or tilt to simply appear as if the background were "scrolling" by. Adding a pan or tilt along with some barrel distortion can create a much more natural integration of 2D backdrops, as well as help them look like larger spaces filmed with a wide-angle lens.

Chromatic Aberration

[Figure 6.22] Chromatic aberration appears as colored fringes around high-contrast edges in a photograph.

A lens artifact closely related to barrel distortion is called *chromatic aberration (CA)*. Chromatic aberration appears in an image as colored fringes around bright lines or high-contrast edges, as shown in Figure 6.22.

CA occurs as light is focused through a lens, because different wavelengths of light are refracted at different angles. For example, red light will refract through the lens at a different angle than blue light, focusing at a different point on the film or sensor. This is the same principle that allows people to split light into a rainbow using a prism. However, in a camera, having different colors of light fall out of alignment on the film or sensor creates colored fringes of CA. Because CA is more prevalent in cheaper lenses, you might simulate it if you're processing your renderings to resemble camcorder footage. You're not likely to see as much CA in background plates shot for feature films.

You can simulate CA using the same kind of outward warping as you would use to simulate barrel distortion, but you'll need to do it one color channel at a time, with slightly more distortion on the red channel and slightly less distortion on the blue channel.

Vignetting

Vignetting is another flaw that is most common in cheap zoom lenses. Vignetting simply makes the edges and corners of the frame darker than the center of the image.

Some directors intentionally produce this effect for creative reasons, such as when showing the point of view of a killer following someone, or in a flashback to make a memory appear more faded. Sometimes, directors will actually smear Vaseline around the edges of a filter in front of the camera, which causes the edges of the frame to become dark and blurry.

Most compositing programs can correct minor vignetting in a background plate or match it by darkening the edges of 3D elements.

Lens Flares and Halation

For years, *lens flares* have been considered an overused cliché in computer graphics. Use lens flares only where they very are clearly motivated, such as when the sun or another very bright light is directly visible in the scene, or in scenes where characters being out in the bright sun is a story point. Figure 6.23 shows a photograph in which the sun's reflection on a building caused a lens flare.

[Figure 6.23]
Even though most 3D artists consider lens flares tacky and overused, they can be used sparingly in places where they are motivated by a bright-enough light.

If you use a lens flare, render it as a separate pass. To do this, simply hide everything else in the scene except the light that is making the lens flare, and render it as a separate file sequence. This way, you can add or screen it over your rendering in a compositing program, and you won't risk rerendering a full scene just to adjust a lens flare.

In many cases, you can avoid lens flares and instead simulate *halation* (also known as *specular bloom*),which is the glow and occasional streaks of light visible around bright light sources. Halation is caused by light reflecting off the back of the film plane of the camera or scattering through the film itself. As with lens flares, it is a good idea to render light glows separately and add them in the composite.

In widescreen movies that are filmed in an anamorphic film format (where a special lens squashes the image horizontally so that it fits on the film), the halation scatters light on the film while the image is squashed. When projected, the halation is stretched out horizontally, so that glows around lights appear to be elongated bars or streaks instead of circular glows.

Use special effects described in this section only in situations where they are really needed. If you find yourself tempted to run your footage through lots of filters to change the look, most likely it is because you aren't happy with the original lighting and shading, and you should go back and fix those problems instead of trying to hide them behind lots of filters. Before you fixate on imitating every possible flaw that could exist in a photograph, try to learn from the best that photography has to offer, and craft well-exposed images where every tone counts.

Exercises

To grow as a 3D artist, take every chance you get to study more about photography and cinematography.

1. Spend some time with a camera that has full manual controls. Try taking a picture of someone or something with the widest f-stop, a middle value, and the narrowest f-stop, and see for yourself how it changes the depth of field and clarity of the image. If you are shooting on film, jot down in a notebook the camera settings you used for each shot. If you

are using a digital camera, all of the exposure information is stored in the EXIF information of the files, which you can read in many image viewers.

2. Load some of your earlier 3D renderings into a program with a histogram function. Were you using all of the tones available? What would the scene look like if you adjusted the levels to change the exposure?

3. Rent a movie and, while watching it, stop and examine some scenes filmed at night or in a dark environment. Where are the brightest and darkest tones? How deep is the depth of field? When the background falls out of focus, can you see any bokeh effects?

4. Start a collection of reference images from movies. Watch DVDs on your computer and use a player that includes a frame grabbing function. When you see a scene whose mood or lighting you admire, store a frame for your personal use. Reference images help guide your own lighting, and are handy for communicating with directors and clients as you plan the look of sequences you are going to light.

[CHAPTER SEVEN]

Composition and Staging

Some of the most important decisions the director and cinematographer make in filming a scene concern composition and staging. *Composition* refers to the layout of the entire shot; *staging* is the arrangement of objects and characters within the frame. Good composition and staging are key ingredients in any compelling professional image. In effect, they act as subtle cues from the director, helping guide a viewer's eye. Composition and staging are governed by a set of artistic rules and cinematic conventions that you can apply in 3D graphics when adjusting your camera, lights, layout, and animation.

Types of Shots

Your first and most basic decision in planning a shot is what will be shown in the frame. If two characters are interacting, will you show both of them in the frame, or just a close-up on one of them? How much of the environment around them will be visible? Do you want to draw the audience's attention to any particular area? Your digital productions can be planned using the vocabulary that filmmakers use to describe each shot.

Shot Sizes

One of the major distinctions between types of shots is the *shot size*, which identifies how large of an area will be visible within the frame. From the smallest area to the largest, here are the five most common shot sizes:

- An *extreme close-up (ECU)* makes a very small detail—such as only part of a character's face—fill the screen.
- A *close-up (CU)* is a shot framed tightly on a specific area, like a character's face.
- A *medium close-up (MCU)* widens the scope further. A character's head and shoulders would constitute a medium close-up.
- A *medium shot (MS)* shows a broader area than a close-up. Often a medium shot shows a character's upper body, arms, and head.
- A *wide shot (WS* or *WIDE)* shows a broad view of an entire location, subject, or action. Often a wide shot will show an entire character from head to toe, or a whole group of characters.

The yellow boxes in Figure 7.1 show the areas of a character typically covered by these shot sizes. These are only general guidelines—actual shot sizes are relative to the size of the subject or environment you are portraying. For example, in an animation of a football game, a wide shot might show the whole stadium, but in a film starring animated insects, a wide shot might cover only a few inches of space.

Wider shots can show whole environments, capture broader actions, or show the positions of multiple characters at once. Before moving in to show close-up detail, you can give your audience an idea of the overall scene with an *establishing shot*. An establishing shot is usually a wide shot that sets up the scene and shows the surroundings that might not be appear in each close-up. For example, an establishing shot might show the exterior of a building, providing context for the location where an interior scene is to follow.

Medium shots and close-ups help draw the audience into the scene, and reveal details or facial expressions. Television has been called a close-up medium, because smaller screens make close-ups especially important. Feature films may use slightly wider shots while still managing to make facial expressions visible.

A *reaction shot* shows a character's response as he or she watches or reacts to some other event. Usually a close-up of the character will be used to show the reaction. Reaction shots in action sequences keep the audience engaged in the human side of a story. Even if you are animating an enormous scope of events, the audience will care more about what is happening if you show the reaction of individual characters being affected by the action.

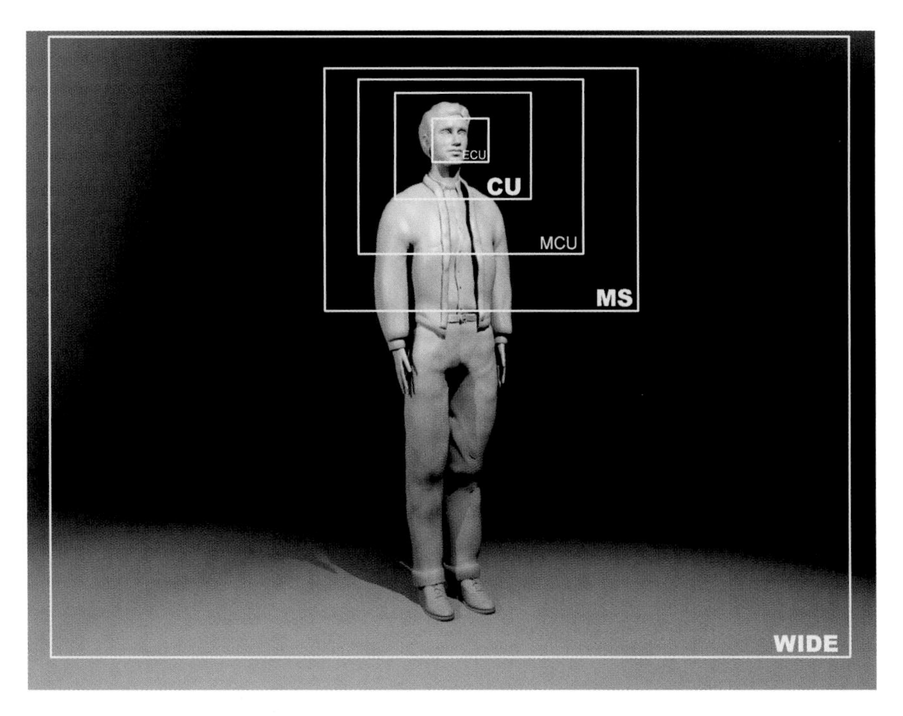

[Figure 7.1] An ECU (extreme close-up), CU (close-up), MCU (medium close-up), MS (medium shot) and WIDE (wide shot) are common shot sizes used for rendering characters.

Z-Axis Blocking

A shot can function as both a close-up and a wide shot at once by using a technique called *z-axis blocking*: populating a scene with subjects at varying distances from the camera. Figure 7.2 shows an example of z-axis blocking, with one character in close-up, walking toward the camera, while other characters remain in the background. Z-axis blocking may sound like a computer graphics term, but in reality cinematographers were using the phrase long before the advent of 3D rendering.

[Figure 7.2]
Z-axis blocking combines a close-up of one character with a wide shot of other characters in this scene staged by Jorge R. Gutierrez.

POV Shots

A *point-of-view shot* (POV) creates the illusion of viewing the scene from a character's perspective.

POV shots are easy to set up in 3D: You just position the camera right between a character's eyes. If a character is moving, group or constrain the camera to follow any character motion, such as by parenting the camera to the head bone, or animate the camera to simulate the character's gaze. Usually you will want to hide the character whose POV is being shown; you don't need to show body parts, such as arms and hands moving as the character walks, in a POV.

Here are some ideas for how POV shots could be useful in your animations:

- Seeing a scene from a character's point of view can help an audience better identify with a character or sympathize with his position in a scene. For example, if something is going to jump out and surprise a character, it might be animated to appear suddenly and leap toward the camera (in other words, from the character's POV), surprising the audience.
- A POV shot can capture an action or event dramatically. For example, if a character were falling down a hole, the camera could be animated to move through space just where her head would be.
- A POV shot can be used for comic effect in some animations, by animating the camera with an attribute of a character. For example, an animated camera might imitate the motion of a staggering drunk or a bounding dog.
- A POV shot can show a character's view when he looks through a gun-sight, telescope, or keyhole. Often POV shots such as these are processed after rendering to imitate the shape of the telescope or keyhole or to simulate the distortion or focus of a viewing device.
- A POV shot can be a convenient "shortcut" because while you are watching through her eyes, the audience doesn't see the character herself, so you don't have to animate or render her in that shot.
- It's a standard horror- and suspense-film convention to show the POV of a killer or monster as it stalks its next victim. The use of the POV shot prevents the audience from seeing the actual killer; they see only the killer's-eye-view of the unwitting victim.

Have fun using POV shots, but remember that they can be very noticeable, and sometimes even distracting, if overused.

The Two-Shot

Specific types of shots can be put together to help you stage a conversation, interview, or other scenes in which two characters are facing each other.

A *two-shot* is simply a shot with two characters, as shown on the left side of Figure 7.3. While this is a convenient, straightforward way to show both characters, it can look flat and uninteresting. To make a scene more visually diverse, you can use a two-shot as an establishing shot, and then cut in to close-ups and *over-the-shoulder* shots.

The Over-the-Shoulder Shot

An *over-the-shoulder shot* (OSS) is a close-up or medium shot that focuses on one of the characters while showing just enough of the other character—a portion of his back and shoulder, generally—to indicate his position. The center and right images in Figure 7.3 illustrate this. Even though you can't see the face of the character whose back appears in the foreground, her presence serves to frame the shot and establish the spatial relationship between characters.

A series of shots that alternate between an OSS of each character, sometimes also including close-ups of the characters, is called *shot/countershot* coverage. This is a common and effective way to capture almost any kind of interaction between two characters, whether they're exchanging words, bullets, kisses, or punches. Once you start looking for it, you will see shot/countershot coverage used over and over in movies and television programs.

Rendering OSS shots of each character and adopting shot/countershot instead of a fixed two-shot for the full scene can create a more engaging, cinematic look for your animation. Rendering an OSS instead of a two-shot through a dialogue scene has an added bonus: You may be able to skip some of the facial animation on one of the characters during that shot, while watching the other character react to what is said.

[Figure 7.3] The shot/countershot structure can start with a two-shot (left) and then alternate between OSS coverage (center, right) of the characters.

Camera Angles

You can change the appearance and function of your shot by where you place the camera. Your *camera angles* come from the positions you choose for the camera and which way it is aimed.

The Line of Action

If you are rendering a scene from several different camera angles and plan to edit the different shots together into a seamless sequence, then it is vital that you make all of your camera angles come from camera positions on the same side of a *line of action*. A line of action is the path along which your subjects are looking or traveling, or an imaginary line between two characters who are interacting. For example, in Figure 7.4, the line of action is shown by the yellow line between the two characters.

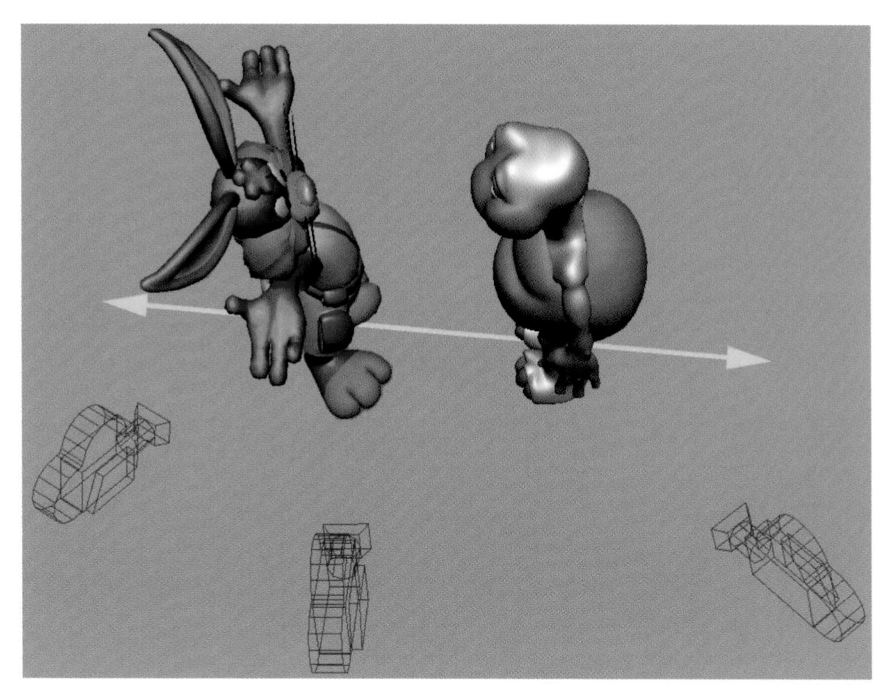

[Figure 7.4]
To maintain screen direction, all camera shots are taken from the same side of an invisible line of action.

You would not want to cut to any angle on the characters filmed from the other side, because that would reverse the direction that the characters appeared to be facing, and could confuse the audience. For example, if a character had been facing toward the right side of the screen, you should not choose a camera angle that suddenly makes her appear to be facing to the left in the next shot, because she will appear to have turned around.

Imagine a character who is traveling or in a chase. If he is running toward the right side of the screen in one shot, then he should continue to appear running toward the right side of the screen in every shot. Unless the character actually turns around, no change of camera angles should be used that would reverse his screen direction.

Football fans are familiar with this concept from the way football games are televised: All of the cameras are normally put on the same side of the stadium. On occasion, a camera will be used on the opposite side, to capture action that would not have been visible otherwise. To avoid confusion, whenever they cut to the camera from the opposite side of the line of action, the words "Reverse Angle" are superimposed on the screen.

Perspective

Perspective is the point of view or position you choose for your camera. Whenever the camera is in a different position, it shows the scene from a different perspective.

Figure 7.5 shows three different perspectives of a person standing in front of a bridge. To maintain a close-up of a similar size from each perspective, a telephoto lens was used when the camera was farther away (left), a normal 60mm lens at 3 meters from the subject (middle), and a wide-angle lens with the camera was close to the subject (right). Although you can notice barrel distortion in the shot taken with the wide-angle lens, the lenses themselves do not change the perspective—they only magnify the scene to make comparison possible on similar size shots.

[Figure 7.5]
A shot from a distant perspective (left) compresses space; a shot from 3 meters away appears more normal (center); and a shot from a close-up perspective tends to expand space and distort features (right).

Notice how the bridge appears to be looming right behind the woman in the left image, but on the right, from a closer perspective, the bridge seems much farther away, and we see more of it. Figure 7.6 shows a similar comparison in 3D. The left image was rendered with the camera far away from the scene, but with a 2-degree angle of view. On the right, the camera has been positioned close to the chess pieces, but given a 120-degree angle of view.

Moving the camera far away from the subject seems to compress or flatten space. This effect could be useful if you wanted to make a character appear lost in a crowd, to make a space seem cramped, or to make objects appear closely stacked together. If you zoom in on a subject from a distant perspective, you will see a much smaller slice of the background behind the subject, which could be useful if there were something in the background you wanted to accentuate.

[Figure 7.6]
Perspective in 3D works just the same as perspective with a real camera: Spaces seem compressed from a distant perspective (left) and expanded from a close-up perspective (right).

Moving the camera close to the subject distorts distance. It can even make a character's facial features appear to stick out farther, such as exaggerating the size of a person's nose. Most photographers back off by about 3 or 4 meters when trying to take a flattering portrait, instead of sticking the camera right in the subject's face. However, you don't want to back off too far, because even though you could compensate for extreme distance with a telephoto lens, doing so would tend to flatten a person's face so that horizontal features such as ears appear to stick out.

When the camera is moved near your characters, and you zoom out to cover the action from the close perspective, there will be a broader view of the background behind the character. Seeing more of the environment around a character could be desirable, but sometimes it requires you to build a more complete set or add more trees to your scene in order to fill up the visible area.

Rendering with the camera near a character can also make any action appear to move more quickly or cover a greater distance. This is especially true for motion directed toward or away from the camera. Getting the camera right into the middle of the action can make animation appear more dynamic, and also puts the audience closer to the perspective of the characters.

Animating a camera's position and field of view at once, in opposite directions, can produce a disturbing effect. For example, if the shots shown in Figure 7.6 had been frames in an animation, simultaneously moving the camera toward the subject while zooming out to compensate, the perspective would shift oddly during the shot. This effect has been used in horror movies to make a hallway appear to grow longer in front of a character as he struggles to run down it.

If you want to choose a natural-looking perspective, a good rule of thumb is to think about where a person might be standing within the 3D space to watch your scene, and position the camera at the same distance. For example, if a scene takes place indoors, the camera should not be much farther back than the size that an actual room would naturally allow.

It is important to note that your perspective on a scene changes only when the camera is moved to a new position. Perspective is not changed by the camera's zoom or field of view. When the camera is left in the same position, the perspective will be the same, no matter how telephoto or wide-angle your lens. Choosing a longer focal length for your camera in 3D graphics gives you just the same perspective as if you had rendered with a short focal length and then cropped the image down to the close-up you wanted.

High-Angle and Low-Angle Shots

The most normal-looking shots will be the ones taken with the camera at eye level. Moving the camera to different heights can create other camera angles that are sometimes more interesting or dramatically useful.

A *low-angle shot*, with the camera positioned below your character, looking up at her, can serve to make a character look bigger, stronger, more honest, or more noble. Low-angle shots can also exaggerate the size of environments and architectural spaces.

A *high-angle shot*, with the camera aimed downward from a position above the character, can make a character look sly, small, young, weak, confused, cute, or childlike. Figure 7.7 shows how a character looks from a low angle (left) and a high angle (right.)

[Figure 7.7] A character will be perceived differently from a high angle (left) than a low angle (right). Images by Andrew Hickinbottom, www.andrewhickinbottom.co.uk.

Camera Moves

If you want to animate more realistic and natural camera moves, it helps to study the most popular types of moves used with a real camera:

- Pan: In a pan, the camera rotates from side to side so that it aims more to the left or right. The camera does not change location in a pan; it needs only to face a different direction. Panning is one of the most common and subtle of all camera moves.
- Tilt: The camera rotates to aim upward or downward, without changing the position where the camera is mounted. Both a tilt and a pan can be done while the camera is mounted on a tripod.
- Zoom: The camera's lens is adjusted to increase or decrease the camera's field of view, magnifying a portion of the scene without moving the camera. A *zoom in* narrows the field of view to create more of a close-up, while a *zoom out* widens the field of view.
- Dolly: The camera's actual position changes, such as to move alongside a subject or to travel closer to a character during a scene. A *dolly in* moves the camera physically closer to the subject, to create more of a close-up. A *dolly out* backs the camera away from the subject. Dollying is considered more dramatic but also more noticeable than zooming, because a dolly actually changes the camera's perspective.
- Rack focus: A camera's focal distance changes during a shot, so that subjects at a different distance from the camera come into or fall out of focus, as shown in Figure 7.8. This is also called a *focus pull.*

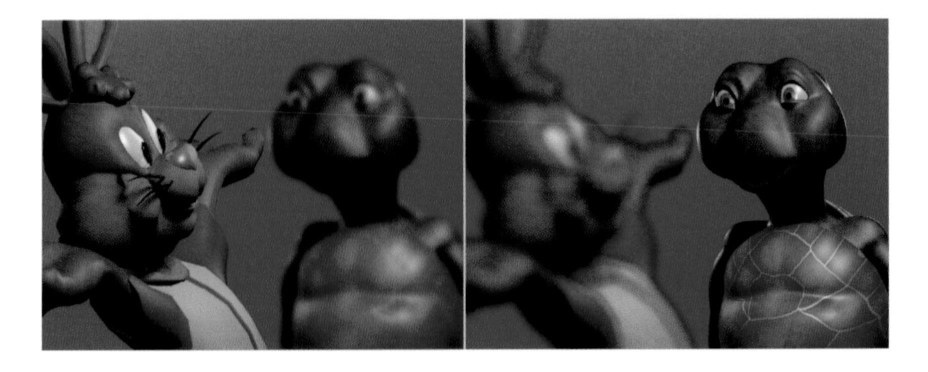

[Figure 7.8] A rack focus directs the audience's attention by changing the focus during the shot.

Note that many of these common types of camera moves do not involve actually changing the camera's position. When the camera pans, tilts, zooms, or rack focuses, it can remain mounted in the same place on a tripod—you only aim the camera in a different direction or adjust the lens.

Motivations for Camera Moves

Constant camera motion can be distracting. A camera move should be used only when it is motivated by an action or event in the story. Here are some times when a camera move might be motivated:

- When a character or vehicle is moving, you can pan or dolly the camera to follow the character's motion.
- POV shots from moving characters and vehicles will require a moving camera.
- A moving camera can dolly into an environment as a way to explore the space, especially for sweeping establishing shots when an environment is first seen.
- For dramatic effect, sometimes a camera can move slowly toward a character to emphasize certain actions or dialogue. When the camera dollies in from a medium shot to a close-up, the audience's attention is focused on the subject being approached.

You don't need to animate the position of the camera if alternatives such as panning to follow your animation, or simply cutting to a new shot, will do just as well. An unmotivated camera move could distract the audience instead of helping you tell the story.

Natural-Looking Camera Moves

An old attitude towards animating the camera in 3D was that you needed to carefully imitate the types of real dollies and cranes on which a movie camera was traditionally moved. 3D artists used to be afraid that if they used any physically impossible camera moves, their animation would seem unrealistic. However, in recent years, filmmakers have begun to use 3D graphics, motion-control camera rigs, digital compositing, and other technologies to create seemingly impossible camera moves in live-action films.

The widespread use of 3D graphics to previsualize motion pictures has further encouraged live-action directors to plan their movies using all kinds of camera motion that in the past would have been seen only in 3D animation or video games. Audiences are growing accustomed to seeing the camera fly through scenes in ways that would have seemed remarkable in previous decades.

Of course, you still need to make sure that any camera motion helps in telling your story instead of distracting from it. Learn to imitate and use old, conventional camera moves when they meet your needs. But, if it fits your story for the camera to fly through a keyhole or follow action out the window of a moving car, go ahead and animate the camera whichever way best fits your scene.

In editing, cutting between two moving camera shots can be particularly distracting. Even if the camera motion within each of the shots looked natural, editing between a camera moving in one direction and a camera moving in a different direction can be jarring in the cut. When animating any camera move, it is a good idea to begin with a well-composed static shot before easing into the move. Upon completing the move, the camera should come to rest at another well-composed static shot.

For natural-looking camera moves, think of the role of a camera operator watching a scene. Often, something needs to begin to happen, such as an actor starting to move, before the camera operator reacts to it and moves the camera to follow the action. Camera motion looks most natural if it begins just after the motion it is intended to follow, as if the operator needed a fraction of a second to react to the motion. Also, when a camera pan comes to an end, it can slightly overshoot its mark and then slightly correct backwards a fraction of a second later, as a human operator often tends to do aiming a handheld camera.

Improving Your Composition

After you have decided on the size and angle of your shot, there are some principles that can help you balance and improve your composition. Where you place key elements within the frame can make the difference between an average or even boring rendering and a rendering with a composition that makes your work look more professional. Careful attention to the composition of a shot also can serve the art of storytelling by helping to direct the viewer's eye to different parts of the image.

The Rule of Thirds

Placing a subject dead-center in a frame does not look very natural or interesting, and generally produces a bad composition. Your rendering will look better composed if you place your subject off-center.

A useful guideline when composing a shot is to picture the frame divided into thirds, both horizontally and vertically, as shown in Figure 7.9. This is known as the *rule of thirds*. Your shot will be better composed if you position the subject along one of the lines (shown in black), or position a subject that you want noticed exactly at a point where two lines intersect (shown in red).

If there is a horizon line in the scene, putting the horizon one-third or two-thirds of the way up the frame can look much better than placing the horizon in the center, which could appear to split the rendering in half.

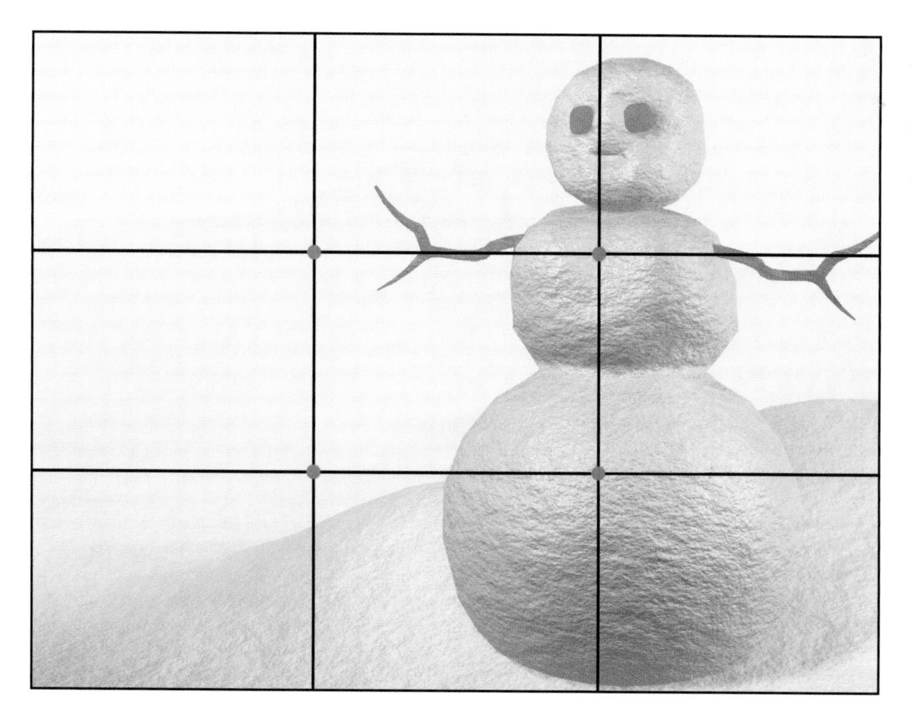

[Figure 7.9]
To follow the rule of thirds, align subjects to break the composition into thirds instead of halves, and put centers of interest at the points marked in red.

Positive and Negative Space

Most images can be said to consist of both positive space and negative space. *Positive space* is the part of the frame showing the main subject or foreground objects. *Negative space* can be considered the background, or the area around the subject. Composition is a balance between the positive and negative space. The left side of Figure 7.10 shows the negative space in black and the positive space in white.

[Figure 7.10]
The negative space (shown in black) and the positive space (white) are equally important shapes in your composition.

Examining your image for positive and negative space can often lead to improving your composition. For example, if all of your positive space is clustered in one area or aligned in a single row, or if large areas of your frame are empty, you might consider reframing the shot. This will allow for more of a balance between positive and negative space.

Sometimes negative space is required in a shot to create a greater sense of balance or closure. For example, in a close-up or medium shot, a character's face or eyes looking to one side creates a powerful vector that directs the audience's attention to one side of the frame. To balance your composition, you usually want to leave negative space in front of your character, in the direction that she is looking. Camera operators sometimes call the extra space left in front of a person *look space* or *nose room*. The top image in Figure 7.11 is a balanced, complete rendering with negative space, giving you room to follow the direction of the character's gaze.

Without look space, or with the negative spaces distributed elsewhere, viewers cannot follow the direction a character is looking, and the composition will seem cropped, unbalanced, or incomplete. In Figure 7.11, a viewer could even interpret the character's pose differently based on the negative space. In the unbalanced lower frame, the woman appears to be deliberately turning away, isolating herself from her surroundings. With no change to her pose, the shift in composition gives the character a more sullen, introspective appearance in the lower frame.

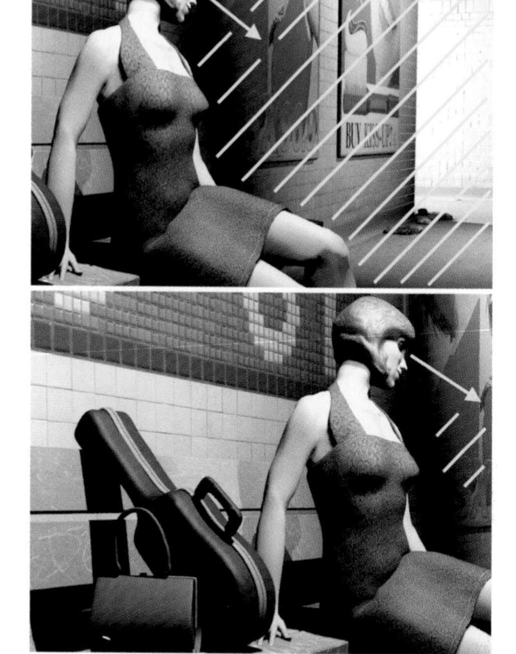

[Figure 7.11] A balanced composition (top) leaves look space for a character (shown in yellow). An unbalanced composition (bottom) can trap your eye in the side of the frame.

Graphic Weight

Everything that appears in your rendering has a *graphic weight*. The graphic weight of an area or object is the amount, relative to other objects in the frame, that it attracts attention or dominates the composition. Bold or bright items that contrast against the surrounding scene have the greatest graphic weight. Sharp edges and shadows have more graphic weight than soft, gradual transitions. People naturally look at other people, so a person in the shot, or parts of the person such as the eyes, are natural centers of interest, which take on greater graphic weight. Larger items have more graphic weight than smaller details. Areas near the edge of the frame also can have a greater graphic weight.

To judge which objects in your scene have the most graphic weight, just glance at the whole rendering, and notice where you find yourself focusing. The objects with a high graphic weight need to be arranged carefully in your frame to achieve a balanced composition.

As with positive and negative space, looking at which parts of your composition have the most graphic weight can help you analyze your composition.

Which parts of the image will first catch your eye when you look at this image? How well distributed are they within the frame? If a viewer were "reading" the image from left to right, would there be anything interesting on the left side to draw the eye back, or would it come to rest on the right side of the frame? There's no right or wrong in terms of where you want to put points of interest within your composition, but the thought process can lead you to find better ways of laying out your scene.

Your lighting can increase or decrease the graphic weight of parts of your scene. Areas of your rendering that are dimly lit, washed out, or lacking contrast will have less graphic weight, while areas with more shading, contrast, or color will stand out. If part of your scene needs more graphic weight, add colored light or extra highlights and contrast.

In a film or television production, motion catches the eye and lends greater graphic weight. When there is a cut from one shot to another, people's eyes will still be looking at an area of attention within the last shot, and continuity is important, especially for rapidly edited sequences. It is a good idea to pick up each new shot with a subject of interest close to where the viewer is already looking. In everyday life, people tend to focus most of their attention on a small area in the center of their visual field, keeping only a vague impression of what is outside that area in their peripheral vision. Allowing viewers of a movie the same comfort, keeping their attention focused through multiple shots allows people to remain immersed in a film instead of being jolted by each shot as if they were constantly being presented with completely different scenes.

Lines

Another way to examine and improve your composition is to picture the dominant lines that can be seen within the shot. Look at any line, whether it is the horizon, a fence, or the edge of a shadow, and think about where it leads. People's eyes naturally follow lines within the image, so placing an interesting subject along a line, or having lines within your composition point to a subject that you want a viewer to notice, will help direct people where you want them to look.

Diagonal lines are dynamic. They add excitement and interest to a composition. Lines that are just horizontal and vertical look boring in comparison. Figure 7.12 shows how much more dramatic a scene looks when it is tilted at an angle (right) instead of relying on purely horizontal and vertical lines (left).

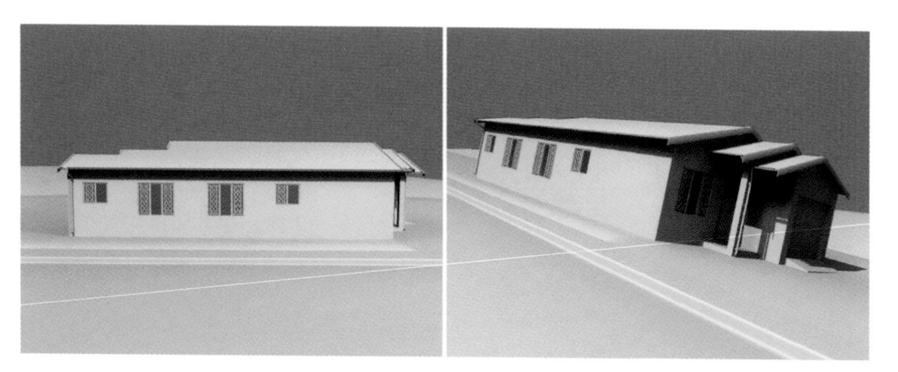

[Figure 7.12] Changing the dominant lines in your image from horizontal (left) to diagonal (right) makes for a more dynamic composition.

Curved lines are soothing. A curve in the shape of an S can even be graceful and elegant. Employ curves when you want to make a scene look organic and natural, and save the straight edges for designs that need to look high-tech or as if they were obviously created with computer graphics.

Jagged lines and sharp corners look threatening. They can add excitement to an image, but they also can make a place or a character look less hospitable. Don't create any angles so sharp that they look as if they could cut you, unless you are trying to make a threatening image.

Tangencies

A *tangency* is a place where two lines meet within your composition, such as where an edge of one object aligns with an edge of another object, or where a shadow falls along an edge in a surface. In 3D graphics, objects often come into perfect alignment by accident, and this can reduce the impact of your composition.

When two lines become tangent, they essentially become the same line in your composition, and that can cause your scene to lose definition. The left side of Figure 7.13 is plagued with undesirable tangencies. The top of the house lines up too perfectly with the horizon behind it, and the house's shadow lines up with the edge of the sidewalk. On the right, both the camera and light are adjusted to fix these problems. Notice how the shape of the house appears better defined on the right, and the shadow looks more natural.

[Figure 7.13] On the left, tangencies between the shadow and the edge of the sidewalk, and between the top of the roof and the horizon, hurt the composition. On the right, changing the camera and light angles fixes the tangencies and makes a stronger image.

Framing for Film and Video

As you work in different media, you need to frame your work for different film and television formats.

Formats and Aspect Ratios

The actual frames in which you arrange your scene can have different proportions, depending on the format of film or television for which you are rendering your graphics. The proportion of the width to the height of an image is called its *aspect ratio*. For example, if the width of an image were exactly twice its height, it would have an aspect ratio of 2:1. Aspect ratios are sometimes written as a single number, the result of dividing the width by the height. For example, 4:3 could be expressed as a 1.33 aspect ratio.

Here are the most popular aspect ratios used in film and television production, in order from the narrowest aspect to the widest:

- 1.33: Standard television sets have a 1.33 aspect ratio (spoken out loud as "one three three"). In many countries, these standard television sets are gradually being replaced by widescreen (16:9) televisions.
- 1.66: Less popular in the United States, but still used in some parts of the world is the 1.66 aspect ratio ("one six six").
- 1.78: HDTV and widescreen advanced television systems have a 1.78 aspect ratio, commonly referred to as 16:9 ("sixteen by nine"). This allows viewers at home to see an aspect ratio closer to some of the most popular widescreen presentations in movie theaters.
- 1.85: The world's most popular aspect ratio for motion pictures is 1.85 ("one eight five").
- 2.35: The second most popular aspect ratio for feature films in the United States is 2.35 ("two three five"). This aspect ratio is sometimes called *Cinemascope* or *Panavision*, which are trademarks for specific formats that use a 2.35 aspect ratio.

When you know the aspect ratio and the horizontal resolution of a shot, you can determine the vertical resolution by division. For example, if you are rendering a film frame that is 2048 pixels across and the aspect ratio is 1.85, the height in pixels would be 2048/1.85, or 1107.

Film Formats

Photographic film is slowly becoming obsolete. Every year, it is replaced to a greater extent by digital photography and digital cinema. However, the transition from film to digital is not a quick "digital revolution" like the switch from records to compact discs. Instead, this is a slow, gradual transition, in large part because many artists continue to shoot film as a matter of personal preference. Movies are still distributed primarily on film as well, because most movie theaters haven't yet invested in digital projectors. Many effects studios offer filmmakers a *digital intermediate process*, in which filmed images are digitized, manipulated, and then recorded onto film again for distribution. Productions that are still shot and distributed on film can benefit from the full range of digital color correction, effects, and compositing. As a result, visual effects professionals are likely to be dealing with a diverse mix of film and digital formats for many years to come.

35mm motion picture film used to be standardized at the 1.33 aspect ratio, and television sets were initially designed with a 1.33 aspect ratio for the sake of compatibility with film. However, in the 1950s Hollywood studios felt threatened by the growing popularity of television and devised widescreen movie formats as a gimmick to differentiate their films from smaller television screens. Different studios, which owned the theater chains as well, developed different methods for fitting a wider image onto regular 35mm film.

Common 2.35 film is shot and projected with an *anamorphic* lens, which is designed to squeeze the image horizontally to fit onto the 35mm film, as shown in Figure 7.14. 2.35 is a popular aspect ratio for films shot outdoors with sweeping panoramas and is often used in bigger-budget films. When anamorphic film is projected, the projector is fitted with an anamorphic lens that will widen the image into its full 2.35 aspect ratio.

[Figure 7.14] An anamorphic widescreen image (left) is scaled down horizontally by a special camera lens to fit on regular 35mm film (right), and requires an anamorphic projector lens to expand it to its original width in the theater.

While 2.35 has its advantages, modern movie theaters are commonly being divided into many smaller screens to show different films at once. A movie screen cannot be made any wider than the size of the theater, so when showing widescreen movies, the width of the screen remains the same as for other aspect ratios, but the image is less tall. A similar thing happens when 2.35 films are adapted for HDTV; either the sides of the image are cropped off beyond the 1.78 frame or the top and bottom of the screen are left black.

When films are shot with a 1.85 aspect ratio, they usually are not shot anamorphically. Instead, the widescreen image is fit into the center of the film frame, as shown on the left side of Figure 7.15. In the theater, only the center part of the film is projected onto the screen. This means that a lot of the film stock is wasted. The center of the film frame—including grain and dirt—is enlarged to fill the screen.

Sometimes the top and bottom of the frame will be masked off, so that only the center part of the frame (what will appear in the theater) is exposed. However, it is becoming more common for films that will be projected in a 1.85 aspect ratio to be exposed *full gate*, as shown on the right side of Figure 7.15. When film is shot full gate, extra image area is recorded above and below what will be seen in theaters, filling the full negative with an image, even though only the center part will be projected in theaters.

[Figure 7.15] A 1.85 widescreen format uses only the center part of the film frame (left) but is often shot full gate (right) to capture extra image area that might be used in visual effects production or made visible in the video release.

When adding visual effects, the entire film frame is often digitized full gate, giving visual effects artists extra image area to work with. Instead of always using the center of the digitized background plate in your final composite, with a full gate image you can shift the entire shot to reframe higher or lower. You can even animate the position of the background image to simulate camera shake or small camera moves, which is very handy for making it appear as if the camera has reacted to a visual effects element or a CG creature that you are adding to the shot.

Shooting full gate also provides extra image area which can be revealed when a widescreen film gets adapted for television.

Adaptation to Television

When films or other widescreen programming are adapted for standard television or home video, the 1.66, 1.85, or 2.35 aspect ratios need to be converted for display on 1.33 screens.

The technique of *letterboxing* is one approach to adapting widescreen images to standard video. A letterboxed image consists of the original widescreen composition shown in its entirety, with a black area above and below the image to fill the rest of the taller-screen format. The left side of Figure 7.16 shows a full 1.85 image as it would appear when letterboxed in a 1.33 television frame. Letterboxing is a faithful way to preserve the composition of a widescreen film, but many home viewers don't like to lose inches off their television picture.

[Figure 7.16] A 1.85 frame can be converted to 1.33 by letterboxing (left) or pan and scan (right).

Another technique, called *pan and scan*, is commonly used to adapt widescreen footage to standard television. This process involves going through a movie and selectively cropping off portions of the left and right of each shot. Usually only the center of the image appears on television. If something significant is happening on the left or right side of the frame, then instead of showing the center, the image can pan sideways to show what had been the left or right side of the widescreen frame. Either way, the picture that fills the TV screen is really just a portion of the full scene that was shown in theaters. The right side of Figure 7.16 shows the cropped 1.33 composition that would result. This practice is seen by some as an unnecessary modification of a filmmaker's original work, especially when it is done to classic films whose directors cannot be a part of the film-to-video conversion.

The pan and scan process also can involve animating the area that gets cropped from each frame. For example, a shot on video might virtually pan across the original film frame, starting by showing the left side of what was filmed and ending by showing the right side of what was filmed. This is supposed to appear similar to the results of the original film camera having panned, but it appears more as if you were scrolling across the image. When watching movies on video (which are not letterboxed), you can sometimes notice small horizontal pans added in the process of converting widescreen films to video.

If a film was shot full gate, then the taller 1.33 aspect image could be cropped from an area that goes beyond the widescreen image. In this case, the television viewer would simply be seeing more of what was above or below the main action than was shown in theaters.

Cropping and Overscan

Unfortunately you can't expect every pixel of your image to make it onto the screen. When digital images are sent to a film recorder, between 15 and 30 rows of pixels can be cropped from each edge of the image in the film recording process. Also, when movies are projected, the theater will adjust the projector so that the image more than completely fills the screen, cropping off even more from the edges of the frame.

In television, a similar cropping problem occurs when a process called *overscanning* crops a portion of a video signal off of the screen. A television picture tube overscans an image by projecting a slightly larger picture than the size of the actual screen. Overscanning was designed into early televisions to hide fluctuations of picture size that could result from variations in the electrical current powering the television receiver. The amount of overscan and the centering of the image vary greatly between televisions.

Important actions should be kept in the center 90 percent of the screen, because some viewers might miss them if they happen too near the edge. Be even more careful if you are putting text or titles on video, because viewers would certainly notice any letters or lines of text that were not visible on the screen. As a rule of thumb, text should be kept in the center 80 percent of the image to keep it safe from overscan. Most 3D software has optional guides to safe image areas that can be displayed in your viewport.

Exercises

Framing and reframing your shots can be done in an infinite number of ways. Study the composition and framing in your favorite movies, and see if you can explore or rethink the composition in your own work.

1. View a scene in a movie on video, and identify the different types of shots used. What shot sizes and angles are used? Can you spot the use of shot/counter-shot coverage, establishing shots, and reaction shots?

2. Load one of your own renderings into a paint program, and experiment with cropping it into smaller frames and details. Does it look better with

a different aspect ratio? If you remove one side of the image and place your subject farther off-center, have you improved or changed your design?

3. Rerender an existing 3D scene from different perspectives. See if you can influence the sense of size and space in the environment with your different renderings. Can your scene be improved if some objects are placed in the foreground, just in front of the camera, while others are left farther back?

[CHAPTER EIGHT]

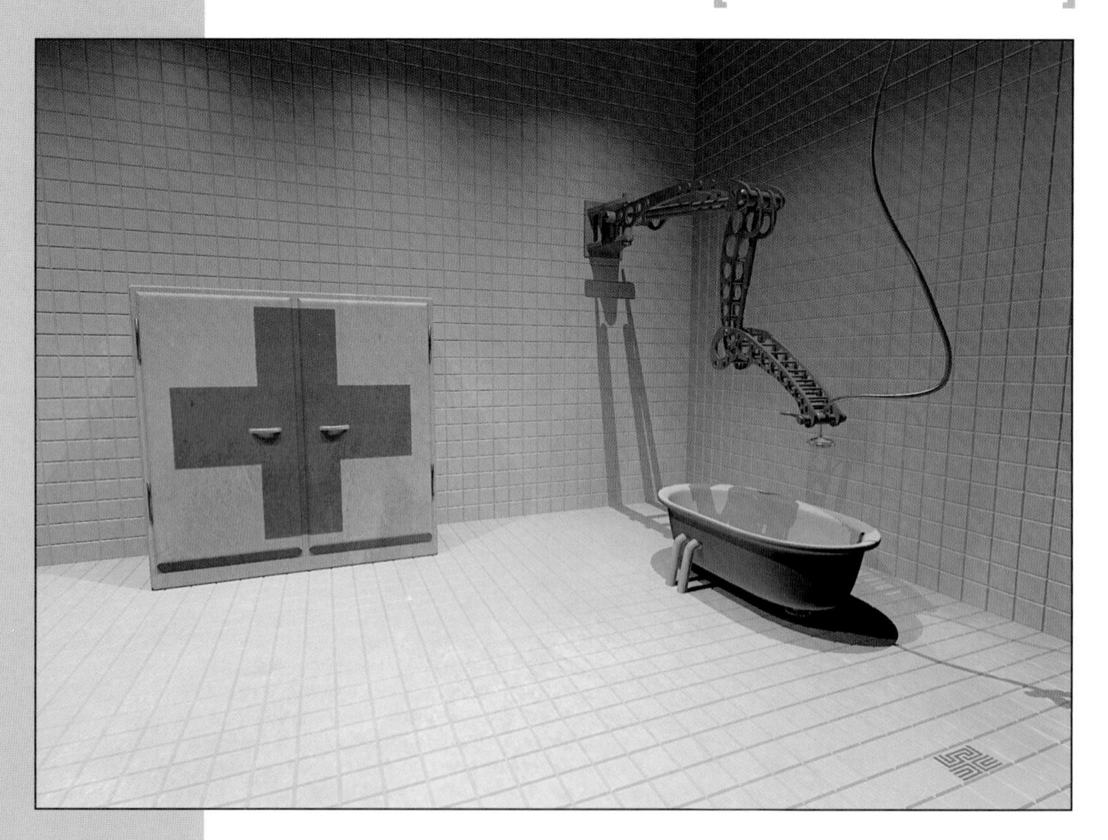

The Art and Science of Color

When you want to play with your audience's emotions, few tools are more powerful than an intelligent use of color. This chapter will explore the visual power of color in your 3D art. The right color scheme can create or enhance a mood, or even change the meaning of an image. But the use of color also has a technical side, and this chapter will also delve into digital color reproduction and how to choose realistic colors for different types of light source.

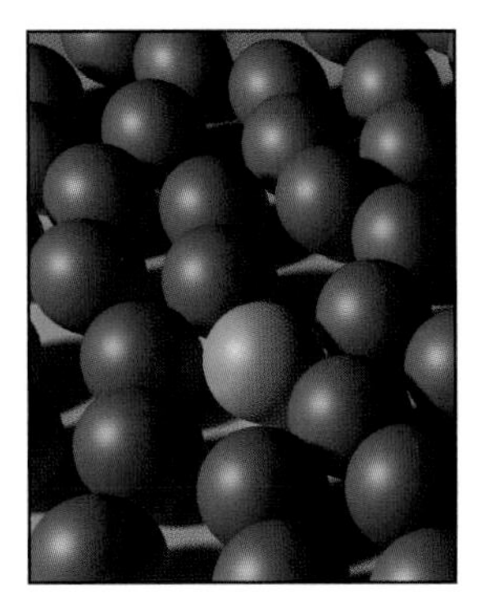

Color Mixing

Colors in 3D graphics software are generally stored as RGB (red, green, blue) values, three numbers representing the levels of red, green, and blue that combine make up the color. In this book, RGB values are shown on a scale of 0 to 1 unless otherwise noted. For example, {0,0,0} represents pure black and {1,1,1} represents pure white.

Additive Color

Red, green, and blue are called the *additive primary colors* because any color of light can be represented by combining red, green, and blue light in varying proportions. When red, green, and blue light are added together in equal proportions in a rendering, they form white light, as seen in Figure 8.1.

[Figure 8.1] The additive primaries combine to form white illumination.

Between the additive primary colors are the *additive secondary colors*, created when any two of the additive primaries are both present in equal amounts. As shown in Figure 8.2, the additive secondary colors are yellow {1,1,0}, cyan {0,1,1}, and magenta {1,0,1}.

The additive secondary colors can also be called the *complements* of the additive primaries. *Complementary* colors are pairs of colors that are opposite from each other on a color wheel. Cyan is the complement of red, magenta is the complement of green, and yellow is the complement of blue.

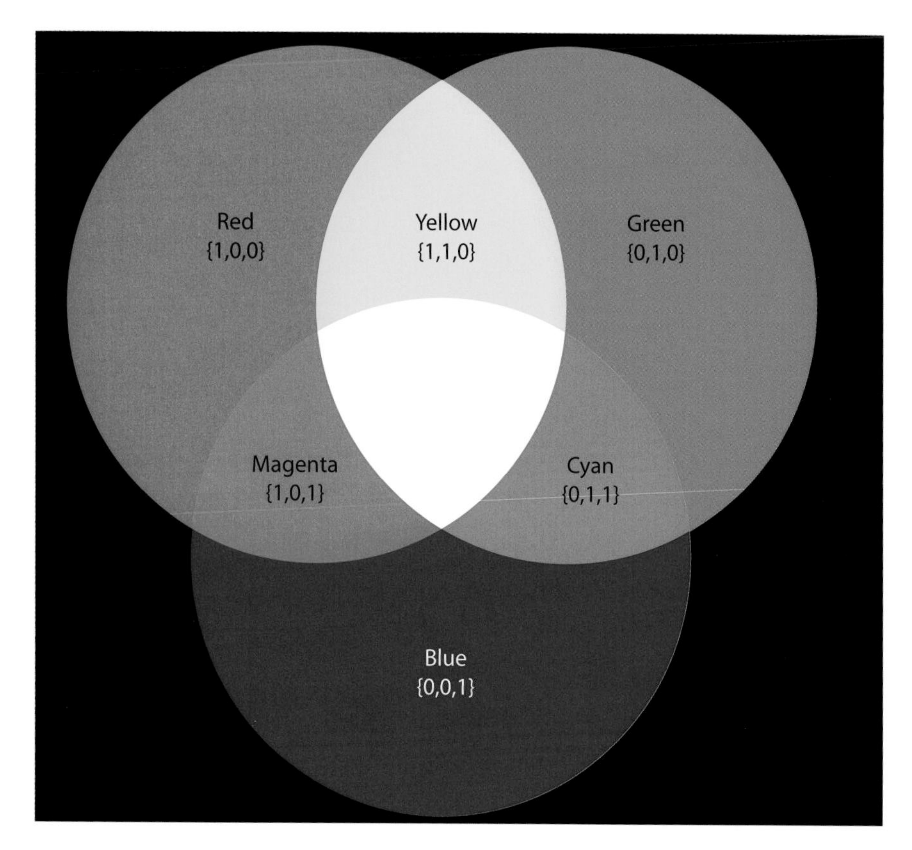

[Figure 8.2]
The additive secondary colors—yellow, magenta, and cyan—exist where any two additive primaries overlap.

Subtractive Color

Printed output creates colors differently than a computer monitor. A monitor starts out black, and then adds red, green, and blue light. A printer starts with white paper, which is darkened with inks in the *subtractive primary colors*: cyan, magenta, and yellow.

The three subtractive primary ink colors can produce any hue, but when combined they produce brown, not black. To compensate for this, most full-color printing uses four ink colors: cyan, magenta, yellow, and black, abbreviated CMYK (yes, the K stands for blacK). The black ink can produce crisp text, and also reinforces the shading of the color image. A conventional four-color printed image is seen up close in Figure 8.3, created by adding cyan, magenta, yellow, and black dots to the paper.

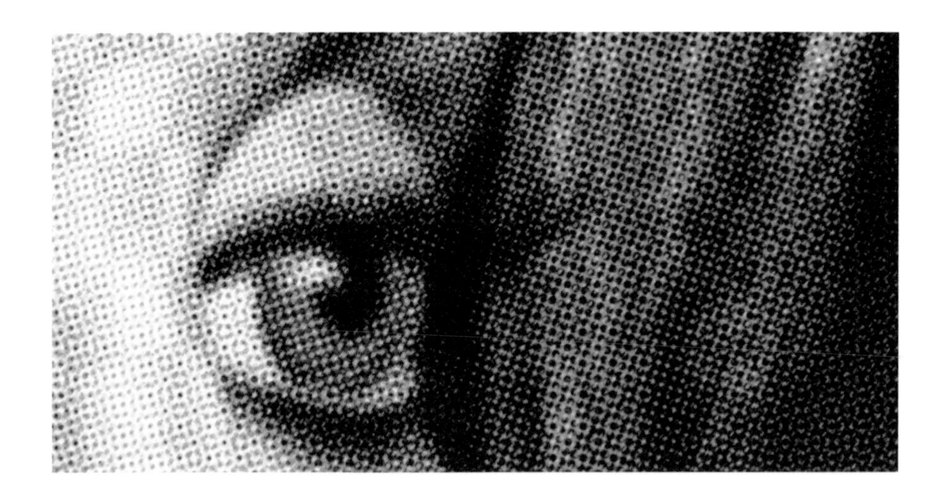

[Figure 8.3]
The subtractive primaries are used in a four-color printing process.

Hue, Saturation, and Value Adjustments

Most graphics programs offer you the option to select colors by HSV (Hue, Saturation, Value) instead of directly setting RGB values. However, HSV color selection is entirely an interface feature in most programs; the values actually stored and used for internal calculations are in RGB.

The advantage of HSV is that it provides a way of selecting colors that is more intuitive to most artists. When we think about colors, we tend to group and describe them based on their hue (is it more red or more orange?), their saturation (is it a pale pink, almost gray, or a bold, saturated red?), and their value (is it dark or bright?). Using hue, saturation, and value as the three ways to organize and describe colors makes sense to us visually. Figure 8.4 shows how colors appear when organized by HSV as opposed to RGB.

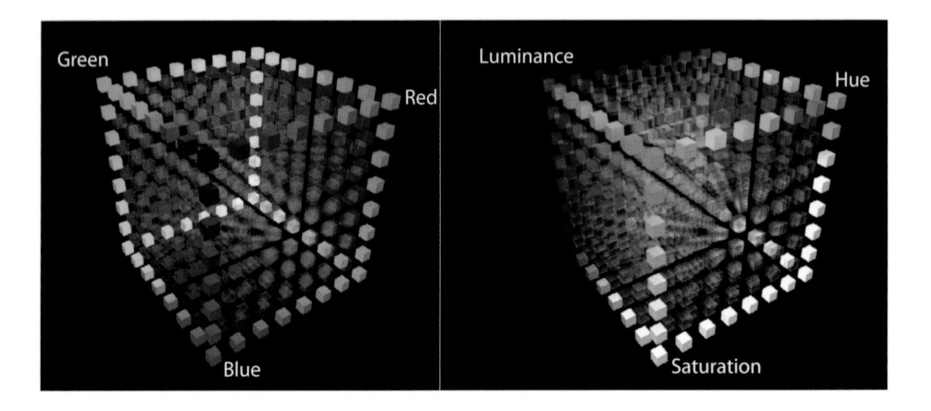

[Figure 8.4]
RGB color (left) mixes red, green, and blue, while HSV (right) varies the hue, luminance, and saturation.

In 3D graphics, internal calculations are done in RGB because it is much quicker and easier to simulate illumination of colored surfaces by colored lights when using only three possible wavelengths of light (red, green, and blue) instead of a continuous spectrum using many possible wavelengths.

When Light Color Meets Surface Color

There are two very different ways that colors are mixed during a rendering. As shown at the beginning of this chapter, when different lights overlap, their colors are *added* together. When colored light illuminates a colored surface, however, the light color is *multiplied* with the surface color. For example, if you make a surface orange {1,.28,.08}, it will reflect 100 percent of the red light that illuminates it, 28 percent of the green light, and 8 percent of the blue light. You can think of a surface color as a filter controlling how much red, green, and blue light an object will reflect.

Note that light colors usually appear less bright when multiplied by surface colors. This is because colors are being multiplied by a fractional value less than one. Some software optionally expresses RGB values on a scale of 0 to 255 instead of 0 to 1, but the renderer's internal color multiplication is still always performed with color values expressed on a scale of 0 to 1. This standard of using a 0 to 255 scale is based on a limitation that no longer exists in most modern rendering software—that there used to be only 256 possible shades of each color. Many 3D programs give you a choice, with either 255 or 1 representing full brightness. And while expressing RGB values in fractions with more digits of accuracy is more precise than the 0 to 255 scale, this interface choice usually won't impact your rendering.

If you set any of the color values for a surface to 0, then the surface will reflect 0 percent of the light of that color. Figure 8.5 shows some of the problems that this can cause. On the left, a white light illuminates spheres of many colors, and all the colors are visible. On the right, the light is pure green {0,1,0}, and where it illuminates a sphere with a pure red {1,0,0} color, the result is black. The result is predictable because the purely red surface reflects 0 percent of the green light, and the light does not emit any red. However, in real life, colors are rarely this pure, and you'd expect a bright enough light to illuminate surfaces of any color.

[Figure 8.5]
A white light uniformly illuminates six Lambert-shaded spheres (left), but some spheres appear black in the render when a green light illuminates them (right).

When you sample colors from an evenly lit photograph, you tend to find that objects usually reflect some amount of red, green, and blue. When you look at something painted bright red, you might not see any green there, but as shown in Figure 8.6, there is a green component of the color.

[Figure 8.6]
RGB colors sampled from a photograph.

Picking colors from a photograph can be a great starting point to root your color scheme in realistic colors. Most graphics programs include an eyedropper or sampler tool. A color sampled from a picture will not exactly match the original surface color, because what you sample is influenced by the lighting in the photograph (as well as by the white balance of the camera—something discussed later in this chapter). Reflections also can tint the colors you sample, especially for surfaces like glass which are reflective but not metallic. In the case of metallic surfaces, reflections tend to be tinted by the surface color. Sampling colors works best from images that are evenly lit with white light.

Often a surface that you would call "black" still reflects at least 15 or 20 percent of the light that hits it, so realistic RGB values for a piece of black rubber might be {0.17,0.16,0.19} instead of {0,0,0}. Likewise, a "white" piece of paper doesn't really reflect 100 percent of the light that hits it, so a color of {0.82,0.76,0.79} could be more realistic than {1,1,1}.

Beginners in 3D graphics often err on the side of choosing surface colors that are too saturated, or too close to pure black or pure white, and thereby create surfaces that don't respond realistically and consistently to light. If you keep most of the red, green, and blue values on surfaces roughly between 0.2 and 0.8, then you'll leave room to use your lighting to determine most of the brightness values in the scene, instead of having some surfaces that always appear much bolder or respond to light differently from others. This is a very generalized rule of thumb; on some projects you might want to use more muted pastel colors, and in other projects bolder colors might be a creative necessity.

Even when you don't use extremely pure RGB colors, if your light color is a complement of your surface color, it will make your surface appear darker. Figure 8.7 shows a rose lit by a red light (left) and a green light (right). In the red light, the petals look bright, but the stem and leaves appear dark. In green light, the stem and leaves appear brighter, but the petals appear dark.

Complementary color lights can also appear to desaturate a surface color. If you used blue light to illuminate a character with pink skin, the skin would look more gray and less saturated than in a white or pink light.

[Figure 8.7]
Lit by red light (left), the petals look brighter, while in green light (right), the leaves look brighter.

With all of the ways that colored lights and differently illuminated surfaces can add complexity to your scene, it's easy to have 3D scenes that are a mishmash of many different tints. As an artist, however, sometimes you need to take control over what colors will appear in your scene, and focus on using colors that come from a clearly defined color scheme.

Color Schemes

The most striking images you can create will have a clearly defined *color scheme* instead of using colors from all over the palette at random. The color scheme—the total set of colors that appear in an image as a whole—creates a first impression and helps set the mood for the scene. When a new scene begins in a movie, the audience perceives the color scheme first, before they even interpret the shapes and subjects depicted in the image.

You can develop a strong color scheme by choosing a small, consistent set of colors, and coloring every element in the scene with one of these specific colors. Often, you'll give different kinds of objects in your scene the same colors to maintain your color scheme. For example, in Figure 8.8, the entire composition consists of a few shades of blue and a few shades of yellow.

Reusing the same set of colors "ties together" the image. The yellow of the moon is picked up and reused for the stars, and similar colored dots appear on the building. Because of the adherence to a limited color scheme, every part of this image is unmistakably unified.

[Figure 8.8]
The color scheme helps unify the composition. Scene by Jorge R. Gutierrez, www.super-macho.com.

When you add a new color to an object or a light, you are not just setting one color, but are also adding to the color scheme of your image. For example, in Figure 8.8 above, the entire scene would have looked different if any object were made bright green or red. People will interpret each color in relation to the rest of the color scheme, so forethought is necessary in order to design the most effective color scheme for your rendering.

Color Contrast

A color scheme can make use of *color contrast* to make some colors seem to "pop" from a scene and grab the viewer's attention. Figure 8.9 is a good example of color contrast: It's hard to look at the image without your eye being drawn immediately to the orange ball. The contrast between the orange and the rest of the color scheme, not just the color's own hue or saturation, makes it pop.

Exclusivity

Concentrating a color in only one area increases color contrast. If orange had been squandered elsewhere in Figure 8.9, then the orange ball would not carry the same graphic weight or attract the viewer's eye as readily.

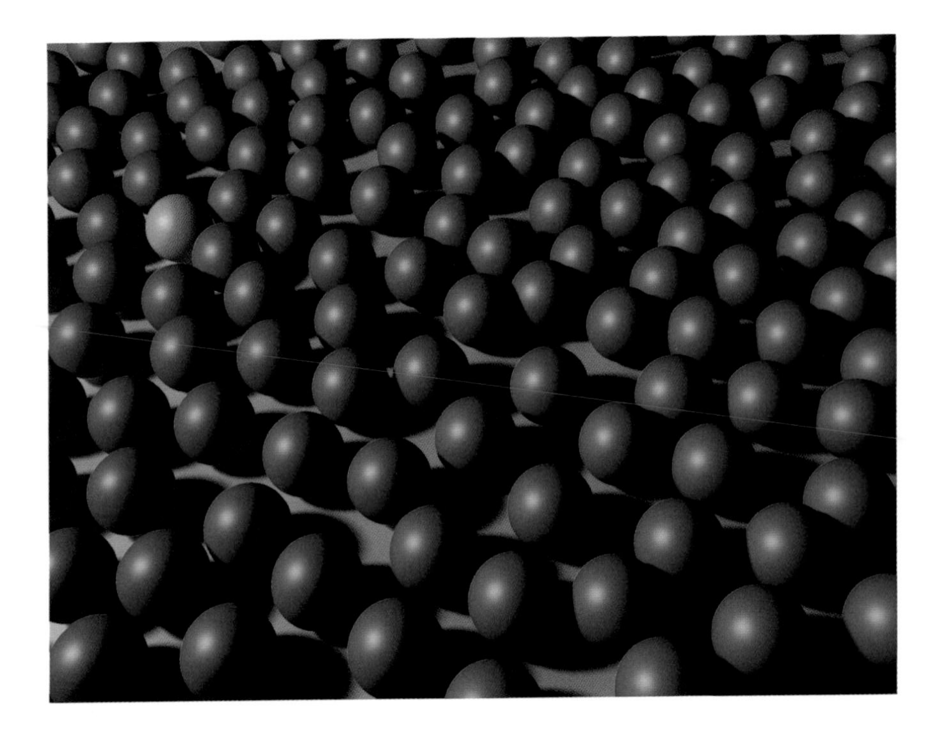

[Figure 8.9] The exclusive use of orange in one part of the image immediately catches your eye.

Complementary Colors

Color contrast is most visible when colors are surrounded by their complements. As noted above, complementary colors are pairs of colors that are opposite from each other on a color wheel, as shown on the left side of Figure 8.10. This provides a maximum amount of contrast, and makes the purple color appear to be an even stronger and more noticeable color.

The reason complementary colors are called "complementary," instead of just "opposite," is that they work so well together. If you are designing two characters who will spend a lot of screen time together, or should look as if they belonged together, consider giving them complementary colors.

Instead of just a pair of two colors, sometimes you can find three or more colors for your color scheme by picking colors evenly spaced around the color wheel, as shown on the right side of Figure 8.10.

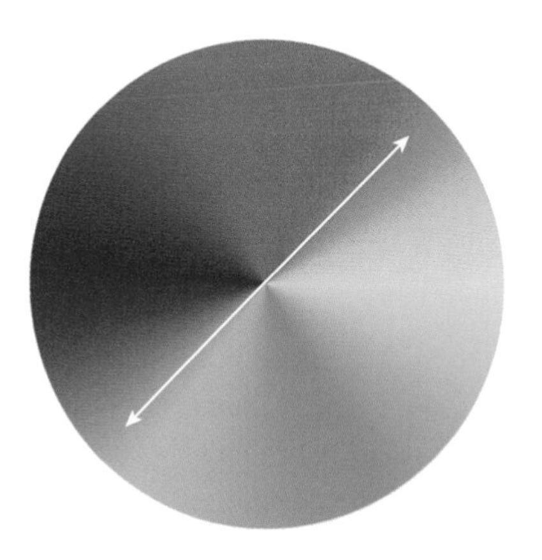

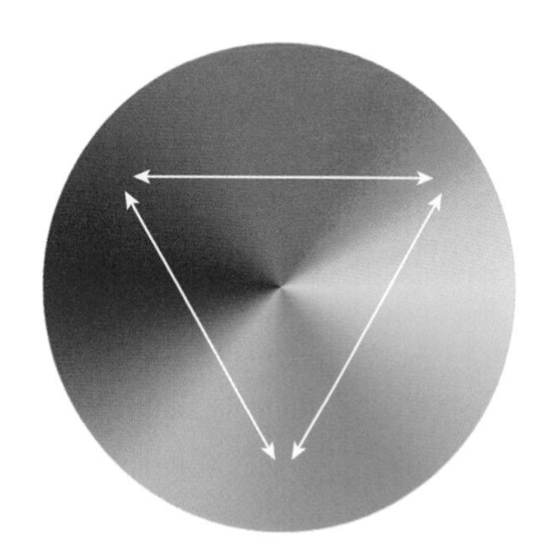

[Figure 8.10] Complementary colors (left) are pairs from opposite sides of the color wheel, but some artists like to pick color schemes from three points around the wheel (right).

There is software available that can help design color schemes. The freeware program Color Schemes, by Eni Oken and Gregg Patton, can follow formulas such as the three equally spaced points around the color wheel shown above, and many other formulas for mixing and matching colors. You can download it from www.oken3d.com/html/tips.html. If you want a supported commercial product, there are also programs such as ColorImpact from Tigercolor.com and ColorSchemer from colorschemer.com. Whether or not you use these programs as a part of your professional work, they can be interesting as educational tools to explore different color schemes.

Contrast Over Time

In animation, planning for how colors will be seen over time can give them greater impact. For example, a bright, fiery explosion of red and yellow looks even more intense if the environment is dark blue before the explosion. The blue soothes the audience, their eyes adjust to the dimly lit scene, and then wham! When the explosion hits them, it looks twice as bright and colorful as it could have without the contrast.

Cutting between scenes presents another chance to take advantage of color contrast. Especially if there are several things going on at once, giving each location a different color scheme will help orient the audience after a cut. For example, if some action takes place in police headquarters while other action is happening in the criminal's base, adding a blue tint to all the scenes in the criminal base would make it easy for the audience to recognize each location instantly.

Meanings of Colors

Why is the logo of a bank, insurance company, or hospital likely to be blue, while the logo of a fast-food restaurant is likely to be yellow or orange? The colors you choose in your color schemes can convey subtle impressions, and trigger different associations in your audience.

Warm and Hot Colors

People generally describe red, orange, and yellow as *warm* colors, as opposed to blue and green, which are *cool* colors. The boldest, most saturated reds and oranges are considered *hot* colors.

Red may trigger alarm because it is the color of blood and fire. People hesitate to go through a red door or push a red button. Signs with strong warnings or prohibitions often use red, as do fire exits. Figure 8.11 shows the different feeling you get from hot colors compared to cool colors.

Hot colors are generally thought to be spicy, exciting, zippy, attention-grabbing colors. A sports car looks faster if it's red. A fast-food restaurant might use orange or yellow in its logo and décor to capture this spirit, or to make customers feel like hurrying up and leaving their tables more quickly.

[Figure 8.11] Hot colors cause excitement (left), while cooler colors suit soothing scenes (right).

Yellow, the color of the sun, is often considered a bright, cheerful color as well. If you cut to a scene that is dominated by bright yellow, the audience expects a happy point to be reached in the story.

While some associations are universally recognized, such as yellow being the color of sunshine, others are very culturally specific. In the United States, the color red is associated with communism so strongly that campaigns on the political left would avoid using predominantly red color schemes in their commercials, posters, or bumper stickers. When they use red at all, it is usually balanced with plenty of blue and white, using all three colors from the American flag. In Canada, however, red and white are the colors of their national flag, so political ads and banners widely feature red-based color schemes and are seen as nothing but patriotic.

Any experience that people have in common can lead to common color associations. The expansion of global media exposes much of the world to a common body of images and color choices, through film, television, art, fashion, and advertising. Red is globally recognized not just as the color of natural constants like blood and fire, but of brand names like Coca-Cola.

Cool Colors

Blue and green are considered soothing and relaxing. In many environments, the water, sky, grass, and trees are composed of blues and greens, and they function as a sort of neutral background.

Deeper, bolder blues can look solid and majestic. This could be one reason that so many banks and insurance companies use blue logos. While a color scheme dominated by red can say "fear me," a deep ocean blue seems to say "trust me."

A scene bathed in blue light can take on a sad feeling. Even very subtle tints in a scene's lighting can help create impressions about a scene. A blue tinted light can create the impression of winter or night air, and make a location or a person look colder.

Green is a fascinating color in that it can look very natural, or very unnatural. Green is the color of much of our natural environment, a symbol of nature itself. However, a person turning green would make her look very sick, a light green is often used in the walls of hospitals, and green-tinted illumination from fluorescent tubes is disturbing. Figure 8.12 takes advantage of a green cast to create an image that suggests sickness. It uses only two small areas of the complementary color red—first on the cabinet, then on one tile in the lower-right corner, to help balance the composition so that your eye isn't stuck at the cabinet.

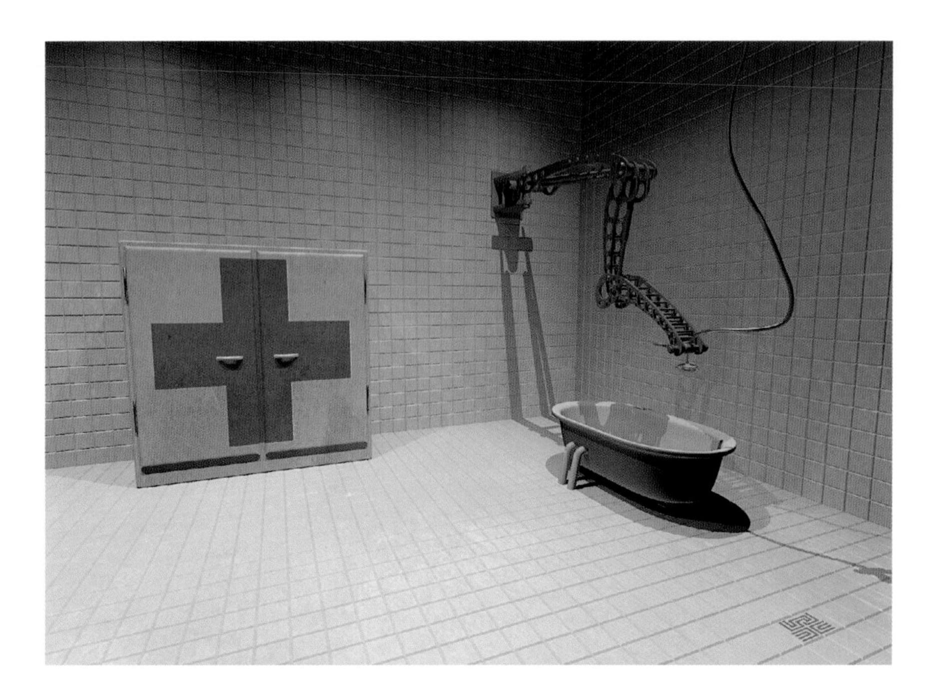

[Figure 8.12] Vaclav Cizkovsky's rendering sets a mood with a green light.

Contextual Associations

Within a narrative film, the meanings of specific colors, like any other symbol, can be redefined. Characters or groups of characters can have their own color schemes in a larger animation, which might be used in their home environment, costumes, props, or even skin colors. Once an audience is subconsciously accustomed to certain colors appearing with your villains, any new element introduced into the film would appear sinister if it used the villains' colors. Like musical motifs, color schemes can follow not just characters, but themes, emotions, or any other recurring aspects of a film.

In storytelling, it can be helpful to occasionally move away from the most obvious color meanings. For example, if you wanted to make a robot look evil or threatening, the most obvious cliché might be to make its eyes glow red. Chances are, however, that your audience has already seen that done before, so you might try something fresher, and have your robot do something evil without flashing a red light.

Color and Depth

Often people perceive cool colors as being farther away, and hot colors as being nearby. For example, even with no other depth cues, most people will find it easier to see the left side of Figure 8.13 as a frame with a hole in the middle, and see the right side as being a small box in front of a larger square.

There are different theories about why this happens. One reason could be that, in natural environments, many subjects are seen against blue sky or green foliage backgrounds, so people naturally consider blue- and green-colored areas to be "background." People might also focus more attention in nature on things with warmer tones, such as a red piece of fruit, a wound, or the flesh tones of a person or animal, than on colors of foliage or sky.

Another reason that blue may appear to be farther away is due to chromatic aberration in people's eyes. When light is refracted through the lens of a human eye, different wavelengths are refracted at different angles. To correct for the difference, human eyes must focus to a slightly closer distance to see a red subject than to see a blue subject in the same position.

[Figure 8.13]
All other factors being equal, red tends to appear closer to us than blue.

In a rendering, washing your background with a blue light and lighting the foreground with red can effectively increase the sense of depth in a scene. Naturally, this is not something that is appropriate or plausible in every scene. In lighting a section of subway tunnel, colored signal lights could have plausibly illuminated the scene with almost any color, but a red foreground and blue background add punch to the scene in Figure 8.14.

[Figure 8.14]
Red light in the foreground enhances the sense of depth in a rendering.

Tinted Black-and-White Images

Even some black-and-white images can benefit from the use of color. You can produce a tinted black-and-white image in almost any paint or compositing program, by first removing any color or saturation, and then assigning a hue and saturation to the entire image.

Even before color film was invented, filmmakers recognized the emotional impact of color. Some early black-and-white movies have scenes tinted with colored dyes. For example, footage of a building on fire would be tinted with a dip in red dye, and then spliced back into the film. Black-and-white photographs are also sometimes tinted with colored oils.

Even without intentional colorization, very old photographs turn yellow with age, and people associate a yellow or sepia tone with an older image. Figure 8.15 is made to appear more nostalgic by being tinted with a sepia tone.

[Figure 8.15]
Tinting a black-and-white image can make it look older or more nostalgic.

Color Balance

If you want to accurately simulate the way a light source would appear if it were really photographed, then you need to start by understanding the idea of *color balance*.

Colors of light do not directly translate into the tints that are reproduced in a photograph. Instead, the colors that appear in a photograph are relative to the color balance of the film that was used.

The color balance of the film determines what color of light will appear to be white light. *Indoor film*, which is film color balanced for use with regular light bulbs, would make light from a regular light bulb look white, but would make what you see outdoors appear blue, as shown in Figure 8.16.

On the other hand, *outdoor film* would make daylight and the outdoors look normal, but indoor light bulbs would appear yellow or red in color, as shown in Figure 8.17.

[Figure 8.16] An indoor (3200K) color balance makes what you see through the door appear blue.

[Figure 8.17] An outdoor (5500K) color balance makes daylight appear normal, but light from indoor bulbs appears red or orange.

Color balancing is not unique to film. A similar adjustment, called *white balance*, is accomplished electronically on video cameras and digital cameras.

Even your own vision automatically adjusts to compensate for different colors of light. For example, imagine that you were wearing a white shirt at night in front of a campfire, where everything was lit by red firelight. Once you have grown accustomed to the light, you would perceive the shirt as being white, even though you see red when you look at the shirt in the red light of a fire. In much the same way that the automatic white balance of a digital camera adjusts the signal to respond to colored light, your brain compensates for different colors of light and manages to perceive a white shirt where it sees red.

Most 3D rendering programs do not have controls to simulate different color balance. Instead, you need to mentally take color balance into account in adjusting the color of your lights. This means that you must know two things before you can pick a realistic light color: the characteristic color of the type of light source you want to represent, and the color balance you want to simulate in your rendering.

The color of a light and the color balance of photographic film are both described by a *color temperature*, which is measured in degrees Kelvin. This is the standard system used by filmmakers and photographers to discuss colors of light. It is worth taking a few minutes to understand color temperatures and photographic color balancing, in order to pick more realistic colors for the lights in your 3D scenes.

Color Temperature

Working in the late 1800s, the British physicist William Kelvin found that as he heated a block of carbon, it glowed in the heat, producing a range of different colors at different temperatures. The black cube first produced a dim red light, increasing to a brighter yellow as the temperature went up, and eventually produced a bright blue-white glow at the highest temperatures.

Today, color temperatures are measured in degrees Kelvin, which are a variation on Centigrade degrees. Instead of starting at the temperature water freezes, the Kelvin scale starts at *absolute zero*, which is –273 Centigrade. Add 273 to a Kelvin temperature, and you get the equivalent in Centigrade.

Color temperatures attributed to different types of lights are not the actual temperature of the light source. They are just a description of the light's color, made by comparing it with the color that would be seen if a block of carbon were heated to that temperature.

Table 8.1 shows the color temperatures correlated with a variety of types of light source that you might encounter in the real world. The low color-temperature values (starting with the match and candle flames) tend to appear a more reddish color, and the higher numbers tend to appear more blue.

[Table 8.1] Color Temperatures of Different Light Sources

SOURCES	Degrees Kelvin (K)
Match flame	1700–1800
Candle flame	1850–1930
Sun, at sunrise or sunset	2000–3000
Household tungsten bulbs	2500–2900
Tungsten lamp 500W–1k	3000
Quartz lights	3200–3500
Fluorescent lights	3200–7500
Tungsten lamp 2k	3275
Tungsten lamp 5k, 10k	3380
Sun, direct at noon	5000–5400
Daylight (sun and sky)	5500–6500
Sun, through clouds/haze	5500–6500
RGB monitor (white point)	6000–7500
Sky, overcast	6500
Outdoor shade areas	7000–8000
Sky, partly cloudy	8000–10000

So, how do we convert these color temperatures into RGB colors for our lights? The answer depends on the color balance of film that you are trying to simulate. If your light source has exactly the same color temperature as the color balance you have chosen for the scene, then your light color could be white or gray. But this isn't usually what happens—in most scenes, you will need a range of different color lights.

Simulating Different Color Balances

Despite the names "indoor" and "outdoor," it is the dominant light source, not the location, that determines your color balance. If you are indoors, but the scene is lit mainly by daylight entering through a window or door, then you might want to use a 5500K color balance despite being indoors. Conversely, if you are outdoors, but a scene is lit mainly by artificial lights (especially at night), then you might want to use a 3200K color balance.

Table 8.2 shows sample RGB values to use for different kinds of lights as seen with an outdoor (5500K) color balance. RGB values are available shown in both 0 to 255 scale and in 0 to 1 scale.

[Table 8.2] RGB Values for Light Sources at 5500K Color Balance

SOURCE	RGB (0–255)	RGB (0–1)
Match flame	177, 94, 88	69, .37, .35
Candle flame	180, 107, 88	.71, .42, .35
Sun, at sunrise or sunset	182, 126, 91	.71, .49, .36
Household tungsten bulbs	184, 144, 93	.72, .56, .36
Tungsten lamp 500W–1k	186, 160, 99	.73, .63, .39
Quartz lights	189, 171, 105	.74, .67, .41
Fluorescent lights	191, 189, 119	.75, .74, .47
Tungsten lamp 2k	192, 186, 138	.75, .73, .54
Tungsten lamp 5k, 10k	192, 189, 158	.75, .74, .62
Sun, direct at noon	192, 191, 173	.75, .75, .68
Daylight (sun and sky)	190, 190, 190	.75, .75, .75
Sun, through clouds/haze	189, 190, 192	.74, .75, .75
RGB monitor (white point)	183, 188, 192	.72, .74, .75
Sky, overcast	174, 183, 190	.68, .72, .75
Outdoor shade areas	165, 178, 187	.65, .70, .73
Sky, partly cloudy	155, 171, 184	.61, .67, .72

Table 8.3 shows sample RGB values to use in simulating indoor (3200K) film. This would typically be used if you wanted to use regular household bulbs to light a scene, and you wanted the bulbs to seem like normal white light.

[Table 8.3] RGB Values for Light Sources at 3200K Color Balance

SOURCES	RGB (0–255)	RGB (0–1)
Match flame	188, 174, 109	.74, .68, .43
Candle flame	191, 181, 120	.75, .71, .47
Sun, at sunrise or sunset	192, 186, 138	.75, .73, .54
Household tungsten bulbs	192, 189, 154	.75, .74, .60
Tungsten lamp 500W–1k	191, 190, 169	.75, .75, .66
Quartz lights	191, 191, 183	.75, .75, .72
Fluorescent lights	191, 197, 189	.75, .77, .74
Tungsten lamp 2k	186, 190, 191	.73, .75, .75
Tungsten lamp 5k, 10k	182, 187, 191	.71, .73, .75
Sun, direct at noon	174, 183, 190	.68, .72, .75
Daylight (sun and sky)	166, 179, 188	.65, .70, .74
Sun, through clouds/haze	159, 173, 184	.62, .68, .72
RGB monitor (white point)	254, 254, 255	1.0, 1.0, 1.0
Sky, overcast	143, 159, 185	.56, .62, .73
Outdoor shade areas	134, 147, 189	.53, .58, .74
Sky, partly cloudy	124, 134, 193	.49, .53, .76

If you don't want to type in RGB values, you can download a version of these tables with columns of RGB colors instead of numbers from www.3dRender.com/light and pick colors directly from the appropriate column.

Caveats Regard Color Temperature

Even in realistic, "accurate" photographs, there is enormous variety in how the hue (and saturation and brightness) of a light can be portrayed. Different kinds of film, different brands of digital cameras, and digital cameras adjusted with different settings will all record colors differently.

The direction that color temperatures run seems counterintuitive to many people. As discussed above, in our common life experience, we think of blue as a cooler color than red. Because of this, the idea that the lowest color temperatures represent red colors, and highest temperatures represent blue colors, is the opposite of what most people would guess. This difference is just because most people's everyday life experiences don't include superheating a block of carbon above 5000 degrees Kelvin until it glows blue.

Color temperatures indicate the shift from red to blue only; they don't tell you about the amount of green in a light. In many cases, a fluorescent light can tend to appear greenish in comparison to other lights. The tables above include the greenish tint in the RGB values listed for fluorescent lights. However, many manufacturers tint their fluorescent tubes to filter out the green and make them more pleasant looking, so different brands of fluorescent tubes have different hues.

Even with stable, consistent types of lights, such as tungsten spotlights, cinematographers can *gel* the lights, placing transparent, colored plastic sheets in front of the light, as in Figure 8.18. Cinematographers can also place gels outside of windows when shooting indoors, and photographers can use colored filters on cameras. Even after scenes are shot, directors have additional creative control through a *digital intermediate process*, a stage in completing a film in which all of the images are processed as digital files. In short, the light colors you see in a movie or on TV will not be the same as the charts above, if the cinematographer doesn't want them to be.

[Figure 8.18]
Colored gels mounted in front of lights can adjust a light's color temperature.

Perhaps the only constant rule that you can determine from studying color temperatures is that a source listed as having a lower color temperature should always appear more red than a source with a higher color temperature. For example, in Figure 8.19, the light coming in from the window appears to be more blue in color than the light from the lamp. In a real photograph, how much more red the lamp light appears than the daylight would vary according to the settings on the camera, the type of bulb, and other factors, but the fact that an interior bulb appears more red than daylight is a constant factor.

[Figure 8.19] In a mixed lighting situation, daylight naturally appears to be more blue than interior lamps.

Some 3D graphics programs include menus of color temperature settings for lights, but not a setting for the color balance of the camera. They may have chosen to always simulate 5500K outdoor film or some other color balance, but be cautious when using these presets, as they might not be based on the color balance most appropriate to your scene. Using a color from one of the tables above, or picking a color from your background plate, could give you a more appropriate color for your lights.

Picking Colors from Pictures

Color temperatures may be your only resource if you are starting from scratch in lighting an all-CG scene. However, if you have an image available to you as a starting point, you should take advantage of it.

In some studios, the art department initially works out colors, and there will be a colored storyboard or some other color illustration of each main scene in your production. Picking colors directly from that image and applying them to lights can be a great starting point. Of course, if you do this, you'll need to test-render and make sure that final colors, including the colors from the shaders as well as the lights, come together to form colors that match the illustration.

Working in visual effects, you will often be integrating a rendered element into a live-action background plate. Picking colors directly from the plate should be your first choice in how to set colors for your lights. Fill or rim light from the sky can be given a color sampled from the sky in the background plate; bounce lights from the ground can be given a color sampled from the ground in the background plate. If some elements such as the sun are not visible in the plate, you may need to make a warmer color for your sunlight based on the color temperature tables above.

Understanding RGB Color

RGB color is a very limited representation of the actual spectrum of colors that can exist in real light. Instead of being able to emit colors of all wavelengths, color televisions and computer monitors use light-emitting phosphors of only three colors: red, green, and blue. Your monitor represents color by varying the intensity of light in these three areas of the spectrum. No light of wavelengths between the colors of the monitor's red, green, and blue phosphors is emitted. As a result, the spectral distribution of light from a monitor could be plotted as shown in Figure 8.20. Instead of a continuous spectrum, it consists of only the red, green, and blue wavelengths, with gaps in between them.

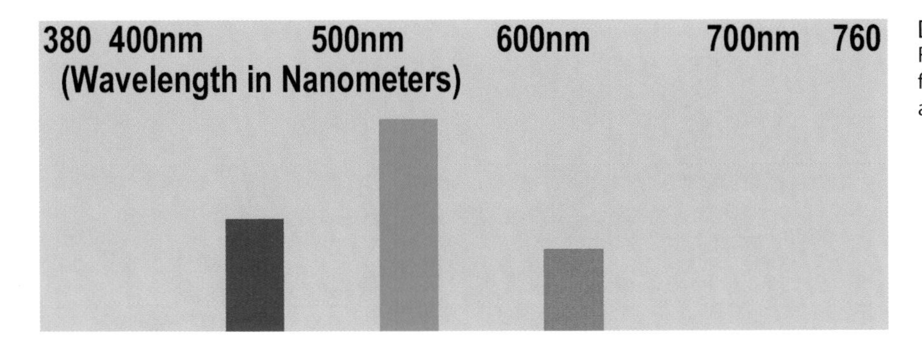

[Figure 8.20]
RGB color re-creates only a few frequencies of light, not a continuous spectrum.

It may seem surprising that such a limited representation is perceived as "full color." The reason that RGB color works convincingly is that people's eyes sample only the intensity of three overlapping, general areas of the spectrum, and perceive colors based on the relative intensity of light within each range of wavelengths. *Cones*—pigmented, light-sensitive cells in people's eyes—are responsible for detecting color. There are three kinds of cones: one type that is pigmented to filter light and respond most strongly to shorter wavelengths (in the area of the spectrum labeled "S" in Figure 8.21), one that best responds to medium wavelengths (labeled "M"), and one that responds to longer waves of light ("L"). Human perception of color is based on the relative strength of the responses from the three types of cones.

Because people sense only the relative intensities of three areas of the spectrum, RGB color's incomplete reproduction of the spectral distribution of light is adequate to represent most colors.

Much of the information that is contained in a color of light is invisible to the naked eye. There can even be cases where different light sources have very different color makeups, but appear identical to a viewer. Splitting the light with a prism would reveal that they consist of very different spectral energy distributions, but there would otherwise be no way to perceive the difference with the naked eye. In Figure 8.22, for example, you see that the plotted spectral distribution of light consists of blue and yellow light, with very little green in between. People still would see the light that is plotted as being green light. If this color were represented on an RGB monitor, the actual spectral distribution of light from the monitor would be more similar to what was shown in Figure 8.20, but the viewer would think he was looking at the same color green.

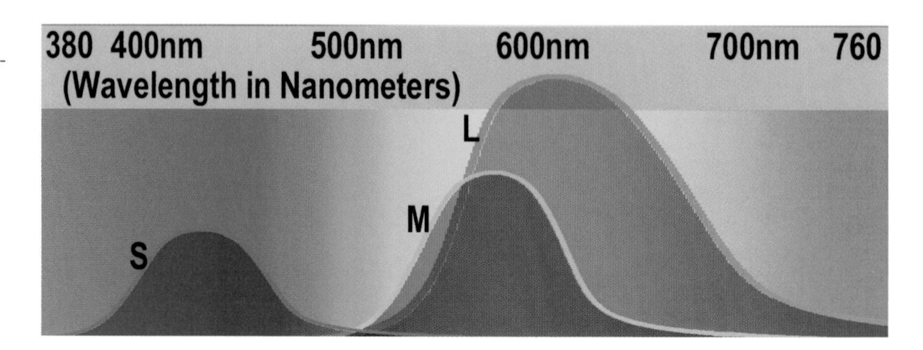

[Figure 8.21]
Humans compare the intensity of light in three areas of the visible spectrum in order to perceive color.

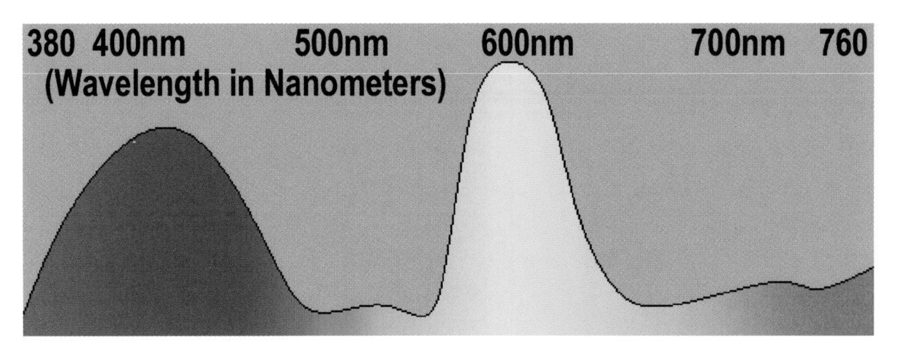

[Figure 8.22]
A complex mixture of wavelengths such as this mix of blue and yellow could be perceived as a pure green.

In music, you can hear the difference between a chord and a note played by itself. With colors, you are blind to the equivalent difference in frequencies. When two colors of light are mixed together, the resulting combination of wavelengths can look the same as a spectrally pure color of an intermediate wavelength. It is as if, when you played an "A" and a "C" at once on the piano keyboard, you could not tell that chord from a single "B" note being played. We don't say that "A and C makes B" in music, but we all have heard art teachers tell us that "red and yellow makes orange."

It might seem as though you're missing a lot of the information available in a color of light, but our simplified perception of wavelengths of light also has its advantages: it is what makes possible RGB color, and all other cases of "color mixing" to simulate intermediate colors with mixed paint, ink, or light.

Importance of Red, Green, and Blue

On an RGB monitor, the red, green, and blue components do not each contribute equally to the brightness of a pixel. Instead, in a pure white light, the green contributes about 55 percent of the brightness, red about 35 percent, and blue about 15 percent.

Many paint programs take the unequal importance of red, green, and blue into account in converting to grayscale, and convert red, green, and blue into different shades of gray. You can verify this in your own paint program by creating pure red, pure green, and pure blue in an RGB image, and then converting the image into monochrome—you'll see a much lighter shade of gray where you had painted green than where you painted blue.

You will also see signs that red, green, and blue are not treated equally in some 3D graphics programs. For example, in Maya, the default *contrast threshold*, which sets the level of contrast that will trigger additional anti-aliasing, has a red level of 0.4, a green level of 0.3, and a blue level of 0.6. This means that small differences in the blue channel are not considered important or visible enough to use a maximum level of anti-aliasing, but an edge that creates a small difference in the green value would be considered more important and get more anti-aliasing. In programs that don't include these values as defaults, you could optionally set them yourself to optimize your anti-aliasing for the colors that contribute most to the brightness of the image.

Digital Color

When rendering final images, professionals render animation as a series of uncompressed images, creating a numbered image file for each frame of an animated sequence. Common file formats include TIFF (.tif), TGA, and the proprietary formats supported by different 3D graphics software. Rendered images generally have at least three channels (red, green, and blue) and usually have a fourth channel when an alpha channel is rendered. Alpha channels store transparency information; Chapter 11, "Rendering Passes and Compositing," describes how useful alpha channels are in compositing.

The amount of accuracy and memory used per channel varies between the most common standard of 8 bits per channel, up to the most versatile alternative of 32-bit-per-channel High Dynamic Range Images (HDRI).

8-bit Color

With 8-bit color, your red, green, blue channels (and an alpha channel if you have one) can each have a range of 256 possible levels, sometimes expressed as a value from 0 to 255 for each channel.

Most 3D images are rendered in 8-bit color. In total, 256 values for each of your red, green, and blue channels gives you over 16 million possible colors, which is generally adequate for most projects.

Don't confuse the number of bits per channel with total bits per pixel. When each pixel has a red, green, blue, and alpha channel, there are four times as many bits per pixel as bits per channel. Graphics cards which use standard 8-bit color (8 bits per channel) are usually advertised as supporting 24-bit color or 32-bit color, which simply means 24 or 32 total bits per pixel, when you add together all the channels.

16-bit Color

16-bit color uses twice as much disk space as 8-bit color, but allows for thousands of possible values for each channel, instead of just 256.

Rendering 16 bits per channel allows for a greater range of adjustment to the colors and tones in an image during the compositing stage of a project. For example, if 3D elements had been rendered to match daylight background plates, but a change in the script required that they be used during sunset, these extreme color changes could be handled better if elements had been rendered at 16 bits per channel rather than the standard 8.

HDRI

High Dynamic Range Images (HDRI) use 32 bits (4 bytes) per channel to store a full floating-point value representing the red, green, and blue values of an image.

Rendering in HDRI takes four times as much disk space as rendering in 8-bit color, but it allows for the most creative control over your elements during compositing.

Switching from 8-bit to 16-bit increases only the *precision* of the data stored, giving you more gradations between 0 (black) and 1 (white). Switching to HDRI gives you more than precision—it increases *dynamic range*, the difference between the brightest and darkest tone that can exist in an image. High Dynamic Range Images store values that can go above 1 (brighter than pure white) or beneath 0 (darker than pure black.)

What good is HDRI? If a value is brighter than the brightest tone a monitor can display, why store it? When you render in 8-bit or 16-bit color, areas that are overexposed in your scene become *clipped*, or rounded down to a value of 1, because they cannot go beyond the highest value those file formats can store. As shown in Figure 8.23, a clipped area has no detail, because all of the pixel values would be 1, without any variation. You can often spot a clipped image by its histogram; the "cliff" on the right side of the histogram shows that tones have built up to a maximum value. If you reduce the brightness of the image after it rendered, the clipped area would become a flat untextured area, as shown on the right side of the figure.

[Figure 8.23]
An 8-bit image is clipped in the overexposed area (left) and the clipped areas lack detail when darkened in a paint or compositing program (right.)

On the other hand, if you render in HDRI, detail and texture are stored in every part of the image, including the overexposed areas, such as the table top in Figure 8.24, where values above 1 are stored at each pixel. In compositing, you could reduce the brightness of overexposed areas, and all of the original texture and detail would be revealed, as shown on the right side of the figure. Chapter 11 will cover other advantages of HDRI.

Switching from 8-bit to 16-bit or HDRI rendering does not greatly increase the amount of computation performed by your renderer, but it does increase the size of the files written out. In some cases, reading and writing larger files can slow down your network, so using HDRI could slow down rendering and compositing simply because of the increased amount of data that needs to be saved and loaded. However, you can easily justify the extra storage and data transfer time if HDRI allows you to do more with the images you rendered instead of needing to render again with different lighting.

[Figure 8.24]
When images are rendered in HDRI (left), even an overexposed image can be darkened to reveal additional detail and texture (right.)

Compact Data Formats

When you render, you will usually be writing out full RGB or RGBA files with 8, 16, or 32 bits per channel, as described above. However, you will sometimes want to covert your images into more compact data formats after rendering.

Monochrome Images

Rendering software will usually output red, green, and blue channels for each image, even if you are rendering a scene in black and white. In processing your images, you could convert the files to monochrome (one channel) images, and they will take up only one-third the size of the three channel files.

Sometimes color rendering is useful even in creating black-and-white images. You might give different colors to different lights in your scene, such as making your key light green and your fill light blue. This gives you more control over the brightness and contrast of each light before you convert to monochrome in a paint or compositing program.

Indexed Color

The least memory-intensive type of digital color is *indexed color,* which means that a limited number of colors are used in your image, and that all the colors used will be included in a color look-up table (CLUT). During the 1980s, indexed color was the only color mode that most personal computers supported, so even 3D graphics had to be rendered into indexed color.

Most paint programs allow you to convert graphics into indexed color for use in interactive gaming and .gif files on websites.

The number of bits used per pixel determines the colors in the CLUT. Table 8.4 shows the number of colors available for each number of bits per pixel.

[Table 8.4] Number of Colors Supported by Bits per Pixel

BITS PER PIXEL	NUMBER OF COLORS
1	2
2	4
3	8
4	16
5	32
6	64
7	128
8	256

The CLUT approach is generally not used above 8 bits per pixel. You could re-create the table above by computing 2^bits to derive the number of colors from the number of bits per pixel. Figure 8.25 shows a CLUT for an image reduced to 8 bits per pixel, or 256 colors.

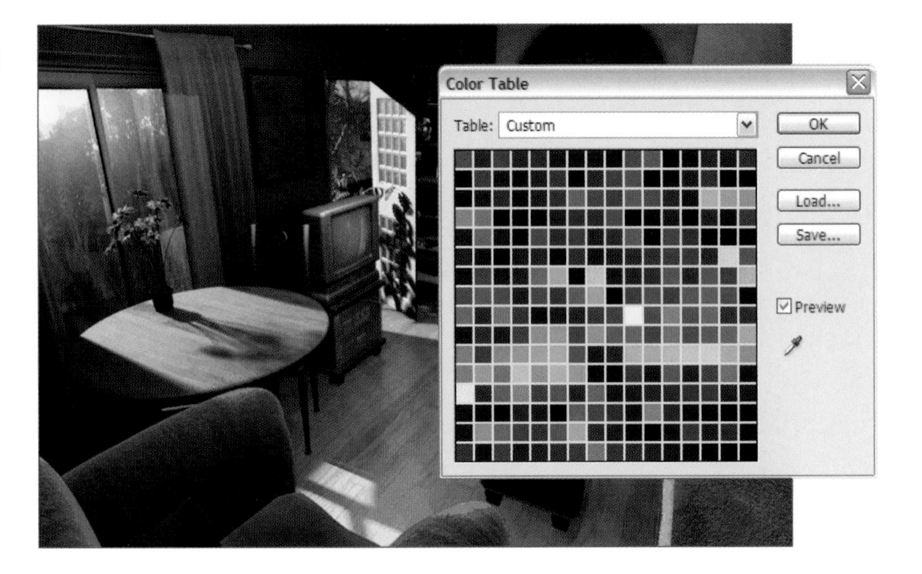

[Figure 8.25] A color look-up table (CLUT) shows the colors that can appear in an indexed color image.

Using indexed color .gif files on websites is useful for icons or diagrams where you want a small file, but you don't want to use any compression that could blur the image.

Compressed Images

After you've rendered your frames, often you'll need to compress them for purposes such as displaying them on the Web. JPEG (.jpg) is by far the most common compressed image format for Internet display. When you save your file as a JPEG, you get to choose between higher quality images that are stored as larger files, and lower quality images that are very compact but can be blurred or have compression artifacts.

Even if a compressed image is your final product, you should also archive your original uncompressed images in case you want to come back to a full-quality copy in the future to edit or print.

Exercises

Color is fun to explore—seize every opportunity to play with color and learn more about its impact on your work.

1. Load a scene you have previously created, and try rendering it with different colors of light. See if you can change the mood of the image to make it more cheerful, sad, or frightening; then make the scene look like it was set at night, or at sunrise. Show your recolored scenes to your friends, and discuss how they respond to the different versions.
2. In a paint program, load a piece of your own work and try removing the color. In many cases, people like some of their own renderings better in black and white, and with increased contrast. Also try tinting the image to different colors. Can you identify a clear color scheme in your renderings?
3. Try lighting a scene with light from two different sources. When a viewer cannot see the light source in the shot, can you make the type of light clear from the colors you use?

[CHAPTER NINE]

Shaders and Rendering Algorithms

This chapter follows your rendering software through the main stages of shading and rendering your scene, and suggests how to get the best quality and software performance along the way. The rendering process starts with *shading*—setting up how your surfaces will respond to light—and we will explore various kinds of shaders and shader adjustments. We will look inside anti-aliasing functions at how your scene is sampled and filtered to produce smooth, high-quality renderings. This chapter will also explore different rendering algorithms, the basic approaches that software uses to produce images, such as raytracing, Reyes algorithms, Z-buffer and scanline rendering, and GPU-acceleration.

Shading Surfaces

Shaders are definitions of how 3D objects respond to light, describing their surface appearance or how they will be rendered. *Shading* is the process of designing, assigning, and adjusting shaders to develop unique looks for the objects in a 3D scene. Figure 9.1 shows some of the variety that can be achieved by assigning different shaders to an object.

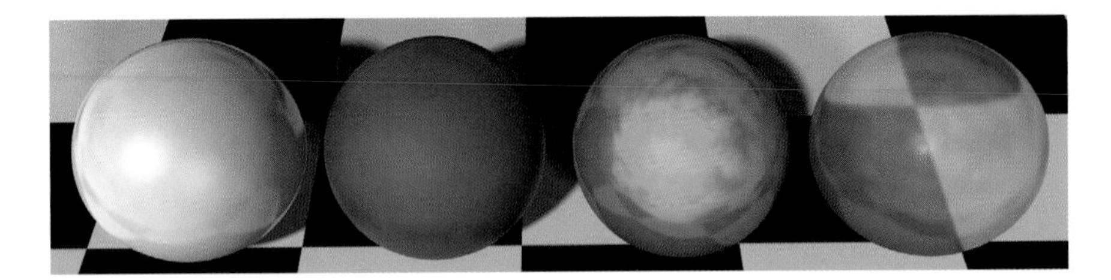

[Figure 9.1]
Four spheres with different shaders respond differently to light. These examples show some of the things that you can do by adjusting attributes discussed in this chapter.

Some 3D programs use the word *material* in reference to their built-in selection of shaders, and use the word *shader* only in reference to the optional plug-ins available for a renderer. While materials and shaders may be listed separately in your software's interface, all definitions of surface appearances provided to the renderer are really shaders.

Diffuse, Glossy, and Specular Reflection

The three most common ways that light reflects off a surface are shown in Figure 9.2. *Diffuse reflection* (left) is when light is scattered uniformly in all directions. *Glossy reflection* (center) will preserve the directionality of light rays, but still cause some scattering or softening. *Specular reflection* (right) perfectly preserves the sharpness of the light and reflects all rays without scattering.

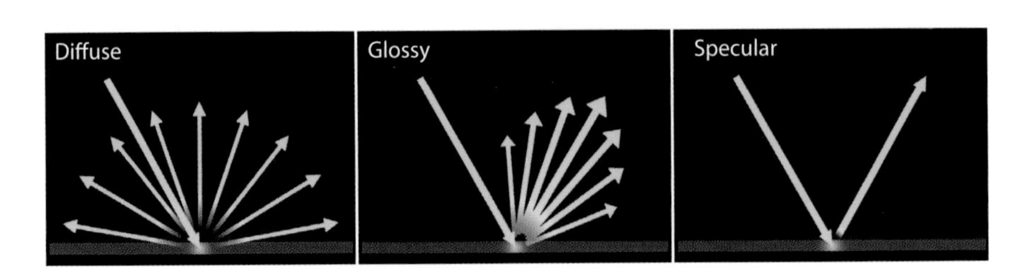

[Figure 9.2]
Light reflects in a diffuse, glossy, or specular manner.

Figure 9.3 shows how diffuse, glossy, and specular reflection appear on surfaces. Diffuse reflection (left) gives materials a matte appearance, so that they don't show any reflections or highlights. Glossy reflections (center) are soft, and diverging rays naturally make reflections appear softer with distance, as you can see in the mug's reflection on the ground. Specular reflections (right) are crisp and mirror-like.

[Figure 9.3]
A scene rendered with entirely diffuse (left), glossy (middle), and specular (right) reflections

Most surfaces show some combination of diffuse, glossy, and specular light transmission. Real surfaces do not reflect light in a perfectly specular way. Even a mirror shows some glossy or diffuse light reflection. Likewise, materials in real life are not completely diffuse.

If you are looking at a real material and you can't spot any reflections or highlights on it, move your head back and forth. As your point of view shifts sideways, you can see highlights and reflections change and travel over the surface, visually separating them from the diffusely reflected light. Moving your head from side to side will readily show you how glossy the pages of this book are. Sometimes you will find a material such as a brown paper bag, and think that it is mainly diffuse, but when you look at it in a well-lit room and shift your head side to side, you can see that there are actually broad highlights on it.

Diffuse, Glossy, and Specular Reflection in Shaders

Many common shader parameters fall into a category of simulating diffuse, glossy, or specular reflection.

Your main surface color controls diffuse shading. When we ask "what color is that?" we mean the color of the diffuse reflection, not the highlights, reflections, or other components of the shading.

Many shaders also have a parameter called *diffuse*, which is simply a multiplier for the surface color. In this case, cutting in half the value of the diffuse setting would reduce your diffuse brightness just the same as cutting in half the brightness of the surface color.

Specular highlights are intended to look like a specular reflection of a light source; however, it may surprise you to hear that most specular highlights are actually a glossy reflection, not a specular one. If a light is a point source, coming from an infinitely small point in space, then a perfectly specular reflection of an infinitely small point of light would be an infinitely small dot, probably much smaller than a pixel. To correct for this, most shaders allow you to adjust the highlight size. While a highlight size could be considered a realistic simulation of the roughness of a surface, most often it is used as a cheat, to hide the fact that your light sources are infinitely small. Once a highlight size is added, the specular highlight actually spreads out to become a glossy reflection of the light source.

Standard raytraced reflections are perfectly specular, which means that they are perfectly focused. *Glossiness*, also called *reflection blur* or *soft reflections*, enables you to make raytraced reflections that blur with distance. See the Raytracing section, later in this chapter, for more on rendering glossy reflections.

Most global illumination techniques (which were described in Chapter 4) can be considered diffuse-to-diffuse light transfer, meaning that the light diffusely reflecting off of one object adds to the diffuse illumination of another. Caustics are an exception—they can be described as specular-to-diffuse light transfer. When light reflects off a surface in a specular or glossy way, caustics carry that illumination into the diffuse shading of other objects.

The Microfacet Model

A *microfacet model* is a way of understanding what makes real materials diffuse, glossy, or specular. A microfacet model simulates the roughness or jaggedness of surfaces on a microscopic level. The tiny details or facets on a rough surface are what scatter the light in different directions to produce a glossy or diffuse light transmission. Several popular shaders, including *cook-torrance*, are programmed based on a microfacet model of surfaces.

Figure 9.4 shows the difference that microscopic roughness can make. On a rough surface (left), parallel rays of light enter and are each reflected to different angles, producing diffuse reflection. On a smoother surface (middle) the rays are scattered less, and retain some of their directionality, producing a glossy reflection. A perfectly smooth surface (right) allows all of the rays to reflect in parallel, producing a perfectly specular reflection.

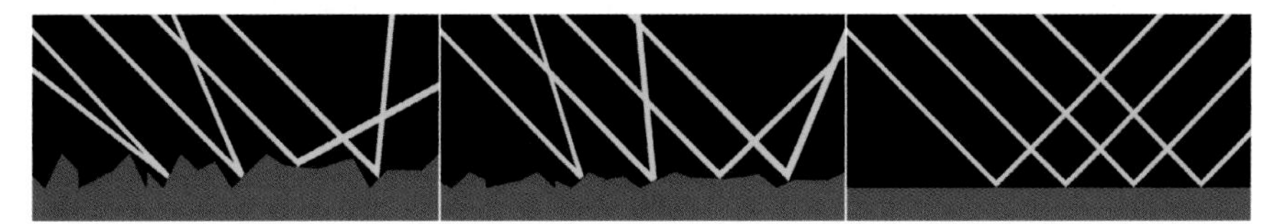

[Figure 9.4]
A microfacet model of diffuse, glossy, and specular reflection

The property of a surface that causes a specular highlight to spread out is called *roughness*. Roughness does not always appear as big, visible bumps. Microscopic roughness in a surface's structure can make a surface appear smooth, while still diffusing reflected light. For example, the surface of a rubber pencil eraser diffuses light due to a microscopic roughness to its structure, even though it looks and feels smooth. In this sense, any surface with a matte finish instead of a glossy finish can be said to be rough.

Specular Highlights

A common misconception is that specular highlights are centered in the brightest point of the diffuse shading. In reality, the positioning of the specular highlights is derived separately from the diffuse shading. The diffuse shading is based on the position of a surface and its angle relative to the light. Specular shading, on the other hand, can be calculated only from a specific camera angle, and is based on the angle between the light, the surface, and the camera. Because of this, specular highlights are an example of *view-dependent shading*.

View-dependent shading is any effect that varies depending on the camera angle from which it was rendered. Specularity, reflections, and refraction are all examples of *view-dependent shading;* they seem to shift across a surface when you view it from different angles. Contrast this with *non-view-dependent shading*, such as diffuse shading and cast shadows, which can be computed without regard for the camera angle.

Realistic Specularity

Big, bright, airbrushed-looking specular highlights are one of the most conspicuous clichés of 3D graphics. Specular highlights appear fake in many renderings because they are often misused or poorly adjusted. However, almost all surfaces in the real world exhibit some degree of specularity, and using it appropriately can add realism to your renderings.

You can improve the quality of your shading if you give your specular highlights an appropriate size, color, shape, and position. Your best bet when adjusting your specular highlights is to find a real-world example of the material you are trying to simulate, and study how it responds to light. By studying reference images or a sample of a real material, you can adjust your specular highlights based on real-world observations, instead of preconceived notions or software presets.

[Figure 9.5] The size of a highlight should be adjusted until it visually matches the size and distance of the light source.

Highlight Size

In real life, the size of a highlight depends on two things: the light source and the surface. A bigger light source, or a light source positioned closer to the surface being lit, will produce a bigger highlight. The type of surface also influences the size of a highlight. Materials with very smooth, hard surfaces, such as metals and glass, have smaller, tighter highlights. Rougher surfaces such as paper and wood have broader (although less intense) highlights.

In many 3D programs, highlight size is adjustable only on shaders, and is not a property of lights. If this is the case, then make sure each highlight really looks like a reflection of the light source that motivates it. If the light source is small or far away, then the highlight should be small, as shown on the top of Figure 9.5. If you are simulating a large light source and it is close to the object, then you would need to increase the highlight size on the shader until you had a very large specular highlight, as shown on the bottom of Figure 9.5.

Specular Color

In most cases, your shader's specular color should be left as a shade of gray. A white or gray specular color means that the color added for specular shading will be based on the color of the light source, which is usually the most natural source of color for a specular highlight.

Colored specularity is necessary only for metallic surfaces. In this case, give the specular color a tint similar to the color of the metal itself. Figure 9.6 is a photograph of a brass fixture. Notice how the highlights and the reflections are all tinted to the brass color. Often metals have a very dark diffuse color, so that they can receive most of their color and shading from the colored specularity.

[Figure 9.6]
Only a metallic reflection uses colored specularity and tints reflections.

The Fresnel Effect

The French physicist Augustin-Jean Fresnel (1788-1827) advanced the wave theory of light through a study of how light was transmitted and propagated by different objects. One of his observations is now known in computer graphics as the *Fresnel effect*—the observation that the amount of light you see reflected from a surface depends on the viewing angle.

For example, note in Figure 9.7 how the side window is full of reflections, so much that you can't see through it. The windshield, on the other hand, does not appear reflective, and is more transparent. Of course, both pieces of glass are equally reflective materials. It is the angle from which you view the glass that changes how much reflection you see.

[Figure 9.7]
The Fresnel effect makes the side window look more reflective than the front in this photograph.

Figure 9.8 shows another common occurrence of the Fresnel effect. If you look straight down at a pool of water, you won't see very much reflected light on the surface of the pool. From the high angle, without seeing reflections, you can see down through the surface to the bottom of the pool. At a glancing angle (looking with your eye level with the water, from the edge of the water surface), you will see much more specularity and reflections on the water surface, and might not be able to see what's under the water at all.

You wouldn't see your reflection in a painted wall if you were looking at it straight on. However, at a glancing angle, as shown in Figure 9.9, you can clearly see reflections of the window and light bulb at the end of the hallway. Many, if not most, surfaces become somewhat reflective when viewed from the correct angle. Even pavement on a street can appear reflective if you are viewing it from a low enough angle.

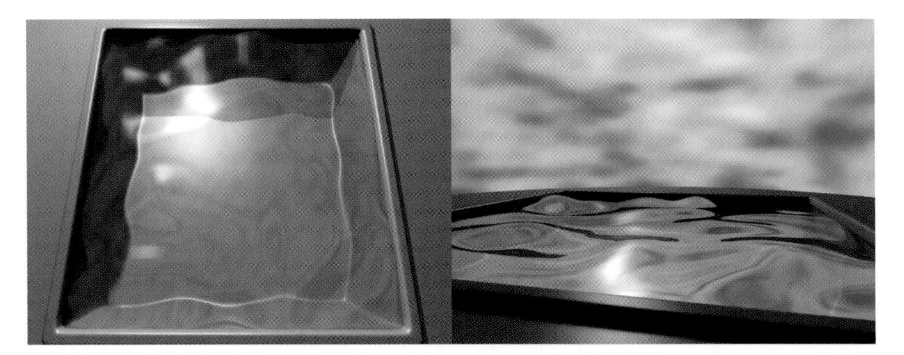

[Figure 9.8]
The Fresnel effect increases reflection and specularity on surfaces viewed at a glancing angle (right).

[Figure 9.9]
Even surfaces that don't look reflective when viewed head-on show reflections at a glancing angle.

A shader that allows you to vary the specularity and other parameters according to the viewing angle of the surface is often called a *Fresnel shader*. A Fresnel shader will let you specify a specular color to be seen on parts of a surface directly facing the camera, and another specular color to be seen on parts of a surface that are perpendicular to the camera. Besides specular color increasing at the edge of an object, the specular highlight size and reflectivity also increase.

Another way the Fresnel effect can be created is by linking the surface angle (or *facing ratio*) of an object to the shader attribute that needs to change, such as the specular brightness, as shown in Figure 9.10.

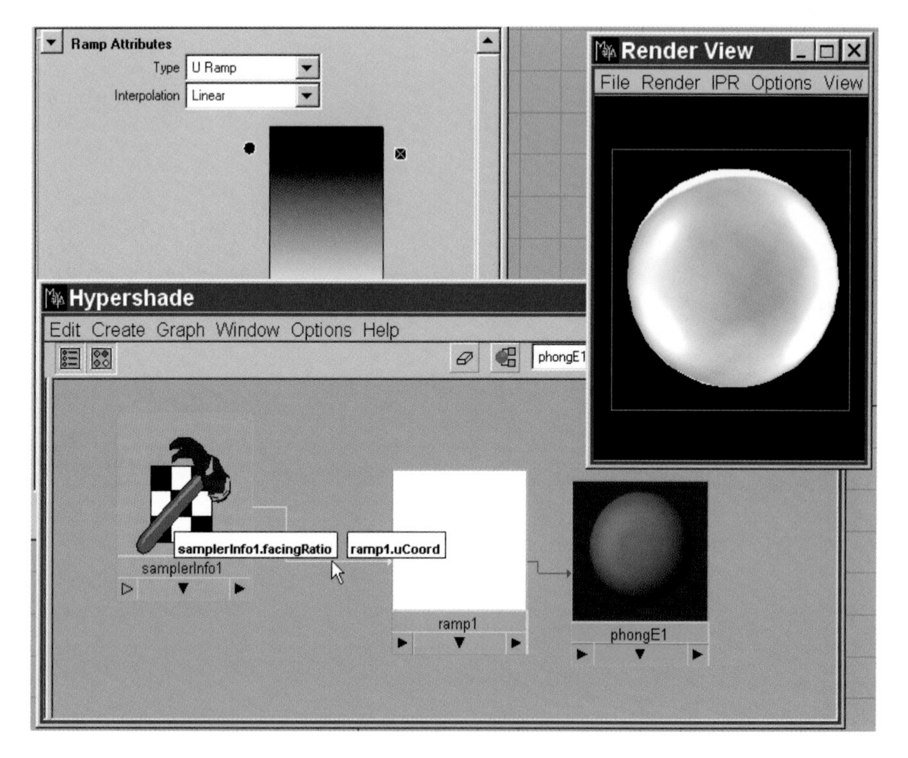

[Figure 9.10] In Maya's Hypershade window, the Facing Ratio attribute of a surface is linked through a ramp into the surface's specularity. The intermediate ramp allows the center-to-edge specularity to be edited as a gradient.

To avoid confusion, note that something else common in film production is also named after Augustin-Jean Fresnel. He invented the Fresnel lens, designed to project beams of light from lighthouses. Still popular today, Fresnel lenses are built into the front of film and television lighting equipment, and filmmakers call this type of focusable lighting instrument a *Fresnel*.

Anisotropic Highlights

The microscopic roughness that is responsible for diffusing light is not always randomly distributed, and doesn't always scatter all light randomly in all directions. Some surfaces have a structure of small grooves or scratches running in a particular direction, instead of random bumpiness. Brushed steel, human hair, phonograph records, DVDs, compact discs, and some wooden objects are examples of surfaces with grooves that affect their shading. Reflections and highlights are stretched-out in a direction perpendicular to the grooves in the surface, for a result called *anisotropic shading*. Surfaces that spread reflected light evenly in all directions are called *isotropic*—you can see the difference in Figure 9.11.

[Figure 9.11] Isotropic shading (left) spreads specular highlights uniformly in all directions, whereas anisotropic shading (right) causes specular highlights to elongate.

On a microfacet level, you can picture rays that run across the grooves getting scattered widely, as shown running across Figure 9.12. However, rays that run along the grooves (vertical in Figure 9.12) will be reflected in parallel without scattering. This broadens the highlights running *across* the grooves, while leaving highlights smaller and more focused where they run *along* the grooves.

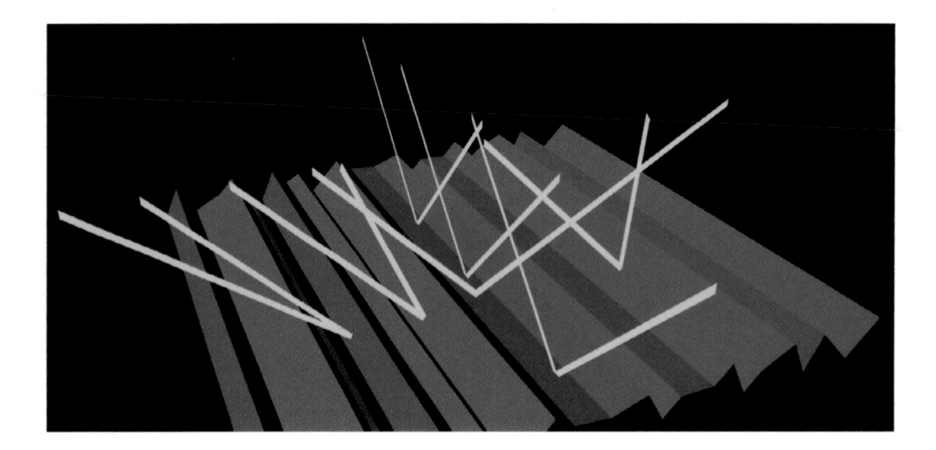

[Figure 9.12] The microfacet structure on an anisotropic surface shows rays scattering only while running across the grain of the surface.

BRDF and BSSRDF

A real surface's *bidirectional reflectance distribution function (BRDF)* describes how it reflects or absorbs light from different angles. Most common shaders, such as Lambert, Phong, and Blinn, provide a simple, generalized BRDF. Some renderers also come with a shader called BRDF, which is designed to mimic real responses to light based on data collected from real-world measurements.

In real life, every material has a unique BRDF that represents how it will reflect or absorb light when illuminated or viewed from different angles. A BRDF can be measured from specific, real-world materials. Researchers have constructed special rigs that can photograph a material sample, or a person's face, from a variety of camera angles, with light hitting it from different angles. From this, they can digitize a *light reflectance field* to be used by a BRDF shader, matching how a real material responds to light from all directions and viewing angles.

BRDF is based on the assumption that light reflects off a surface at the same point where it hits. As discussed in Chapter 5, "Lighting Creatures, Characters, and Animation," translucent materials rendered with subsurface scattering are brightened by light that hit the opposite side or another point on the object, and have been transmitted through it. When you add scattering to a BRDF, you get a *bidirectional surface scattering reflectance distribution function (BSSRDF)*. This is quite a mouthful, but all it means is a shader that can be based on measured data about realistic light transmission, and also includes support for realistic translucency.

Anti-Aliasing

Anti-aliasing is a critical component of high-quality rendering. Without anti-aliasing, jaggy or stair-stepped artifacts appear along diagonal edges, and textures can appear to crawl or jitter during animation. Anti-aliasing makes rendered images look smooth, natural, and more similar to a photograph.

The two main components of anti-aliasing are *over-sampling* and *filtering*.

Over-Sampling

Over-sampling means collecting more data than you need. When a renderer over-samples a scene, it computes more points or rays than the number of pixels in the final image.

Figure 9.13 shows an area of 8 pixels by 8 pixels, in which a polygon needs to be displayed. To render the image without over-sampling, only one sample (shown as a yellow dot in the left side of the figure) is taken per pixel. If the sample hits the polygon, the corresponding pixel takes on the sampled color from the polygon. If the sample hits the background, then the pixel gets the background color. The right side of the figure shows the results. Without over-sampling, the polygon is represented in a blocky, stair-stepped manner.

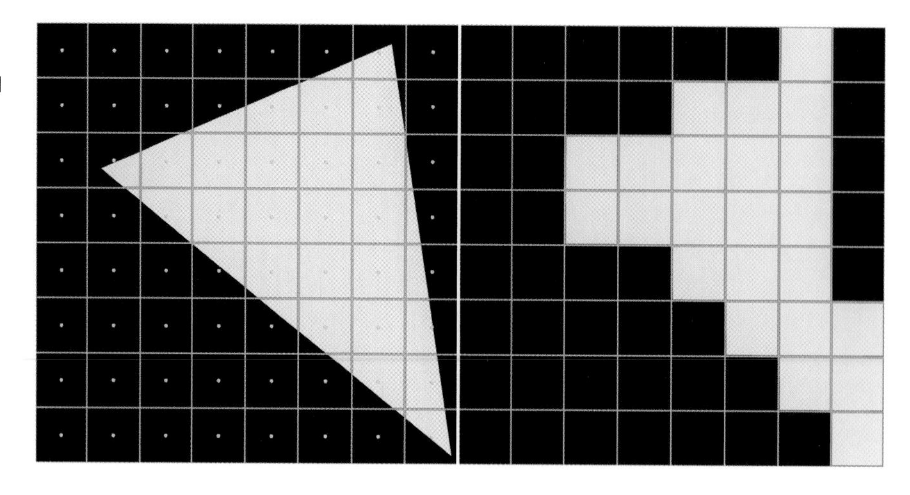

[Figure 9.13]
A single sample per pixel (left) produces stair-stepped output (right).

Figure 9.14 shows a small amount of over-sampling, using four samples per pixel. Where the edge of the polygon passes through a pixel, some of the samples hit it, and others miss. The results are averaged together for each pixel, producing intermediate shades of gray. On the right side of Figure 9.14 you can see the output shaded with an average of four samples per pixel.

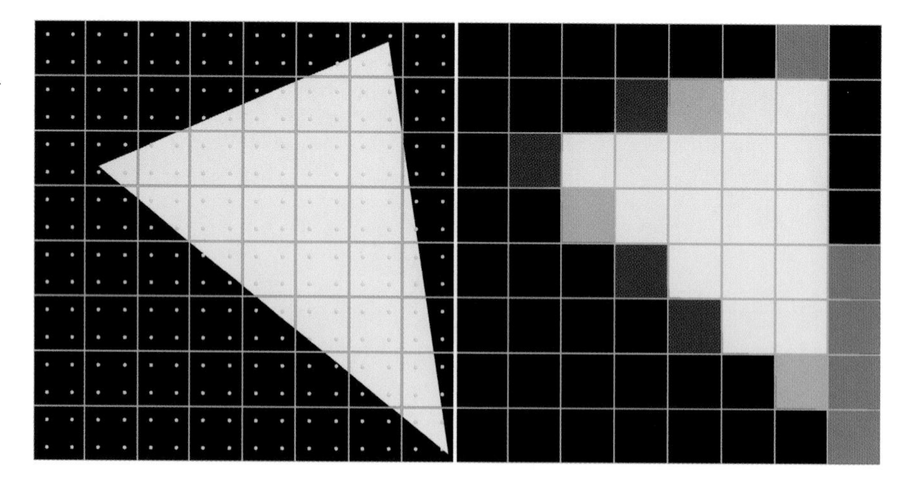

[Figure 9.14]
Four samples per pixel (left) produce more accurate anti-aliased output (right).

Anti-aliasing through over-sampling does not blur your image. It actually uses shading to represent a subpixel level of detail, adding detail to your image. Using more over-sampling will never make your image softer—it will only make it more accurate. The only downside to over-sampling is that more samples take longer to compute and slow down your rendering.

Adaptive Over-Sampling

Adaptive over-sampling varies the number of samples taken in different parts of the image. The renderer would take more samples where there are significant edges that need anti-aliasing, and fewer samples in smooth areas where over-sampling is unlikely to make much of a difference. With adaptive anti-aliasing, instead of setting one number for a consistent amount of over-sampling, you choose both a minimum and a maximum level.

The renderer would begin by taking the minimum number of samples, shown as large red dots in Figure 9.15. The renderer then needs to determine where additional samples are needed. A common way to do this is by measuring contrast between the samples. The renderer compares the colors of each sample with its neighbors to see how different their color values are. Where neighboring samples differ in color by more than a *contrast threshold* that you set, more samples need to be taken. The yellow dots show the additional samples that are taken in high-contrast areas. The process continues until the level of contrast between new samples is less than the contrast threshold, or the maximum amount of over-sampling has been achieved.

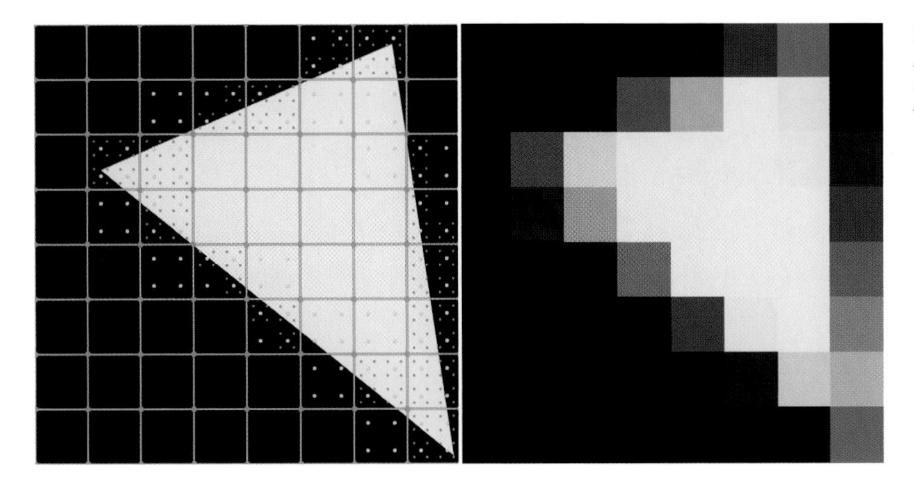

[Figure 9.15] Adaptive over-sampling uses extra samples only where they are needed.

Notice that only the minimum samples (red) are placed uniformly over the image. The next level of samples (yellow) appears only where there was contrast between the initial samples. The samples taken at the maximum level (green) appear only where contrast existed between previous samples. All of these samples will be averaged together to compute a color for each pixel. As a result, the edge of the polygon has been thoroughly sampled, but extra time hasn't been wasted taking too many samples of empty space.

This example shows over-sampling based on screen space, taking extra samples per pixel. In many programs, you can specify that a particular surface should be over-sampled more than the rest of the scene, so that over-sampling is increased where it encounters a particular shader, texture, or object.

Adjusting the Contrast Threshold

When you lower your contrast threshold, you tend to get more anti-aliasing. As you raise the contrast threshold, more subtle color changes are less likely to trigger additional over-sampling, so you tend to get less anti-aliasing.

Most renderers let you set the contrast threshold as a set of red, green, and blue values. For maximum efficiency, you have to remember that red, green, and blue are not equally important. In an RGB image, the brightness is not derived equally from the three color channels. Instead, a white image will get about 59 percent of its brightness from the green, 30 percent from the red, and the remaining 11 percent from the blue. As a result, a small change in your green channel will be much more noticeable than a numerically equivalent change in your blue channel.

Instead of setting the red, green, and blue of the contrast threshold to the same number, you can choose values that take the importance of the different color channels into account, such as a contrast threshold of 0.2 red, 0.15 green, and 0.3 blue.

If you are able to set a contrast threshold for differences in the alpha channel as well, this should be the lowest number, such as half the green value.

Under-Sampling

Under-sampling means sampling fewer points or rays than the number of pixels being rendered. This can cause blurry images or lower image quality.

However, under-sampling is often used in conjunction with adaptive over-sampling. For example, in Mental Ray, where negative numbers refer to under-sampling, the minimum number of samples is often set to –2, with the maximum at 0 or 1, in order to render quick tests or previews. This way the renderer will begin sampling the image with an initial under-sampling pass, but then in areas of high contrast it will take more samples, heading into an area of over-sampling where needed.

There is a danger that the initial under-sampling could entirely miss thin lines, causing gaps within the animation. Even when used as an adaptive minimum, under-sampling is safe only for tests, not final production work.

Filtering

Filtering is the process of constructing the final image out of your subpixel samples. Most programs offer a choice of different filtering types, which are ways to reconstruct your image, most of them weighted to rely most on samples within the pixel, but also factoring in local samples from adjacent pixels.

Using filtering takes relatively little extra rendering time, compared to over-sampling. Filtering lets you get the smoothest possible image from a limited number of samples.

When used in small amounts, a little filtering can smooth out jagged edges and help create a more natural image. However, on a subpixel level, filtering is very similar to blurring an image with a Photoshop filter. As a result, too much filtering can make your image blurry. Any time you activate or increase the level of filtering, test-render at least a small portion of your image to make sure you haven't turned it up too high and softened the image too much.

Rendering at Higher Resolutions

An alternative way to achieve good anti-aliasing is to render at a higher resolution than you will need for your final product. For example, if your final image was going to be 720 pixels wide, you might render at 1440 pixels. Using an even multiple such as 200 percent or 400 percent of your final image size can lead to smoother results. When you are finished rendering and compositing your shot, the last step in your composite can be to scale down the image to your final size. Some of that render speed that you lose in rendering at higher resolutions can be regained by using lower quality anti-aliasing.

Rendering at a higher resolution and then scaling down is a manual way to make your own over-sampling. Of course, if you render the entire image at four times the resolution, the over-sampling you create will not be adaptive, but the quality can be just as high. If you also wanted to create some filtering, you could blur the high-resolution image a bit before scaling down.

If you worked this way, your image files will be much bigger, using up more network bandwidth, I/O time, and storage space. However, it will allow you to work at a higher resolution during compositing and retouching, and scale down only after image processing is completed. This provides you with potentially higher quality in the compositing process, if operations such as rotations or matte extraction can be done at high resolution before the image is scaled down.

Raytracing

Raytracing is an optional part of the rendering process that simulates the natural reflection, refraction, and shadowing of light by 3D surfaces.

The process of raytracing is backwards in comparison to real life. In real life, light originates at a light source, bounces around the scene, and eventually reaches the camera. In raytracing, rays begin at the camera and are fired from the camera out into the scene.

To begin a raytracing process, the renderer divides the camera's field of view into an array of pixels, based on the resolution of the image being rendered. For each pixel, a ray is projected from the camera, sampling one point from any objects that it hits, as shown in Figure 9.16. With anti-aliasing, more than one point may be sampled per pixel, further multiplying the amount of work your raytracer needs to do.

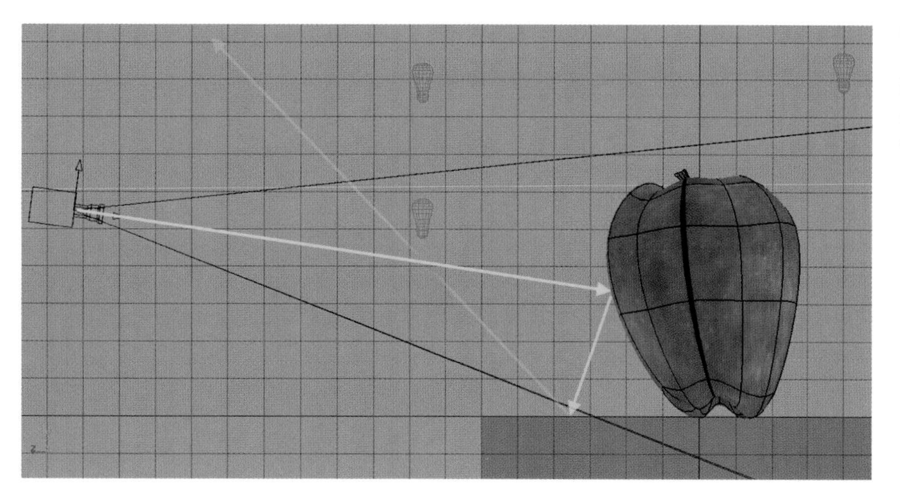

[Figure 9.16]
In raytracing, a ray (shown in yellow) starts at the camera, then bounces off visible objects.

When the ray hits an object, the object is checked to see if it is reflective or refractive, or may be receiving shadows, which need to be computed by sampling other rays. If the object were reflective, for example, then after computing the diffuse and specular shading of the point on the surface, an additional ray would be traced bouncing off the object into 3D space, checking if any other object's reflection would appear at the point being rendered.

If another reflective object was encountered, then another ray would be cast from that object, further extending the amount of rendering work done for that pixel.

Raytracing Acceleration Structures

Raytracing software spends a great deal of time searching through space to

- Find out whether a ray would hit any model between a light and a point on a surface that might receive a raytraced shadow
- Find out which object will appear in a particular pixel of a reflection
- Find out what objects a ray will hit after refracting through glass

All of this searching must be done for each bounce of each ray, for every pixel in your scene.

To quickly determine which objects are present in a particular area of 3D space, a raytracer needs to sort all of the geometry in the scene into lists of polygons or other basic components, based on their location. These lists are called *raytracing acceleration structures*. They take time to compute and they use up a lot of your computer's memory, but without them raytracing would take much longer than it already does.

A renderer begins creating raytracing acceleration structures by tessellating all of the surfaces in the scene into polygons. Any NURBS or subdivision surfaces are divided into polygons, and any displacement mapping is divided into more polygons. All of these polygons are then sorted into lists. These lists of polygons are sorted into smaller lists, by subdividing the space they occupy. The process continues until all of the lists are reasonably short, or until a limit to the depth of sorting is reached.

Adjusting your raytracing *recursion depth* or *oct tree depth* is a trade-off between memory use and rendering speed. If you have enough free RAM during your rendering process, and you want to potentially speed up the ray-tracing a little bit, they can be increased. If your raytracing is using up all of your computer's memory, so that it is crashing or swapping data out from the hard disk, then turning them down could help save some memory and avoid swapping. However, turning the recursion depth down too low if you weren't out of memory could lead to slower render times.

Raytraced Reflections

Raytraced reflections serve a very similar role to specular shading. Raytraced reflections are specular reflections of other objects in the scene, while specular shading is a specular reflection of a light source.

Often a raytraced reflection of something bright makes a more realistic highlight than a specular highlight from a light, because you can better control the shape of a raytraced reflection. Figure 9.17 shows a comparison of an apple with only a specular highlight and an apple with a raytraced reflection of a window. To add a reflection, just build a simple model in the shape you want, and position it near a light source. The model built to appear in the reflection could be just one polygon, and could be given any texture map. As long as it is bright enough, and the rendered surface is reflective, your custom shape will show up in your rendering.

[Figure 9.17]
An object can show reflected light with a specular highlight (left), a raytraced reflection (middle), or both (right).

Integrating Reflections and Specular Highlights

Often you'll want both specular highlights and raytraced reflections on a surface. The key is to make sure that reflections and highlights work together, so that they look like part of the same reflection.

If you use colored reflectivity to simulate a metallic surface, usually the color of the reflection should be the same as the specular color.

If you look at the scene reflected in a surface, you should see a complete scene in the reflection, with highlights visible only in the places where a light source would be reflected.

The Surrounding Environment

If a reflective object were surrounded by empty black space, no reflection would appear, and the object would simply get darker the more reflective you made it. When you are using raytraced reflections, you must give reflective objects something to reflect.

A common beginner's mistake with raytraced reflections is failing to build a complete scene that goes all the way around your model. Some 3D artists are in the habit of building rooms with only three walls, leaving the fourth side open so that the camera can look through the opening. A reflective object in such a three-walled room would have a black square missing from its reflection. If the camera needs to look through the fourth wall, you can set it to be invisible to *primary rays* or *primary visibility*, but leave it visible in reflections.

Glossy Reflections

Standard raytraced reflections produce perfectly specular reflections of other objects. Often the reflections can appear unrealistically crisp.

Glossiness, also called *reflection blur* or *reflection softness*, is an option in most raytracers that scatters or randomizes reflected rays to produce a naturally blurred reflection. When glossiness is applied, rays are randomized to shoot in slightly different directions in rendering a reflection. Initially this can cause some dithering or noise, from all of the randomly scattered reflection rays. To correct this, you also need to raise the number of rays that are cast in the reflection. Calculating more rays can greatly increase rendering time, but will produce a smoother, more realistic reflection.

Reflection Limits

In a scene where there any many reflective or refractive surfaces, there is a risk that a raytracer could get caught in an infinite loop, forever tracing a ray from one surface to another surface. Figure 9.18 shows a situation where mirrors on each wall of a room reflect one another. In order to render the mirror on the right, the raytracer must include the reflection of the left mirror, which in turn requires a calculation of the left mirror's reflection of the right mirror, which again reflects the left mirror, and so on. As the rays of light seem to bounce infinitely between mirrors, the scene could take an infinite amount of time to raytrace.

[Figure 9.18] Mirrors facing each other could create an infinite loop in raytracing.

To prevent the renderer from endlessly looping, the number of raytracing steps is strictly limited. Because it can have such a huge impact on your rendering time, many programs limit the number of reflections twice. First, it is limited globally in your rendering settings, where you set a maximum number of reflections and total raytracing steps. Second, it is also limited per shader, where a reflective shader will have a *reflection limit* (also called a *recursion depth* or *trace depth*) set as a raytracing option.

If you don't need reflections of reflections, setting the number of reflections to 1 either globally or in the shader will speed up your rendering time. If you need to see light interreflect several times between surfaces, use a higher number on both the shaders and your global settings, but be prepared to wait.

Shadows

Chapter 3, "Shadows and Occlusion," described how raytraced shadows differ from *shadow-mapped* (also called *depth-map*) shadows. Here is a summary of the main differences:

- Shadow-mapped shadows generally render more quickly and use less memory than raytraced shadows.
- Raytraced shadows can remain crisp and accurate at any resolution rendering, while shadow maps have a limited resolution.
- Transparent and transparency-mapped objects can cast transparent shadows with raytracing. Most implementations of shadow maps ignore the level of transparency in an object.
- When raytraced shadows are made soft, they become diffused with distance in a very realistic way—but at a substantial cost in rendering time. Soft shadow maps are filtered uniformly and appear less realistic.

Flip back to Chapter 3 if you want to read more about shadows.

Depth Map Shadows and Raytracing

Depth map shadows are completely compatible with raytracing. You can continue to use depth map shadows when you switch over to using raytracing, and they can be seen in raytraced reflections and through refractive surfaces, without any special adjustments.

If a scene is already using raytracing for other effects such as reflections or refraction, then the extra memory taken up by raytracing has already been used, and using raytraced shadows could be just as efficient a solution as depth maps. However, if your scene includes elements such as hair, fur, or dense foliage, you may want to exclude those from any raytracing, and use depth mapped shadows for the shadows of those elements.

Trace Depth and Number of Shadows

Raytraced shadows do not necessarily appear in reflections or through refractive surfaces, unless the light's *ray depth limit* (also called *trace depth* or number of shadows) is high enough. A level of 1 will make the shadow appear when seen directly, but not in reflections. A level of 2 will make the shadow also appear indirectly in reflections or refractions. Going higher would make the shadow visible even through multiple layers of refractive glass or in a reflection of a reflection, as long as you add a level for each layer of glass.

Transparency and Refraction

When making an object transparent, you have the same concern as with raytraced reflections: The object's surroundings will affect the shading. A transparent surface left in limbo in an all-black environment will only appear darker as it becomes more transparent. Make sure that there is another object or background behind the transparent object that you will be able to see once the object becomes transparent.

Refraction is a raytracing effect that adds a lens-like distortion to the image seen through a transparent surface. Just like an optical lens, when using refraction your 3D models will focus rays differently depending on their shape and proportions. The models in Figure 9.19 focus rays differently due to their different shapes. How concave or convex a model is, and whether you look through a single surface or both a front and back surface, will produce completely different refractions.

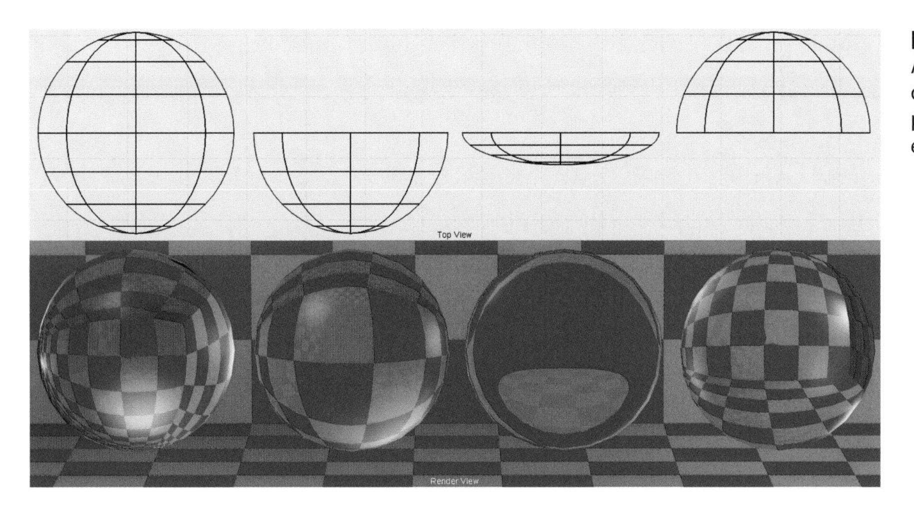

[Figure 9.19]
All using an IOR of 1.44, differently shaped models produce different refraction effects.

Index of Refraction

Besides the shape of the model, the other factor governing refraction is a number called the *index of refraction (IOR)*. Figure 9.20 shows an object rendered with several different index of refraction values. A value of 1 gives you no refraction, allowing rays to pass straight through the object. As you set values further above or below 1, the amount of refraction increases. For a convex surface, such as a sphere, values above 1 will make it enlarge the refracted image, like a magnifying glass, while values below 1 will make the refracted image shrink.

[Figure 9.20]
From left to right, vases are rendered with an index of refraction of 1.0 (no refraction), 1.04, 1.15, and 1.44 (glass). There is no difference in the transparency of the vases—the black edges appearing on the right are purely a function of refraction from the environment.

Table 9.1 lists some common materials and their indices of refraction (IORs). Refraction happens when light leaves one kind of material and enters another, such as leaving air and entering glass, or leaving water and entering air. Because of this, IOR values are all relative to two materials; they describe light bending as it travels out of one material and into another. The values in Table 9.1 are based on the listed material surrounded by air, with one exception: The listing of "Air (from under water)" might be used at a water surface when looking up at air, or on bubbles of air seen under water.

[Table 9.1] Useful Index of Refraction (IOR) Settings for Materials

MATERIAL	IOR
Air (from under water)	0.75
Air/Neutral	1.00
Smoke	1.02
Ice	1.30
Water	1.33
Glass	1.44
Quartz	1.55
Ruby	1.77
Crystal	2.00
Diamond	2.42

The numbers in Table 9.1 should be useful starting points, but you will probably make most adjustments based on sight. You need to see the refraction on your own model before you can be sure that the index of refraction gives you the look you want.

Colored Refraction

In real life, different frequencies of light refract at different angles. You'll recall from Chapter 6, "Cameras and Exposure," that this difference is what's responsible for chromatic aberration in lenses. Blue light tends to refract as if a material had a slightly higher index of refraction, and red light tends to refract as if there were a slightly lower index of refraction. The rainbows of colors that you see through a prism or in a diamond come from this effect in refraction.

Some shaders contain an option called *dispersion* or *chromatic aberration* that adds multicolored refraction. Figure 9.21 shows the difference that colored refraction makes. If your renderer doesn't support this effect, you could fake it yourself by rendering your surface in three passes: red light with a slightly lower index of refraction, green light with a normal index of refraction, and blue light with a slightly higher index of refraction. Composite together the red, green, and blue passes to simulate optical dispersion.

[Figure 9.21] Without optical dispersion (left) refraction works in black and white, whereas with optical dispersion (right) you see different wavelengths of light refracted differently.

Simulating optical dispersion is one case that gives away the flaws in rendering with RGB color, simulating only three wavelengths of light, instead of calculating a continuous spectrum and simulating many wavelengths of light. If you see banding artifacts (red, green, and blue stripes) when you simulate optical dispersion, then you are running into these limits. A few renderers allow a simulation of a continuous spectrum, but rendering in RGB remains the standard in most of the CG industry. Figure 9.21 was rendered in RGB but used a soft refraction effect to prevent visible banding.

Refraction Limits

As with reflections and raytraced shadows, refraction also must be limited. However, there are times when refraction limits need to be quite high in order to see through all of the refractive surfaces in a scene. Figure 9.22 shows a scene where a refraction limit of 2 (left) is not enough to see through a rack of glass plates. Upping the limit to 8 (right) allows up to look through all of the plates.

[Figure 9.22] Too low a trace depth (left) makes some objects seem less transparent, whereas a higher trace depth (right) lets you see through all the refractive objects.

Count how many surfaces you need to see through that are refractive, and set the refraction limits on the shader. Set global limits on the number of refraction steps to be high enough to see through all of the layers in your scene.

The number of refractive steps will not limit a transparent surface that is not refractive. If some of the transparent surfaces that you need to see through don't really need to refract, then make another glass shader for those surfaces with refraction turned off, and you won't need to crank up your refraction limits too high.

Reyes Algorithms

A *Reyes algorithm* is the heart of Pixar's RenderMan, which has for years been considered the leading rendering software for high-end feature film work. Other renderers have also adopted Reyes and Reyes-type algorithms.

The core elements of a Reyes renderer were originally developed in the 1980s by Lucasfilm's Computer Graphics Research Group, the initial group of people who later became Pixar Animation Studios.

Reyes stands for *Renders Everything You Ever Saw*. That acronym was conceived by a researcher while swimming in the waters of Point Reyes, an area near Lucasfilm in Marin County, California. The algorithm was designed to make possible a high level of detail, smooth curved surfaces, displacement mapping with pixel-level detail, motion blur, and depth of field—all key aspects of producing realistic graphics for film—within the speed and memory limitations of that era's computers.

Reyes renders curved surfaces, such as those represented by NURBS or subdivision surfaces, by dividing them into *micropolygons*, small quadrilaterals each about one pixel in size or smaller. Each curved surface is divided into exactly enough micropolygons to appear completely smooth at the rendered resolution. If a shader is applying displacement mapping, the displacement will also be broken down into micropolygons.

Next, the shader is evaluated to assign a color and opacity to each micropolygon. All of your lighting, shadows, and texture mapping are applied at this stage. For example, a specular highlight might cause a white micropolygon. If a part of a texture map contains a green pixel, it could contribute to a green micropolygon.

Shaded micropolygons are sampled in screen space to produce the rendered image. Sampling the micropolygons after they have been shaded does not take very long. This is important to contrast with conventional raytracers, which need to shoot twice as many rays into the scene, requiring twice the render time, in order to double the amount of over-sampling. As a result, fine quality anti-aliasing can be achieved easily with a Reyes algorithm. Rendering effects such as motion blur and depth of field, which typically require a large number of samples to render smoothly, can also be achieved without adding inordinately to the rendering time.

A Reyes algorithm typically divides an image into *buckets*, or groups of about 16 pixels by 16 pixels. Division into micropolygons, shading, and rendering are done one bucket at a time. As a result, entire objects or scenes of micropolygons do not need to be stored in memory at once, but instead can be created as needed for each bucket, and then cleared from memory after the bucket is rendered.

The RenderMan Interface Standard

When Pixar created RenderMan, they didn't just create a piece of rendering software. They also created the *RenderMan Interface Standard*. In much the same way that HTML is a language to describe websites or PostScript describes printed pages, the RenderMan Interface Standard was created as a way to describe a 3D scene to be rendered.

Key components of the RenderMan Interface Standard are

- .rib (RenderMan Interface Bytestream) files, which contain scene descriptions
- A shading language to describe RenderMan shaders in .sl files

Companies other than Pixar also make their own *RenderMan-compliant renderers*, which follow the RenderMan Interface Standard and can produce renderings from the same files as Pixar's RenderMan. These other RenderMan-compliant renderers include RenderDotC, 3Delight, Gelato (discussed below), and Aqsis (which is free.) Most major animation and modeling packages can output files to be rendered in a RenderMan-compliant renderer, either natively or through a plug-in.

Reyes and Raytracing

Traditionally, most Reyes rendering has been done without raytracing. In many feature films that you have seen rendered with Reyes algorithms, all of the shadows have been depth mapped shadows and all reflections have been reflection maps. A main idea behind Reyes algorithms, rendering one bucket at a time without needing to hold polygons in memory for the whole scene, works well if rays are not bouncing around the scene requiring random access to other objects in a reflection, refraction, or shadow.

In the past five years, computers have become faster and have enough memory that raytracing is finally becoming more common in feature film production. Full support for raytracing and global illumination have been added to Pixar's RenderMan and other RenderMan-compliant renderers, so that today raytracing often coexists with the Reyes algorithm. However, studios still employ raytracing only when it is needed, and try to avoid it on complex scenes involving hair and vegetation.

Z-Buffer Rendering

Z-buffer rendering is an approach to rendering usually taken by graphics cards for real-time display, and also used for rendering animation tests.

In the early days of 3D graphics, one of the great challenges was finding efficient algorithms for *hidden surface removal*—the tasks of making sure that surfaces in the foreground appeared in front of surfaces in the background. Some of the early solutions were very slow, such as sorting all of the polygons in the scene in order from back to front before drawing them.

Z-buffer rendering is a solution to the problem of real-time hidden surface removal that allows objects to be drawn rapidly without regard for the order in which polygons are rendered, and without regard for camera angle. The z-buffer is an area of memory that stores the depth information about your image.

As the first polygon is drawn, colored pixels are added to a frame buffer, and at the same time, depth information is added to the z-buffer, recording the distance from the camera to each point on the polygon being drawn. When other polygons are drawn, their depth at each pixel is compared to the depth information in the z-buffer. If a polygon is closer to the camera than any polygons already drawn in that area, then it will be drawn into the frame buffer. If any part of the polygon is farther away from the camera from a polygon already drawn into the frame buffer, then part of the polygon will be hidden, based on a comparison of its depth to the value in the z-buffer.

Scanline Rendering

Scanline rendering is a rendering process that renders on a pixel-by-pixel basis, instead of a polygon-by-polygon basis. After each line of a horizontal line of pixels (or *scanline*) is completed, the renderer moves on to the next line until the image is complete. This process could be done on a graphics card as an alternate way to perform z-buffer rendering, or it could be done in software as a basic type of rendering for animation.

Scanline rendering usually refers to a plain, no-frills rendering that does not use techniques such as raytracing or global illumination.

GPU-Accelerated and Hardware Rendering

Most modern personal computers contain two types of processors:

- The central processing unit (CPU) is responsible for most of the computer's calculations, including 3D rendering.
- On your graphics card is the graphics processing unit (GPU), which is a chip dedicated to processes needed in real-time graphics display. The GPU is responsible for real-time, interactive graphics, from video games to the shaded displays in your 3D program's viewports.

The GPU in modern graphics cards is a flexible, programmable chip, so some graphics software takes advantage of it for uses other than playing games. The GPU can be used for *hardware rendering, interactive previewing,* or *hardware acceleration* of a software rendering process.

Hardware Rendering

Hardware rendering refers to using the images output by your graphics card as the final output of your rendering process.

Graphics cards are designed to create images that can be drawn in real time for interactive graphics. Freed from the limitation of needing to complete 30 to 60 frames per second, graphics cards can actually produce higher quality images than what appears in a videogame. Furthermore, the images that are hardware rendered can be used as layers or passes in a multipass composite.

At the present time, full hardware rendering is used widely in previsualization, and in test renderings of animation and simulation, but is not up to the quality requirements of television or feature film production work.

GPU Acceleration

GPU acceleration means rendering with software that takes advantage of the processing power of your GPU as an added resource to speed up some operations. GPU acceleration does not mean settling for a reduced-quality rendering. It means only that a GPU is one of the processors used in computing pixel values for a full-quality software rendering. GPU acceleration requires a GPU, but makes selective use of it only for certain types of calculation.

As of this writing, GPU acceleration is a technique that is either implemented in or being considered by most high-end renderers. It holds the promise of taking fuller advantage of the resources of an artist's machine, and providing faster rendering than would be possible on the CPU alone.

There are some drawbacks to GPU rendering. One is that GPUs are designed to access data loaded into the memory of the graphics card, not the computer's main memory. Extra time needs to be spent loading textures and other data into the graphics card's memory.

Programming for two different types of processors at once is very challenging. It is already a challenge to adapt rendering software to work well in multiple threads on multiple cores or CPUs, but to add to that the extra complexity of having different tasks running simultaneously on different types of processors makes it very hard to write and debug rendering software.

Finally, there is the issue of being dependent on graphics cards. In major studios, *render farms* consist of thousands of rack-mounted computers which generally don't have graphics cards.

Despite these challenges, in recent years, GPUs have been advancing more rapidly than CPUs. If this trend continues, GPU-accelerated rendering is certain to look more and more attractive the farther GPUs pull ahead of CPUs in computing power. The graphics card manufacturer nVidia is developing a GPU-accelerated renderer, Gelato (http://film.nvidia.com), so it is likely that future GPUs will also become more suitable for accelerating full-quality rendering processes.

Interactive Previewing

Interactive previewing allows lighting artists to get more work done in a limited time and, more importantly, to refine their work more completely and accurately in a limited amount of time.

Interactive previewing of lighting is different from real-time rendering in that only the lights are being changed, while the models, camera, and shaders remain the same. Usually there is a prerendering phase to interactive previewing, in which certain information about each pixel is precomputed. The prerender might take minutes or hours, but can be done without supervision. After the prerendering is done, the GPU and CPU work together to interactively update the scene while the user moves and adjusts lights, shadows, and reflections.

If you are developing a lighting set-up that will appear in multiple shots, some interactive previewing systems can use prerendered data from several shots at once, showing how moving or adjusting a light would appear in each of them.

The final product from interactive previewing is not a rendered image, but an improved 3D scene, which can then be rendered overnight on the render farm after lighting changes have been made.

Using GPUs to accelerate interactive previewing, then allowing the final frames to render overnight, allows for the studios to remain consistent with what's been called *Blinn's Law*. Blinn's Law states that at a film studio, frame rendering times will remain constant despite any advances in hardware or software. If a studio considered 8 hours per frame acceptable 10 or 15 years ago, it will continue to invest 8 hours a frame this year. The only thing that will change is that they will expect higher quality, more complex scenes, and use more ambitious algorithms every year, using up any advantage gained by having faster computers. Blinn's Law has held true at most studios for many years.

Exercises

To be become truly obsessive about realistic rendering, try to think throughout the day of how you would render everything that you see around you.

1. Look at the surfaces in the room around you. If you were recreating them in 3D, how many of them would need to be reflective? Of those, how many would use a glossy reflection? For the surfaces that you didn't

see as reflective, do any of them become more reflective when viewed at a glancing angle?

2. Figure 9.1 at the beginning of this chapter showed four differently shaded spheres. Try to re-create them in your 3D software. Pay attention to issues discussed in this chapter such as specular and glossy reflections, refraction, specular size and color, and the Fresnel effect.

3. As a test of whether your shaders really look like the materials you're trying to represent, show them to someone else in a scene that does not make the material obvious through context. Ask other people what material they think a ball is made of, and you might find situations where people would have called something metal if it has been assigned to a model of a car or a teapot, but out of context will tell you that it looks like plastic.

[CHAPTER TEN]

Designing and Assigning Textures

Texture mapping is the art of adding variation and detail to 3D surfaces that goes beyond the level of detail modeled into the geometry. Creating texture maps is a process where your skills in 2D painting, photography, and image manipulation can add to your 3D scene. You can create textures to make your models look as if they were built out of any kind of material, from cinder blocks to human skin, and use texture to determine whether objects are old or new, clean or dirty, polished or dented. Every attribute of a shader discussed in the last chapter can be replaced with a texture map, varying it and modulating it in different parts of the surface. This chapter will discuss the types of textures you can create, different ways to create textures, and how to align textures with your models.

Types of Texture Mapping

Textures can be used to control many different attributes of a surface, to produce different effects in your rendering. The seven most common mapping techniques are:

- Color
- Specular
- Incandescence
- Transparency
- Displacement
- Bump
- Normal

Color Mapping

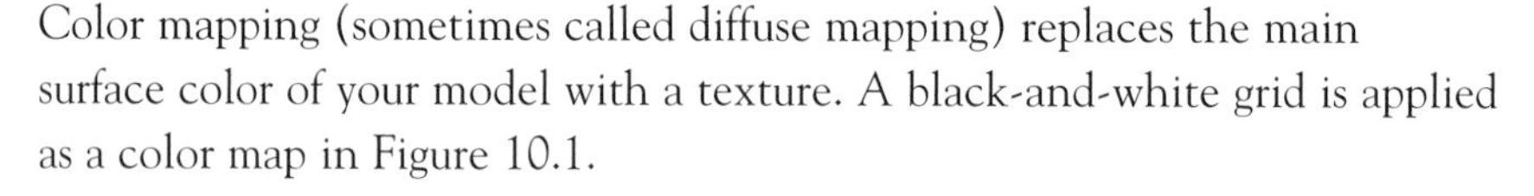

Color mapping (sometimes called diffuse mapping) replaces the main surface color of your model with a texture. A black-and-white grid is applied as a color map in Figure 10.1.

[Figure 10.1] A sphere with a basic color map

Your color map sets the tint and intensity of diffuse light reflectance by a surface. In some renderers, color mapping and diffuse mapping are listed as two different kinds of maps. In this case, the tones of the color map are multiplied by the tones of the diffuse map. For example, a 50 percent gray in a diffuse map would cut the brightness of the color map in half.

Color mapping replaces the object color used in diffuse illumination, but does not override your lighting and shading. It is best to avoid having highlights, shadows, or lighting variations appear in the color maps themselves—when you render, lighting will be added by the lights. A highlight mapped onto your model as a part of a color map could look fake, as if it were just painted onto the object's surface. As a result, the best color maps usually look very flat when viewed by themselves, such as the color map for a man's face shown in Figure 10.2.

In a realistic rendering, object colors usually should not include pure black or pure white, and should avoid completely saturated red, green, or blue colors. A 100 percent white color would mean that 100 percent of the light hitting the surface was diffusely reflected, which does not occur in the real world. Similarly, a pure black surface would show no diffuse light reflectance, which is also unrealistic. In most cases, it's a good idea to keep the red, green, and blue color values in your texture maps between 15 and 85 percent. While your texture maps may look a bit flat by themselves, your final render will gain contrast and directionality from your lighting, as shown in Figure 10.3.

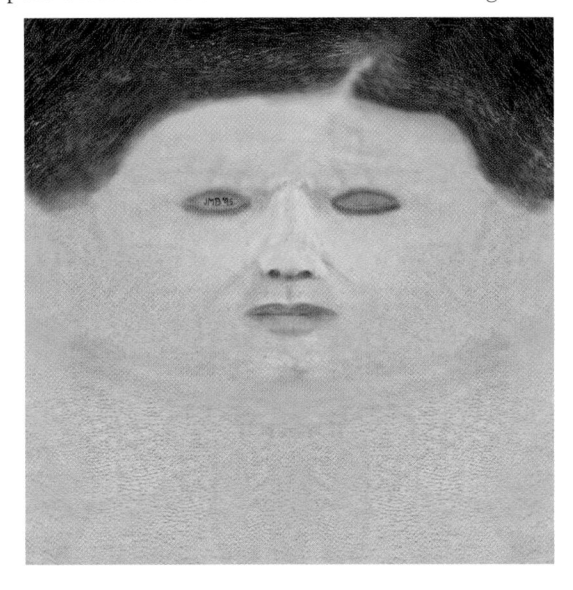

[Figure 10.2]
Color maps should not show any built-in lighting.

[Figure 10.3]
A head model textured with the color map from Figure 10.2

Specular Mapping

Specular mapping varies the brightness and color of the specular highlights on different parts of an object's surface. A checkered pattern is applied as a specular map around the entire object in Figure 10.4, but its influence is seen only in the area of the specular highlight.

Your specular map will not create specular highlights by itself; highlights still need to come from light sources. Your specular map can tint the highlights, change their brightness, or even block them completely from a particular part of your model. However, the effects of specular mapping will be visible only in places where a specular highlight would have appeared anyway.

Bright areas in your specular map make highlights brighter, creating a glossier or shinier area on your object. Dark tones of a specular map make highlights less visible, and pure black in a specular map completely prevents highlights from showing up on the corresponding parts of your model. For example, Figure 10.5 shows a specular map for a man's face. White areas of the map produce a shiny forehead and nose, while dark areas prevent highlights on the stubble of his chin and cheeks.

[Figure 10.4] A sphere with a grid as a specular map

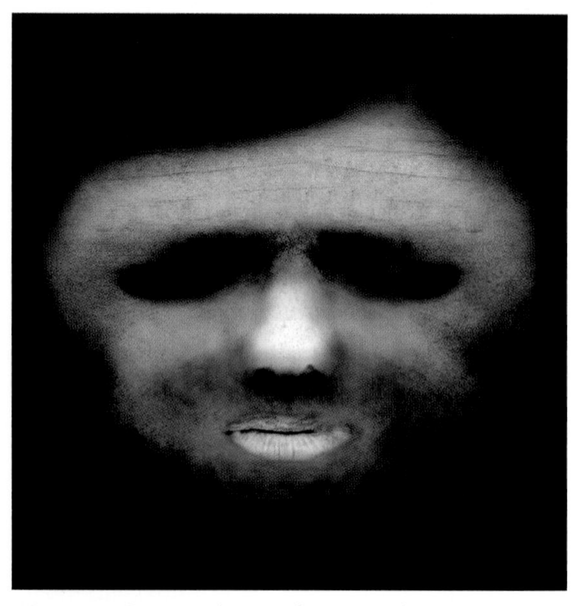

[Figure 10.5] A specular map for a man's face shows where it is dull or shiny.

The effects of a specular map are visible only in areas of your model that would already receive a specular highlight. To thoroughly evaluate what the map is doing all around your model, you need to render a *turntable test*, an animated loop showing the model rotating 360 degrees in front of the camera. Because the camera and lights remain in place, you will see the highlights travel across the surface of the model as it spins, and you'll be able to spot where the highlights are brighter, where they are less bright, and which areas don't receive highlights at all.

Closely related to a specular map is a reflectivity map. Because specular highlights represent the reflection of light sources, you generally expect to see specularity in the same places that you see other reflections. Reflectivity maps determine how reflective a surface is in reflecting other objects or the environment around it. Often a specularity map can perform a double function in also being linked to the reflectivity of a surface. In other cases there may be differences between them, such as for sparkly car paint, where you might want sparkles to appear in the specularity, while mirror-like reflectivity might be limited to the areas in between the sparkles.

Incandescence Mapping

Incandescence mapping (also called luminosity, ambience, or constant mapping) uses a texture map to simulate self-illuminating properties of an object. The colors in an incandescence map are added to the colors in your final rendering, without regard for your lighting. As shown in Figure 10.6, incandescence maps are visible on a surface even in shadow areas; they don't need a light source to illuminate them.

[Figure 10.6] A sphere with a grid as an incandescence map

Incandescence maps are perfect for tasks like adding illuminated lights to the side of a building or ship, adding the glowing picture to a television or monitor, or texturing the surface of a light bulb. Incandescence maps are also handy if you want to combine 2D pictures with your 3D renderings, and have the pictures keep their own lighting, without needing lights in your scene to illuminate them.

If an incandescence map is applied to an object that has no specularity (pure black specular color) and no diffuse shading (pure black diffuse color), then it can produce a flat area of color, with the exact shades and tones from the source map being output in the rendering of the object. Some renderers have a separate option to render with a surface shader or lightsource material, which produces this same effect, although these may not be as easy to blend with other shading effects as an incandescence map.

In Alias software, mapping the ambient color is different from mapping the incandescence in that the ambient color gets multiplied by the main shader color before it is added to your illumination. Figure 10.7 shows an example of this. If you brighten the lampshade with a map on the ambient color (left), the ambient color gets multiplied by the color map, and the texture is preserved and reinforced. Brightening the lampshade with an incandescence map (right) makes the surface brighter but is not filtered through the color map.

[Figure 10.7]
An ambience map (left) is multiplied by the color map, while an incandescence map (right) is added without regard for surface color.

Transparency Mapping

Transparency mapping has several useful functions. The simplest function of a transparency map is to create a pattern in a surface's transparency. Instead of making a surface uniformly transparent, you can make parts of it less transparent, such as if a window were dirty, or give it different colors of transparency, such as to create a stained glass window.

Figure 10.8 shows a white and black checkerboard applied to a surface's transparency. Dark areas of a transparency map will make a surface less transparent, and light areas make the surface more clear.

Transparency mapping can also be used to cut out detailed shapes and patterns from a surface. Figure 10.9 shows a transparency map designed to simulate hairs or eyelashes. Most 3D programs can use a texture map's alpha channel to determine the level of transparency in a textured surface. The eyelash texture map contains color information, which can be applied as a color map, and also contains transparency information in its alpha channel.

[Figure 10.8] A sphere is transparency mapped with a checkerboard pattern.

The eyelash texture creates the eyelashes and ear hairs for the hippo in Figure 10.10. The eyelash texture map creates the illusion of separate lashes or hairs by hiding parts of the eyelash surface in stripes of transparency. The same technique could be used to make a row of grass that sticks up from a lawn, the bangs of a character's hair, or a distant tree line on a hillside.

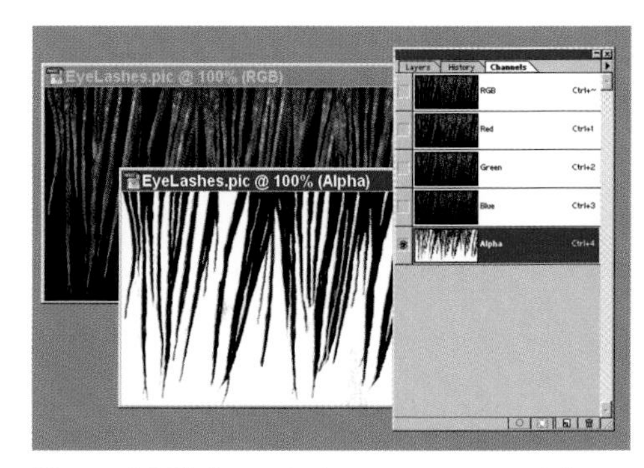

[Figure 10.9] An eyelash texture uses an alpha channel for transparency.

A transparent area of a surface will not necessarily be invisible. Reflections, refraction, and specular highlights are still visible on a transparent surface. If you want to be sure transparent parts of your surface are completely invisible, you can reuse the transparency map to map the specularity and reflectivity, to make them both become 0 wherever the transparency is 1.

The technique of replacing a complex 3D object with a transparency-mapped flat surface is called *billboarding*. You can billboard a 3D object by rendering the object that needs to be replaced, and then applying the rendered image as a color map on a flat surface, with the rendered alpha channel as your transparency map. Billboarding might not work when the camera is near the surface, but can look convincing for more distant objects, and saves a lot of memory and rendering time when used to replace complex models.

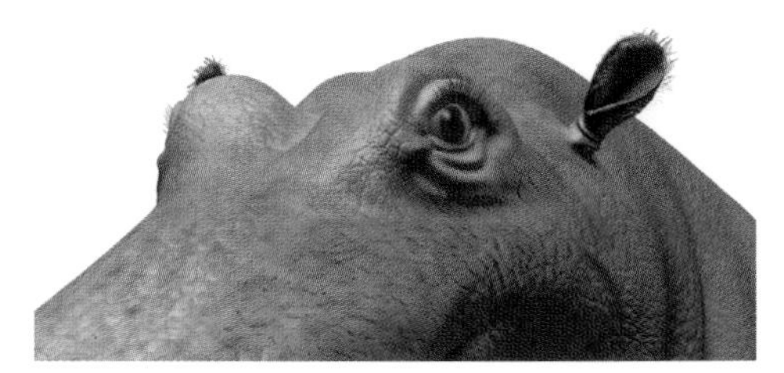

[Figure 10.10] Ear hair and eyelashes are created with transparency mapping.

Displacement Mapping

The brightness of a displacement map is used to change the shape of a surface. The brighter the tone in a displacement map, the farther out a point on the surface will be displaced. Figure 10.11 shows the checker pattern displacement mapped onto a sphere. The change to the shape of the sphere is most noticeable at the edges.

Displacement height determines how far in or out a displacement map should push your surface. In many shaders, you also have an offset parameter to set how much displacement you start with where the map is pure black. You might leave the offset at 0 so that black in the displacement map has no effect, or you might make it start at a value of –0.5 so that black displaces the surface inward and a middle gray is used where you want the map to have no effect.

A detailed displacement map will require that a surface be tessellated (subdivided into many small polygons) during the rendering using a much higher polygon count than would be used without a displacement map. Using too little subdivision on a displacement-mapped surface can result in a blocky, jagged, or poorly defined displacement. Increasing the subdivision or displacement map quality on a surface can give you a more detailed, accurate representation of the map, but can add greatly to the memory and time required to complete your rendering.

[Figure 10.11] A sphere's shape is changed by a displacement map.

In a Reyes renderer, such as Pixar's Renderman, tessellation adjustments are not needed; as long as your shading rate is low enough, displacement maps are rendered accurately at any resolution. At shading rates below 1, the displacement is even smaller than a pixel. Your only concerns in rendering with displacement maps in a Reyes renderer are to make sure that a shader's displacement bounds reflect the maximum height of your displacement map, and that any shadows of the object are evaluating the displaced shader so that the displaced object shadows correctly.

Because displacement maps don't change the shape of a surface until render time, animators will not see the displacement while posing a character. Be very careful about applying displacement to ground surfaces or skin surfaces where accurate contact is needed; without seeing the displacement, an animator might make the character's feet cut through parts of the ground that displace upward, or float above parts of the ground that displace downward. Sometimes you may need to provide animators with a polygon mesh representing the shape that a surface will be displaced into, as reference for the appearance of the displacement map.

Bump Mapping

Bump mapping is a trick that simulates small details on an object's surface, without actually displacing the geometry. Figure 10.12 shows the influence of a checkerboard as a bump map. Bump mapping isn't as convincing as displacement mapping, but can render much more quickly.

Bump mapping works by changing the surface's shading as if small details had been present. The shading of a surface is based on an angle called the *surface normal*, which is usually perpendicular to the geometric surface of an object. A bump map changes the surface normals, making the object respond to light as if additional details had been present in the geometry.

[Figure 10.12] A bump map simulates ridges without changing the shape of the sphere.

Bump maps are encoded with brighter tones representing higher elevations, and darker tones representing lower elevations. A white dot would represent a bump up from the surface, and a dark dot would represent a depression into the surface. A transition from dark to light would create a ridge between different altitudes. People often use a neutral 50 percent gray as a starting point for a bump map, but any flat tone will work the same way. In a bump map, an area of constant color, with no variation in shading, will have no effect on a surface.

Because bump mapping does not actually change the shape of your geometry, it has some limitations:

- The outline or silhouette of an object is not changed by a bump map, and will remain smooth or straight even if the map simulates a very rough surface. For example, a sphere with a bump map still has a perfectly circular outline.
- Shadows cast by a bump-mapped object will still have their original shape.
- Shadows received on a bump-mapped surface will remain straight, and will not be distorted as if they really landed on rough ground.
- Unlike modeled or displaced details, details added to a surface via a bump map do not cast attached shadows onto the surface.
- The line where a bump-mapped object intersects with another object is not changed by a bump map, and can give away the real shapes of the objects.

These limitations are all corrected with displacement mapping, because displacement actually changes a surface's shape. However, bump mapping is a useful cheat for times that you aren't bothered by these limitations. Here are the main effects that a bump map can accurately simulate:

- Diffuse shading is varied as if the bumps really existed in the surface.
- Specular highlights are broken-up and scattered. Tiny highlights can even appear on individual bumps caused by a bright pixel in a bump map.
- Reflections (raytraced or reflection mapped) are distorted and broken up.
- Refraction (the view through transparent, raytraced surfaces) is correctly modified and distorted.

Figure 10.13 shows how a bump map breaks up highlights and reflections. The water surface starts out perfectly smooth and uniform with no bump map (left), but when a bump map is applied (right) the raytraced reflections are rippled and distorted. Additional highlights are also added on the right, and thanks to the bump map they are broken up into blotchy shapes instead of appearing as perfect circles. For a subtle effect such as distorting the highlights and reflections on a surface, bump mapping can be a convincing and convenient tool.

[Figure 10.13] The water is a smooth surface (left), but adding a bump map distorts reflections and highlights (right) in this scene by Gladys Leung (www.runtoglad.com).

Normal Mapping

Normal mapping is similar to bump mapping in that it cheats your shading without actually changing the shape of the model.

Compared to bump mapping, normal mapping is a more direct, specific way to perturb surface normals. In bump mapping, pixel brightness is interpreted as a height, and a slope derived from the heights of adjacent pixels determines the angle assigned to surface normals. In a normal map, a 3D angle for a normal is directly specified by three values per pixel, stored as three color channels in the map.

The most common use for normal mapping is to mask the difference between a high-resolution, detailed model and a low-polygon model. Figure 10.14 shows a high resolution model (left), a simplified low-polygon model without any textures (center), and the model with a normal map (right). On the right, the model looks almost as if it were made of far more polygons, although the faceted edges of the model give away that the geometry hasn't really changed.

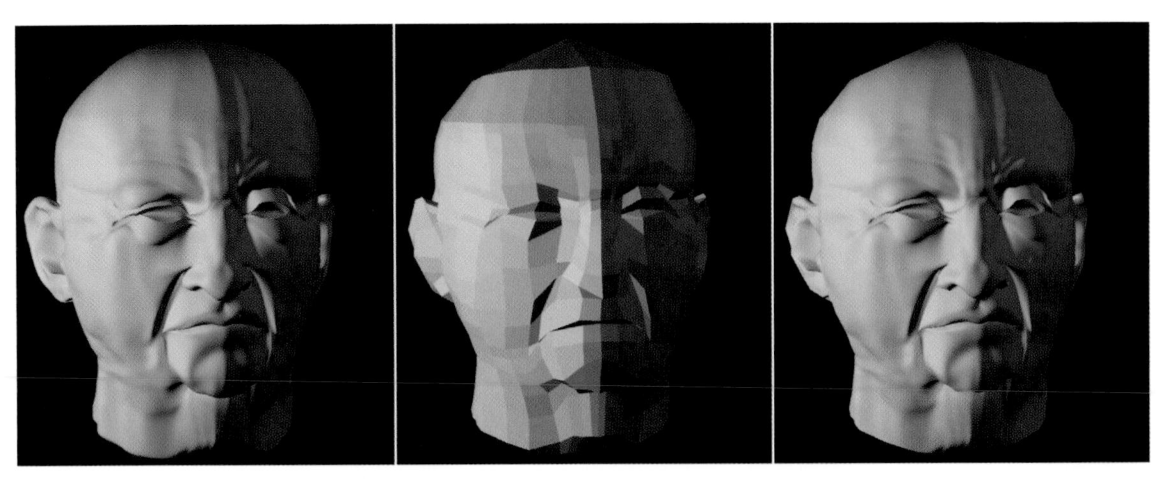

[Figure 10.14] A high polygon model (left) can be replaced by a low polygon model (center) if it is made to look higher resolution with a normal map (right).

Normal maps can be computed automatically based on the difference between two versions of a model. The normal map shown in Figure 10.15 represents the difference between the low-polygon model and a higher resolution model. Normal mapping allows video game developers to use low-polygon models while creating the appearance of higher levels of detail. Normal mapping is not used as widely in film and television production, but could be used for small background objects within complex scenes.

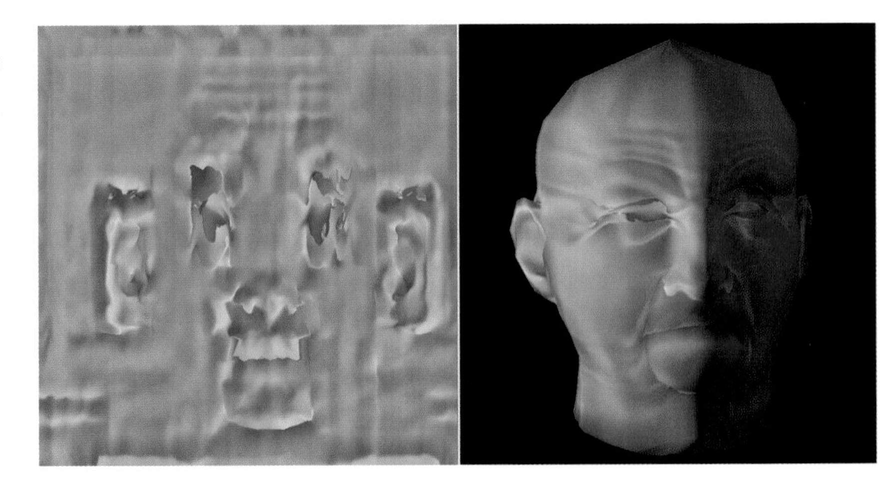

[Figure 10.15] This normal map represents the difference between the low polygon and high polygon models. On the right it is shown as a color map on the low resolution model.

Polynomial Texture Mapping

Polynomial texture mapping (PTM) is another cheat to your shading, like bump mapping and normal mapping. Compared to bump mapping, PTM is a newer, more sophisticated, and more realistic way to simulate small details on a surface. Unlike bump mapping, PTM simulates the shadowing between bumps, translucency of details such as small grains of rice, and even the interreflection of light between surface features. PTM can simulate fine textures such as the weave of a fabric or towel, including the illumination shared between fibers, in a more subtle and accurate way than displacement mapping or bump mapping.

Instead of a single grayscale image, like a bump map, a PTM starts with six channels, which could be stored as a six-channel TIFF file, or as two files each with red, green, and blue channels. PTM data can be acquired via light probes that digitize a real material while lighting it from many different angles with an array of strobe lights. PTM data can also be baked in 3D, based on a source displacement map with assigned material characteristics.

At the time of this writing, PTM is a published technique that can be used at studios that write their own shaders, but most users are still waiting for their software to support PTM. Many users feel the need for a more modern and complete alternative to bump mapping. Hopefully PTM, or something similar, will become widely available in commercial software in the near future.

Other Mapping Techniques

The number of effects that texture maps can govern is virtually unlimited. Specific maps may be used to control almost any kind of visual effect possible in your software. For example, some programs use a specific type of map to control the shape and color of a lens flare or the surface appearance of a particle. Even a plug-in might use its own type of texture maps for special purposes, such as determining the length, direction, and curliness of hairs emitted from a surface.

Photographic Textures

Most professional texture painters make heavy use of digitized images in painting textures. When creating original textures for a creature, character, vehicle, or environment, you can give a huge boost to the level of realism in your maps by including portions of images photographed or scanned from real surfaces. Even if you paint textures yourself instead of using parts of the photographs directly in the map, collecting high-quality reference images is an essential part of beginning your texture-mapping project.

There is a richness to real life that is worth going out to capture for each production, even when rendering a fictional subject. The actual subject you shoot may just be an analogy to what you are making. For example, you might texture the hull of a UFO with maps derived from panels of a city bus, or take close-ups of leftovers from a seafood restaurant to texture an alien creature.

Besides improving the quality and believability of your maps, photographic textures can also save time in creating all of the maps you need for a particular production. No amount of digitizing will eliminate the need to do some work putting together textures in a paint program, but having great shots of real surfaces that look like what you are trying to create is a terrific starting point that can get you better maps in less time.

Shooting Tips

Not every photograph will be equally useful in making texture maps. Try to follow these six tips when going out with your camera to collect textures:

- To capture surface color textures, try to avoid highlights, shadows, or lighting variation in your photographs. Sometimes you'll find uniform lighting in the shade, with the sun behind your subject, or when the sun is behind a cloud. If you can't avoid having a highlight, such as on a close-up of a person's eye, try to make it a small, concentrated one that will be easier to retouch out, not a broad soft light that covers a big area.

- Shoot surfaces straight on, not from an angle. Take a moment to level and straighten the camera and make sure that the horizontal parts of your shot are really horizontal. You may need to stand on a bridge or pier to get a straight-down view of sand, dirt, or street surfaces.
- Try to reduce lens distortion. Get to know your camera and lens by shooting a few test shots of a brick wall or gridlike pattern. Many zoom lenses create barrel distortion when they are zoomed out, and provide less distortion at medium or telephoto settings. It is easier to choose your distance and zoom settings in the field than to straighten out warped lines in a paint program.
- Shoot edges, not just the center of surfaces. Textures often change when you get near the edge of a surface, such as where a wall meets the ground. Focus on any area where two materials meet or intersect and get extra texture shots there. You may find later that some of these areas need their own maps.
- Collect texture maps in whole families, or groups of related textures taken from the same location. For example, if you need oak leaves, collect several different leaves from the same tree, so that your oak tree can have a natural variety in its foliage.
- Take some shots both wider and closer than you think you need. Close-up or macro photography of a subject reveals a different world of textures and patterns. Wider shots showing textures in context are vital to checking the scale of your textures. For example, you will need to decide during texture mapping how many bricks tall a house's walls are, and a wide shot could be an ideal reference to help get the texture scale right.

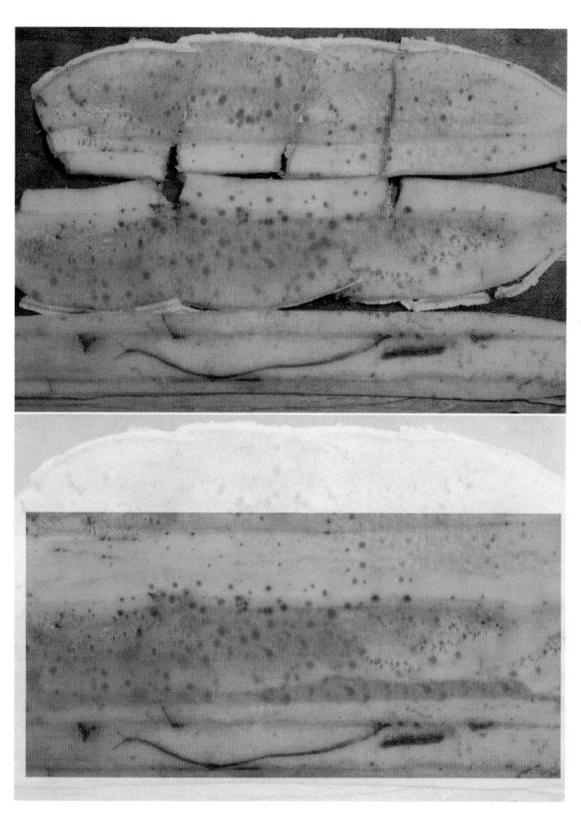

[Figure 10.16] A banana texture shot from a peel (top) is cloned into a complete texture (bottom).

Following these guidelines sometimes takes some extra work and set-up time. For example, to achieve uniform lighting and a straight-on camera angle in shooting a banana texture, I had to peel it and lay out the peel on a cutting board, as shown on the top of Figure 10.16. To make a complete texture map, I covered the gaps using the cloning tool in Photoshop and cropped the resulting image, as shown on the bottom of the figure.

Shoot liberally when you are out photographing images for texture maps. Assuming that you are using a digital camera, there's no reason not to shoot a few dozen extra shots of whatever you find interesting in an environment. As you archive your shots from many productions, you'll find older images useful again and again. Figure 10.17 is an extreme close-up of the white of an eye that I have used in textures for several creatures and characters since shooting it.

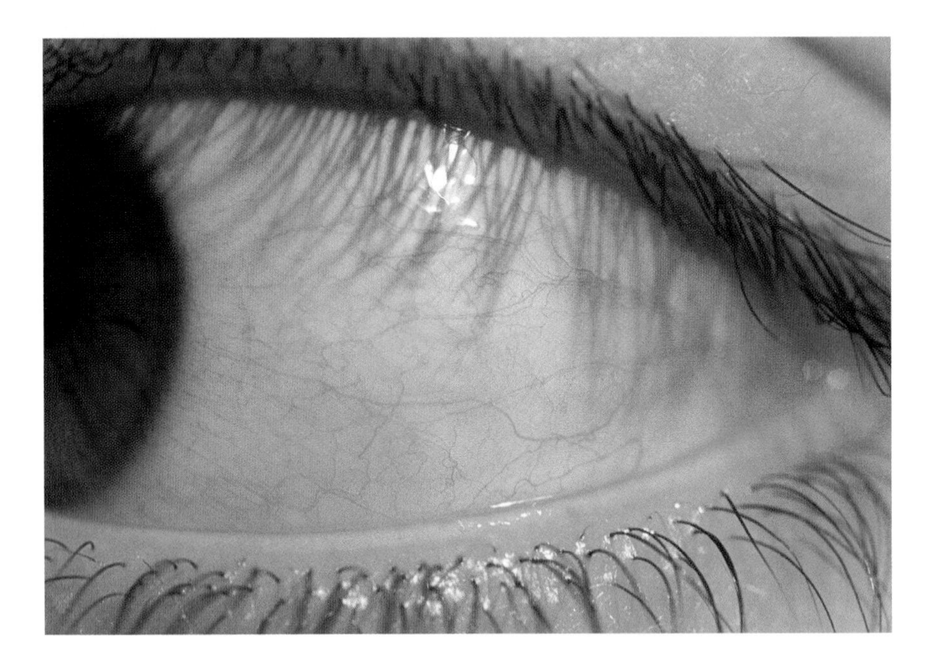

[Figure 10.17] Incredibly useful vein textures from an extreme close-up of an eye

Flatbed Scans

A flatbed scanner is a useful peripheral often overlooked by modern 3D artists. While scanners might not be as quick or as much fun to use as a digital camera, they can produce images with completely uniform lighting, an absolutely flat perspective, and perfect focus from edge to edge, providing ideal source material for creating texture maps.

Flatbed scanners tend to have very high resolutions compared to digital cameras. If you scan an 8-inch by 8-inch fabric sample at 600 dpi (dots per inch), that would be a 4800 × 4800 resolution scan, or 23 megapixels, all with no blurring or distortion.

Flatbed scanners are great for scanning clothing, fabric and wallpaper samples, flat artwork, photographs, or any other materials that are flat and fit on the document-sized glass plate of the scanner. Even odd subjects, such as raw meat, kimchi, or a toupee, can be laid flat on a scanner and scanned at high resolutions. Figure 10.18 shows a hair texture created by laying a hairpiece directly on a flatbed scanner.

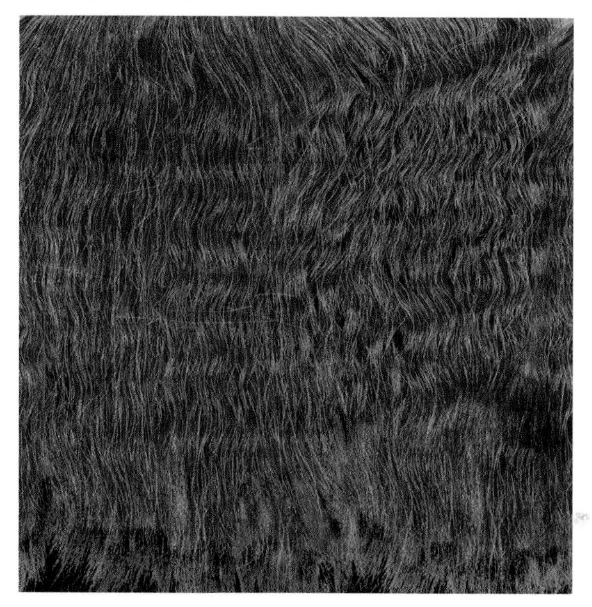

[Figure 10.18] Hair texture scanned on a flatbed scanner

Stylized Textures

For some projects, there are merits to painting every map from scratch, without letting real-world imagery intrude on your scene. This approach is especially useful if you have experience drawing and painting in traditional media. While hand-painted maps may be created in almost any visual style, they are especially important for nonrealistic, fanciful, and illustrative renderings. Figure 10.19 was textured with hand-painted maps created in a 2D paint program.

[Figure 10.19] Hand-painted texture maps maintain the illustrative style of a fanciful scene Eni Oken (www.oken3d.com) created using 3D Studio Max.

The models underneath your texture maps may be very simple, like the buildings in Figure 10.20. The texture maps add richness to the scene, while preserving the fanciful, ornamental style of the modeling.

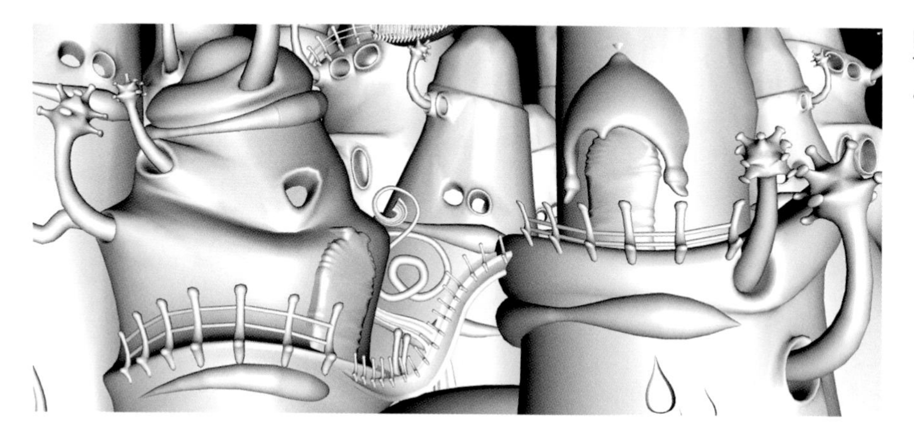

[Figure 10.20]
The untextured buildings are simple forms.

Figure 10.21 shows one of the texture maps being applied to the awning of a building. The map matches the shape of the geometry, and adds appropriate colors and ornamental details to the awning. Colors in the map are carefully chosen to integrate with the scene's color scheme, using the same purple, yellow, and orange tones that are picked up in many other surfaces.

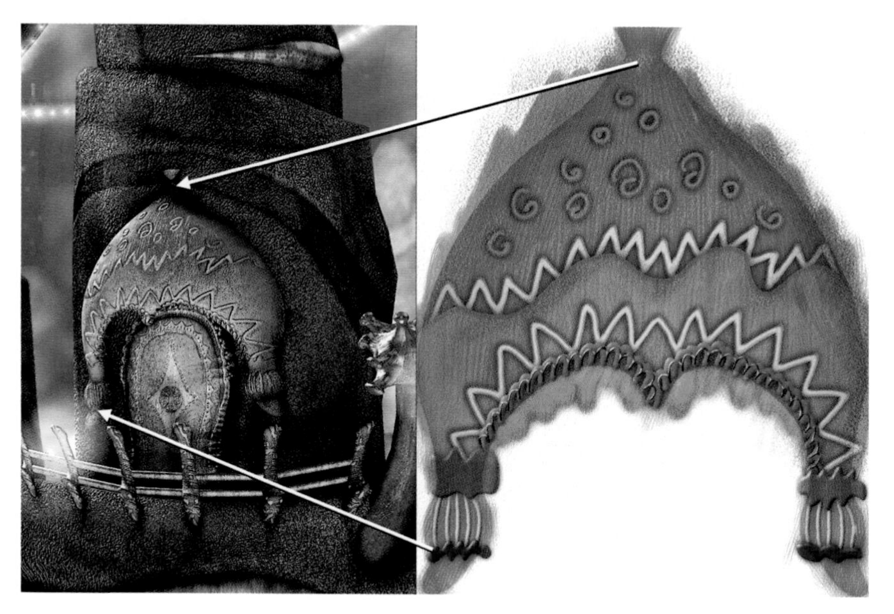

[Figure 10.21]
Ornamental texture maps are added to the color and bump of the buildings.

Light and shadows are painted into these maps in order to reinforce the lighting in the scene or simulate details and dimensionality that never existed in the underlying geometry. Note how the door texture map in Figure 10.22 already contains shading and shadows. In the final rendering, these are added together with the shading and shadows of the geometry.

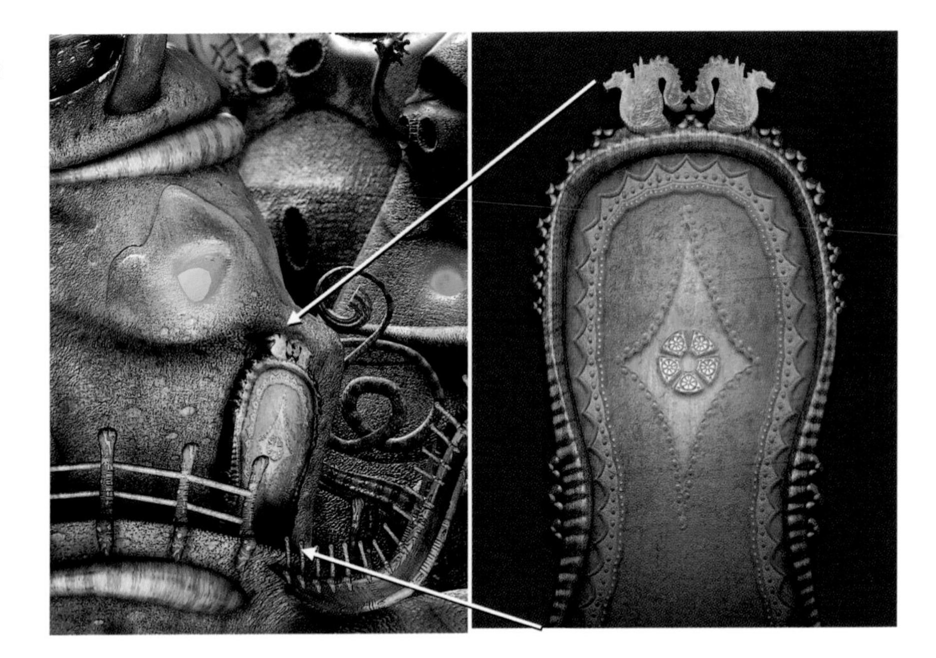

[Figure 10.22]
Color maps for the stylized rendering already contain shading and shadows.

Texture Map Resolution

How high does the resolution of your texture maps need to be?

Start by thinking about the resolution of your final output. You would need higher resolution textures if you were rendering for film (or the best quality HDTV) at 1920 pixels across than if you were rendering video frames at 720 pixels across.

Some texture maps can be lower resolution than your rendered frames. If your texture map covers a small object that will fill only half the frame, then it needs to be only half the output resolution. If a map repeats three times across a surface, then the map needs to be only a third of the resolution.

However, there are times when you need higher resolution maps. If a map wraps all the way around a character's head, then only a portion of the map will texture the character's face. In a full-screen close-up, the face itself needs to have enough detail to fill the screen. If a texture map covers a mountain or a whole planet, then close-ups on a small part of the object would require maps many times the resolution of the screen—although in extreme cases you'd probably use a separate map for close-ups.

Most graphics cards, and many renderers, work most efficiently with texture maps whose dimensions are a power of 2, such as 256, 512, 1024, or 2048. In fact, some software and hardware internally scales up maps of other dimensions to the next power of two. Table 10.1 shows some of the most common texture-map resolutions, and their RAM use for a 4-channel file.

[Table 10.1] Texture Map Memory Use

MAP RESOLUTION	MEMORY USED
256 x 256	256 KB
512 x 512	1 MB
1024 x 512	2 MB
1024 x 1024	4 MB
2048 x 1024	8 MB
2048 x 2048	16 MB
4096 x 4096	64 MB

When you digitize a map, or work with it in a paint program, try to design your textures at a higher resolution than the final maps you'll need in 3D. For example, if you are going to use a 512 × 512 map, start with an original file at least 1024 pixels across. Many steps you make in a paint program, such as rotating the image, can slightly lower the image quality. If you start with a higher resolution than you really need, then all of your image editing can appear seamless after the map is scaled down to its final size.

Your texture maps have a limited amount of detail. If a texture map is too low a resolution for your needs, you can't gain detail by scaling up the map—scaling up a low-resolution map only produces a softer image. On the other hand, making textures that are higher resolution than you need allows you to scale a map down later if you want a smaller map that uses less memory.

The only kind of resolution that matters in your completed texture maps is the size in pixels. The dpi setting on a completed texture map won't matter in 3D, so you can leave it at whatever value happens to appear there; 72 is a common default. If you are using a device (like a flatbed scanner or slide scanner) with an adjustable dpi for scanning, then use whatever dpi setting provides you with the number of pixels that you need to create your map.

Alignment Strategies

Whether you will be painting your texture maps from scratch or processing digitized images, you need a good strategy for aligning textures with your surfaces. When you look at a texture map, you need to know which pixels in the map will appear on which points on the surface of your 3D model. There are several different approaches to this problem.

Tiling Maps

A *tiling map* is a texture map designed so that it can be repeated multiple times on a surface, and each repetition will fit together seamlessly with the adjacent copies, like a pattern printed on wallpaper. The left edge of a tiling map will line up seamlessly with its right edge, and its top will align with its bottom, so that you can't tell where one repetition ends and another one starts, as shown in Figure 10.23. The white crosses indicate the four corners of the repeating shingle texture—if they weren't superimposed, you wouldn't be able to tell where the pattern repeats.

[Figure 10.23] White crosses indicate corners of a seamless tiling map.

You can make a tiling map in almost any paint program. Begin by cropping the photograph or painted map that needs to tile so that the top and bottom, and the left and right, appear to be cropped at a similar point on the texture. You should see nothing but a consistent texture within the frame.

The next step is to offset the image so that you can see how the opposite edges fit together. Figure 10.24 shows how you can use Photoshop's Filter > Other > Offset command, starting with a cropped texture image (left). The image is slid by half its width to the right, and down by half its height. Pixels that slide off one edge of the frame wrap around to appear on the opposite edge. The right side of the figure shows that, after the Offset operation, what used to be the four corners of the image are now all in the center of the frame. Notice that the reddish leaves that were in the upper-left corner are now just below and to the right of the center point. After the offset, opposite edges will all fit together seamlessly in a tiling map; the only seams that need to be fixed are the ones now visible in the center of the image.

There are several approaches to covering over the seams. You could use the cloning tool or healing patch, either of which will copy other parts of the texture over the seams. The cloning brush enables you to paint the area being cloned with different levels of opacity, while the healing patch copies a whole region at a time, but also color-corrects the region so that it blends seamlessly with its surroundings. You could also start with two copies of your layer, as shown in Figure 10.25, with the offset layer on top of the original, and create a layer mask hiding the seams from the top layer. These techniques can be combined, starting with the layered approach and then flattening the image and cloning any remaining areas.

[Figure 10.24] The original image (left) is offset (right) to make it seamless at the edges, and draw the seams into the center.

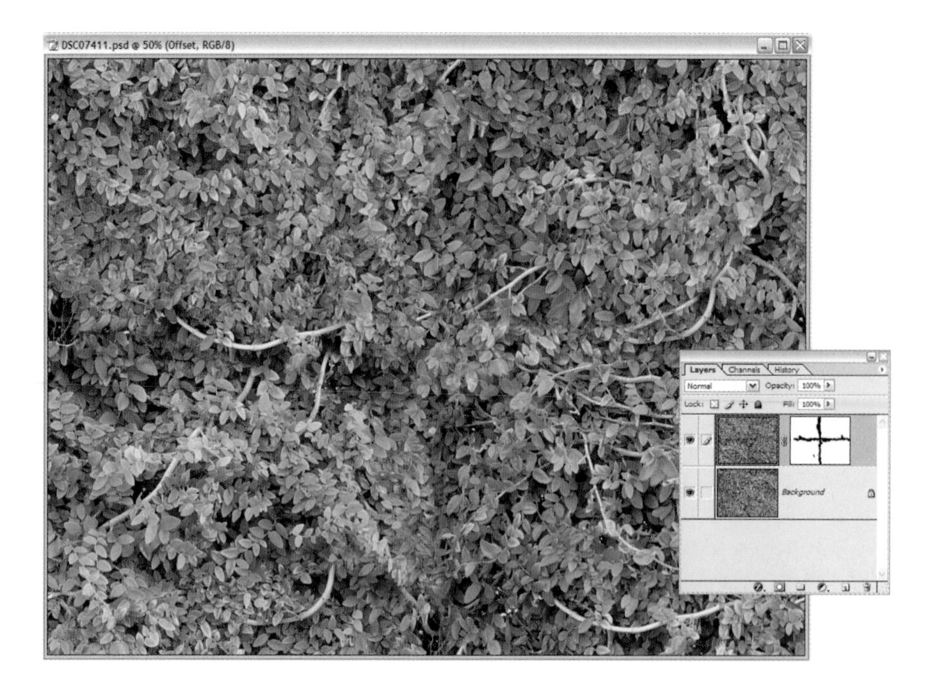

[Figure 10.25] Seams in the top layer are hidden by painting a layer mask.

As a test to see if your map is truly seamless, you can roll the image around, using the Offset filter with different amounts horizontally and vertically to see where seams or discontinuities remain. For a test that actually shows you multiple repetitions, you can scale the map down to a smaller size, define it as a pattern, and use that pattern to fill the background of a larger image file.

Correcting Luminance and Color Shifts

If you are starting with photographed elements, correcting any overall shifts in brightness or color is a huge concern in preparing a tiling map. Often a photograph will be brighter in the center than on the edges, or there will be an overall gradient shifting one side to a different color than the other. Even if a map like this were made seamless at the edges, when applied with many repetitions in 3D, you would see the brightness or color shifting back and forth with each repetition across a surface, creating a visible pattern from a distance.

Figure 10.26 shows a picture of a tree that has been cropped (left) and offset (right) in preparation for making a tiling tree bark texture. There was an overall shift in brightness and color running across the original image. The offset makes this especially visible along the center seam.

To correct overall color shifts, you could use the gradient tool to paint gradient selection masks, and then adjust the levels on different parts of the image.

Another great tool to equalize the brightness and colors in a map is the Filter > Other > Highpass filter. If you apply a Highpass filter before you do the offset, you can cancel out all of the overall variation in a layer, while preserving the detail and texture smaller than a specified blur radius. Highpass is a very heavy-handed filter, which will greatly reduce your image's overall contrast. After using Highpass, you'll need to adjust the levels of red, green, and blue to restore the color and contrast of your texture.

If you want more control than a Highpass filter offers, you can create a similar result for yourself. Make a copy of the layer that needs its colors and tones equalized. Blur the copy using a big enough radius to hide the texture, and then invert the layer. If you mix the inverted layer at 50 percent opacity, then you have re-created the results of a Highpass filter, as shown in Figure 10.27.

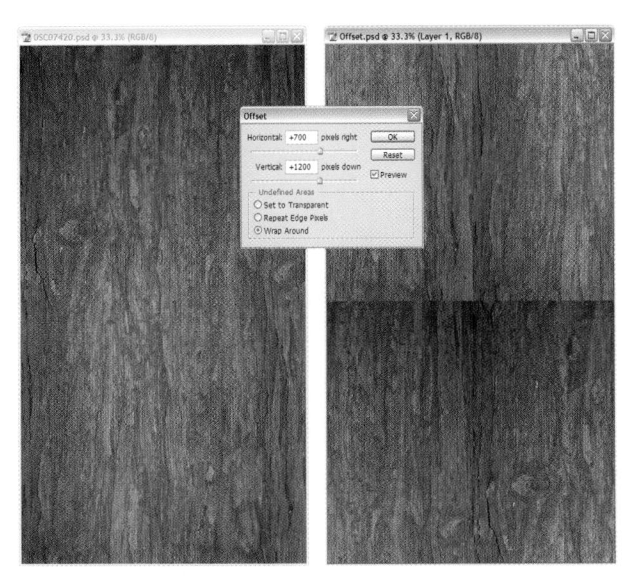

[Figure 10.26] Color and luminance shifts are revealed by the Offset filter.

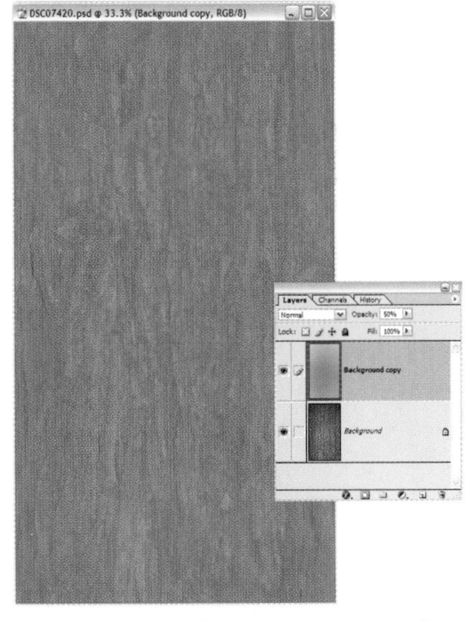

[Figure 10.27] Simulating a Highpass filter with multiple layers gives you more control over the process.

After building a Highpass-like result for yourself, you have the freedom to adjust the opacity of the top layer to less than 50 percent for a more subtle effect, or use a blending mode such as luminance if you don't want to cancel out the colors. After you have merged the layers, you will probably still be left with a low-contrast image, and you may need to increase the contrast of the image or use Auto Levels in order to bring out the contrast and variety of the texture map. The corrected map repeats three times across Figure 10.28 without shifting brighter or darker.

Expanding a Tiling Map

When you look at several repetitions of a tiling map, sometimes you see distinctive features that repeat too often, calling attention to the repetition of the map. For example, Figure 10.29 shows a tiling map of a brick wall with a variety of discolored bricks. It repeats four times across the figure, and the colored bricks form an obvious repeating pattern instead of looking random.

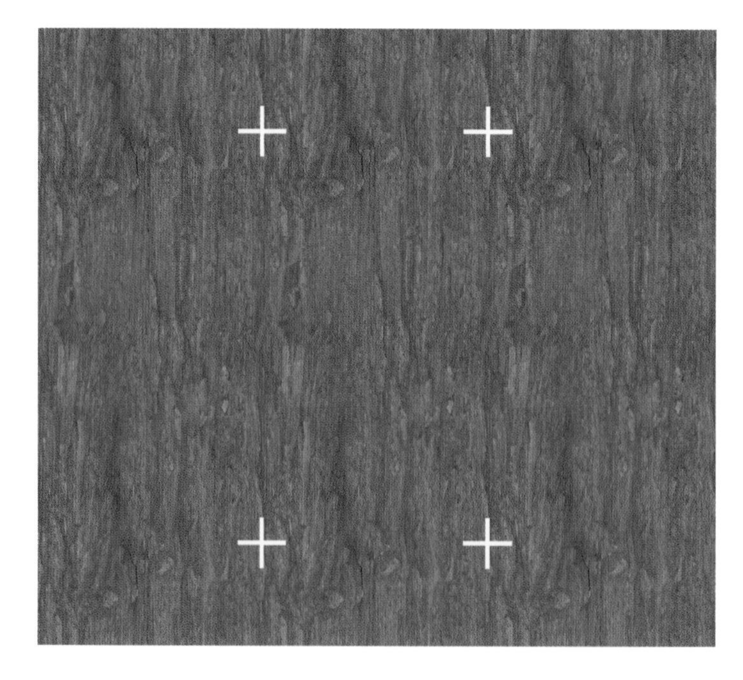

[Figure 10.28] After luminance equalization, the map repeats without shifts in tone. White crosses mark a single instance of the map.

[Figure 10.29]
Repetition is too obvious in this tiling brick texture.

One way to reduce this problem is to expand the texture map. To expand the map, you create a new image with twice the width and twice the height of the original. Paste four copies of the original into the new image, so that they fit together to form four repetitions of the pattern, as shown on the left side of Figure 10.30. The copies can all be flattened onto the same layer. At this point, you can use the cloning tool (or lasso, cut, and paste) to move around some of the bricks. You might also change some of their colors, or anything else that will break up the repetition of the pattern. Results are shown on the right of the figure. This new, expanded tiling map will be able to cover larger areas without visible repetitions.

[Figure 10.30]
Four repetitions of a tiling texture are pasted together (left) and then edited to make a larger texture that repeats less often (right).

[Figure 10.31] Making a more realistic transition from the wall to the ground, this map tiles horizontally but not vertically.

Before you start expanding a map, however, it's a good idea to test-render it in your 3D scene. Sometimes repetitions appear obvious to you when you preview the tiling in a paint program, but when a surface is broken up with different illumination and shadows, and parts of it are covered up by other texture maps or other objects, you can get away with a lot more repetitions of a map without a pattern becoming too obvious.

Horizontal and Vertical Tiling

Maps don't always need to repeat both horizontally and vertically. You can make some maps that are designed to tile only in a horizontal direction, or just in a vertical direction. Figure 10.31 shows a map covering the lower edge of a cinderblock wall. It tiles only horizontally, and would just run along the lower level of a surface.

Decals

In texturing a detailed or realistic object, you will usually need to layer together more than one texture map. Some of the maps will be assigned to different attributes, such as your color map, your bump map, and so on. Some of the maps will be applied to different regions of your model, for example, if you use separate maps near edges of a surface. If you want to add a unique detail to a specific position of an object, even in a region where you already have other textures applied to the same attribute, then you may want to create a decal.

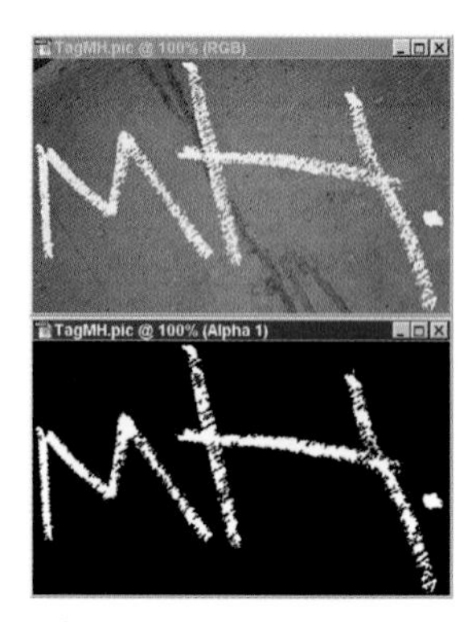

[Figure 10.32] A decal map is created along with an alpha channel to control how it is layered over other maps.

A *decal* (sometimes called a *layered texture*, *stencil*, or *label map*) is a texture map that has been masked-out for layering on top of other textures, to add a unique detail to a specific position on an object. As shown in Figure 10.32, creating a decal usually requires both a color image (top) and a mask (below). The color image will contain the texture of the decal area, and the mask will contain white areas where the decal image should appear, and black where the background material should be visible. The mask is usually stored in the alpha channel of the color map, but might be a separate image file.

Using alpha channel layering, many decal maps can be layered on top of one another, building up more detailed scenes, as shown in Figure 10.33.

[Figure 10.33]
Arrows indicate some of the locations where the map from Figure 10.32 is used throughout the scene.

Dirt

One of the most useful purposes for decals is adding dirt to your models. You can make maps that represent dirt, smudges, and other surface imperfections, and layer them on top of other textures. Figure 10.34 shows a map of a water stain (left), designed to repeat vertically, and masked with an alpha channel mask (right). A vertical map like this could help break up and add variety to a horizontal map like the one in Figure 10.31.

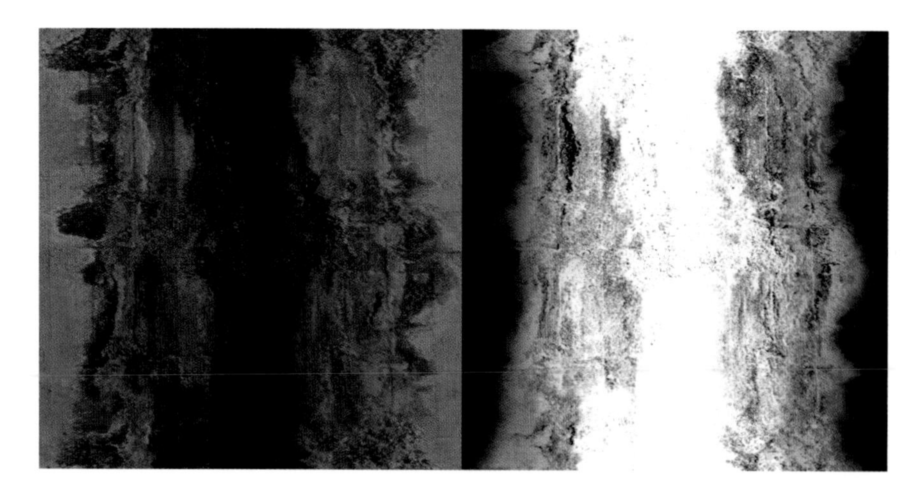

[Figure 10.34]
This vertically tiling water stain texture (left) is layered via an alpha channel (right) over other textures.

Use dirt to add "signal," not "noise." When you need to make something dirty, don't just superimpose random noise on it. Instead, choose dirt maps that add specific, motivated detail to your objects. Think through the story behind all the stains and imperfections on a surface—something has to cause any dirt, scratches, or stains that you would see. Here are few examples of motivations that would influence the design and position of dirt maps:

- Scratches don't appear randomly on a floor, they are more likely to appear in an area that gets scraped when a door opens.
- Carpets are most worn in the path where people walk.
- Mildew grows darkest near cracks and corners.
- Water leaves stains in the path where it drips down a surface, or where its surface reaches a high-water mark.

Figure 10.35 shows a photograph of rust stains on a cement wall. Notice that they are not random; the streaks are concentrated below metal posts, the source of the rust. This kind of thinking is especially important in making a fantasy world or imaginary environment believable. You need to imagine the whole history of what has happened in an environment in order to invent convincing dirt for it.

[Figure 10.35]
Rust stains appear where water drips from metal fixtures.

Also, dirt isn't all dark. Dirtying up your surface doesn't just mean darkening it, or just making it less saturated. Some kinds of dirt make your surface lighter in color, such as dust, scratches, water stains, and bird droppings. Rust, rot, and fungus can even add richness and color to an aging surface.

Projections

A *projection* is a way to cast a 2D image into 3D space. A projection like a movie projector projecting film into a theater—which starts small at the lens and expands as it moves through space—is a *camera projection*. In 3D graphics, besides camera projection, you can also choose from *planar, cylindrical, spherical projection*, and often several other types.

Planar Projections

A planar projection casts your texture map onto a model so that it retains the same size and orientation as it is projected through 3D space. A planar projection will project a texture onto a model exactly as you would see if you had painted it over a front, side, or other orthogonal view of your model.

If you are painting a planar projection map, you'll want to bring an orthogonal view of your model into your paint program for reference. For example, to paint a map that will be projected onto the front of a character's head, you'd bring a front view of the character into your paint program. If you are

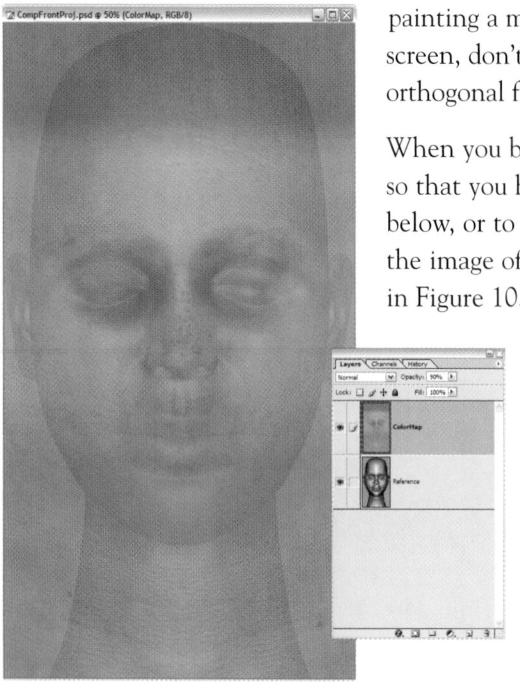

[Figure 10.36] A front view is used for reference in the background, while the color map (top layer, partially transparent) is composited together on top.

painting a map that will be higher resolution than your monitor screen, don't just use a screen grab. Instead, render the head using an orthogonal front view as the camera, matching the map's resolution.

When you bring the image into the paint program, crop it precisely so that you have the entire model in the map, but no black above, below, or to either side. You can then create a new layer, leaving the image of the head in the background for reference, as shown in Figure 10.36. This enables you to work in your paint program, painting or compositing together the texture map, and when you position a freckle on the character's nose, you can see where to put it relative to the character's nose in the background image. You can flatten the image and save it without the background when you bring your texture map into your 3D application.

The main advantage of planar projection maps is their simple compatibility with flat painting. Another advantage, compared to other ways of texturing a character, is that projections are separate from the geometry, so even if you edit the model, the map can still be projected on the same way.

Figure 10.37 is a render of the head using the map shown above. One of the problems with planar projections is that a projection that perfectly covers the front of a model tends to stretch out or turn into streaks along the sides. You can see some streaking in front of the ear and along the left edge of the neck. The other problem with planar projections is that they go all the way through the model, so that a face projected onto the front of the head would also appear on the back.

Because planar projections only do a good job of covering one side of a model, you will often need more than one planar projection to texture a model all the way around. For example, you might paint one texture for the front of the head, and another for the side of the head.

To combine a front and side projection, you could assign different maps to different polygons in your model, or you could blend them more organically with an alpha channel mask.

Some programs have a function that will convert projections into file maps that directly follow a surface's UV coordinates, such as Maya's Convert to File Texture command. If you have two or more projections and convert them each into a UV map, then you could use a paint program to combine them into one texture.

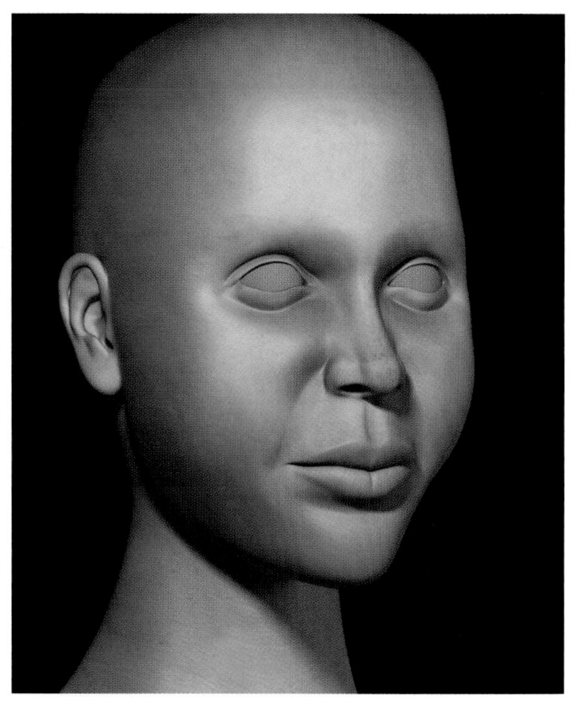

[Figure 10.37] A planar projection aligns with the front of the head, but stretches out along the sides.

Cylindrical and Spherical Projections

Cylindrical and spherical projections cast an image inwards from a sphere or cylinder positioned around the model. Figure 10.38 shows a head model with a grid applied in cylindrical (left) and spherical projection (right). Note that they are similar except that the poles of the sphere come together to a point, projecting the top and bottom of the map more uniformly on the top and bottom of the model. If you weren't going to see the top surface, then a cylinder might be a better choice to wrap around a head without distortion.

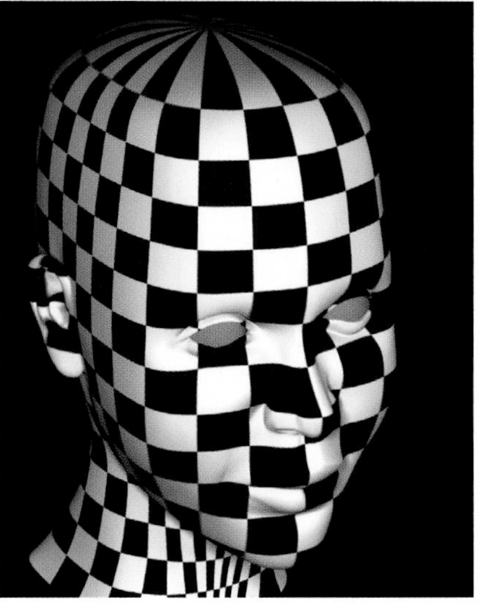

[Figure 10.38] A head mapped in cylindrical projection (left) and spherical projection (right).

Cylindrical and spherical projections do not exactly match any window view of your 3D program, so they are not as easy to paint in alignment with a reference image as a planar projection. However, they can be perfect for wrapping a skin texture around a character's arm or leg. You may need to use several of them in texturing a body, with a cylinder around each limb.

Camera Projections

Camera projection (also called *perspective* or *front projection*), which is most similar to a movie projector or slide projector, can exactly match the view of a specific camera in your scene. If you were painting or compositing together a digital matte painting, this kind of projection would let you paint over the actual geometry, as rendered, and then project new images into the scene in a way that would exactly align with the geometry seen by the camera.

A camera projection is also useful for projecting your background plate into a 3D scene, so that surfaces will be textured with a view exactly matching what the camera sees. This can be useful in making reflections match real-world environments. Figure 10.39 shows a camera projection of a real scene onto simple matched geometry. When it appears in raytraced reflections, it creates reflections on 3D objects that appear to reflect the environment into which they are composited.

[Figure 10.39]
A cube is textured with the background plate using camera projection (left) so that CG objects can realistically reflect the environment (right).

Other Projections

Different software supports different projection types. Many programs offer *cubic projection*, which combines several planar projections from different angles. Also useful are *custom* or *deformable projections*, which you can bend or edit to project the texture from just about any shape.

UV Coordinates

Coordinates in U and V describe a position on a surface in much the same way that X and Y describe a pixel location in a texture map. While some people think of the V as standing for vertical, they are really named UV coordinates because U, V, and W are the three letters before X, Y, and Z.

There are two basic kinds of UV coordinates: *implicit UV coordinates*, the kind built-in to NURBS surfaces, and *explicit UV coordinates*, which are user-specified, as used on polygon meshes and subdivision surfaces.

Implicit UV Coordinates

NURBS surfaces have *implicit* (or "built-in") UV coordinates. From the moment a NURBS surface is created, it has implicit UV coordinates at each point. No matter how you edit a NURBS surface, there will always be a unique UV coordinate for each point on the surface. Figure 10.40 shows a map marked with unique colors and numbers (left) applied to the UV coordinates of a NURBS surface (right).

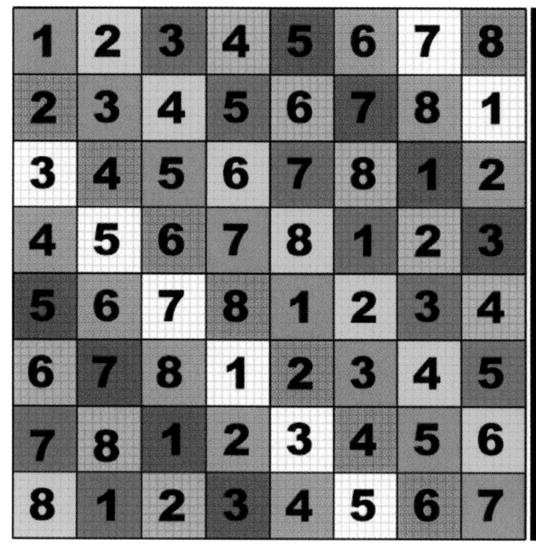

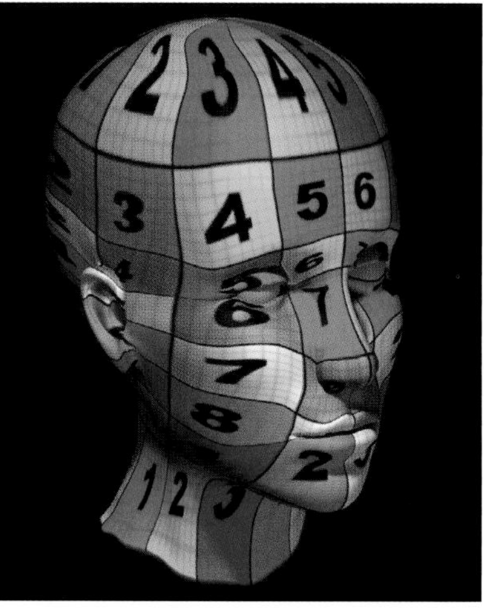

[Figure 10.40] A map designed to show alignment (left) follows the UV coordinates of a NURBS head (right).

The built-in UV coordinates are made possible by the structure of a NURBS surface, which is always a grid. A NURBS surface is made up of a set of curves running in a direction called U, intersecting a set of curves running in the other direction, called V. Each point has its own UV coordinate value describing its position within the grid structure of the surface. Even though the surface can be bent and reshaped flexibly, it will always remain a grid. To preserve the grid structure, NURBS modeling software does not allow individual points to be deleted; the entire row or column of points would need to be deleted at once.

A map applied to a NURBS surface will follow its UV coordinates, usually with the X (horizontal) dimension of the texture map running along the U direction, and the Y (vertical) dimension of the texture map running along the V direction. This way, each pixel in the map will appear exactly once, somewhere on the surface.

The way you construct a NURBS surface will determine how your UV coordinates are distributed on your model. Figure 10.41 shows how a differently built NURBS model will receive the map used in the last figure. This time, the model is built with the mouth as one pole of the geometry, so one edge of the map converges at the mouth.

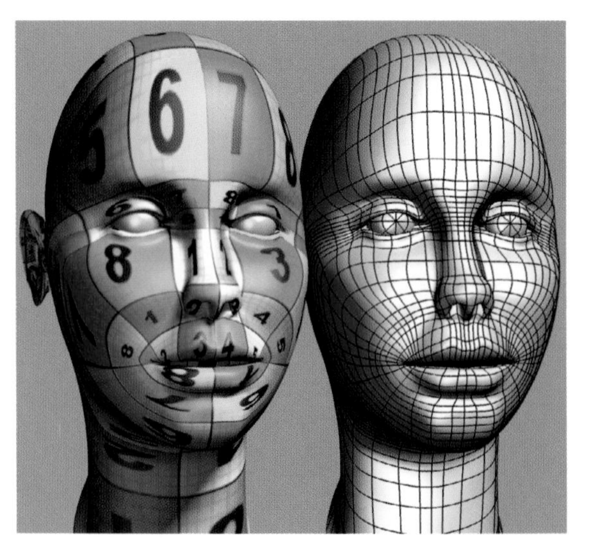

[Figure 10.41] The map radiates out from the mouth in mouth-centered geometry.

Explicit UV Coordinates

Polygon meshes and subdivision surfaces have a free-form geometric structure that does not have to be a grid and does not necessarily consist of four-sided polygons. Because there is no grid structure implicit in their geometry, polygon meshes do not have implicit UV coordinates like NURBS. Instead, polygon meshes use *explicit* (or assigned) UV coordinates. Subdivision surfaces that are smoothed starting with a polygonal control mesh also use explicit coordinates, usually based on the coordinates assigned to the control mesh.

Explicit UV coordinates are stored along with each vertex of a mesh. You can assign whatever UV coordinates you want to each vertex, even if some parts of a mesh reuse the same coordinate values. Where coordinate values repeat, a portion of your texture map may be repeated. Game developers sometimes do this intentionally, in order to reuse a part of a map on more than one part of a model, and thereby get more use out of a limited size texture map. In film and television work, you are more likely to want each part of your model to have a unique UV coordinate, so that you can paint into any part of it without having your painted details appear more than once on the surface.

Even if your software provides you with UV coordinates as a starting point when you initially create a new polygon mesh, these UV coordinates will be made incomplete as soon as you begin editing the surface. Modeling functions that add polygons to the mesh will create polygons that don't have UV coordinates.

Explicit UV coordinates generally need to be assigned after a model is completed. To assign new UV coordinates, you generally start with a choice of projection types that will be a basis for how the UV coordinates are distributed through space. Most 3D programs include a UV Texture Editor window, as shown in Figure 10.42, which shows an unfolded view of the object's geometry superimposed over the map. Moving points in this view changes their UV coordinates, giving them a different alignment with the texture map.

The unfolded view of the polygons seen in the UV Texture Editor is also useful when copied as a background layer into your paint program, to serve as reference in painting or editing texture maps.

The improving mapping tools in today's 3D programs are making the distinction between implicit and explicit textures less of an issue than it used to be. Even when texturing NURBS surfaces, which have implicit UV coordinates, some systems allow users to explicitly redefine or edit the UV values of a point.

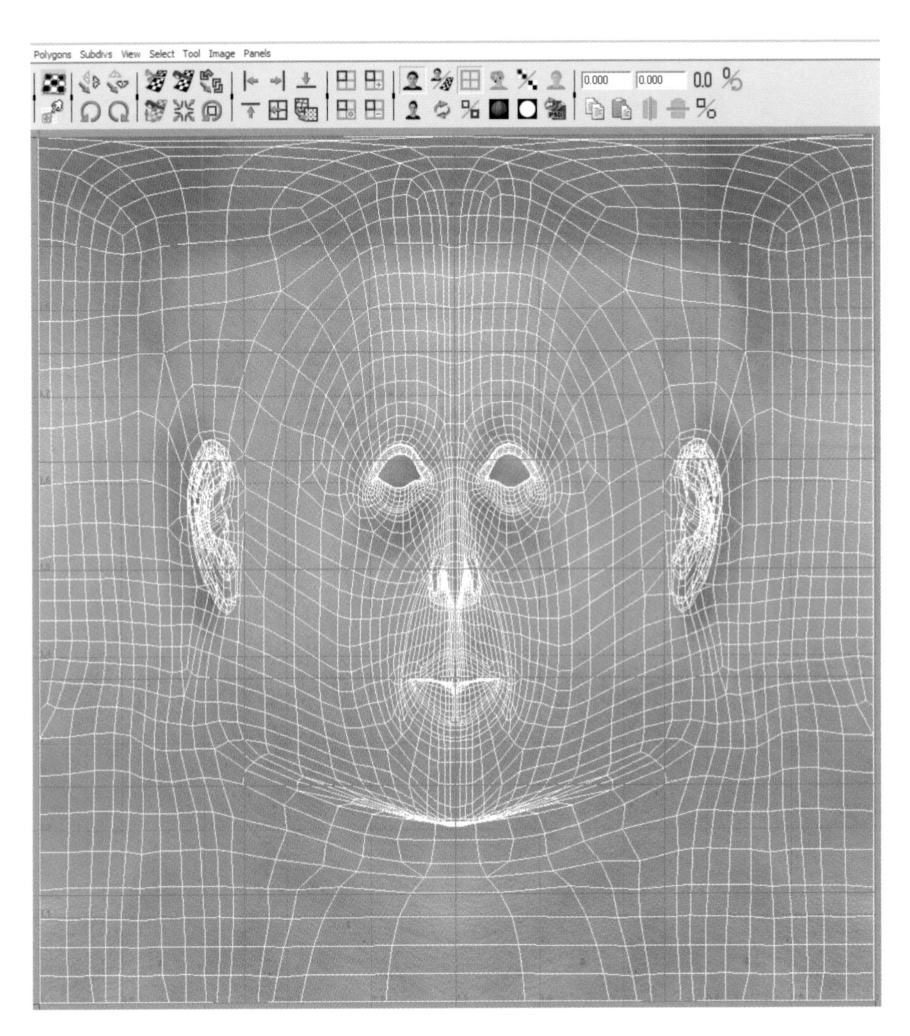

[Figure 10.42]
The UV Texture Editor shows an unfolded view of the polygons as they align with the texture map.

Multiple UV Sets

It is possible to create multiple UV sets for a model, so that different texture maps follow differently edited UV coordinates. For example, with multiple UV sets, you could have one texture map representing a fabric texture on a garment, uniformly covering each panel of the fabric. Another UV set could follow the edges of the fabric and guide where a stitching pattern was to be applied. By having different UV sets, both maps can be repeated and aligned in different ways.

Texturing Poles

Poles are places where an entire side of a texture map gets pinched together into a single point. Poles occur at the top and bottom of a spherical projection, and also happen in UV coordinates in at the geometric poles of a NURBS surface.

You can use the Photoshop function Filter > Distort > Polar Coordinates to switch a map from having a pole in the center of the image to representing the pole as one edge of the image. Figure 10.43 shows a texture map of an eye before the filter is applied (left), and after (right). If the eyeball had been off center, then instead of horizontal lines the edge of the iris would appear wavy.

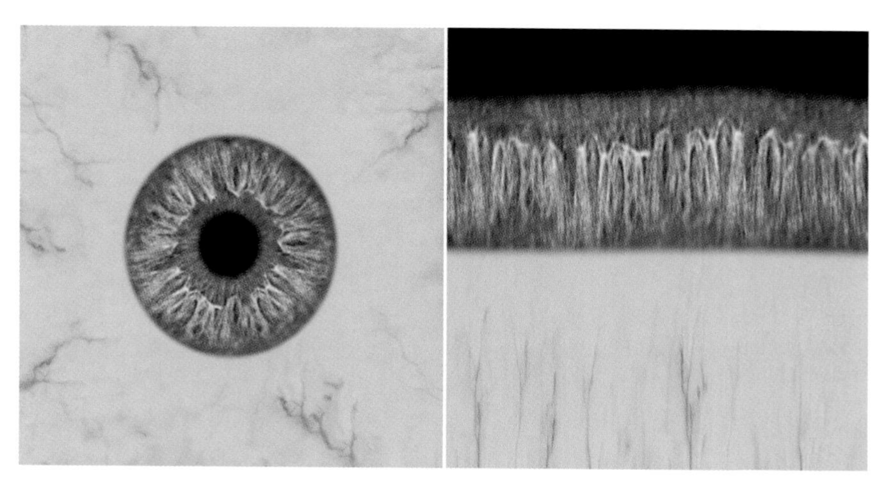

[Figure 10.43]
An eyeball texture map made for planar projections (left) and designed to radiate out from a pole (right)

This conversion optimizes an eyeball texture map for being applied according to the UV coordinates of a spherical eyeball with the pole facing outward. Another benefit to the conversion is that it makes it easier to retouch a highlight or eyelash out of a picture, because you could just clone or copy other parts of the texture from the left or right of the area. If you want to work this way only temporarily, the filter can also convert in the opposite direction to reverse this effect.

Texturing an apple is another situation where parts of your map will cover poles. A NURBS apple, shown on the left side of Figure 10.44, will have poles at the top and bottom. The geometry converges at the bottom pole to a single point (center), but needs to be textured without the texture appearing to pinch together, as rendered on the right of the figure.

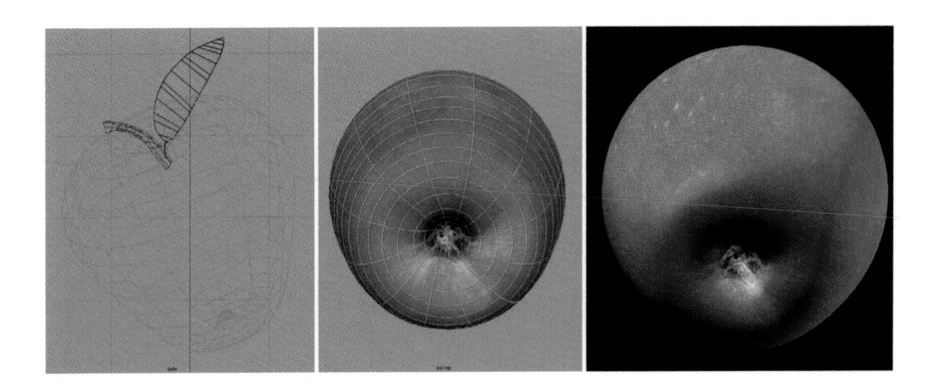

[Figure 10.44]
A NURBS apple (left) features a pole at the bottom (center) that needs to be seamlessly textured (right).

To cover the apple, a map is used that stretches out at the top and bottom pole, shown in Figure 10.45. The top and bottom were created using the Polar Coordinates filter.

[Figure 10.45]
The color map for the apple includes textures for the poles at the top and bottom.

Figure 10.46 shows a photograph of the bottom of an apple (left) that was converted with the Polar Coordinates filter (right). This result was scaled down to a smaller height to fit into the bottom part of the map.

[Figure 10.46]
The source picture of the lower apple (left) is converted to polar coordinates (right).

3D Paint Programs

Painting texture maps in a 3D paint program is designed to be a simple, direct process. You generally start by importing a 3D model that has UV coordinates worked out, and either paint directly onto the surface or onto a layer that gets projected onto the surface each time you rotate the model to a new angle.

3D paint programs can be used to create complete, final texture maps. However, many 3D artists prefer having the control of seeing and working with textures in a regular 2D paint program, and want to work with texture maps in a full-featured program like Adobe Photoshop. A compromise approach is to use a 3D paint program to paint a "markup map" onto the model, making a texture that only indicates the location of each major feature on your model. For example, you might paint colored lines around the edges of the lips, nose, eyelids, and jawline of a head model, and then use that markup map as a background layer in a 2D paint program to guide the creation of your final texture map.

Procedural Textures

A *procedural texture* is an algorithm in the computer that can generate a colored pattern based on input parameters, without needing to load an image file. You can think of procedural textures as an alternative to creating texture maps, although most people use them in combination with texture maps instead of as a complete replacement.

Compared to texture maps, procedural textures have some advantages and some disadvantages.

Resolution Independence

Procedural textures are resolution independent. When you make a high resolution rendering, or zoom in to an extreme close-up, a procedural texture can reveal more and more detail, and will never become blurry like an overstretched texture map. Most procedural patterns can be mathematically derived at any scale, although some have a setting for the number of iterations or levels of detail to be computed.

Due to their resolution independence, procedural textures are well suited for covering broad areas of a scene, such as for a landscape or terrain. A procedural texture could cover an infinitely large ground surface without ever repeating.

However, the resolution independence of procedural textures is not a guarantee that the close-up appearance of a texture will meet your needs or expectations. No matter which kind of texturing you use, designing a 3D scene to appear realistic and detailed in extreme close-ups requires a study of how your subject appears at very close range, followed by test-rendering and development of appropriately detailed textures.

3D Textures

Some procedural textures are *3D textures*, also called *solid textures*. Instead of being two-dimensional like a texture map, a 3D texture is a procedure that produces a pattern based on a three-dimensional position in space. You can model any shape object, and a 3D texture will always be applied evenly to every part of it. For example, the marble texture in Figure 10.47 wraps seamlessly from one side of the cube to another, and even into holes cutting through the object. This would require effort to set up if each surface were textured with a texture map, but happens automatically with 3D textures.

Many programs also support 2D procedural textures, which can be projected or applied to UV coordinates, just like a texture map.

[Figure 10.47] A 3D procedural texture uniformly textures all surfaces within its 3D space.

Animation

Procedural textures are controlled by adjusting numeric parameters. You can animate parameters so that when they change over time, your texture will change in all sorts of ways. Animated procedural textures can produce unique appearances that can be used in visual effects, transitions, or even as abstract animated backgrounds to appear behind titles and logos.

Appearance

While features such as resolution independence, seamless 3D texturing of complex models, and animatable parameters are great technical advantages, the most important consideration in choosing an approach to your texturing is the final appearance you can create. Most 3D programs come with a set of general-purpose procedural textures that add different types of noise and patterns to a surface. If you are working on putting together scenes very quickly, and want to create textures without needing to leave your 3D program, then assigning a general-purpose procedural texture to a surface can be a quick way of putting colored patterns onto different objects.

General-purpose 3D textures seldom look exactly like what you are approximating with them. For example, a procedural wood texture can look somewhat like wood, or perhaps more like a simulated wood pattern, but it isn't likely to look like antique oak furniture or softwood cedar or maple or anything more specific. If you care about getting the look exactly right, you should probably be creating texture maps instead of relying of procedural textures. Figure 10.48 shows a comparison between a general-purpose procedural texture (left) and a custom bitmap texture (right). While the procedural texture might not look as realistic, it was created in a tiny fraction of the time.

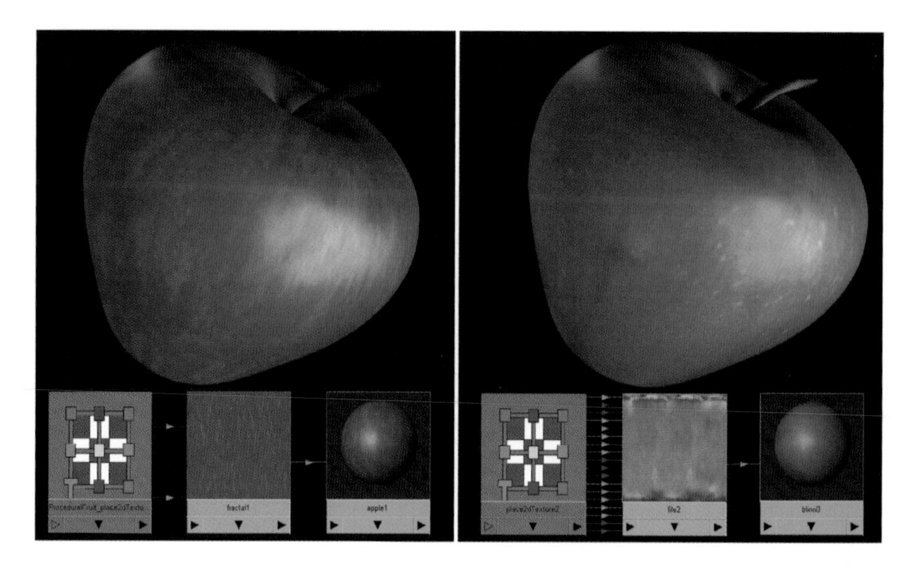

[Figure 10.48] A procedural approach to texturing an apple (left) is simpler to create than a bitmap texture (right).

Artists working on quality-oriented productions sometimes use procedural textures in combination with texture maps. For example, you create a texture map for an apple based on photographs, but map the specular color of the apple with a procedural noise to simulate variable amounts of shininess on the surface. When multiple procedural textures are used together and combined with texture maps, procedural textures can be a useful tool.

Another way that procedural textures are used in high-end productions is through custom shader development. All large studios and many smaller companies employ programmers or shading technical directors who write custom shaders. Custom shaders are shaders written for the needs of a specific production, and may include procedural textures developed to achieve specific looks for a particular type of surface. While writing custom shaders can take longer than painting a texture map, they are useful because they can cover an entire planet or other large or varied objects with non-repeating patterns.

Baking Procedural Textures into Texture Maps

A procedural texture can be baked into a texture map. In Maya, for example, the Convert to File Texture function in Hypershade will convert any procedural texture into a bitmap texture. If your software doesn't have any baking or conversion functions, a universal way to turn procedural textures into texture maps is to apply the procedural texture to a flat surface, and make a rendering of the surface. The rendered texture can then be applied as a map on different objects.

The main reason to convert procedural textures into bitmaps is to gain additional creative control. The procedural pattern might be a main part of your texture, but you might want to paint in different details around particular areas, such as stretching out part of the texture around a joint, or adding unique wounds or imperfections to a texture.

While the general purpose textures that ship with most 3D software might not meet all of your needs in texturing, they can sometimes be great starting points in painting a more detailed or interesting texture. Instead of using the random noise function in your paint program, baking textures in your 3D program gives you access to a much bigger library of noise and other procedural patterns to use as starting points in painting maps. Even when a procedural texture is too simple or regular to use as the final texture, it might still be a useful starting point to bake into a bitmap and bring into your paint program.

Another reason to convert procedural textures into bitmaps is to move textured models between different programs. Different software will have different procedural textures available, but every program should be able to render a texture map.

Converting to a bitmap might make some textures render more quickly, especially when sampled over time with motion blur. However, this depends on how complex the original procedural texture was, and how high resolution the texture map becomes. For example, if you convert your procedural texture into a bitmap 4096 pixels across, it might take more memory and rendering time than the original procedure.

Both procedural and bitmap textures have their place in production. Texture maps may be more popular because they offer additional control and random access to coloring specific points on an object, but you should never overlook the possibility that a procedural texture might be the best tool for a particular job.

Looks Development

Looks development means developing the overall appearance of a surface, including the shader and all of the texture maps. Some programs, like 3D Studio Max, use the word *Material* in reference to a shader with all of the textures attached.

All of the types of textures discussed in this chapter may be used together, along with different types of shaders as described in the previous chapter, to create new looks for your surfaces. The question is, when putting together maps of several different types, how do the components all work together? How do you plan and execute a complex surface appearance that requires a color map, a bump map, and a specularity map all aligned with each other? Where do you start?

There are several different approaches to creating a complex material. In general, the main approaches can be called painting in layers, color first, and displacement first.

Painting in Layers

One of the great advantages of painting your textures from scratch, instead of processing photographs or scans into texture maps, is that different elements of your textures can be painted onto different layers in your paint program.

As an example, in painting a skin texture, features such as freckles, pores, hairs, dirt, and tan lines can each be painted onto different layers. The fact that these features are each painted on separate layers makes it vastly easier to create other types of maps based on your color map. In creating a bump map, you can decide which features will be a part of a bump map, and which will not. Freckles only represent a color change, so a freckles layer can be omitted from the bump map. Pores are depressions into the skin, so they would be turned into dark spots on the bump map. Razor stubble on a man's chin bumps outwards, so that layer should be turned white and added as white dots in the bump map.

When painting dirt into textures, sometimes custom brushes can be made starting with photographic images, and these custom brushes can add realistic detail to the layers being painted. Dirt tends to influence several of the texture maps on a surface. Of course dirt can change the color of a surface, but it also can make the surface less shiny, so dirt can be represented as a darkened area in a specular or reflectivity map. The texture of a dirt pattern or stain is sometimes added to a bump map as well, and if a surface is transparent, then dirt tends to create a darker area (less transparency) in the transparency map.

For every feature, every piece of dirt or scratch on a surface, you need to decide which texture maps the feature will appear in. Usually studying a real example of the material you are trying to recreate is the best guide. For each surface feature, ask yourself how it influences the shininess, the bump, the transparency, or other attributes of a surface before putting that feature into additional texture maps. By having features appear in several types of maps, the different maps you apply to the surface reinforce each other in creating a more believable look.

Color First

The color-first approach just means starting with a color map before making any of the other kinds of maps that will complement it. Textures derived from photographs or scans tend to fall into this category.

Sometimes, looking at a color map, you might decide that lighter tones in the map tend to appear where a surface is higher, and darker areas appear where the surface is lower, so that you can let your color map double as a bump map. If dark features on your color map represent things that actually bump higher, then you could invert your color map to make a bump map. For example, a brick wall with white mortar between dark red bricks would need to be inverted so that the mortar appeared darker before it would make a good bump map for the wall. Often, however, you'll see some details in your color map that shouldn't cause any change of height at all, so you will need to retouch these out of the map before using it as a bump, while emphasizing the features that should bump more visibly in or out from the surface.

A specular map can sometimes start as a black-and-white version of your color map. You need to think, however, about whether each feature in your color map would really affect your specularity. Many features do not, if they are simply color changes without any change to the shininess of the surface. If a feature shouldn't affect the specularity of the surface, then you should retouch it out of the color map before using it as a specular map.

The process of deciding what belongs in your color map, your bump map, or your specular map is the same when you start with a color map as if you started with a multi-layer painting. The difference is that all of the different types of features are together in a single image, so any attempt to sort them out needs to be done through retouching and image processing, instead of just creating a new layer set with a different combination of features made visible.

Displacement First

Painting displacement first (also called bump first) is an approach where the basic structure of a map is painted before the color is assigned. For example, if you were creating the look of a stained glass window, you might start by painting the structure of the metal frames that go around the individual pieces of glass. This map could be used as a bump map. It also would be the starting point for painting the color map, which would be made by filling in the areas between the metal frames with different colors. A transparency map could be made by filling in gray between the metal frames, perhaps with some dirt painted in dark tones around the edges. As a result, a complete look that varies several attributes is painted starting with the basic structure contained in the bump or displacement map.

Painting displacement maps in a paint program is difficult. You are trying to visualize a complex 3D surface being deformed into a new shape, but all you see are tones of gray painted into a flat image. Small adjustments to the gamma of your image can make the difference between a sharp ridge and a rounded or flat top to a peak in your displacement, but getting these adjustments right can be a slow trial-and-error process moving versions of your map between your paint program and your 3D application. Luckily, there are other choices for how to create complex displacement maps.

Organic Modeling Tools

Organic modeling tools, such as Pixologic ZBrush and SensAble Technologies' ClayTools, are becoming increasingly popular ways to create geometry with displacement maps. They offer an interface where 3D surfaces can be manipulated like clay with different types of sculpting tools, allowing you to paint or sculpt displaced surfaces interactively.

Once a richly displaced surface has been created in an organic modeling program, it can be exported into other 3D applications as both a simplified base mesh, and a displacement map (or optionally a normal map) representing additional pixel-level detail in the surface. These displacement maps can be highly accurate 32-bit images, which store more detail than maps you paint in a regular paint program and explicitly communicate the actual displacement height at each point, instead of just varying from black and white and requiring you to adjust the displacement height in your 3D software.

Baking Geometry into Displacement Maps

Another way to make a displacement map is to start with a 3D model, and make a rendering based on its height or depth. The left side of Figure 10.49 shows a 3D model that will be converted into a displacement map for a coin. You want it to render white at the highest point and black at the lowest point. In this case, a gradient is projected down from the top to assign colors to the model. When it is rendered (right) it forms a displacement map with all of the height detail from the model.

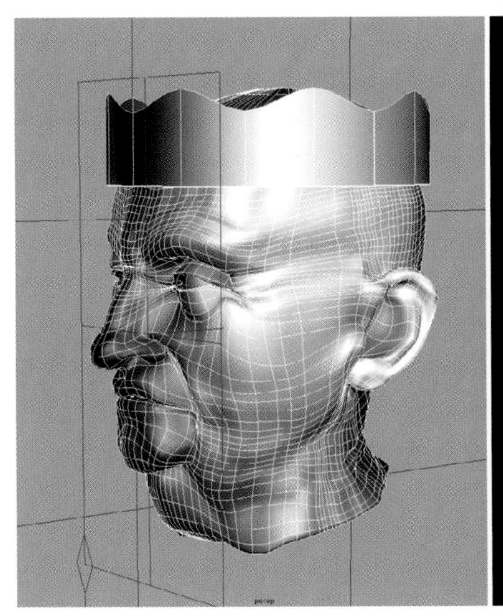

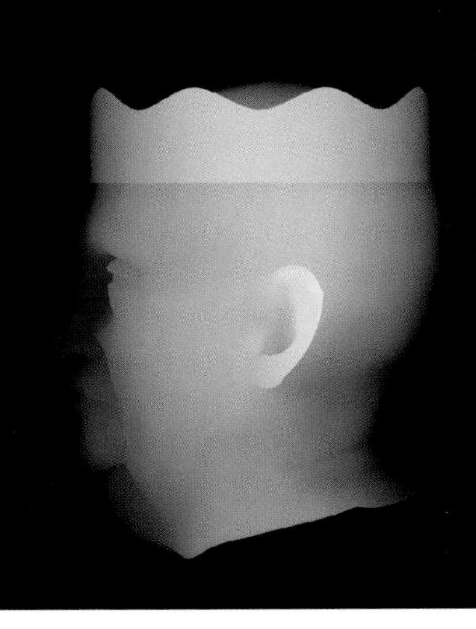

[Figure 10.49]
A head model (left) is converted into a displacement map (right).

The image from the right side of Figure 10.50 is the starting point for the look of the coin. More detail and text is added in a paint program. This could be rendered as a displacement map for close-ups or as a bump map in wider shots.

[Figure 10.50]
The displacement map from Figure 10.49 is applied to a coin.

Great texture maps can come from almost any kind of image, whether it was rendered in 3D, baked from a procedure, photographed, scanned, or painted. The keys to successful texture mapping are learning to visualize what you want, and being flexible about how you accomplish your goals.

Exercises

1. Find a small outdoor area—it could be the area around a tree stump, a fire hydrant, a potted plant, or any space about a meter across. Photograph it with a digital camera, shooting some wider shots from multiple angles for modeling reference, and then an extensive set of close-up pictures for texture map development. Model and texture map that area to reproduce it as completely as possible.

2. Find a surface that you normally consider to be blank or devoid of texture, such as a white wall. How can you tell by sight what material it is made of? For example, how would you tell when looking at the surface whether it was paper, plastic, or plaster? What kinds of texture mapping would you use to represent the surface, and how would you create it?

3. The next time you build a 3D model, think carefully about which details you really need to model, and which you might be able to replace with a texture map. For example, if there is detail carved into the surface that could be replaced with a bump map, or if a complex edge or cutout pattern could be replaced by a transparency map, then try building a simpler model and using texture mapping to add the detail.

The passes I used in this book's cover image include a global illumination pass, rim and specular pass, key light lighting pass, ambient pass, effects layer with fog, and an ambient occlusion pass.

Rendering Passes and Compositing

Film and television production companies are continually asked to render scenes that seem to be beyond the limits of their software and hardware. To complete ambitious 3D renderings with the required complexity, quality, and speed, almost all professional productions are rendered in multiple *layers* or *passes* and finished though *compositing*. Compositing is the art of combining multiple images into a unified final scene. Multipass rendering and compositing allow for more efficient rendering, increased creative control, convincing integration with live-action footage, and rapid revisions of shots.

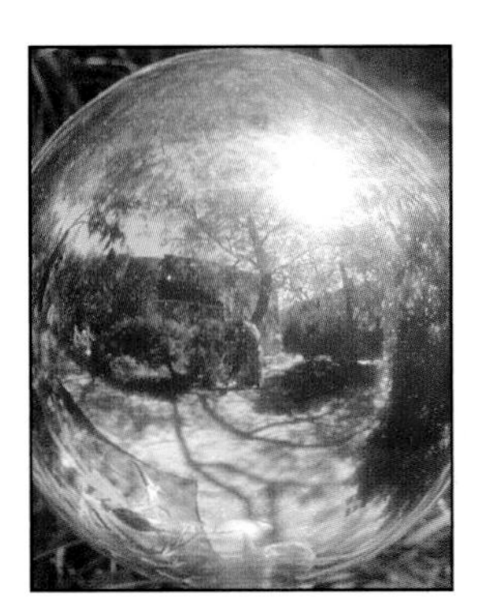

Rendering in Layers

Rendering in layers is the process of rendering different objects in your scene into different image files that will be composited together.

As a simple example of rendering in layers, Figure 11.1 shows a spaceship landing on a planet. The spaceship is rendered as the foreground layer, and the planet rendered separately as a background layer.

[Figure 11.1] A separately rendered background layer (the planet), and foreground layer (the spaceship) form a complete composite.

The foreground and background layers start out as part of the same 3D scene, and are staged and animated together. During rendering, however, you can render the background layer by itself. Many 3D programs have software support for organizing objects into different layers and selecting which will be rendered. If you don't have that support, you can organize objects into different groups and display the layer to be rendered while hiding the other groups of objects.

The foreground spaceship layer is rendered over a black background, as shown in Figure 11.2. The figure also shows the *alpha channel*—the channel of the image file that stores transparency information—rendered along with the spaceship. In compositing, the white pixels in the alpha channel mark where the layer is opaque, making the spaceship appear, and the black pixels mark parts of the layer that will be transparent, making the background layer visible. Alpha channels will be covered in depth below.

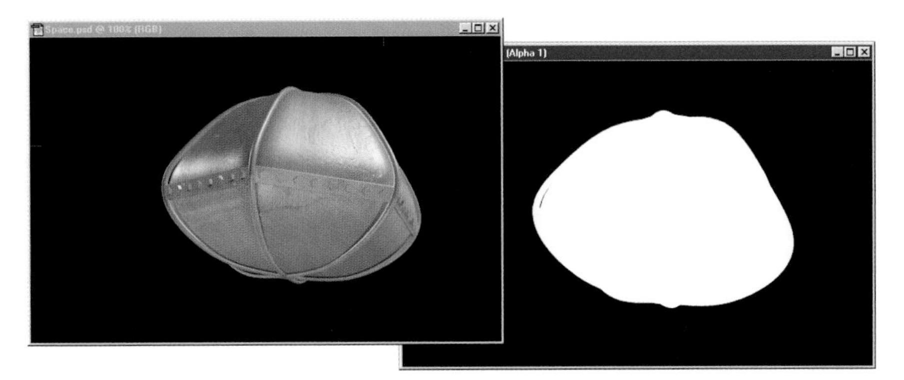

[Figure 11.2] The foreground layer (left) is rendered along with an alpha channel (right).

Background Layers

As long as the camera does not move during the shot, and no part of the planet is animated, the planet could be rendered as a *held layer*. A held layer is a still image that only needs to be rendered once, usually at the first frame, and then can be composited into every frame of the shot, along with the animated layers.

In addition to saving render time, using held layers enables you to retouch or add detail to your background using a paint program.

A sky is often split into its own layer and rendered separately. You may want motion in the sky, such as drifting clouds or twinkling stars, even if the rest of your set or environment is a held background layer.

When a sky is much brighter than the layer in front of it, sometimes it creates a visible glow that wraps around the edges of other layers. When the contrast between the horizon and the sky seems too sharp, as on the top of Figure 11.3, adding a glow around the sky can make the transition more natural, as shown on the lower half of the figure.

[Figure 11.3] When a bright sky is composited behind a subject (top), sometimes it helps to add a glow around the edge of the sky (bottom).

Matte Objects

The easiest way to break down your scene into layers is to start with the farthest back, and work your way toward the front of the scene. However, sometimes objects don't fit neatly into a back-to-front ordering. For example, imagine if you were splitting the grass into a different layer from the egg in Figure 11.4, where the grass is both in front of and behind the egg.

When one layer surrounds another in space, instead of being clearly in front of or behind it, some of the objects may need to be rendered as a *matte object*. A matte object is an object that renders pure black, and also appears pure black in the alpha channel. Many shaders have an *alpha* or *matte opacity* setting that can be turned down to pure black for a black alpha.

Figure 11.5 shows the grass rendered with the egg as a matte object. In this case, the grass layer can be composited over the egg layer to produce the result seen in Figure 11.4. Even though the grass layer is composited over the egg, the hole in the grass layer cut by the matte object ensures that the egg will appear to be in front of some of the grass.

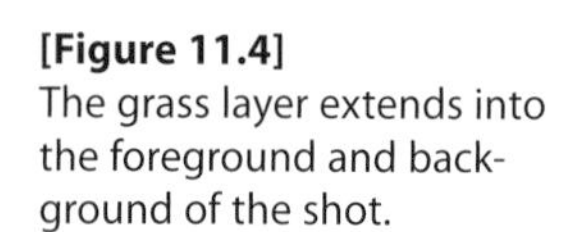

[Figure 11.4]
The grass layer extends into the foreground and background of the shot.

[Figure 11.5] Rendering the egg as a matte object, it appears as a black hole in the grass layer (left) and its alpha channel (right).

You could achieve similar results if you render the egg with the grass as a matte object, so that the egg had the grass cut out of it. In that case, you would composite the egg layer over the grass layer, instead of the other way around. Using the ground and ground coverings as a matte object is common in rendering animated characters, so that when their feet are composited over the ground the bottoms of the feet can be occluded by appropriate parts of the terrain.

Finally, you have the option of rendering both layers with all of the geometry visible, but rendering the grass with the egg as a matte object, and the egg with the grass as a matte object. If you take this approach, then you don't even need to use the alpha channels to combine the layers; simply adding them together will result in a perfect composite.

Effects Layers

An *effects layer* (sometimes called an *effects pass*) is a separate rendering of a visual effect. It might be rain, snow, splashing water, smoke, fire, or even an optical effect such as a light bloom or lens flare. Splitting effects elements into separate layers gives you a great deal more control over their appearance in the final composite, and is a good idea for almost any shot that contains any kind of visual effect.

Why Bother With Layers?

Rendering in layers clearly involves more setup work than rendering all the objects in a scene at once. You might wonder why most professional productions are rendered in multiple layers at all. Couldn't busy professionals skip the process of rendering in layers, and then save more time by not needing to composite? There are actually several advantages to rendering in layers:

- Rendering in layers makes large, complex scenes possible. Your computer's memory could be overloaded if all objects had to be rendered at once. Without layers, huge projects would either slow down the computer as it swapped data from its hard drive, or crash it completely.
- Using held layers saves rendering time compared to rerendering static objects for each frame of your animation.
- For high-quality character animation, most of your rerenders are likely to apply to the character, not the background. In this case, you can quickly rerender the character as a foreground layer, without rerendering the full scene.
- For a soft-focused background, you can sometimes get away with blurring the background layer in your compositing program, instead of rendering with a slow depth-of-field (DOF) effect in 3D.
- For maximum rendering efficiency, you can render different layers using different software settings. For example, you might use motion blur and raytracing on layers where they were needed. More distant objects, or objects that you plan to blur during compositing, might be rendered in a manner more optimized for speed.
- You can reuse separately rendered elements in multiple places and times, so you don't need to render as many elements. For example, you might recycle a cloud of smoke or an exploding fireball that had been rendered for a different shot.
- You can perform last-minute fixes, such as adjusting the color or brightness of a part of your scene, more easily by adjusting individual layers in your composite, rather than rerendering your whole scene.
- To work around bugs, limitations, or incompatibilities in your software, split different effects into different render layers. For example, if you use an effect that does not render through a transparent surface, you could render the effect as a separate layer, then composite the transparent foreground layer over it.

While including layer rendering and compositing in your pipeline takes an investment to set up, it can save an enormous amount of time and money once it becomes a regular part of your workflow.

Optical Effects

Optical effects are phenomena such as lens flares or streaks radiating from a light, which simulate effects that could occur in and around a camera's lens or film. During compositing, optical effects are usually added last, superimposed over other elements.

By themselves, most optical effects are very quick to render. However, as you wouldn't want to repeatedly rerender a complex scene just to see different adjustments to a lens flare, it is better to develop its look as a separate layer that can be rendered and adjusted quickly.

Optical effects that become too visible can make your scenes look fake and tacky. Having them as a separate layer gives you a chance to adjust, diminish, or even delete the effects later if you change your mind about their importance in your scene.

Particle Effects

The appearance of particles can be greatly enhanced if you render them in separate layers. You can use rendered particles as masks to control different image-processing effects, manipulate their color and opacity, and combine them in different ways with the background image.

Figure 11.6 shows a very simple cloud of particles. Using the particle cloud as a mask for a distortion effect, the background is distorted by the particles, as though the particles were causing refraction. Finally, the particles are colored green and keyed over the background, behind the ship that emitted them.

When particles are widely distributed throughout a scene, some of them may appear in front of other objects, and some of them behind other objects. Objects surrounded by particles often need to be rendered as matte objects within a particle layer.

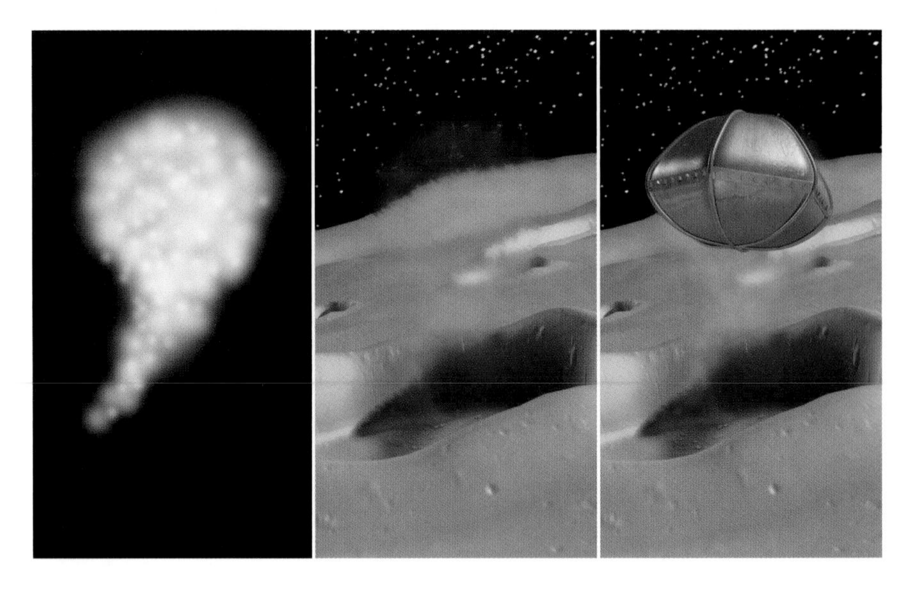

[Figure 11.6] An effects layer (left) can be used as a mask for a displacement effect (middle) to add simulated refraction to a composite (right).

Alpha Channel Issues

An alpha channel represents transparency or coverage of an image layer. Where alpha channel pixels are white, or a value of 1, they represent full coverage by a layer, meaning that the corresponding color pixels should be fully opaque. Where the alpha channel is black, or storing a value of 0, it represents pixels that are transparent, or not covered by that layer. Alpha channel values between 0 and 1 represent varying degrees of transparency.

In a rendered image, pixels can be said to be transparent or have partial coverage in areas where a transparent shader is used, along the edges of objects where they are anti-aliased against the background, and in the streak of a moving object rendered with motion blur. Partial transparency is always evident in the alpha channel. Whether partial transparency is also evident in the color channel depends on whether your image is premultiplied.

Most 3D rendering uses a *premultiplied alpha channel*. Rendering over a black background with a premultiplied (or *premult*) alpha channel is the default behavior of most 3D graphics software, and the most common way that layers and passes are rendered in professional production work.

When an image has a premultiplied alpha channel, it means that the alpha channel exactly fits together with the red, green, and blue channels of the image. In images with a *non-premultiplied alpha channel* (or *straight alpha channel*), the alpha channel is completely independent from the color channel, and could be any matte or mask.

In many renderers, there is a premultiply option that can be turned off if you do not want a premultiplied image. Figure 11.7 shows an image rendered premultiplied (left) and not premultiplied (center). In areas with anti-aliased edges, motion blur, and transparency, you can see that the premultiplied image looks more smooth and realistic.

The alpha channel, shown on the right of the figure, does not change between premultiplied and straight renderings. In the premultiplied color image, objects appear anti-aliased against the black background, and motion blur blends the spoon with the background color. Without premultiplication, the coverage and transparency is stored exclusively in the alpha channel, and the colored pixels in the image are never blended with the background. You can see this difference in the transparent bowl, the moving spoon, and all of the anti-aliased edges.

[Figure 11.7] Motion blur, transparency, and anti-aliasing blend smoothly with the background in a premultiplied image (left), but do not blend with the background color in a non-premultiplied image (center). The alpha channel (right) does not change.

Compositing With Straight Alpha Channels

Non-premultiplied alpha channels come from a tradition of matting or masking in live-action compositing. When images are filmed or photographed, they don't include an alpha channel. In the compositing process, mattes that are rotoscoped or keyed off a green screen can be stored in an alpha channel, but this does not change the color channels in the original image. As a result, compositing processes designed for dealing with filmed elements tend to expect an alpha channel to be a separate, arbitrary mask, with no direct connection to the color channels in the image.

Different programs have different ways of dealing with straight alpha channels. Adobe Photoshop is built around the assumption that all alpha channels and layer masks are straight. When you import an element into Adobe After Effects, it lets you specify whether the element has a straight or premultiplied alpha channel. In node-based compositing programs such as Shake, a straight alpha channel can be used as the mask input to a keymix node, using the alpha channel just as if it were the output of a keying operation.

Rendering with straight alpha channels limits your compositing in several ways. Here are some of the drawbacks to working with straight alphas:

- Images will not appear anti-aliased until they are multiplied with the alpha channel.
- A pair of layers, each matting the objects shown by the other layer, would not add together correctly if they weren't rendered premult, because the color channels would not be anti-aliased against the matte objects.
- If you blur your images during the composite, such as to simulate depth of field or motion blur, the color can fall out of alignment with the alpha, causing colored fringes around your images.

However, there can be advantages as well:

- Some editing and simpler compositing programs handle straight alphas more easily than premultiplied.
- Some color correction operations can be applied more accurately to color channels that are not premultiplied. For example, if you gamma correct an image, an edge pixel that is 50 percent transparent in the alpha would receive the appropriate color correction in a straight image, but might be mishandled as if it represented a darker tone when applied to a premultiplied image.
- Images that will be multiplied with the background during compositing generally don't need to be premultiplied in rendering. Elements such as occlusion passes (discussed below) should be rendered without premultiplication.

Compositing With Premultiplied Alpha Channels

Compositing with premultiplied alpha channels is generally faster and simpler than working with images that have not been premultiplied. Multiplication with the alpha channel is a part of the arithmetic used when layers are composited together, so some compositors premultiply all elements in order to save compositing time.

In Shake, an Over node works perfectly for putting together layers with premultiplied alpha channels. Adobe Photoshop doesn't expect alpha channels to be premultiplied, but if you use a premultiplied alpha channel to delete the background from a layer, the function Matting > Remove Black Matte will perfect the key according to the premultiplied alpha channel.

If you render premultiplied layers, you can always switch them to un-premultiplied and back in a compositing program. Figure 11.8 shows the MDiv (matte divide, as in un-premultiply) and MMult (premultiply) nodes in Shake. You don't need to use these often. They would be useful, however, if you encountered a color correction operation that didn't look consistent in half-transparent edge pixels around a layer. If some combination of extensive color correction operations left you with visible fringes around the edges of a premultiplied layer, you could fix this problem by un-premultiplying before the color correction and premultiplying again after it, as shown on the right side of Figure 11.8.

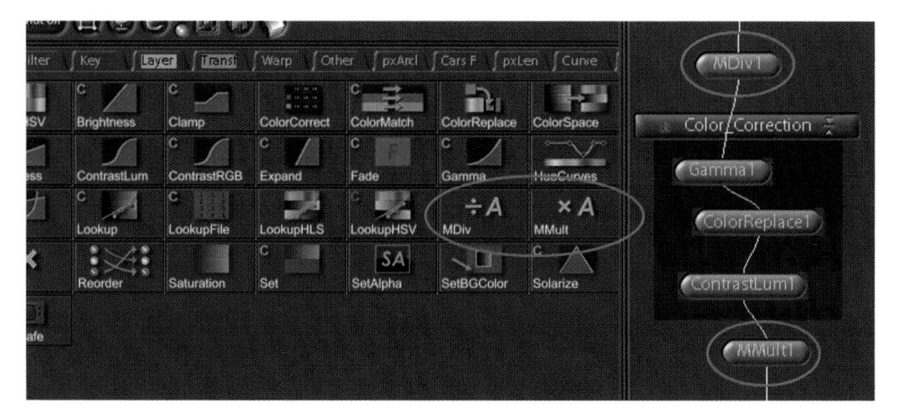

[Figure 11.8] When needed, you can un-premultiply an image prior to color correction, and premultiply it again afterward.

If you are rendering 3D graphics and passing layers off to someone else for compositing, you will sometimes encounter compositors who are more used to working with straight alphas than premult. Warning signs that your compositor is unfamiliar with premultiplied graphics will come if you hear a comment such as, "Your mattes were a little off, but we fixed them" (this means they may have pushed the edges in by a pixel or two, which would not really fix a problem and could badly degrade motion blurred frames) or "Could you possibly render this over a different color than black?" (which means that they are having problems separating the image from the background, being unaccustomed to premultiplied alpha channels).

A good test to make sure that your alpha channel compositing is working flawlessly is to render a scene of a white object in a white environment, as shown in Figure 11.9. If you render the foreground object against a black background as one layer, and render the environment as another layer, you should be able to composite the two together seamlessly, without any darkness creeping into the edge pixels around the foreground object.

[Figure 11.9] Check to avoid black matte lines in a composite, even between two white objects.

If you aren't sure how to get a particular compositing program to work with premultiplied alpha channels, there is a fallback solution that will work in any application. Instead of using the alpha channel to layer your foreground over the background, use the alpha channel to cut a black hole in the background, as shown in Figure 11.10.

With the black hole cut in the background, you can then add your foreground as the layer on top. Figure 11.11 shows how a simple "add" operation (or "linear dodge" in Photoshop), without using any matte or mask, will put your foreground over the background without any dark fringes or matting errors.

[Figure 11.10]
Using an alpha to cut a hole in the background prepares it for the addition of another layer.

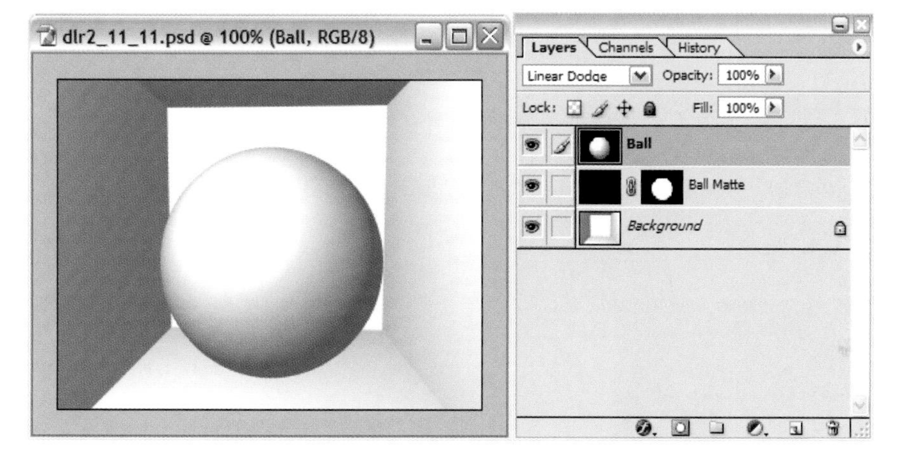

[Figure 11.11]
A layer can be added on top of a composite, without needing any masks, if its alpha has already been used to black out the background.

Rendering in Passes

Rendering in passes is the process of rendering different attributes of your scene separately. Passes are often named after the attribute of the scene that they isolate, such as a shadow pass, which would show just the shadows in the scene. Whereas rendering in layers just means rendering different objects separately, rendering in passes isolates aspects of the scene such as parts of your lighting, shadows, or depth information. The ten most common types of passes that you can render are:

- Diffuse
- Specular
- Reflection
- Shadow
- Ambient
- Occlusion
- Beauty
- Global Illumination
- Mask
- Depth

Rendering in passes is not exclusive of rendering in layers—you can do both at the same time, such as rendering a specular pass for your foreground character layer. In some programs, the system for managing layers is also used to set up all of your passes.

Diffuse Passes

A *diffuse pass* is the full-color rendering of your subject, including diffuse illumination, color, and texture, but *not* including reflections, highlights, or shadows, which will be rendered as separate passes. Because a diffuse pass includes the diffuse illumination from lights, surfaces are shaded brighter where they face a light source and darker where they face away from a light source. Figure 11.12 is the diffuse pass for the spaceship; it includes the basic texture and shading, but lacks highlights and reflections.

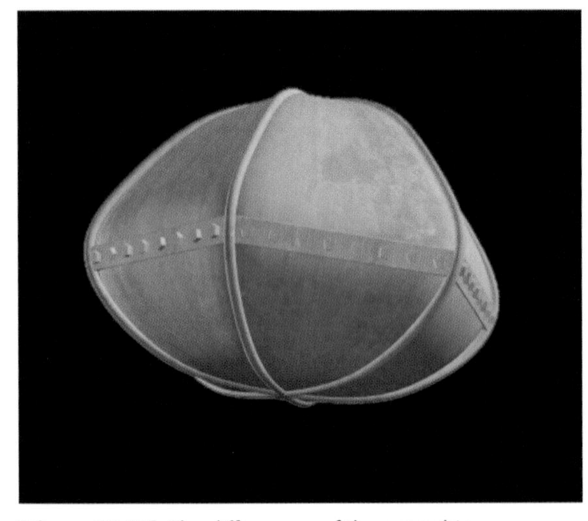

[Figure 11.12] The diffuse pass of the spaceship

Many programs include a preset to render a diffuse pass as a single function. If you need to set up diffuse pass rendering without a preset, you can do it by modifying the shaders not to be reflective or have specular highlights, and by setting the lights not to cast shadows. Another approach to setting up a diffuse pass is to modify the lights not to emit specularity, and globally turn off raytraced reflections.

Specular Passes

Specular passes (or *highlight passes*) isolate the specular highlights from your objects. You can render specular passes by turning off any ambient light and making the object's diffuse shading and color mapping pure black. The result, as shown in Figure 11.13, will be a rendering of all the specular highlights in the scene, without any other types of shading.

[Figure 11.13] The specular pass of the spaceship

Rendering a separate specular pass allows you more creative control over how the highlights are rendered. For example, in Figure 11.13, a bump map was added to vary and soften the highlights. The bump map was not there in rendering the diffuse pass; it was applied only for the highlights. You may also move your lights to different positions if it makes better highlights. Naturally the lights should come from the same general angle as the lighting that is used in the diffuse pass and shadow passes, but there's nothing wrong with cheating a little bit to make a better-looking rendering.

During your composite, having specular highlights as a separate pass will allow control over their color and brightness, so that you can adjust the highlights to match the rest of your composited scene. Don't clip large areas of your highlights into pure white. Your specular pass will work best if highlights run through different shades of gray, which will allow it to look realistic when added together with other passes.

You can also use separately rendered highlights to control visual effects, such as glows added in compositing. Adding a blurred copy of your specular pass will create glows around your highlights, as shown in Figure 11.14. This way, glows do not take any test-renders to adjust, and they can be adjusted in context with the final composite.

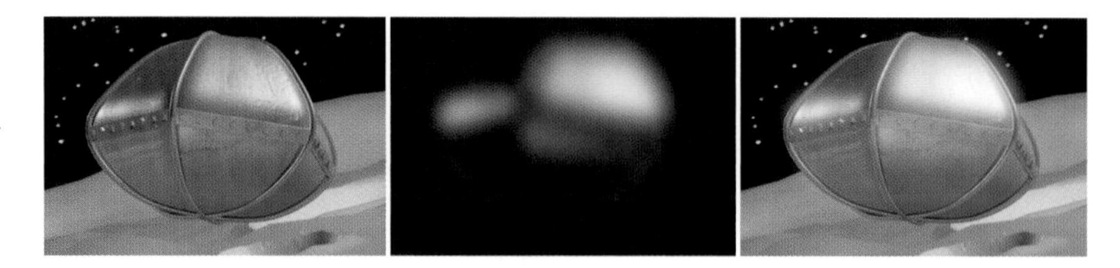

[Figure 11.14] Adding together the spaceship image (left) with a blurred copy of the specular pass (middle) creates a glow effect around its highlights (right).

Reflection Passes

A *reflection pass* can include self-reflections, reflections of other objects, or reflections of the surrounding environment. Often you need to render several reflection passes, especially if you want to isolate raytraced reflections on different objects.

To set up a reflection pass showing the reflections of the environment onto the spaceship, the spaceship is given a shader that does not show diffuse illumination or specular highlights (it is given a black color and a highlight size of 0), but is reflective. The objects that it needs to reflect are made invisible to primary visibility, but are left visible in reflections. The result shows only the reflections on the spaceship, without any diffuse or specular illumination. The reflection pass for the spaceship is separate from any other reflection passes that might be needed later, such as if you rendered reflections of the ship on a reflective ground surface.

Compositing Reflections

Reflection passes, diffuse passes, and specular passes can all be composited together with an Add operation (or Linear Dodge in Photoshop), as shown in Figure 11.15. This way, lighter areas of your reflection and specular passes will brighten your diffuse pass, and black areas will have no effect.

Some people use Screen instead of Add as the compositing mode when combining these passes. Instead of adding the values as $a+b$, a Screen operation calculates $1-(1-a)*(1-b)$. The result looks similar, but not as bright. While Add is truer to the results of rendering diffuse, specular, and reflections at once in a 3D program, Screen is less likely to reach pure white and suffer from clipping problems in bright areas. When two values are added and they each reach medium gray, the result is pure white. When two medium gray values are screened together, they are a light gray, and it takes brighter values to reach pure white.

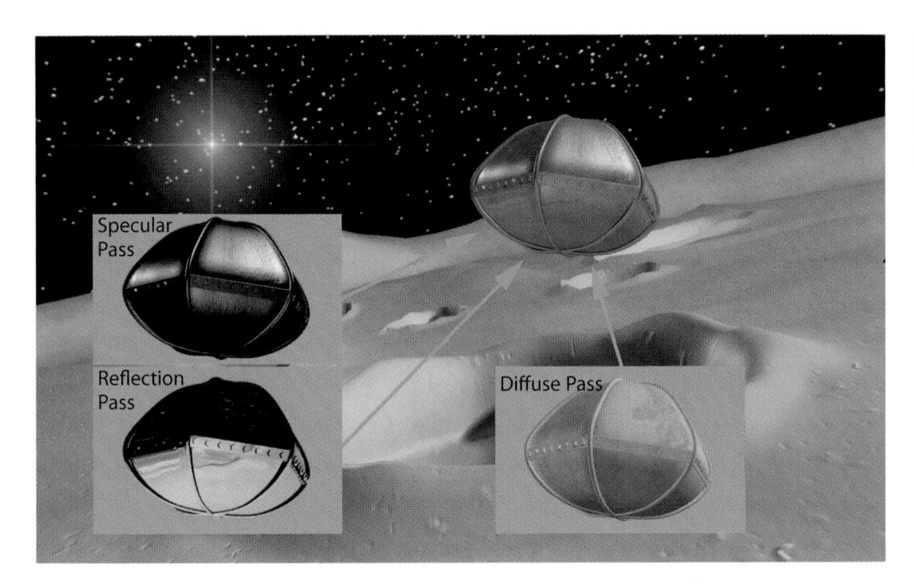

[Figure 11.15] Diffuse, specular, and reflection passes are added together in the final composite.

In some cases, you will get the best results by blurring your reflection pass slightly in your compositing program. If you're going to do this, sometimes you can save rendering time by using less anti-aliasing or fewer samples in your reflection. Even if your reflection pass doesn't look perfectly refined when rendered, it can still look good after it is blurred in your compositing program.

Adding Reflections to Real Objects

Sometimes your 3D object will cast a reflection onto a real-world surface, such as a shiny floor, countertop, or water surface. In this case, render the cast reflection as a separate reflection pass received by a 3D model of the real surface, such as the grid in Figure 11.16.

For the effect of rippling water, you might add a bump map to a reflective water surface object, which distorts a reflection as shown in Figure 11.17.

[Figure 11.16]
A plane is positioned to receive a reflection pass.

[Figure 11.17]
Bump mapping distorts the reflection to make it more watery (right).

When keying the reflection over a surface, adjust it in your compositing program to match the tones of existing reflections on the surface, as in Figure 11.18. Reflections that have too much color and contrast can look unrealistic, so color correction is usually necessary to match any real background sequence.

[Figure 11.18]
The reflection is graded to match the water's colors.

Shadow Passes

A *shadow pass* is a rendering that shows the locations of shadows in a scene.

In scenes with overlapping shadows, it is important to keep the different shadows separated when rendering shadow passes, so that you can control their appearance, color, and softness separately during the composite.

The scene on the left side of Figure 11.19 is lit by multiple light sources. A shadow pass that lumped them all together (right) would not allow you to isolate them and manipulate them separately in the composite. This kind of shadow pass is a quick preset in some programs, but it puts all of your shadows together into the alpha channel of the shadow pass image. If you have to use a preset like this, try to render several of them, one for each of your lights, to avoid lumping multiple shadows together.

[Figure 11.19] A scene with several overlapping lights (left) could produce an unmanageable number of overlaps in a shadow pass (right).

Colored Shadow Passes

An alternate way to render a shadow pass is to set up lights with different shadow colors, such as red, green, and blue. With the light's color set to black, the colored shadows are all that appear in the pass. If you render a colored shadow pass as shown in Figure 11.20, then you can separate the red, green, and blue channels during the composite, and use them as three separate shadow passes.

[Figure 11.20] Shadows split into red, green, and blue pack three shadow passes into one.

The trick of using a black light color and a red, green, or blue shadow color doesn't work in every program. You may need a workaround, such as giving the light a negative intensity and a negative shadow color. Regardless of how you set it up, packing three shadows into each shadow pass is more efficient than rendering shadow passes with only one shadow, or a shadow pass in which the shadows cannot be separated.

Even with the shadows isolated into different color channels, for complete control over your shadows you also need to separate the *cast shadows* (shadows from one object onto another) from the *attached shadows* (where objects shadow themselves). To do this, you should make the objects that cast the shadows invisible to primary rays, so they are only present in the pass to cast shadows, as in Figure 11.21. Having shadow objects cast shadows without being directly visible in a layer also helps you include shadows cast from one layer into another.

Attached shadows don't always need to be included in a shadow pass at all. Sometimes you can render attached shadows as a part of the object's diffuse and specular passes, and only worry about the cast shadows in your shadow passes. It's a good idea to render different shadow passes for different layers. Especially in a scene with transparent objects, rendering a shadow pass for the foreground objects, and another for the background, would be more manageable than rendering them all together.

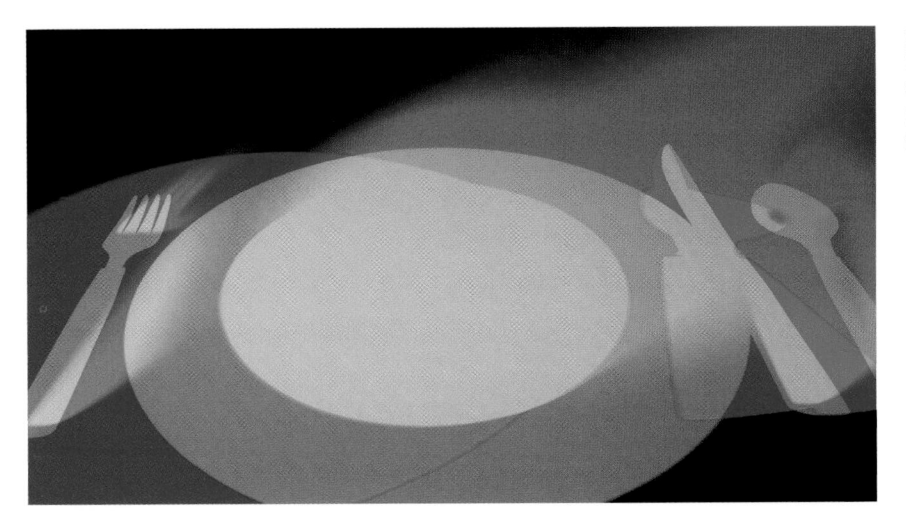

[Figure 11.21] Isolating shadows on the table allows them to be blurred separately from the foreground geometry.

There are many ways to actually use a shadow pass in compositing. Some people lay the shadow pass over other passes, so that they cover the background with black in the areas where their alpha channels are more solid. Other compositors treat a shadow pass as a mask for a darkening adjustment. Another popular approach is to invert the shadow pass (so that it becomes a black shadow on a white background) and multiply it with the colored image. If you plan to multiply your shadow pass with other elements, you might want to render it straight instead of premultiplied, to avoid matte lines building up in your composite.

Blurring and Distorting Shadow Passes

Shadows sometimes look better when the shadow pass is blurred during compositing. If you are rendering a shadow pass that you know will be blurred later anyway, you might use less anti-aliasing on the shadow pass, turn down the number of shadow samples or shadow rays on soft shadows, or use a lower resolution shadow map. Figure 11.22 shows the scene with the shadows on the table blurred during the composite.

If your shadow pass is cast onto a flat, smooth surface, then blurring the shadow pass will create a realistic result that looks as if you had rendered a soft shadow. If the surface receiving the shadow is rough, jagged, or has any complex shape, then you run the risk that parts of the shadow will get blurred out of alignment with the geometry, darkening inappropriate parts of the scene. If your shadow isn't cast onto a flat surface, then make sure your shadow is rendered with the amount of softness you need, because you will be limited in how much you can blur it in compositing.

[Figure 11.22] Because the shadows on the table were a separate pass, they can be left crisp (left) or blurred in the composite (right).

Separating the shadows that fall onto the ground is especially important if you are integrating CG with photographs or filmed backgrounds. In adding shadow passes to live-action plates, sometimes an extra displacement is applied during the composite, such as using the luminance of the background plate to shift parts of the shadow by a few pixels. This can make the edges of your shadows appear rougher where they fall onto rocks, grass, or other details on a real ground surface.

Doubled Shadows

A common problem in compositing visual effects shots is *doubled shadows*. As shown in Figure 11.23, doubled shadows occur where a shadow pass further darkens an area that was already shadowed from the same light source. When combining two shadow passes that represent the blocking of the same light, be sure to composite the passes together first in a lighten-only or darken-only mode, and then use the merged shadows to darken the background plate.

Doubled shadows can be a problem when adding a shadow pass to a live-action background plate. Especially for exterior scenes where the sun provides a single source for shadows, doubled shadows would look highly unrealistic. The shadow pass must not darken areas that are already darkened by a real shadow. The real shadow needs to be masked out, so that your shadow pass darkens only the areas that weren't already in shadow. Your shadow pass should appear to extend the area of the real shadow, extending its area with the same shadow tone.

[Figure 11.23] Shadows motivated by the same light source should not double-darken an area where they overlap (left) but should blend seamlessly together (right).

Ambient Passes

An *ambient pass* (also known as a *color pass*) shows the color and texture maps on your surfaces, but does not include any diffuse shading, specular highlights, shadows, or reflections. An ambient pass shows every object as if it were uniformly lit by ambient light, so objects appear in a consistently flat, uniform tone, as shown in Figure 11.24. There will not be any shading to brighten or darken parts of the surface, as there would be in a diffuse pass. The colors in rendered pixels in an ambient pass will be the exact color taken from the corresponding pixel of a texture map, or the exact surface color of untextured objects, without any influence from lighting.

[Figure 11.24] An ambient pass is a flat, uniformly shaded reproduction of the scene's colors.

In Maya, you need to add a type of light called an Ambient Light to make an ambient pass, with its Ambient Shade parameter set to 0. Other than this, you generally do not need any light sources present in an ambient pass. An ambient pass will look the same no matter how your scene is lit. To create an ambient pass in 3D Studio Max, turn all other lights off, and add a light set to ambient only. You can also create an ambient pass by rendering a diffuse pass with Diffuse Texture Element Lighting unchecked.

Occlusion Passes

An *occlusion pass* is a close cousin of the shadow pass, only it represents ambient occlusion instead of a shadow. Figure 11.25 shows an occlusion pass for a complete scene.

[Figure 11.25]
An occlusion pass captures the distance between each of the surfaces in the scene.

In your composite, you can multiply occlusion passes with an entire scene, or with a diffuse, specular, reflection, or ambient pass. Figure 11.26 shows an ambient pass of the scene before and after it is multiplied with the occlusion. Multiplying an ambient pass with an occlusion pass can provide a terrific replacement for very soft fill lighting, because the result resembles very soft illumination with soft shadows.

[Figure 11.26]
An ambient pass (left) is shown multiplied with the occlusion pass (right).

Because occlusion passes are usually multiplied with other passes, they should be rendered without premultiplication. You wouldn't want a spaceship to get darker when it moved more rapidly with motion blur, for example, which is what could happen if you rendered an occlusion pass premultiplied, and then multiplied it with the ship's ambient or diffuse pass. Empty areas of occlusion passes should show a pure white background.

If you render separate occlusion passes for different layers of geometry, then you can separately adjust the occlusion from the ground onto the subject, or from the subject onto the ground. If you are compositing a character into a real environment, darkening the ground under the character with an occlusion pass is vital to achieving a realistic composite.

As discussed in Chapter 3, "Shadows and Occlusion," ambient occlusion shoots rays out from each point on each surface as it is rendered. It leaves the area white if the rays don't hit any other objects, or darkens points on a surface from which many rays are blocked. In theory, this simulates light from a bright hazy sky or evenly lit room, which brightens everything except for areas where the light is blocked by nearby objects.

Ambient occlusion shades the scene based on the proximity of nearby objects, without taking into account their brightness, color, or transparency. In some cases, you might want to remove objects from the occlusion pass, so that they don't darken surfaces under or near them. For example, if an object is supposed to be an illuminated light bulb or made of transparent glass, you could leave it out of the occlusion pass. You can also set objects to be visible to primary rays, so they appear in the pass, but set them not to be visible in reflections or casting shadows, so they don't occlude other objects.

Beauty Passes

A *beauty pass* is really just a name for a complete rendering of your scene, complete with all of the attributes such as reflections, highlights, and shadows. Whether you knew it or not, when you were rendering your scene before you broke it down into passes, you were rendering a beauty pass.

A beauty pass is made redundant if you render other passes that can be composited together to recreate it. For example, if you have rendered a diffuse pass, a specular pass, and a shadow pass, then by adding together the diffuse and specular pass, and compositing over or multiplying the shadow pass, you could entirely recreate the beauty pass in your compositing program.

Global Illumination Passes

A *global illumination* pass isolates the indirect light added to your scene by global illumination, as shown in Figure 11.27. This pass can also include raytraced reflections and refractions, and can be a useful way to isolate them into separate passes.

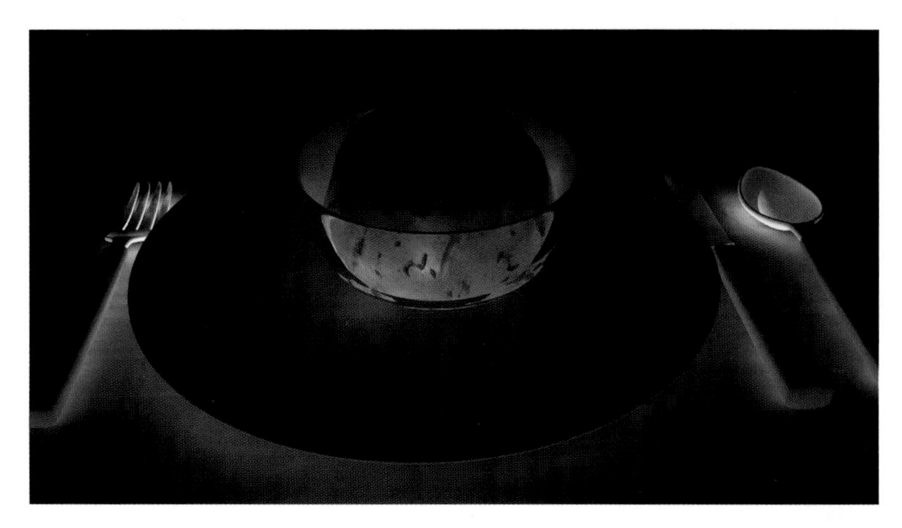

[Figure 11.27] A global illumination pass shows only indirect light.

Usually you would use a global illumination pass in combination with other passes that did not include global illumination. This way, you can adjust the balance of direct and indirect light in your rendering. Figure 11.28 shows a beauty pass (top) without global illumination, and then two possible composites adding different amounts of global illumination from the global illumination pass.

Adjusting the balance between direct and indirect light in your scene could be a very slow process if you had to rerender your scene with global illumination for every change, adjusting the intensity of the global illumination or photons each time. It is much easier to get your scene looking the way you want it if you have your global illumination rendered separately, so that it can be brightened, darkened, or tinted interactively in the composite.

[Figure 11.28] A beauty pass (top) with a global illumination pass added (center) and the global illumination made brighter (lower)

If you are using caustics, those too might benefit from being rendered as a separate pass. Particularly if your shadows and occlusion are being rendered as separate passes, getting the intensity of the caustics might require some tweaking during the composite.

Mask Passes

A *mask pass* (sometimes called a *matte pass* or *alpha pass*) is a pass that provides you with masks showing the location of different objects in your scene.

You already get an alpha channel with each layer you render, which can be used as a mask for any kind of effect in your compositing program. If you want to render more masks at once, the key is to use more of the channels of your image. By giving one object a solid red color, another a solid blue color, and another a solid green color, you get three extra channels of masking information, in addition to your alpha, in a single pass. Figure 11.29 shows two possible mask passes that use all three channels to mask out all of the significant areas of the scene.

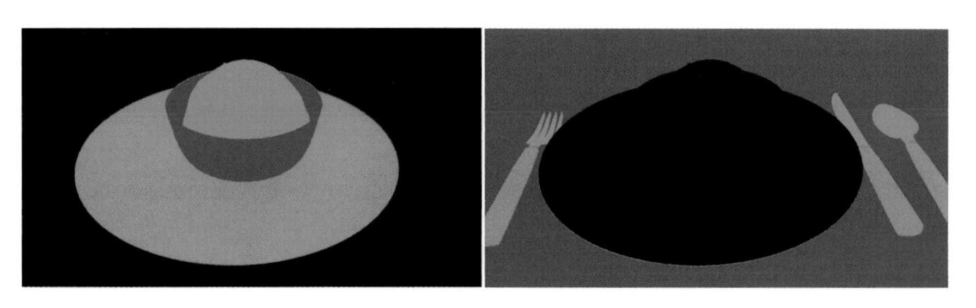

[Figure 11.29]
Two mask passes use their red, green, and blue channels to matte geometry in the scene.

In a compositing program, you can split the red, green, blue, and alpha channels into separate masks to control color correction, or any other effects or adjustments that you want to confine to specific objects in your scene. Depending on how many objects or types of objects require separate masks, you may need to render several mask passes for a scene.

Depth Passes

A *depth pass* (also called *Z-depth* or a *depth map*) stores depth information at each point in your scene. A depth pass is an array of values, measuring the distance from the camera to the closest subject rendered at each pixel.

This type of pass gives you added control over tinting and processing the more distant parts of the scene differently from the foreground. It's especially effective for larger outdoor scenes. A depth pass of the space scene is shown in Figure 11.30. Brighter shades of gray represent parts of the scene that are closer to the camera.

Using a Depth Pass

You can use a depth pass as a mask for any kind of image processing effect. Figure 11.31 used the depth pass to mask a blur of the background and to tint the background with a cool, gray color. This enhances the sense of depth in the scene by simulating a camera's limited depth of field, and also simulates atmospheric perspective as though looking through dust that dulled the color of the distant rocks.

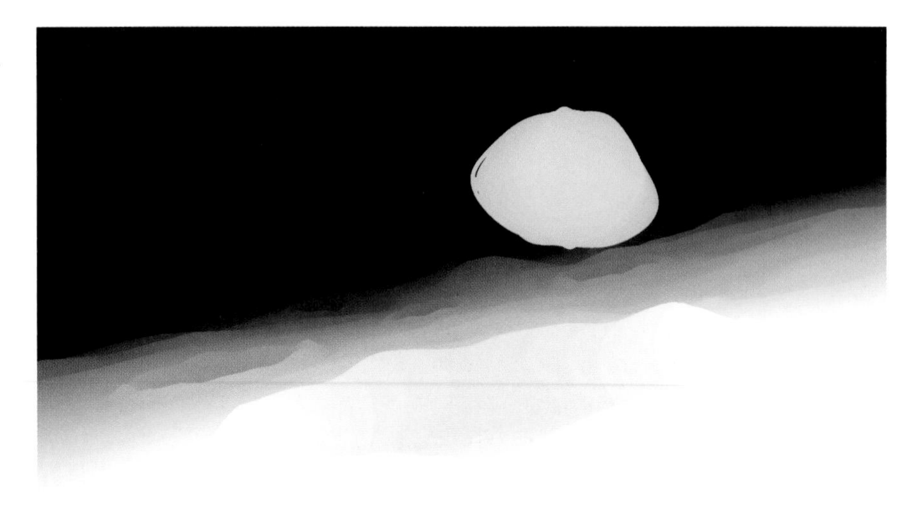

[Figure 11.30]
A simulated depth pass rendered with fog

[Figure 11.31]
Using the depth pass as a mask for atmospheric perspective and DOF

Depth maps are worth rendering for any environment that needs atmospheric or depth of field effects to be simulated during compositing. Even for scenes where there is not much visible fog or dust, having a depth map lets you tint your scene to cooler or less saturated colors with distance, adding an impression of *atmospheric perspective*—the color shift that you are used to seeing in natural environments.

Types of Depth Passes

A true depth pass is not an image. The value stored for each pixel location is not a color or shade, but a floating-point accurate number representing the camera-to-subject distance. If a true depth map is converted into a viewable grayscale image, with only 256 levels of gray, then the accuracy is limited compared to the original distance measurements.

To produce anti-aliased output from a scene's depth, you can make a rendering that is sometimes called a *simulated depth pass*. Simulated depth passes are really the output of a regular rendering. They do not involve floating-point distance measurements. To set-up a simulated depth pass rendering, all of the objects in your scene need to be given a flat, constant white color, with no shading. Then you must activate a *depth-fading* or *fog effect* to fade your scene toward black at greater distances from the camera. The results will be something like those shown in Figure 11.30.

You can also render a simulated depth pass by texture mapping a ramp or gradient projected across all the geometry in the scene, so that closer geometry is white and more distant geometry is black.

Pass Management Features

An old way to set up passes is to modify your whole scene for each pass you want to render. For example, making a specular pass, you would change all the shaders in the scene to black out the diffuse illumination, and show only specular highlights. This works in any program and enables you to set up any pass you need, but it is not very efficient. You may end up saving several versions of your scene, one modified to render each pass that you need. If there is a change in the modeling or animation, you would then need to modify each of these scene versions before rerendering your passes. While 3D artists have set up multipass rendering manually like this for many years, and it does work, most modern 3D software has added pass management features that make dealing with passes much easier and more efficient.

Most high-end 3D programs include pass management functions which can speed and simplify rendering in passes. The advantages of having pass management built into the software are that you can configure and maintain many pass descriptions at once in a 3D scene. Different passes and layers may include different shaders, lights, and objects, or could include overrides to change render settings, shader values, or attributes of specific objects. As a result, you can have one scene, but flip through different layers and passes, each ready to render as soon as a version of your animation is complete.

You may render passes into many separate image files or into one large multilayer file. While writing many passes and layers into a single file can be convenient, most studios render each pass as a separate file. If each of your passes is a separate file, then you have random access to choose which passes to delete, rerender, render on different machines, or save in multiple versions. If a rendering task crashes before it completes every pass, with separate files you don't need to start again from the beginning.

Rendering Many Passes at Once

Most 3D software can render at least a color image, an alpha channel, and a depth pass at the same time. To render more passes than that, sometimes passes must be rendered in serial, one after another. Some renderers can be programmed to output many passes at the same time, instead of each pass being a separate rendering task. Renderman's support for Arbitrary Output Variables is an example of this. While rendering one main image (the beauty pass), Renderman can simultaneously write out many other image files, containing specularity, reflections, shadows, multiple masks, or even different lights in isolation. If you want to render different layers, with different objects visible, you would still need to render them in serial. But if rendering many passes in parallel is an option for you, it saves a huge amount of time.

Lighting in the Composite

To a greater and greater extent, the appearance of your scene's lighting can be adjusted during the compositing process. While nothing done during compositing can completely replace the process of adjusting and aiming your actual lights prior to rendering, an increasing number of quick fixes can be made interactively during compositing, sometimes saving a production from needing to relight and rerender scenes.

Rendering Lights as Separate Passes

A *lighting pass* is an optional part of multipass rendering that adds a great deal of flexibility and control to the compositing process. Instead of rendering a beauty pass all at once, you could instead render multiple lighting passes, as shown in Figure 11.32. An individual lighting pass shows the influence of one light (or one group of lights) on a layer. You can create it by rendering with just one of your lights visible, and all the other lights hidden.

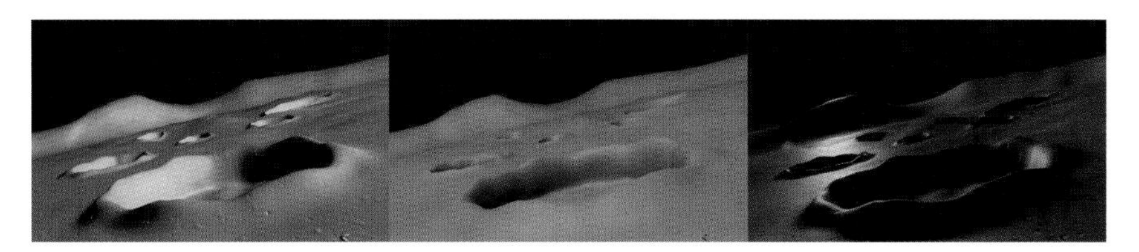

[Figure 11.32]
The key (left), fill (middle), and rim lights (right) rendered as separate passes

The three passes in the figure can be added together during compositing. Use the Add or Screen mode in your compositing program, in just the same way that you would composite a specular or reflection pass. During the composite, you can separately tweak the brightness and color of each of the lighting passes to produce different lighting effects, as shown in Figure 11.33.

[Figure 11.33]
A range of appearances can be interactively created by combining the lighting passes with different adjustments.

You probably won't have time to render separate lighting passes from each light on each layer in your scene. Here are some of the situations where it is worthwhile to render separate lighting passes:

- Your key light is usually worth isolating. This way, you can multiply your other lights with an occlusion pass, but have the key light blocked exclusively by its own shadows to preserve directionality.

- Lights that will be processed in any way during the composite, such as a specular light that will trigger a glow effect, should always be separated.
- Lights that you plan to animate or turn on or off during the composite need to be isolated. For example, a flash of light from an explosion could be rendered as a separate lighting pass. This allows the animated lighting to be precisely matched in color and timing to the source that motivates it, once all of your effects have been composited into the scene.
- Any light which might become so bright that it overexposes the shot should be a separate pass, so that you can err on the side of turning its intensity too low, and then brighten it as needed during the composite.
- Render a separate lighting pass for any objects brightened with ambience or incandescence. For your other lighting passes, override these parameters of the shaders. You don't want any areas to build up by adding brightness to multiple lighting passes, or they would appear too bright when the passes were added together.

In compositing, you can always increase the brightness or saturation of a pass if you need to. Rendering lights in separate passes lets you be conservative about how bright or how saturated your lights will be, with the knowledge that you can boost them if you need to during the composite.

Relighting Tools

Tools or plug-ins in some compositing programs allow you to virtually relight rendered layers. To use any such tool, you must render out information about the surface normals in your 3D scene, showing the direction that each point on a surface was facing when it was rendered. This information, sometimes called a *normal pass*, then allows light from different directions to be simulated during the composite. Figure 11.34 shows a normal pass of the ice cream scene.

There are serious limits to what lighting changes can be made without rerendering. If you need a shadow to be cast in a different shape or direction, then that rendering process depends on going back to the 3D model. High quality rendering depends on sub-pixel level detail and anti-aliasing that can't be maintained by functions that simulate lighting in the compositing software. Layers that are covered in hair or grass often depend on surface normals that vary on a scale smaller than a pixel, so relighting complex or furry scenes might not work well.

[Figure 11.34]
A normal pass provides surface angle information for relighting during the composite.

Matching Live-Action Background Plates

A *background plate* is usually a sequence of frames digitized from live-action film or video, into which you will add your computer graphics elements.

Many 3D programs have an option to view background plates within an animation window (an *image plane* or *rotoscope background*), showing how your subject will be aligned with the background. Once your 3D scene is aligned with the camera angles from the real-world shot, you face the challenge of matching the lighting from the real-world environment. Matching the direction, color, and tone of the light sources in the real scene is essential to integrating your 3D rendered passes with the photographed background plate.

Reference Balls and Light Probes

A set of reflective and matte balls can be ideal reference objects to help measure the position and color of lights on a location. Mirrored balls are sold as lawn ornaments, ball bearings, and as housings for ceiling-mounted security cameras. For a ball with a matte finish, plaster is ideal, but a Styrofoam ball from a craft store could be more portable and affordable. You may need to paint the ball gray and to attach a piece of wire to hold it in place.

Matte Balls

A photograph showing the matte ball in a lighting environment can be great for picking the color of light reaching your subject from each direction, as shown in Figure 11.35. Ideally, this image should be shot with the same camera as your final background plate, and digitized at the same time with the same settings.

For the most accurate color matches, pick specific RGB color values from the image of the ball, as shown in Figure 11.36. You can then assign these RGB colors directly as colors for your lights from corresponding directions.

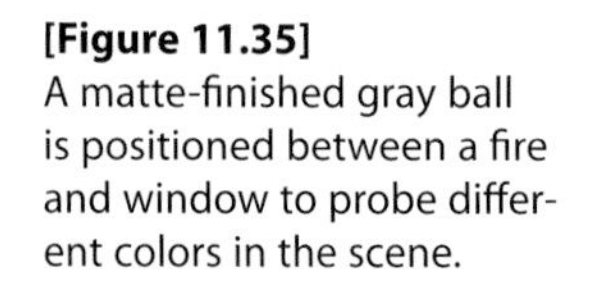

[Figure 11.35]
A matte-finished gray ball is positioned between a fire and window to probe different colors in the scene.

When developing the scene's lighting, you can import the ball image as a background in your 3D program, and create a 3D sphere in front of it. Using your 3D sphere as a reference, adjust infinite or directional lights from each direction to make the shading of the 3D sphere match the shading of the ball in the background plate.

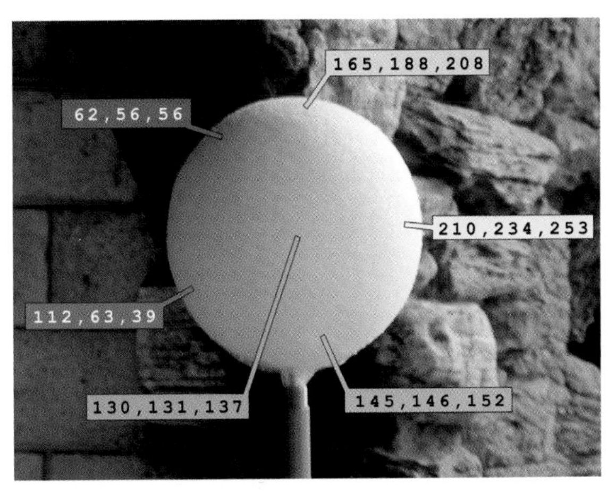

[Figure 11.36] RGB colors picked off the reference ball will give an accurate color match to 3D lights.

Studying the colors reaching a point in a real-world environment is a great exercise for anyone working in 3D lighting. Even if you don't need to match the lighting of a background plate right now, this process could be worth trying a few times, just to get a better feel for the colors of real-world lights.

Mirror Balls

A picture of a reflective ball in an environment, like the one shown in Figure 11.37, helps you more precisely determine the angle and relative brightness of each light, and guides you in creating highlights and reflections for your object. It is best if the reflective ball is shot from the same camera position as your final background plate.

[Figure 11.37] A mirror ball captures a reflected image of the surrounding environment for reference or for use as a reflection map.

As with the matte ball image, the reflective ball image can be brought into your 3D program. If you make a shiny 3D sphere, you should be able to see highlights from your brighter lights, and match these to the highlights in the reflective ball.

An added bonus to having a picture of a reflective sphere in your environment is that you can use it to develop a reflection map for your object, as shown in Figure 11.38. In many programs, the best way to project your acquired image is as a planar projection onto the side of a large sphere surrounding your 3D scene; make the sphere render reflections only.

[Figure 11.38]
The image from the mirror ball makes a perfect reflection map.

Light Probe Images

The traditional approach to matching natural light from a real environment is to use an array of infinite or directional lights, as described above. Once each light is properly adjusted to match the color and brightness from each direction, this approach can produce realistic renderings and seamless lighting matches.

Another approach to re-creating a real-world lighting environment is to use a *light probe image* recorded on the same location as your background plate. A light probe image captures the lighting from all angles around a subject, which can be created by photographing a reflective ball at the shooting location. The light probe image can then be used to illuminate objects with all the recorded colors and tones of real-world light. From only one light probe image, illumination will reach 3D objects from all angles, as though the light source were a giant sphere wrapped around the entire 3D scene.

[Figure 11.39]
A high dynamic range image will indicate accurate colors at multiple levels of exposure.

Unlike ordinary photographs of a reflective ball, light probe images are *high dynamic range images (HDRI)*, meaning that they can capture an exposure latitude greatly exceeding the range of one visible image. To photograph light probe images, cameras are programmed to shoot a series of images at different exposure settings, exposing for the brightest light sources all the way down to the darkest, as shown in Figure 11.39. Without using HDRI, all of the brighter lights in a scene might appear clipped as pure white highlights, with no record of their relative brightness or color. Using HDRI, a light probe image can accurately record the color and relative brightness of every light source.

Other Approaches to Matching Lighting

You can't always use probes and reflective balls on the set, nor can you expect every production to stop and wait for you to set up special reference shots. Sometimes you won't even be able to visit the location where background plates were photographed.

Even if you do get to measure the lighting with different kinds of balls, the lighting in the scene may change without being remeasured. Also, balls in one location in a scene may fail to give you the information you need about lighting in another point—you'd need an infinite number of probes to fully measure the light at every point in space.

If you can go to the set or shooting location, you can use other techniques to assist in matching the lighting:

- **Bring a camera to the set.** Take reference pictures of the set and the lighting around it. Take flat-on pictures of walls or floors for possible use in texture mapping. Take wide-angle or panoramic pictures to create reflection maps.
- **Bring a measuring tape to the set.** Ask early in the production if you can have blueprints for the set, but don't trust the original plans to be accurate. Bring a measuring tape and record enough information so that you can build an accurate 3D model of the set if necessary.
- **Watch for changes during the course of the production.** In a studio, lights are adjusted, and even the walls and set pieces are moved between shots. Outside, the weather and time of day create more changes.

If you cannot go to the shooting location, or your background plate comes from stock footage or other sources, you still can match the lighting using other techniques:

- **Study shadows in the background plate.** When you have matched their length and direction in 3D, your lights will be in the right places.
- **Use an object in the background plate to find light colors.** Try to find a white or gray object in the background plate from which you can pick RGB values.
- **Try to find reference objects in the background plate that can be made into a matching 3D model.** By aligning the 3D model with the real object, you can compare how illumination and highlights hit your 3D model until it receives the same illumination as the background plate.

Every production will create different challenges, but with this basic set of tricks, you should be able to match the lights from any background plate.

Exercises

1. In most projects, you only render the passes you really need, without any redundancy. As an exercise, try rendering all 10 of the common pass types above, and see if you can reassemble the other passes to match the beauty pass.

2. Rent a movie in which 3D renderings have been composited over live-action background plates. Examining a still frame, ask yourself: How well do the composited shadow passes match and merge with the shadows that already existed in the background plate? Do the black levels and dark tones of the 3D elements match the live action? Is the level of color saturation consistent?

3. Load any 3D scene that you previously rendered in a single pass, and try splitting it up into multiple layers and passes. Try to improve each aspect of your rendering as you render it separately, such as achieving the most realistic highlights you can in your highlight pass. Composite the results in a paint or compositing program, adjust the layers, and see how much you can improve upon your original rendering.

[CHAPTER TWELVE]

Production Pipelines and Professional Practices

Launching a career in 3D lighting and rendering involves a lot of decisions. Will you specialize in just lighting, or also try to master other crafts? Which other skills would best complement lighting? Should you accept a job doing something else, like rotoscoping, and hope to work your way up to being a lighting technical director? This chapter presents some of the issues and challenges you will encounter in the working world, including understanding and integrating yourself into the sometimes-complex production pipelines of film studios, developing a lighting showreel, and getting a job.

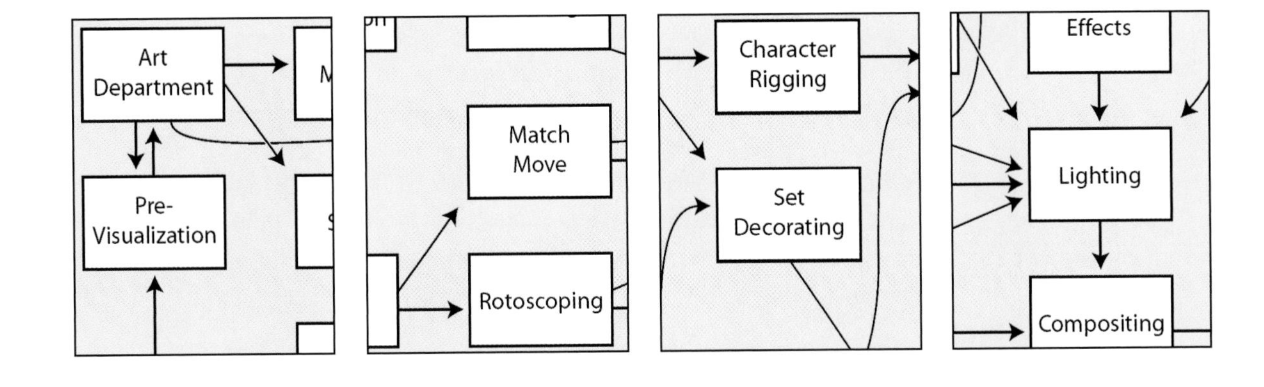

Production Pipelines

If you've been working on computer graphics at home, at school, or in a small company, you may not be familiar with all of the positions that exist within a large studio producing animated features or feature film visual effects.

Companies must organize hundreds of employees to complete large amounts of animation and effects on ambitious schedules. At this scale, a *production pipeline*—the system whereby artists across departments contribute to a computer graphics production—is necessary.

This section outlines the positions and departments typically found in either visual effects studios or computer animation studios, and how they work together as part of a production pipeline.

Planning an Animated Feature

In an animation studio, the story department works with the director and editor to plan out how the story will develop, be told, and be broken down into individual shots and sequences. The layout department then sets up all of the shots in the movie with their composition, camera angles, and camera moves.

Story

Story is one of the most important of all departments. If a story is not engaging, it won't matter to the audience how great the modeling or animation or lighting is; high production values cannot save a weak story.

A *story artist* works primarily on paper. He comes up with ideas for how a sequence or portion of the story could be presented, draws *storyboards* (small sketches of each shot in a sequence), and presents his ideas (in what's called a *pitch*) to the director. Stories go through many revisions, so even an approved sequence is likely to have changes made over time. It is traditional in the world of animation for animators to work out the stories to their films in storyboard form. In some studios, producers insist that screenplays be written and approved before a film begins production, just as if they were planning a live-action film. However, even if there is an initial screenplay, the planning and telling of the story will be worked out and revised in storyboard form before animation begins.

The *story reel* (also called an *animatic*) is a preview of the entire movie, initially put together before the film is animated. Working with the film's editorial staff, the story department creates the story reel by digitizing the drawings of each shot from their storyboards, and editing them together into a preview of each sequence in the film. If there is a camera motion that is not well represented by a single drawing, the story department also creates moving graphics using compositing programs or simplified 3D graphics. To get an idea of what they look like, you can see portions of a film's story reel if you watch the deleted scenes featured on DVD along with many animated features.

The director usually watches many versions of the story reel, trying to develop a well-paced telling of the film's story before animation begins. Sometimes sequences are shortened, consolidated, or eliminated to help move the story forward or shorten the film. On large productions, it can save many millions of dollars to make these decisions while sequences exist only as little digitized pencil drawings instead of being fully animated and rendered.

Over the course of the film's production, the editor continues revising and updating the story reel. When shots are animated, the editor replaces the still pictures digitized from the storyboards with moving shots, and sometimes makes small adjustments to the timing. Eventually, fully lit and rendered footage replaces the animation tests. The soundtracks to story reels often start out with dialog performed by the director, animators, or other available crew, but once final casting has been done professional actors are used to replace them.

As the reel becomes a more and more complete preview of the film, it can be screened to solicit feedback from real audiences, and more changes are sometimes made based on test screenings. Eventually, the edited reel becomes the final cut of the film that will be shown in theaters.

Layout

After the story department has completed storyboards and added them to the reel, *layout artists* are responsible for positioning or animating the 3D camera to compose shots. Layout artists are the first in the pipeline to actually create a 3D scene for each shot in the movie. Using storyboards or story reels as a guide, they work in close consultation with the director to frame each shot. Sometimes a layout artist will make several different versions of a camera move so that the director can pick the best way to cover a scene. After the modeling department has built sets and character models, layout artists also load the necessary models into the shot, and put them into position.

Sometimes a layout artist will roughly animate a character, at least translating the character from one place to another if that motion is an important part of the shot. Even though the temporary motion they add will be replaced with full character animation by an animator, the composition and animated camera moves made by a layout artist will be a part of the final film. Sometimes a layout artist will also adjust the depth of field (DOF) for all of the shots in a sequence, to ensure that this aspect of the camera work is done consistently.

Preparing for Visual Effects Shots

Visual effects studios start their productions differently than feature animation studios. Instead of creating sequences from scratch like an animation studio, effects studios are focused on integrating computer graphics with live-action film.

There would not be a story department in a visual effects studio; the story was probably written long before the studio was hired to add visual effects to the film. In a visual effects studio, a *previsualization department* helps plan how effects will be integrated with live-action, as well as helps directors plan their live-action filming.

Instead of having camera moves designed by a layout department as in animation, the camera angles and camera moves in a visual effects studio are usually copied from a live-action camera by a *match move department*. Finally, elements of the live-action film are traced and matted out by a *rotoscoping department*.

Previsualization

Previsualization, or *previs*, is a way of previewing live-action or visual effects shots with simplified 3D graphics, to plan sequences and camera moves before they are filmed. Some companies offer previsualization services to directors to help plan complex sequences prior to filming. Some directors even previsualize an entire feature film before shooting it. Using previsualization, directors can work out camera angles, figure out exactly how action scenes or stunts should be staged, and generally make live-action film production faster and more efficient.

The best previsualization is done before any footage is shot, but visual effects studios also do previs of visual effects sequences for shots where background plates have already been filmed. Previsualization helps determine where 3D elements and effects will appear, which models or miniatures need to be built, and how *practical effects* (effects elements filmed in real life such as smoke or explosions) should be filmed.

Previsualization artists must be able to work quickly and responsively, and frequently need to work alongside the director, moving the camera and changing elements of the scene at the director's request.

Match Move and Virtual Sets

When 3D creatures or effects are combined with live-action film, the match move department does the work of aligning the 3D camera with the real camera.

If the cinematographer shooting the live-action footage moved the camera during the shot, then match move artists will create a 3D scene with an animated camera that duplicates the real camera's motion, frame by frame. This task is called *3D camera tracking* and can be done with commercially available software such as 3D Equalizer (www.3dequalizer.com), built-in features of some 3D animation packages, or proprietary software at some studios.

Besides matching the camera itself, match move artists also create *virtual set models* (sometimes also called *match move geometry*), which are carefully measured models of the sets that were used in filming a live-action scene. For example, if a scene shows 3D creatures chasing real actors through a real house, then match move artists would create an accurately built reproduction of the floor, walls, and other main surfaces that were visible in the live-action footage. Match move artists will superimpose their virtual set models over the filmed footage, as in Figure 12.1. If the wireframe models remain in alignment with the filmed set throughout the shot, then this verifies that the 3D camera is accurately matched with the real camera.

[Figure 12.1]
The match move department checks 3D camera alignment by superimposing match move geometry over the original background plates.

Even though the virtual set models will not be visible in the final product, other departments will use them to maintain integration with the live-action footage. For example, character animators will stage action and position characters relative to the virtual set. Effects artists may use virtual set models as a part of the dynamic simulation of smoke, fire, water, or other effects that would be limited by walls and furniture. Lighting artists will use the virtual set to align light positions with windows and lamps in the real set. They will also render shadow and reflection passes using the virtual set geometry, so that the composited shadows and reflections will follow the shape of walls, doors, or terrain visible in the shot.

Match move artists are an important part of modern visual effects. Historically, visual effects shots were often filmed from a locked-off camera that remained motionless whenever two images were aligned for a visual effect. In today's feature films, filmmakers can move the camera on visual effects shots just as freely as in any other shot. This better integrates the effects into the film, and preserves the creative freedom of the cinematographer.

Being a match move artist is often considered an entry-level position. After someone starts in match move, he can gain experience working in the pipeline and working with the company's software, and may later move into other departments such as modeling, animation, or lighting.

The head of the match move department is usually one of the few visual effects studio employees who travel to different shooting locations along with the crew. On location, he can take detailed measurements of the real set and camera location, measure distances, or survey the terrain of the shooting location. For some shots, the department head may place tracking markers in the scene that will appear in the footage to facilitate 3D camera tracking. These markers will be retouched out of the shot later by the rotoscoping department.

Rotoscoping

In shots that combine 3D animation with live-action footage, sometimes the 3D creature or character needs to appear in the background, behind actors or objects that were filmed in the real world. To accomplish this, a *matte* needs to be created at each frame of the shot, indicating the exact shape and location of the real-world people or objects that appear in the foreground. Drawing these animated mattes is called *rotoscoping* (or *roto*).

Once a *rotoscoper* (or *roto artist*) creates animated mattes for actors in the foreground, it makes it easy for compositors to insert 3D elements behind them. Roto elements are also used for other effects, such as casting the shadow of a 3D character onto a human actor or blurring, sharpening, or color-correcting different parts of a scene.

It would be very difficult to preview the interaction of a 3D character and a human actor if you couldn't see them composited together, so animators need roto elements as early in production as possible, even for test-renders of their animation. Lighters also need a preview of the final shot, including seeing 3D elements behind rotoscoped live-action elements. Often a very rough, quick version of the roto is developed first, and distributed to lighters and animators to help preview the appearance of the shot as it is developed. Eventually, a more final, accurate roto will need to be developed, before the compositor begins to combine the final elements.

Rotoscoping can be very labor intensive, because it involves tracing the outlines of moving people on a frame-by-frame basis, trying to match every aspect of the movement and the motion blur. Being a roto artist is often an entry-level position at a studio, and after starting in roto, employees are often promoted to texture painting, compositing, or other positions. Besides rotoscoping animated mattes, roto artists also do routine retouching such as removing dust and scratches from digitized film frames, or removing tracking points from the shot.

Core Departments

Thus far we have focused on the differences between animated feature production and visual effects production. However, once you get beyond the initial starting points of the pipeline, many of the same core departments will be involved in any computer graphics pipeline, for common tasks such as designing and building models, animating characters and effects, and determining the look of the rendered images.

Art Department

The art department is responsible for developing concepts and designs for all of the scenes, creatures, characters, and effects that will be produced at the studio.

Work produced by artists in the art department can include concept sketches showing what a scene or character might look like; small sculptures called *maquettes*, which convey the final designs for characters; and color storyboards (sometimes called *color scripts*), which define the color schemes to be used throughout the production.

Traditional artists do most of the work in the art department. Many work without computers, drawing on paper or sculpting models out of clay. Others use digital tools such as 2D paint programs to illustrate their designs. However, almost all of the work ends up in digital form, either by scanning flat artwork into digital images, or by using 3D scanners to digitized hand-sculpted maquettes into 3D models. In some cases, the artists are credited as *concept artists* (who develop designs for imaginary environments, creatures, or vehicles) or *character designers*. All of the work that the art department produces is ultimately subject to approval by the director of the film, who can make suggestions, request changes, or ask for new versions.

Designing on paper saves time compared to designing everything in 3D. For example, if a script calls for a dog character, a concept artist could draw several pictures of what the dog could look like, and show them to the director. If the director wants some changes, new drawings can be made quickly, with artists sometimes making new sketches or modifying existing drawings as they talk. If people jumped straight into 3D without an approved character design on paper, the process of modeling the dog in 3D, texturing it, rigging it, and adding fur could take weeks of work. All of this work would be wasted if the director wanted a redesign.

A key position on any film is the *art director,* who helps the director create the look and feel of the film. In live-action film, an art director is involved in all aspects of costume design, set design, set decoration, matte paintings, make-up, and other creative aspects of the film. In a computer animated film, the art director is involved in all of the issues that would need to be art directed in a live-action film, as well as approving the modeling, shading, textures, and lighting.

After the colors and appearance of each sequence are initially planned in the color script or concept art from the art department, scenes will still evolve substantially as they are actually shaded and lit. The art director will stay involved, giving feedback in reviews of lighting and shading, but the director ultimately guides the development of the final shot.

Modeling

The modeling department can begin building digital versions of creatures, characters, and environments as soon as the director approves the art department's designs.

At some large studios, modeling is split into two or more departments. Often, companies split modelers into organic modeling and hard surface modeling departments. *Organic modelers* tend to have a sculpture background and build characters and other freeform surfaces, whereas *hard surface modelers* often have an industrial design or architecture background and model vehicles, weapons, props, and buildings. Other studios split departments into *character modelers*, who build the characters and set up their facial expressions, and *set/prop modelers*, who build everything else that will appear in a film, including buildings, vehicles, props, weapons, terrains, and foliage.

Modelers work with a variety of starting points. In some cases, they will be given detailed designs for their models from the art department; in other cases, they will be asked to find reference images and build things according to those images. Modelers also sometimes begin with digitized data made by putting an actor, a maquette, or other models into a 3D scanner. The modeler then needs to clean up the data, fill in any areas that were not digitized correctly, and make sure that the topology and level of detail meets the production's needs. In any situation, there is a need for judgment and creativity on the part of the modelers. They usually need to shepherd a model through several different revisions before everyone is happy, having each version reviewed, and then responding to different notes and feedback from the director and art director.

There are two common ways to show a model for review. One way is a *turntable test*, which is just short looping animation showing a model rotating 360 degrees in front of the camera. Another way is to place the model in context within a scene, and show it from the actual camera angles that will be used in the production.

After the model is approved, it will be made available to the rigging and texture paint departments, who will prepare it for animation and rendering. With luck, the model will move through the production pipeline without coming back for modeling fixes, although some amount of model fixes are inevitable. Problems with models sometimes don't appear until the model appears in your rendering, in which case a lighter will request model fixes.

Because modeling happens early in the production, it is a good complementary skill to have in addition to lighting and rendering. At many companies, there are people who work as modelers early in a production, and then do lighting and rendering later on.

As soon as completed models are approved, they will all go to the shading department. The prop models will also become available to the set decorating department and the character models will go on to rigging.

Set Decorating

In an animated feature, or for many visual effects sequences, a complex 3D world needs to be arranged and populated with many 3D models. After modelers have built models of household items, trees, plants, and other objects that will appear in a movie, it is the job of a *set decorator* to place many copies of these models throughout the scene.

Set decorators rely on sketches and feedback from the art department, as well as their own aesthetic judgment, to go from a small library of plant species models into a full jungle, or from a directory of household props into a cluttered room that looks as if it belongs in the story.

Set decorators are very aware of where the camera is positioned and how it moves throughout a sequence. They try to dress detail into the specific areas that will be visible in the shot, filling in background areas with larger objects only where necessary. If a location is going to be visible only in a single shot, then a set decorator may follow the cone of the camera and dress props or foliage only into the area that will be visible, as shown in Figure 12.2. Even for a single shot, it's a good idea to have vegetation slightly beyond the camera's view because it could still cast shadows that are visible in the shot, and any shot may need to survive reframing to a different aspect ratio.

[Figure 12.2]
Set decorators fill a 3D scene with models where the camera is aimed (camera is shown in green), sometimes leaving other areas blank.

Technical Directors

Several departments, at different points along the pipeline, use the common job title *Technical Director,* or *TD*. Some companies use this title for several different jobs:

- Lighting TDs (the most popular use of the word) light and render 3D scenes.
- Character TDs are responsible for rigging a character with a skeleton, clothing, hair, and deformation controls.
- Shader TDs write and adjust shaders to determine the appearance of models, and prepare objects to be painted by the texture painters.

At some companies, TDs do modeling in earlier stages of a production and later are involved in compositing and effects animation. Some companies even have *pipeline TDs* involved in developing the architecture that links all of the departments together.

A TD isn't primarily a technical position, nor is it exactly a director. Most TDs are really artists in the production pipeline doing portions of the creative work that happen to also require some computer skills. TD positions require a balance of artistic sensibility, technical savvy, a good eye, and good problem-solving skills. Almost all TDs are able to work with different operating systems, including being proficient in common Unix shell commands. Many know how to write scripts in different scripting languages, such as MEL, Tcl, Perl, or Python. Among the TDs who have scripting or programming skills, most spend their time working on specific characters or shots, and doing scripting or programming only when needed to speed up their work or solve a production problem. Some TDs are programmers, but most are not.

The name TD is applied to many different people working in studios, so don't be surprised that it shows up several times in descriptions of otherwise unrelated departments below.

Character Rigging

Once a character has been modeled, the process of turning it into an animate-able character is called *character rigging* or *character setup*. Assigning a skeleton to the character's geometry is central to the process; an animator will pick icons for bones and joints on the screen and drag them to pose the character. Sliders, which control dozens of factors— such as how wide a creature's left upper eyelid is opened, or how much extra bulge is given to a particular muscle—also need to be set up so that any attribute of a character can be animated easily. Taken together, the skeleton and all of the controls for a character are called a *rig*.

The people designing and testing rigs are usually called *character TDs*, but they are known by more colorful names such as physiquer, rigger, or puppeteer at different companies. A character TD will make test animations showing how a creature or character appears when deformed into different poses. Based on these tests, corrective adjustments are often made. For example, if the initial result of rotating a character's arms upward produced awkwardly deformed shoulders, the character TD might adjust the skeletal structure of the character, or might resculpt the shoulders and rig that shape to appear when the arm was rotated upward.

To be a character TD, you must be very familiar with the company's animation package. While switching between brands of animation software might take only a few weeks of training for an animator, a character TD will need to master more of the minutia of the package.

Throughout a production, issues will arise in viewing specific shots that the character TD will need to address. Also, specific gags or effects throughout a production may require rigs to add controls or deformations for a specific shot.

Character Animation

Character animation has been practiced since the early days of motion pictures, using hand-drawn animation (also called 2D) and stop-motion animation (posing models, dolls, or clay figures at different frames). In modern production companies, the practice of meticulously planning a character's performance frame by frame is applied in 3D graphics using the same basic principles and aesthetic judgments that were first developed in 2D and stop-motion animation. If motion capture is used at the studio to digitize the motion of real actors, then a great deal of an animator's time will also be spent cleaning up the motion captured performance and completing the portions of the motion such as the eyes and hands that may not have been digitized.

Every year there are fewer and fewer jobs for traditional animators who draw without a computer. However, the art of hand-drawn animation remains a valuable skill for anyone who wants to enter the field of character animation, because it exposes people to so many of the principles and practices of the field.

The most common interaction between character animators and lighters occurs when lighting reveals mistakes in the animation that were not visible to the animator. For example, if a foot were floating in the air instead of fully planted on the ground, the error might not have been noticed in animation test renders, but would become visible when the scene was rendered with shadows and occlusion. At this point, either the lighting artist finds a way to cheat or fix the problem (such as moving the character or the ground) or else the shot is sent back to the animation department to be fixed. There are also times when animated lighting needs to be coordinated between lighting artists and animators, if a character turns on a light, a car flashes its turn signals, or a glint of light reflecting off a mirror needs to be animated on a wall. However, these are the exceptions—it is most common for the lighter's work to come as a total surprise to the animators when they finally see the shots they animated fully lit and rendered.

Effects

It is the job of an *effects TD* (sometimes called an effects animator or effects artist) to produce elements such as flowing or splashing water, dust, avalanches, hurricanes, smoke, flames, and sometimes hair and fabric motion. Effects animation often relies on dynamic simulations, procedures used to calculate motion based on the physical parameters of the effect being simulated. Effects TDs may use a commercial package such as Maya or Houdini to set up a simulation, or proprietary software developed at their company.

A few effects TDs are usually involved in a production from the very beginning, helping to design and set up effects that will be used in a film. Once the production starts, a larger group of effects TDs will join the team, creating effects for specific shots.

Effects need tight integration with character animation, and generally an artist working on effects for a shot doesn't start until the character animation is completed. For example, if an animated whale is going to spray water off its tail, the effects TD producing the water spray needs to start with the character animation as the basis of her dynamic simulation. If the character animation were changed, the effect would probably need to be redone. With every effect, from hair and clothing motion to volcanic explosions, the exact timing must look right relative to the other action in the scene.

Effects TDs need to work closely with the lighting department. Often effects elements such as smoke will need to be lit in special ways or will require certain kinds of shadows, and there will be notes given to the lighting TD about how to deal with and light the effects. The design of water or rain effects often rely largely on how they are lit; lighting TDs might work out a good way to add rim lights or reflections that make the water visible. The effects TD may have experience lighting and be able to make recommendations about how to best bring out an effect's appearance.

Lighters also need to do a lot of work illuminating a scene as if the effects elements were really there. Sparks, fire, explosions, and laser beams are not just effects elements, they are also motivations for animated lighting that will need to be added to the scene.

Shading

As described in Chapter 9, "Shaders and Rendering Algorithms," shading is the process of developing shaders or surface descriptions that determine how each model will respond to light. As soon as the modeling department completes a model and it is approved, the shading department goes to work creating shaders for the surfaces. The work of assigning shaders to surfaces is generally the work of a shading TD.

For many common objects, pre-existing shaders can be assigned and adjusted to represent common surfaces, especially if they are just props or set pieces. For other jobs, especially characters or special surfaces, custom shaders are written. This allows a production to take advantage of the latest technology and specify the unique reactions to light from an individual surface. Because some surfaces require new, unique shaders while others can be shaded using older code, you will find that some shading TDs are programmers with advanced computer skills, while others are basically artists who can get their work done entirely by linking together and adjusting existing shading nodes.

In many cases, shading TDs will also assign texture maps to surfaces. In some companies, the same people do texture mapping and shading. At large studios, painting original texture maps may be done by texture painters, but a shading TD may do basic texturing, such creating a tiling metal texture to help a surface look like metal.

Texture Paint

As soon as shaders are created on a surface, *texture painters* go to work creating maps for it.

Texture painters develop texture maps using a variety of tools and sources. Some of the image sources include:

- Painting maps from scratch in a 2D or 3D paint program.
- Basing all or part of a map on a scan or photograph of a real-world surface.
- Starting the map with a photograph of a painted maquette from the art department.
- Projecting images from the live-action portion of a film onto 3D models, and modifying as needed.
- Mixing procedural patterns and noises.

These techniques can be used in various combinations depending on the type of maps that need to be created. Even when digitized or procedural sources are used, texture painters almost always need to paint into and manipulate an image to produce their final set of texture maps.

With maps assigned to the model, the texture painter will create a turntable test to show the mapping from all sides. A frame from a live-action scene can be used as the background image in the test, to show how well the model integrates with the real environment.

Lighting

A *lighting artist* (also called a lighter, lighting TD, or lighting animator) working within a production pipeline has to think first and foremost about lighting, but also about bringing together all of the elements of a shot that other departments created. In most companies, lighting TDs put together the latest version of the animation, the effects, the camera moves, the shaders and textures into scenes that they render every day.

Most lighting TDs show their work each morning in screenings called *dailies*, where they receive feedback on the lighting of their shots. By the end of the day, the TD will have created a new version of the lighting that addresses each of the concerns mentioned in dailies. Shots are then left to render overnight, so that they can be ready to screen the next day in dailies. This cycle repeats until the shot is approved.

While a lighting TD is revising the lighting, artists in other departments may also be making changes to the animation, the shaders, the effects, or other aspects of the shot, because they too are being asked to make changes during dailies. Being in a later part of the production pipeline means that changes can be inherited from many different people. At times it seems that the farther down the production pipeline you are, the more people could potentially make a mistake that causes problems with your shot. However, most studios have developed systems for managing different versions of their assets (an asset is anything someone has created, such as a model, an animation, a shader) so that a TD will have the ability to select an earlier version of an asset if a new version causes problems. An asset management system should also help prevent changes that are made while a shot is rendering from appearing in some frames but not others.

Eventually the lights created by lighting TDs become assets that are stored in different versions in a studio's asset management system. Groups of lights designed to light a particular set or character, called *rigs*, are set up and then shared between lighting TDs who are working on different shots, in order to save time and improve continuity.

Compositing

Compositors take rendered images from lighting TDs, and sometimes also start with compositing scripts that TDs developed in order to initially comp together their dailies. Compositors also rely on mattes that the rotoscoping department created.

If 3D elements were rendered in multiple passes of diffuse shading, highlights, and reflections, then compositors will begin to composite these together along with any live-action plates, to form a complete image. Then image processing is applied, such as slightly blurring the edges of the 3D model where it needs to blend with the filmed imagery, color-correcting any of the passes, and adding film grain to match the live-action footage. In visual effects studios, compositors also need to composite and manipulate live-action footage. They might add shadows of a 3D character, composite in dust kicks where a character's foot hits the ground, or remove any elements from the shot that do not belong in the film, such as telephone lines that accidentally appear in a historical drama.

Some visual effects studios provide a *digital intermediate process* to filmmakers: digitizing filmed footage for general retouching, color correction, timing adjustments, and other 2D manipulation, and then outputting to film again. These services give directors who shoot film access to most of the creative possibilities of working with digital images. A digital intermediate process would not involve all of the 3D-graphics-related department, so the compositors would be working with footage that has not gone through the rest of the pipeline.

In animation studios, compositing can be a much simpler process than it usually is in visual effects studios. At times, all that a compositor needs to do is layer together a background and perhaps midground and foreground layers, and perhaps add glows around some of the light sources. In many animation studios, lighting TDs do their own compositing and there is no compositing department. However, the visual sophistication of animated films grows every year. Effects artists make sophisticated effects like fluids, fireballs, or force fields that are built out of multiple passes and distort the area behind them in sophisticated ways, requiring a large number of compositing operations. Some studios render elements in many passes and adjust the appearance of the lighting in the scene during the composite. As a result, even companies that don't need to combine computer graphics with live-action are still dealing with increasingly sophisticated compositing.

Film I/O

A *film I/O* department (also called *photoscience* or *scanning and recording*) is the department that manages the scanning of film frames into digital files and the recording of final images back onto film. As productions start to rely less on film and more on digital production and digital distribution, this department may take on a new moniker.

Animation studios that don't create visual effects may not have the equipment to digitize film frames, but still need a department to focus on outputting final images onto film, digital cinema, and different video formats, while trying to maintain the highest possible quality and a consistent look on each format.

This department also deals with the challenging issue of keeping color displays accurately calibrated throughout the studio, so that everyone can see images as close as possible to the final output.

Visualizing Production Pipelines

Using the departments described above, you can imagine the production pipeline of a visual effects studio as shown in Figure 12.3. In general, each department is waiting for materials from the department before it in the pipeline, before it can begin its own work on a shot. However, departments are often working on shots simultaneously, with animators, effects artists, lighters, and compositors potentially working on different aspects of the same shot at the same time.

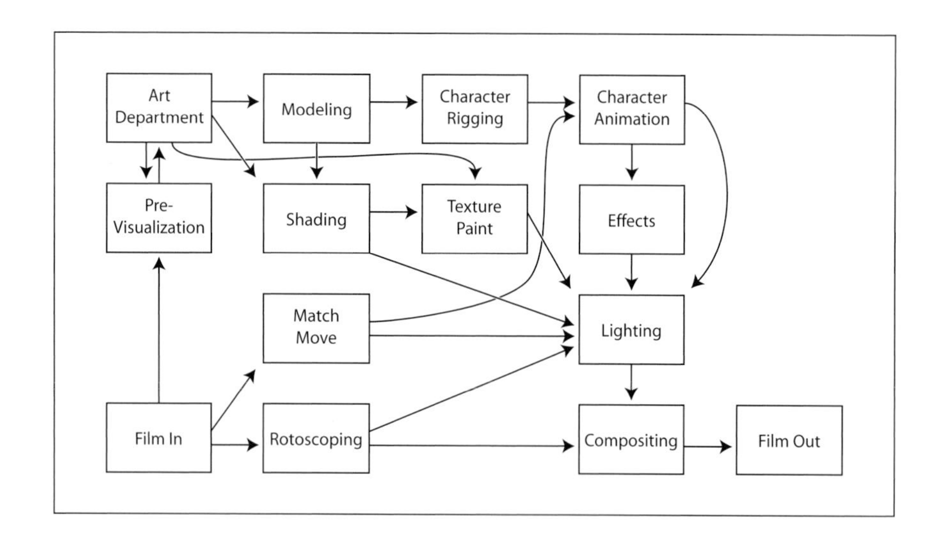

[Figure 12.3] A visual effects pipeline is focused on integrating computer graphics with live-action film.

At an animation studio, on the other hand, the pipeline would not be centered around live-action film, but instead on developing original art and stories, and putting together computer-generated shots. A generalized pipeline for an animation studio is shown in Figure 12.4.

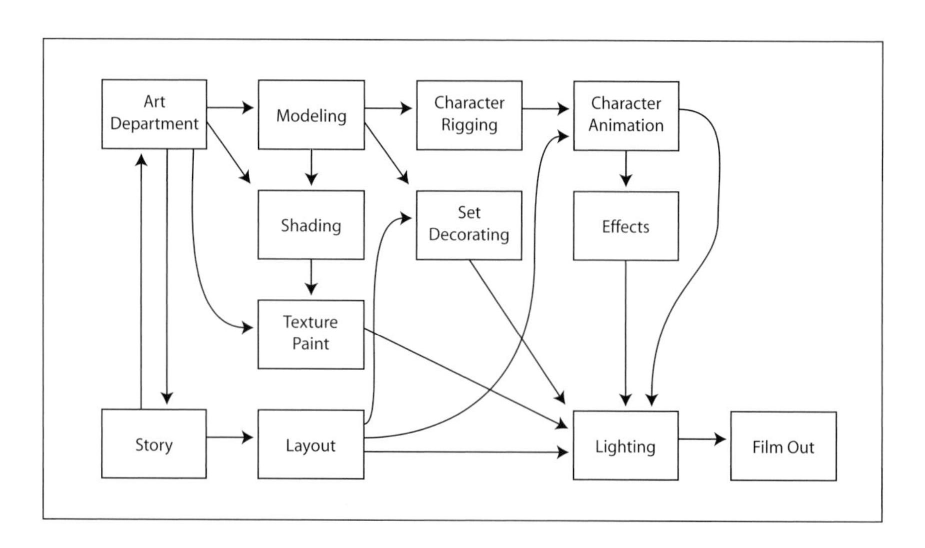

[Figure 12.4] An animated feature pipeline is focused on creating an original story and art.

As a production moves through the pipeline, the workflow is flexible. For example, there might be more people working in modeling near the beginning of a production (when there are a lot of models to be built), and more people in lighting toward the end of the production (when there are more shots to be lit).

Although you see similar jobs at many places, no two studios have exactly the same pipeline. Some studios have other departments to fill specific needs, such as a creature department that builds physical models to use on film sets. Other companies provide film and television editing services to clients as well as effects. Studios can change their pipelines and add new departments at any time. For example, a particular film might need a department dedicated to clothing and hair simulation, or another film might need a department focused on rerendering shots as stereo pairs for a release in a stereoscopic 3D film format. Also, many small studios—and some large ones—are consolidating several jobs into one wherever they think it would improve efficiency.

Getting Work Approved

At the heart of any computer graphics production is an approval process in which supervisors, the director, or a client approve artists' work at each stage of the production.

Working with Clients

If you are doing freelance work or have started your own company, you quickly learn that running your own business does *not* mean that you are your own boss. All it means is that you are working for different bosses on each project. Learning to get along with your clients is often the key to a successful business.

Setting Expectations

Imagine if you were going to have surgery in a hospital, and you had no special knowledge of medicine. You would expect the doctors and medical staff to tell you clearly how much the procedure was going to cost, how long the process was going to take, what to expect during it, and what the results or expected outcomes could be. While your doctor may have spent most of her life studying or practicing medicine, you expect everything to be explained in plain English. When you deal with a client or employer who is not an expert in computer graphics, it's your job to be the doctor and explain the process to him, as clearly and patiently as possible.

Early in a production, you want to clearly establish what—and when—you will deliver to your client. Set up a calendar of when each stage of the project will be shown and approved. Stages could include model construction, texturing, animation, effects, lighting and rendering, or any other key work that your project will need.

Scheduling the approval process in stages means that you can get feedback on test versions or portions of the project before you commit to a final rendering. You don't want to wait until the end of your production schedule, when you have completed your work, to hear from your client that some earlier part of your work needs to be changed.

Make sure your client knows what to expect in terms of an untextured model, a textured model, animation tests, and final renders, and that he is clear on which issues should or shouldn't be commented upon at each stage. It is a good habit to start any presentation with clear statements such as "This is what we are working on now" or "These are the things we'll still be able to change later" in order to set the context for what you are presenting.

Never make any footage shown to your client appear to be further ahead than it really is. For example, if the texture maps on your models aren't final yet and you want comments only on the animation, you might want to show the footage to your client in black and white, in order to avoid calling attention to the temporary rendered appearance of the surfaces.

Dealing with Changes

When you schedule presentations for your client, allow time to make changes based on his feedback. A client will almost never approve the first version of something he's shown. However, you should also make it clear from the beginning that new requests during the production, which take significant extra time, could constitute an overage for which he will be charged. The best way to be paid or to bill a client is in a rate per day or week of work. Your time has value, and your equipment depreciation and expenses can be computed per week, so basing your initial bid and your overage charges on your time is always a fair approach.

One answer you should never give to any request is "that's impossible." Instead, explain to your client the extra costs or lengthy production delays that could be involved and suggest alternate routes that might better fit the client's budget and schedule. If you try to convince a client that something they want is impossible, you may be embarrassed when you figure out how to do it the next week, or when the client asks elsewhere and eventually finds what she wants.

If you are showing two versions of an image after making fixes and enhancements, the best way to present your modifications is to show before/after comparison in the same window, flipping back and forth between the old version the client saw before and the new version with your modifications. Changes are always most visible when they appear as motion between frames instead of the two versions simply being shown side by side.

Finally, every version that gets shown to a client should always be carefully backed up, including images, 3D scenes, and textures used to produce it. Even versions that the client didn't seem to like should be stored in case they change their mind or ask for something similar.

Supervising Lighters

In a large production with many lighting artists working on a project, showing each version of a shot directly to the client or director each day can be cumbersome. The best approach in this case is to have a *lead lighter* or *supervising lighter* meet with all of the other lighting artists and approve their shots for review, before they are shown to the director.

Some of the elements shown to a supervising lighter will be the same as what would be shown to a client, such as playing the shot in motion and before/after comparisons of any changes or progress in a shot. If you are test-rendering shots at a lower resolution than the final product, then in addition to the animation of the shot in motion at low resolution, there should usually also be a few high-resolution frames to inspect how all of the texture, light, shadows, and other details hold up at full resolution.

Most studios have software that will break down the shot to show each light source or significant group of lights rendered into a separate image. The lead lighter can then look through each of the light sources used in the scene one at a time, or combine them together in different proportions to preview how the scene would look if some of the lights had a different brightness or color. As technology progresses, more and more companies are developing interactive lighting tools to preview lighting changes in real time, allowing a lead lighter a more complete picture of potential changes.

The supervising lighter should always keep in mind the big picture of what's important to a sequence. The director may have given notes on the overall visual goals, such as showing that a main character is in a strange, inhospitable environment. There might be an overall progression, such as having more contrast in the lighting as the intensity of an argument increases. Individual shots always need to be viewed as a part of the overall scene, and a supervising lighter should frequently screen or compare multiple shots for continuity.

The Chain of Command

In film productions, a lead lighter can look at the work of each lighter to review the progress of shots on a daily basis, and then, when each shot is ready, have it shown to the director and art director. Once the director approves a shot, it is considered final and, unless changes are made late in the game, it will appear in the movie.

In TV commercials, the chain of command is more complex. Once you have pleased the art director and director, there are still many people who could request changes. The director of the TV commercial has to answer to the creative employees at the advertising agency that hired her production company to make the commercial.

Getting a Job in 3D Lighting

If you are already working in the industry, then you know that your performance at the companies where you've worked and the people that you have worked with are most important to moving ahead and getting your next job.

If you are a student or just trying to break into the industry for the first time, however, your first priority is developing a showreel to demonstrate your skills.

A Lighting Showreel

A *showreel* (also called a *demo reel*) is a short video showing your best work related to the job you are applying for. To demonstrate your skills in lighting, your showreel should show that you can integrate elements into a live-action environment, and also that you can light fully CG environments.

To show matching and integration, it is good to include projects in which you composite a 3D creature, character, or vehicle into a live-action or photographed environment. Show that you can get the colors, lighting, shadows, and reflections to match between a real environment and something that you have lit in 3D. If possible, demonstrate your range by lighting and rendering a variety of subjects, including some that are reflective, some that are organically textured or translucent, and some that are furry or have hair.

Some work on your reel should show that you can light entirely 3D environments, including interior and exterior environments. Include props, characters, and vegetation. Pay attention to the way your lighting makes people feel, whether the scene is supposed to feel foreboding, cheerful, sad, inviting, or scary. The mood of the shot should be reflected in the lighting and colors as well as the content of the scene.

In addition to still images, it is a good idea to include some animation. This isn't to prove that you are an animator, but only because most professional work involves dealing with moving footage. If you don't have any animated characters, you could animate aspects of your environment such as the time of day, or different weather or seasons. Moving objects such as curtains, tree branches, or doors can cast different shadows and change the lighting during the shot. Some of the best lighting demonstrations involve studying a single location as the time or weather or mood changes; this shows how much lighting can add to a scene. If you are also interested in an effects TD position, then some effects animation—such as water, fire, or smoke—could be a good addition to your reel as well.

Originality is important in your work. Developing something original, unique, or personal will make your showreel more memorable and reflect well on you as an artist. When you work professionally, the content of your scenes will usually be determined by a client or director, so while you are a student or hobbyist you should seize the opportunity to create something that you really care about.

Credits

A showreel should be accompanied by a breakdown sheet that lists which shots or projects are included in the reel, where or for what client or project you created them, and exactly what you did on each shot. If you did everything in creating a shot, then say that and mention which software you used.

There are nothing wrong with using premade models, or collaborating with others in a group project. If you worked on a shot only in doing lighting, rendering, or other positions, then say exactly what you did to contribute to the shot. Your only concern in joining a group project is to make sure that the work will look better than anything that you could have done by yourself. In most cases, having a good team of people working in specific areas such as modeling and animation can greatly speed your work and allow you to focus on quality lighting and rendering. However, at some schools group projects may be done on limited schedules or without adequate merit-based selection of people to work in each position, producing projects that don't look as good as a talented individual could have made.

Brief informative titles can also be added before each shot or project on your reel itself, containing pertinent information about what you did and what software was used.

Be careful about putting any pertinent information on the soundtrack of your showreel. At many companies lighting showreels are viewed with the volume turned down or all the way off, so voice-over narration may go unheard.

The most important credit to put on your work is your own. Be sure to put your name and contact information on each piece of your application, including your resume, your reel, the cover to your reel, and the breakdown sheet. When the human resources department loans out your reel to people in relevant departments for review, there is always a chance that materials will be lost or separated, so putting your contact information on everything is a good practice.

Quality over Quantity

Your first concern in making a professional showreel is creating professional quality work. If you are deciding between a short 15-second project and a long 2-minute project, consider how much more professional and polished you could make the shorter project.

As a student, while you are still learning the software and trying techniques for the first time, naturally projects will take you longer than they would if you were more experienced. However, your first goal should be learning professional level skills and techniques—practicing them at a higher speed will come later.

There are already more than enough bad computer graphics in the world. Showing an employer a bad showreel with the excuse that you made it all very quickly is not likely to get you a job. Depending on how experienced you are, showreels that run less than 2 minutes are generally fine for students; most experienced professionals can usually benefit from keeping their showreels down to 2 or 3 minutes as well.

If you're not sure whether any particular shot belongs on your reel, the first rule of editing is "if in doubt, leave it out."

Starting Strong

Many employers watch only the first 15 or 20 seconds of a showreel if it doesn't demonstrate the quality they are seeking. If you put your best work first, it makes people more likely to continue watching all the way through.

If you deliver your showreel on DVD, be sure that it starts playing your best work right away, without requiring any menus, lengthy title sequences, or other delays before the first shot plays. If you have some reason to include a menu on a DVD, put it at the end of the showreel instead of the beginning.

Some companies still request showreels on videotape instead of DVD. The first 5 to 10 seconds of a VHS tape often have poor picture quality, so a small amount of black before the showreel begins may be necessary. However, you do not need more than 10 seconds of black, and certainly don't need color bars or a lengthy title sequence to precede your showreel.

Do I Need to Specialize?

There are many people who create 3D animation and visual effects by themselves, doing the work of all of the departments and positions listed above. It is also common at small companies for a team of a few people to complete projects, with some employees doing animation and other employees doing modeling and rendering work.

As a general statement, larger studios need to be more structured, and are usually divided into more departments than smaller companies. Even at larger studios, people who have more than one talent—such as being able to do modeling, rigging, or effects as well as lighting—can be more valuable as long-term employees, because they can move to different departments as needed.

At a larger studio, you will have to choose (or have chosen for you) one position that you will perform in the pipeline. If you enjoy the creative process of creating 3D scenes as a whole and are looking for a job that has lots of variety instead of doing the same thing every day, then you may feel reluctant to specialize into any of the departments, and may prefer to work in smaller companies where individuals do a more flexible range of tasks.

It benefits a 3D artist to experience the entire process of creating an animated 3D scene, rendering and compositing it. Working through projects by yourself is the best way to learn, and the experience will make you more conversant with people in other departments. Many of the 3D artists who have specialized positions in a large studio have worked in other jobs previously in which they were less specialized, and have a level of understanding of the entire production process.

The advantage of specializing is the opportunity to focus on and achieve excellence in a craft. Most character animators, for example, seem happy to live with character animation as a full-time job. They practice week after week animating different shots, having their work critiqued, solving problems, refining their work, and learning new techniques. For a character animator to stop and spend time with a modeling, lighting, or software issue seems like a distraction, not a welcomed departure.

If there is a fixed requirement in getting a job, it is that you should do at least one thing at a professional level. If you can do more than one thing, that's fine, but until you can achieve excellence in at least one area, you won't be able to make an impressive showreel.

Internal Promotion

Computer graphics production companies rely heavily on internal promotion to fill many positions. When a position becomes available, the first choice of most managers is to hire from within the company. As a second choice, previous freelancers may be called. Searching through a box of showreels and trying to hire someone new would actually be a last choice and becomes necessary only when a company needs to replace people or is growing.

For the production company, it makes a lot of sense to hire and promote from within. They can get employees whom they already know and who know the pipeline, and it gives incentive to entry-level employees to know that they might get promoted to a more creative position on a future film. In most cases, studios allow workers to practice and learn new software and skills on their own time, to help improve their chances of moving into another job.

This means that if you apply to a studio wanting to be a lighting TD, but they offer you a position in rotoscoping or match move instead, then taking the entry-level job might not be such a bad place to start. By studying the work of people whose department you want to join, learning the software, and demonstrating skill in the areas you are interested in, you can often move up within a production company.

When companies promote people from within, they also tend to save money. They know how much you were getting paid before they promoted you and that you are likely to take the promotion you have been working toward, even if it is accompanied by only a small raise. In many cases, people find that they have to switch companies in order to command a more substantial pay raise.

Job Security

When people ask how to achieve job security in computer graphics, the short answer is that you can't. Nobody is guaranteed a job that won't go away, and many positions are hired on a per-project basis or subject to layoffs when business is slow.

Some companies are better than others at maintaining employees for the long term. Studios that work on longer-term projects need to keep employees around, and try to make a livable environment in which employees will stay and work on several films, building a talent pool of more experienced employees. Studios offer benefits such as stock options that vest over the course of 4 or 5 years, meaning that you get more benefits if you stay at the job longer. But, even if you land a job in one of the few studios with a reputation for being a relatively stable long-term employer, you are still likely to be engaged in *at-will employment*, which means that you can be laid off or may choose to resign at any time without violating any contract.

Visual effects studios and companies working on television commercials have work only when they are the winning bid on a project, so inevitably there will be times when they are unusually busy and other times when things are slow. No studio can keep paying employees' salaries for too long when there is no work for them to do and no income to the company. Thus a portion of the workforce is often hired on a per-project basis—and, of course, there is always the risk that a wave of layoffs will follow the completion of a big project if there isn't an equally big project starting right after it.

More than security in any single job, you need to think about *career security*. Maintaining and continually improving your skills, your showreel, your website, and your connections within the industry are a must for your career security. If you have a portfolio to be proud of and are respected by your supervisors and coworkers, then even if your current position ends, you should always be able to find new opportunities.

Another key aspect in career security is where you live. If you take a job in a city that has only one or two computer graphics studios, then losing your job would mean having to move. Living in an area where there is a vibrant industry provides much better career security than being isolated.

Advancing in Your Career

Working in computer graphics puts every artist in the "Alice in Wonderland" situation of having to run very fast just to stay in the same place. Keeping up with today's technology requires that you rethink and revise even your most tried-and-true techniques, and invest the time in testing new ones. To move your career forward, you should always be learning and growing.

Even after a project is delivered, before you put away your files, load up the scenes (no matter how sick you are of them) and experiment with a few more renderings. You may want to render a high-resolution print of the scene for your own portfolio, or experiment with other ways the scene could look, without needing to match your client's expectations.

If possible, work on personal projects, no matter how brief or simple, to stretch what you can achieve. You may have some down time in between major projects to do your own work. Perhaps you are fortunate enough to be reading this book while you are still a student, so that you can experiment with each of the techniques and concepts covered here. Whether you are creating images for pay or for pleasure, never stop creating new images and trying new techniques.

Index

C

E

F

G

H

I

J

K

L

M

N

S

T

U

V

W

Z